Basics
of
Classical Syriac

Basics *of* Classical Syriac

COMPLETE GRAMMAR, WORKBOOK, AND LEXICON

STEVEN C. HALLAM

ZONDERVAN®

ZONDERVAN

Basics of Classical Syriac

Requests for information should be addressed to:

Zondervan, *3900 Sparks Dr. SE, Grand Rapids, Michigan 49546*

Library of Congress Cataloging-in-Publication Data

Names: Hallam, Steven C., 1982- author.
Title: Basics of Classical Syriac : complete grammar, workbook, and lexicon / Steven C. Hallam
Description: Grand Rapids, MI : Zondervan, 2016. | In English and Syriac. |
Includes bibliographical references.
Identifiers: LCCN 2016015699 | ISBN 9780310527862 (softcover)
Subjects: LCSH: Syriac language--Grammar. | Syriac language--Dictionaries.
Classification: LCC PJ5421 .H355 2016 | DDC 492/.382421--dc23 LC record available at https://lccn.loc.gov/2016015699

Interior design: Matthew Van Zomeren

Printed in the United States of America

16 17 18 19 20 21 22 23 24 /PHP/ 20 19 18 17 16 15 14 13 12 11 10 9 8 7 6 5 4 3 2 1

To:

Lindsay
My best friend.

Table of Contents

Verbal System: Weak Verbs

Appendices

Preface

There are several reasons that have motivated the writing of this grammar. Primarily, it is the hope that this grammar will introduce the concepts of Syriac in a format that is easy to understand for the beginner. It is with this goal in mind that the grammar has been purposefully written with several characteristics that may appear somewhat odd to the seasoned reader, and require brief explanation:[1]

1. The script that is used in this text is a mix of Estrangela script with Western vowel pointing. To the beginner, note that this is not a typical combination of text and vowel pointing. The reasoning behind combining these two for use in the grammar is based on the following: (1) Since the Estrangela script is the oldest in Classical Syriac, it remains one of the most important to know for biblical studies. (2) It is also the easiest script to read in terms of recognizing various letters which very often get mistaken for one another (such as *qōp* and *waw*, or *rēš* and *dālat*). (3) The Western vowel pointing is often the easiest pointing for the beginning student to recognize due to the fact that it is based off of the Greek alphabet. Additionally, it is used most frequently in academic writings and is useful to know. This is not to downplay the importance of the Eastern vowel pointing—as it is regarded as the more ancient pronunciation in many respects—but for basic familiarity of the language, there are many advantages to using the Western pointing in the beginning.
2. As this grammar is written primarily with the biblical text in mind, all of the exercises will have the biblical references provided. It is assumed that students will have access to some sort of Bible software. Even if a formal Bible software package is not available, there are many resources freely available on the Internet that grant access to helpful tools important in the development of learning the language. It is recommended that students make use of these tools when a difficult parsing or translation requires additional help. This reduces the stress and frustration while still in the formative years of learning the language. It is suggested that the student translate what they can, and then utilize other resources when necessary. There is no better way to learn a language, besides speaking it, than with trial and error through translation of large portions of text.
3. The ܩܽܘܫܳܝܳܐ (*quššāyā*) and ܪܽܘܟܳܟܳܐ (*rukkākā*) (dots above or below the *begadkepat* letters) have been left out of the paradigms, but not the actual biblical text cited in homework and examples. Reasoning for this is twofold: (1) The minimalism of the basic text void of additional markings seems to provide a simplified platform for

1. Note: To the beginning student, please do not get bogged down in the details here. These are simply explaining the decisions of some of the finer points within the grammar that might be considered odd or strange by one who is familiar with the language.

learning, allowing the student to focus more clearly on the larger structural rules of the text. (2) One goal of this grammar is to get the student to a point of familiarity that he or she might begin reading texts that do not have vowel pointing. Not having these features will hopefully increase familiarity with the simplified form of the text.

4. For the same reasons as mentioned above, the soft and hard pronunciations will not be marked in the transliterations (a soft pronunciation is denoted with a line under the letter, as in *ṯ*) in order to promote a simplified form of the phonetics. The more precise pronunciation is obtained from reading the text.

One main objective of this grammar is to get the student into the biblical text as quickly as possible, and it is important to note the limitations of this particular endeavor. It is in no way intended to be an exhaustive examination of the Syriac language. It is intended to be a friendly and accessible generalization of the language. Please recognize that certain nuances and grammatical characteristics exist beyond what are mentioned in this text. Because of this, it is recommended that a reference grammar, such as *Compendious Syriac Grammar* by Theodor Nöldeke, be consulted in conjunction with this grammar in order to shed light on the generalizations that are present in this introduction to the language.

Additionally, to the beginning student, one of the most important things to recognize is that this grammar centers on translational Syriac. Its presentation, therefore, shows significant influence from the languages surrounding its composition. This is evident in the New Testament translations, where Greek influence is readily apparent, and is in contrast to a more pure form of the language that is written in nonbiblical texts. The Syriac written corpus is vast, and the intent is that this grammar will serve as a jumping-off point in order to explore the rich tradition of the Syriac language.

This grammar can be broken into four distinct parts. The first part (chs. 1–6) covers the basics of the noun and adjective and familiarizes the student with simple sentences. The second part (chs. 7–11) introduces the basic structure of the Syriac verbal system according to the peal stem. The third part (chs. 12–16) addresses the derived stems, and the fourth part (chs. 17–23) familiarizes the student with the function and form of the weak verbs.

As for the exercises, the purpose of these is two-fold. First, the particular passages have been chosen because they highlight the aspect of Syriac grammar that is being covered in the chapter or as a review for material covered in previous chapters. The next purpose of the exercises is to build familiarity with the language. The best way to do this is simply through translating large amounts of text and therefore, each exercise was chosen in order to maximize the familiarity with Syriac through as much translation as possible.

Six appendices have been included. *Reading Eastern and Western Texts* serves as additional information to these two distinct Syriac scripts. Following this is a very brief introduction to numbers and dates. *Next Steps* offers some direction for the student who has just finished the grammar and is looking for resources and guidance to continue sharpening their Syriac. Also included is a brief Syriac-Hebrew comparison chart offering a quick-glance of the two languages. Following this are charts of the peal verb with pronominal endings. These paradigms are not found in the text because the student is encouraged to learn the basic structures of the pronominal endings as opposed to rote memorization of the conjugations. Finally, I have included a concise Syriac-English lexicon that covers the vocabulary words found in the grammar.

A brief note to professors or instructors who are using this grammar as a textbook. The contents have been separated with a traditional semester timeline in mind. It would be a very lofty task to try and fit the entire grammar into a single semester. Therefore chapters 1–11 (nouns and verbs) are intended for use in a first semester class and chapters 12–23 (derived stems and weak verbs) are intended for use in a second semester class.

Finally, I owe a huge thank you to my family, Marsha and Curt Hallam, my brother Chris, and Lindsay Hallam, to whom the book is dedicated, for their support through this undertaking. In addition, I'd like to thank the late Verlyn Verbrugge who was the first to give encouragement for the project. And to Nancy Erickson, for her excellent work as editor of the grammar, and James Spinti, for his editorial hand, thank you. Thanks also to Matthew Van Zomeren for his care in typesetting. I owe a large debt of gratitude to Joseph Hermiz, who first introduced me to the Syriac language and who has provided me with literature and friendship in the years after.

It is truly my hope that this grammar will spark learning into an often neglected, and very beautiful language. ܫܠܡܐ ܥܡܟܘܢ (*šlāmā ʿamkon*, peace with you).

1

Alphabet

ܠܫܢܐ ܣܘܪܝܝܐ — *Leššānā Suryāyā* — The Syriac Language

Introduction

Syriac is a dialect of the Aramaic family of ancient East Semitic languages. Given this, it is read from right to left (←). The alphabet is composed of twenty-two letters that follow generally the same values as their Hebrew counterparts.[1] There are three main scripts used in writing:

Esṭrangelā (ܐܶܣܛܪܰܢܓܶܠܳܐ)[2] – This is the oldest form of the Syriac script. Due to its importance in biblical studies, this is the font that will be used throughout this grammar. It was originally written without vowel pointing. For ease in pronunciation, vowel pointing will be added to the script, but recognize that typically it is absent in Estrangela.

In the fifth century AD, christological controversies (and political boundaries) caused a split within the Syriac-speaking church, and after some time two independent scripts developed:

Western Script (ܣܶܪܛܳܐ, *serṭā*, "line"): Known inaccurately as the Jacobite script. In general, this has become the adopted script for scholarly writings and publications. The vowel pointing used in this volume will follow the *serṭā* style.

Eastern Script (ܡܰܕܢܚܳܝܳܐ, *madnḥāyā*, "Eastern"): Also known as ܣܘܳܕܳܝܳܐ, *swādāyā* ("conversational"), Assyrian, or ܟܰܠܕܳܐ, *kaldā* (Chaldean). In the past, it was branded as the Nestorian script, which is inaccurate.

---

1. While the two are very similar, it is important to note that Aramaic did not develop *out of* Hebrew, but rather *in conjunction with* Hebrew. Both are members of the ancient Semitic family (Hebrew being Northwest Semitic, while Aramaic is East Semitic), and so they share similar grammatical-syntactical structures, as well as some similar vocabulary. However, to best understand the Syriac language, it needs to be recognized and treated on its own.
2. The word Estrangela has no precise translation. Its suggested meanings range from "gospel writing" (from its common usage in biblical texts) to a transliteration of the Greek, meaning "rounded."

The Letters[3]

Before reviewing the Syriac alphabet, it may be helpful for those familiar with Hebrew to examine the comparative Syriac-Hebrew chart in the appendix. Note that Syriac developed independently of Hebrew, and therefore the name and transliteration of some of the letters vary slightly.

There are a few phonetic symbols in the table on the following page that some students may not be familiar with. For those familiar with Hebrew, the transliterations and pronunciations will be familiar. Note the following guide on the more obscure markings.

- *ḥēt* = *ḥ*. Note that there is a small dot beneath the letter *h*. This indicates that the letter is produced in a much harsher tone than the traditional pronunciation of the letter *h*. There is no real English equivalent of this sound, but it is often described as a *fricative h*. It is often rendered phonetically as *kh* or *ch* to communicate the idea.
- *ṭēt* = *ṭ*. The dot beneath the *t* indicates a similar articulation to that of the *ṣādē* below. When pronouncing a *ṭēt*, the tongue is raised high near the top of the mouth. This is a slight distinction, and should not be overemphasized.
- *ʿē* = ʿ. This phonetic symbol resembles a superscripted *c* and is another vocalization in which there is no English equivalent. In fact, this sound is probably the furthest from having any English equivalent. It is described as almost choking on your own throat muscles. To make the sound, try producing the sound of a short *e*, but with the throat tightly constricted.
- *ṣādē* = *ṣ*. The dot beneath the letter *s* indicates that the letter is to be pronounced similar to an *s*, but with a slightly nuanced articulation that is produced by raising the tongue in the mouth. Note that this is sometimes inaccurately represented as a *ts* sound. The sound produced here bears a greater similarity with a simple *s* than it does a *ts*.
- *šīn* = *š*. The addition of an upside down circumflex above the letter *s* indicates that this letter makes the *sh* sound, as in *sh*arp.

3. On the following chart, the asterisk next to a letter indicates that the script has an extra *yūd* attached to it (either before or behind) in order to indicate how the letter looks when next to another letter in a word.

Letter	Name	Transliteration
ܐ	*ālap*	–
ܒ	*bēth*	*b*
ܓ	*gāmal*	*g*
ܕ	*dālat*	*d*
ܗ	*hē*	*h*
ܘ	*waw*	*w*
ܙ	*zayn*	*z*
ܚ	*ḥēt*	*ḥ*
ܛ	*ṭēt*	*ṭ*
ܝ	*yūd*	*y*
ܟ	*kāp** (Initial/Midial)	*k*
ܟ	*kāp* (Final)	*k*
ܠ	*lāmad*	*l*
ܡ	*mīm** (Initial/Medial)	*m*
ܡ	*mīm* (Final)	*m*
ܢ	*nūn** (Initial/Medial)	*n*
ܢ	*nūn* (Final, no connecting prefix)	*n*
ܣ	*semkat*	*s*
ܥ	*ʿē*	ʿ
ܦ	*pē*	*p*
ܨ	*ṣādē*	*ṣ*
ܩ	*qop*	*q*
ܪ	*rīš*	*r*
ܫ	*šīn*	*š*
ܬ	*taw*	*t*

Initial, Medial, and Final Forms

There are three letters in Syriac where the shape of the letter changes depending on where it is placed in the word: *kāp*, *mīm*, and *nūn*.[4] While these changes are not drastic enough to alter the general character of the letter, it is worth noting them. The changes in these three consonants are not unlike those found in the corresponding letters of the Hebrew alphabet.

1. Note the *kāp* in:

   ܟܬܒܐ — *ktābā* — book

   ܗܠܟ — *hallek* — to walk

2. Note the *mīm* in:

   ܡܠܟܐ — *malkā* — king

   ܟܠܡܕܡ — *kollmeddem* — everything

3. Note the *nūn* in:

   ܢܦܠ — *npal* — to fall

   ܬܡܢ — *tamman* — there

   ܐܗܪܘܢ — *ahron* — Aaron

Cursive Font

The Syriac script is written in cursive, with most of the characters connecting to the preceding letter. However, some are written with a break in the connection to the following letter (the letter on the left). These are easy to recognize in the basic forms of the characters because they do not have marks that easily continue the flow of a pen to the left of the letter:

ܕ	*dālat*
ܗ	*hē*
ܘ	*waw*
ܙ	*zayn*
ܨ	*ṣādē*
ܪ	*rīš*
ܬ	*taw*

For example, note how the various letters are connected in Matthew 1:1:[5]

ܟܬܒܐ ܕܬܘܠܕܬܗ ܕܝܫܘܥ ܡܫܝܚܐ. ܒܪܗ ܕܕܘܝܕ ܒܪܗ ܕܐܒܪܗܡ

It is not necessary to memorize this chart, as this will become self-evident as the student

4. Note that this analysis pertains specifically to Estrangela, as the Eastern and Western scripts will sometimes have letters change their shape depending on what letter comes after them, such as a *lāmad* and *ālap* combination in Western Syriac script.
5. Burkitt, F. Crawford, *Euangelion Da-Mepharreshe: The Old Syriac Version of the Four Gospels*, vol. 1. (Piscataway, NJ: Gorgias Press, 2003).

becomes familiar with reading Syriac texts, and will come naturally. For the time being, it is enough to acknowledge the differences.

Memorizing the Alphabet

A helpful tool in memorizing the alphabet is to memorize six words formed by stringing the letters of the alphabet together in order (also note how the cursive connections interact with the proceeding letters):[6]

ܐܒܓܕ ܗܘܙ ܚܛܝ ܟܠܡܢ ܣܥܦܨ ܩܪܫܬ

Abgad Hawaz Ḥaṭṭi Kulman Sa'Paṣ Qaršat

Pronunciation

The consonants which make up the acronym *begadkepat* can be pronounced with hard or soft readings. This is similar to Hebrew. When there is a dot placed above the letter it is given the *hard* pronunciation (also known as a *stop*), and when there is a dot placed below it is given a *soft* pronunciation (also known as a *spirant*). Some of these are voiced, while others are unvoiced.

Hard		Soft	
ܒ݁	*b*	ܒ݂	*v*
ܓ݁	*g*	ܓ݂	*j*
ܕ݁	*d*	ܕ݂	*dh*
ܟ݁	*k*	ܟ݂	*kh*
ܦ݁	*p*	ܦ݂	*ph*
ܬ݁	*t*	ܬ݂	*th*

Note: The pointing for the *begadkepat* letters will be left out of the paradigms in this grammar in order to familiarize the student with a simpler form of the text. But in order to reflect accurately the original manuscripts, pointing will appear in the cited biblical texts for homework and examples.

Along these lines, note that the transliterations in this grammar do not take into account the hard or soft pronunciations of these consonants. For example, note the following word with its transliteration and translation:

ܟܬܳܒܳܐ	*ktābā*	book

This word should actually be pronounced *kthāvā* (or more accurately, *kṯāḇā*) but will show in this grammar as *ktābā*. Remember that when using this grammar it will be up to

6. These words have no meaning but are just a way to memorize the order of the alphabet.

the student to read the Syriac and be aware of the soft or hard pronunciation of the letters in the text.

Gutturals

Some letters in Syriac tend to function differently than typical consonants. These are known as gutturals. The gutturals in Syriac behave much the same way that they do in Hebrew. They include the following letters.

ܐ	ܗ	ܚ	ܥ	ܪ
ālap	*hē*	*ḥēt*	*ʿē*	*rīš*

For now, it is important to simply note them. Later in the grammar, special attention will be given to these letters and how their presence will modify the pronunciation of a word. This is especially true when it comes to conjugating verbs, as verbs that end in a guttural will take an *a*-vowel, and this can make certain words conjugate differently than others.

Vocabulary / Exercises

List of Proper Nouns: Below is a list of proper nouns that will be used throughout the grammar. Do your best to identify the Syriac letters introduced in this chapter and become familiar with the script. Next, try to sound out the words and compare them to their English equivalents. How are they similar? How are they different?

Keep this list handy, because inevitably as you progress in your Syriac studies you will come across a word that will be difficult to parse, spending hours upon hours trying to figure out the meaning, only to sound it out and realize that it is a proper noun. Proper nouns will not be marked in this text, so use this list as a reference.

ܐܒܪܗܡ	Abraham	ܟܦܪܢܚܘܡ	Capernaum
ܐܘܪܫܠܡ	Jerusalem	ܡܘܫܐ	Moses
ܐܝܣܚܩ	Isaac	ܡܨܪܝܢ	Egypt
ܐܦܣܘܣ	Ephesus	ܡܪܝܡ	Mary
ܐܫܥܝܐ	Isaiah	ܡܪܬܐ	Martha
ܒܥܠܙܒܘܒ	Beelzebub	ܡܫܝܚܐ	Christ (Messiah)
ܒܪ ܐܒܐ	Barabbas	ܢܨܪܬ	Nazareth
ܓܠܝܠܐ	Galilee	ܢܝܩܕܡܘܣ	Nicodemus
ܕܘܝܕ	David	ܣܦܪܐ	scribes
ܗܪܘܕܣ	Herod	ܣܛܢܐ	satan
ܝܘܚܢܢ	John	ܦܘܠܘܣ	Paul
ܝܘܢܢ	Jonah	ܦܝܠܛܘܣ	Pilate
ܝܘܣܦ	Joseph	ܦܪܝܫܐ	Pharisees
ܝܗܘܕܝܐ	Jews	ܨܗܝܘܢ	Zion
ܝܗܘܕܐ	Judas	ܩܪܢܠܝܘܣ	Cornelius
ܝܣܪܝܠ	Israel	ܩܝܦܐ	Caiaphas
ܝܥܩܘܒ	Jacob	ܩܣܪ	Caesar
ܝܫܘܥ	Jesus	ܫܡܥܘܢ	Simon
ܟܐܦܐ	Peter (Cephas)	ܫܡܪܝܢ	Samaria

2

Vowels

Introduction

Estrangela Syriac words were originally written without vowel pointing. Given this, it is important for the student to learn the Syriac vocabulary without the aid of these diacritical marks. The vowel marks developed independently within each branch of the Syriac church.

Syriac Vowels

Western Vowels

The Western / *serto* convention developed alongside the Greek vocabulary and therefore used Greek letters as diacritical marks. This is the convention that will be used in the grammar.[1] In this chart, the *yūd* is used only as a reference point.

	Name	Transliteration	English Pronunciation
ܝܰ	*ptāḥā*	*a*	like the "a" in bat
ܝܶ	*rbāṣā*	*e*	like the "e" in pet
ܝܺ	*hbāṣā*	*i*	like the "ee" in bee
ܝܳ	*zqāpā*	*ā*	like the "a" in father (think of it sort of like an "o" or "ah")
ܝܽܘ	*ʿṣāṣā*	*u*	like the "oo" in moon

Pronunciation of *zqapa*: The Eastern and Western traditions within the Syriac church developed independent phonetics when it comes to the pronunciation of the *zqapa* vowel.[2] The Eastern pronounces it with a long *a* (as in father) and the Western pronounces it as an *o* (as in role). This is why the Eastern church calls it the *Peshitta*, and the Western the *Peshitto.*

---

1. Please note that the combination of Estrangela text and Western vowel pointing is used here for ease in learning. Students generally become used to the Western vowel pointing quicker than the Eastern vowels.
2. The split between the Syriac church is generally dated to around the mid-fifth century AD, in conjunction with the many christological controversies that divided the church. The two scripts developed somewhat independently of one another after that point.

Eastern Vowels

The Eastern convention of vowel pointing developed along with more traditional Eastern scripts. This grammar briefly introduces the Eastern script, but it is highly recommended that steps be taken to become proficient with this important style after completion of the grammar. These vowels are again placed over the *yūd* consonant as a reference point.

	Name	Transliteration	English Pronunciation
ܝܵ	*zeqāpā*	*ā*	like the "a" in father
ܝܲ	*petāḥā*	*a*	like the "a" in bat
ܝܸ	*zelama pšiqā*	*e*	like the "i" in sit
ܝܹ	*zelama qišyā*	*ē*	like the "ay" in day
ܝܼ	*ḥevāṣā*	*i*	like the "ee" in bee
ܘܿ	*rewaḥā*	*o*	like the "o" in home
ܘܼ	*rewaṣā*	*u*	like the "oo" in moon

Eastern and Western Vowel Equivalents

Below is a rough estimate of the typical vowel equivalents in the Eastern and Western script. The Eastern vowel pointing is more nuanced in terms of the sounds that are designated so this chart can not be exact in comparison. Remember, the two dialects developed independently from one another, so use this chart as a point of reference only. Additionally, these are only generalizations, as there is generally a lot of flexiblity between the transliteration from one dialect to the other.

Eastern	Pronunciation	Western
ܝܵ	*ā* as in father	ܝܳ
ܝܲ	*a* as in bat	ܝܰ
ܝܸ	*e* as in pet	ܝܶ
ܝܹ or ܒܹܝ	*ē* as in there	ܒܶܝ or ܒܺܝ
ܝܼ	*i as* in bee	ܒܺܝ
ܘܿ	*o* as in home	ܘܳ
ܘܼ	*u* as in moon	ܘܽ

In specific cases, this grammar will also use a *rewaḥā*, ܘܿ, to represent the *o* sound in Western pointed texts. This is used when the *o* sound is more accurate for pronunciation, as the Western texts only attest a *u* sound. In these instances, both pronunciations will be shown.

Quiescent Consonants

There are three consonants which can function as vowels within a word: *ālap*, *yūd*, and *waw*. The technical term for this is quiescent, meaning they take the vocalization of the vowel that preceeds the letter.

ܐ (*ālap*) is always quiescent and has no vocalization outside of the vowel that is associated with it:

Initial *ālap*

ܐܳܕܳܡ *ādām* = Adam

ܐܶܟ݂ܳܠ *ekāl* = to eat

Final *ālap*

ܣܰܝܦܳܐ *saypā* = sword

ܝ (*yūd*) can function as a consonant (*y*) or a vowel (*i* or *e*). If the *yūd* is preceded by or paired with an *i*-vowel, then it carries the vowel sound. If it is preceded by an *e*-vowel, then it lengthens the *e* into a long *ē* and is pronounced like the "ay" in day. Any other pairing retains the *y* pronunciation.

Consonantal *yūd*

ܝܰܘܣܶܦ *yawsep* = Joseph

Quiescent *yūd*

ܡܺܝܬ݂ܶܐ *mite* = dead (pl.)

ܠܟ݂ܶܝܢ *lkēn* = to you (pl.)

ܝܺܕܰܥ *idaʿ* = to know

Additionally, the combination of *ālap-yūd* at the beginning of a word forms the vowel (*i* or *e*)

ܐܝܼܠܳܢܶܐ *ilāne* = trees (pl.)

ܘ (*waw*) can function as a consonant (*w*) or a vowel (*o* or *u*). As with *yūd*, this is dependent on which vowel the *waw* is paired with. If it is preceeded by a *u*-vowel, it carries the *u* pronunciation. Any other vowel retains the consonant.

Consonantal *waw*

ܘܳܠܶܐ *wāle* = it is necessary for

Quiescent *waw*

ܫܽܘܦܪܳܐ *šurpā* = beauty

Likewise, the combination of *ālap-waw* at the beginning of a word forms the vowel (*o* or *u*)

ܐܽܘܪܺܫܠܶܡ *urišlem* = Jerusalem

Writing Vowels

Sometimes the vowel pointing on the top of a word can make the word crowded, especially if there are additional diacritical marks present. If this is the case, some scribes will write the vowel pointing beneath the letter. This does not change the pronunciation at all; it only makes some space for the vowels to be seen more clearly. There is no set way for each vowel to be written, whether above or below, and mainly relies on the scribe's preference. For example, notice the vowel placements below.

ܐܠܗܐ *alāhā* = God

or

ܐܠܗܐ *alāhā* = God

ܪܘܚܐ *ruḥā* = spirit

or

ܪܘܚܐ *ruḥā* = spirit

Pronunciation

The rules for pronunciation and syllabification in Syriac are vast. Here, only the basics will be covered in order to grasp the fundamentals of pronunciation. The best help for pronunciation is to hear the language spoken, but in the absence of this the following rules can be used as a baseline.

When beginning to read the text, start by pairing each consonant with its respective vowel, pronouncing the consonant first. If a consonant appears without a vowel above it then there is an implied *shewa*, a short *ĕ* sound, which is paired with the letter. The sound breaks up the consonants for ease in pronunciation, but it is not marked in the Syriac text. The term *shewa* is borrowed from other Semitic languages (such as Hebrew)[3] since the Syriac language has no sign or name corresponding to the short vowel.[4] For the purposes of this introductory grammar it is enough to simply note the assumption of a short *e* sound when two consonants are next to one another. A *shewa* will not be marked in transliterations in this grammar outside of the discussion here.

In Syriac, syllables can only begin with a single consonant followed by either its accompanying vowel (long or short) or an assumed *shewa*. For example, if we were to pair each consonant with its corresponding vowel in the word below, it would look as follows:

ܟܬܒܐ

kə-ṯā-ḇā

the book

3. In Hebrew, the *shewa* represents either a very short *ĕ* sound (vocal shewa) or no sound at all (silent *shewa*). The vowel is marked in the language with two vertical dots under a letter.
4. Thomas Arayathinal, *Aramaic Grammar*, 2 vols. (Kerala State: India, St. Josephs Press, 1957), 1:24.

Also, if a word begins with a vowel then pronounce only the vowel sound followed by a glottal stop. For example, ܐܡܪ (emar, "to say, speak") would be syllabified as: *e-mar*. Note in this example that syllables can also end in a consonant. If a syllable ends in a consonant it is called "closed" and if it ends in a vowel then it is called "open."

Lastly, if a letter is doubled, then the consonant will both end the previous syllable and start the next one. For example, the word ܫܡܝܐ would be pronounced as: *šə-may-yā*.

Vocabulary

This is the first chapter where formal vocabulary lists are introduced. The vocabulary words have been selected based primarily on frequency of usage in Syriac texts and with a secondary consideration to how they fit within the overall framework of the grammar.[5] The idea behind this is to become familiar with the most prominent vocabulary as early as possible, even if such things like parsing for verbs have not been covered. For example, I have tried to generally use only strong verbs early on, but if there is a widely used weak verb that is important to become familiar with later on in the grammar, it has been introduced in order to build familiarity with the word.

Nouns

ܐܚܐ	*aḥā*	brother
ܐܝܕܐ	*idā*	hand
ܐܪܥܐ	*arʿā*	earth, country, ground, land
ܓܒܪܐ	*gabrā*	man, husband
ܗܝܡܢܘܬܐ	*haymānutā*	faith, belief
ܝܘܡܐ	*yawmā*	day
ܡܕܡ	*meddem*	something
ܡܠܟܐ	*malkā*	king
ܡܠܟܘܬܐ	*malkutā*	kingdom
ܡܠܬܐ	*melltā*	word
ܥܡܐ	*ʿamā*	people, nation
ܫܡܐ	*šmā*	name
ܫܡܝܐ	*šmayyā*	heaven, sky
ܬܠܡܝܕܐ	*talmidā*	disciple

5. The data for word frequency is obtained from George Kiraz, *Lexical Tools to the Syriac New Testament* (Piscataway, NJ: Gorgias Press, 2002).

Other

ܕܝܢ	*dēn*	but, yet, for, then, however
ܠܐ	*lā*	no, not
ܡܢ	*men*	from
ܥܠ	*ʿal*	on, against, over

Exercises

The following passage is from Matthew 6:9b–13 in Syriac. It is the Lord's Prayer, or *Abun D'Bashmaya*, named for the first two words of the prayer. The text is from the *Peshitta* version of the New Testament and has gained notoriety as possibly the closest text known to the actual words that Jesus uttered during the prayer. Transliterate the text and practice the pronunciation of each word. For example, the first two words would be transliterated as *abun d-bašmayyā*.

ܐܒܘܢ ܕܒܫܡܝܐ ܢܬܩܕܫ ܫܡܟ

ܬܐܬܐ ܡܠܟܘܬܟ ܢܗܘܐ ܨܒܝܢܟ ܐܝܟܢܐ ܕܒܫܡܝܐ ܐܦ ܒܐܪܥܐ

ܗܒ ܠܢ ܠܚܡܐ ܕܣܘܢܩܢܢ ܝܘܡܢܐ

ܘܫܒܘܩ ܠܢ ܚܘܒܝܢ ܐܝܟܢܐ ܕܐܦ ܚܢܢ ܫܒܩܢ ܠܚܝܒܝܢ

ܘܠܐ ܬܥܠܢ ܠܢܣܝܘܢܐ ܐܠܐ ܦܨܢ ܡܢ ܒܝܫܐ ܡܛܠ ܕܕܝܠܟ ܗܝ

ܡܠܟܘܬܐ ܘܚܝܠܐ ܘܬܫܒܘܚܬܐ ܠܥܠܡ ܥܠܡܝܢ[6]

Additional Practice

Spend at least ten minutes a day reading Syriac. One of the toughest obstacles to overcome initially with Syriac is that the script is completely foreign to that of English. Therefore, it is important that you spend as much time reading early on as you can.

In addition, if you have access to a Syriac text, begin by copying it word-for-word on some paper. You will get good practice at familiarization with the written forms of the letters, and you will also see how hard of a job the scribes had when they were copying texts. It puts you in a great lineage of text-copyists who have struggled to read and accurately copy certain letters correctly.

---

6. All biblical texts used in this grammar, unless otherwise noted, will be cited from: *The Leiden Peshitta* (Leiden: Brill, 1972); it is also available online at http://cal1.cn.huc.edu/.

3

Nouns and Adjectives

Introduction

Like other languages in the Semitic family, a word can be modified by either adding to the end of it (suffix) or by adding to the beginning of it (prefix). Adding endings to a word is known as inflection, and the inflection will show the state of the noun or adjective. In Syriac there are three states: emphatic, absolute, and construct. Each state is built off of a triconsonantal root that forms the foundation of the noun or adjective that it represents.

Nouns

The Emphatic State

As Syriac (and Aramaic) developed, the emphatic state became the normal form of the noun. The emphatic state is used to a far greater degree than the absolute or construct states. Due to its prominence, more time will be spent discussing this particular inflection.

Definiteness / Indefiniteness

In Syriac there is no inflection to distinguish between a definite and indefinite noun. In English, definite nouns are marked by the word *the* to suggest that a specific or particular thing is in mind. To express an indefinite noun the letter *a* is used. For example:

Indefinite Noun	Definite Noun
A dog is furry.	***The*** dog is furry.
(as in any dog, none in particular)	(as in the specific dog that the author has in mind)

In Syriac, the context must provide the student with the *definiteness* of the noun that is being represented. For example:

ܥܳܠܡܳܐ *ʿālmā* = world

This could be translated as "*a* world" or "*the* world."

While there is no nominal inflection to make the distinction between an indefinite or a definite noun in Syriac, there is a way that authors sometimes allude to the indefiniteness of a noun. This was done by adding the number one (*ḥad*) next to the noun. It can be translated loosely as "a." Note the use in Matthew 8:5:

ܩܶܢܛܪܽܘܢܳܐ ܚܰܕ

qenṭrunā ḥad

Literally: "one centurion"

Translation: "a centurion"

Gender

Syriac nouns have two genders — masculine and feminine. As in other languages, these are purely grammatical genders and should not be confused with physical gender. While the grammatical gender will often follow the physical gender, it would be incorrect to base an observation of physical gender solely on a noun's grammatical gender. For example, the word for spirit in Syriac, *ruḥā*, is of a feminine grammatical gender, but this is not a commentary on the physical gender of the spirit.[1]

Determining a masculine or a feminine noun in the emphatic state is relatively easy to do. There are some irregular nouns (like *ruḥā*), but for the most part (in the emphatic state) if the word ends in *-ā*, then the word is masculine. If the word ends in *-tā*, then it is feminine. For example:

Root:

ܡܠܟ = ruler

ܡܰܠܟܳܐ	ܡܰܠܟܬ݂ܳܐ
malkā = king	*malktā* = queen

1. The later translators of the *Peshitta* treated the term spirit, when it related to the Holy Spirit, as a masculine noun in several places, despite its feminine grammatical gender; see Sebastian P. Brock, "The Holy Spirit as Feminine in Early Syriac Literature," in *After Eve: Women, Theology and the Christian Tradition*, ed. Janet Martin Soskice (London: Marshall-Pickering, 1990), 73–88.

Number

Nouns in Syriac can be numbered either as a single or as a plural noun. The singular can be identified with the *-ā* (ms) or *-tā* (fs) ending, as discussed above. The plural is easily identified by adding an *-e* on the end of the word in the masculine gender. For the feminine, it is a little more nuanced. While in the singular the feminine ending is *-tā*, in the plural the feminine ending is *-atā*. For example:

ܡܰܠܟܳܐ= ruler

ܡܰܠܟܹ̈ܐ	ܡܰܠܟܳ̈ܬܳܐ
malke = kings	*malkātā* = queens

Seyame: While it might seem difficult to identify the feminine plural, it is made easier by the addition of the *seyame*, two dots above the noun. These are present above the *kāp* in the two words above, and are placed above nouns to signify that they are plural. Being able to identify the *seyame* will become an important practice as the earlier manuscripts do not have vowel pointing, making this the only way to identify a plural. For example:

ܡܠܟ̈ܬܐ

malkātā

queens

In the emphatic state, the paradigm for the noun endings looks as follows:

	Masculine		Feminine	
	Singular	Plural	Singular	Plural
Emphatic	◌ܳܐ *-ā*	◌ܶܐ *-e*	ܬܳܐ *-tā*	◌ܳܬܳܐ *-ātā*

The Construct State

In early Semitic languages, such as Biblical Hebrew, the construct state was the primary way to show nominal possession (also known as a genitive). An author would string nouns together that were in the construct state in order to form a construct chain. In Syriac, a *dālat* prefix is added to the word (see chapter 4) to indicate possession.[2] For example:

ܐܠܗܐ	+	ܕ	=	ܕܐܠܗܐ
God		of		of God
alāhā		*d-*		*dalāhā*

The construct state does appear in Syriac, but it is reserved mainly for set phrases or idioms. The presence of the construct state will often reveal that the phrase is still in use from an older period of the language. For example:

ܒܪ ܐܢܫܐ	*bar našā*	son of man (person)
ܡܠܟ ܡܠܟܐ	*mlek malke*	king of kings
ܒܪ ܝܘܢܢ	*bar yawnān*	son of Jonah

Note that the forms in the above examples are identical to the emphatic state, with the exception that they do not have the *-ā* ending. When two words are grouped in a construct chain, the noun in the construct state is immediately followed by a noun that is often in the emphatic state. When translating, the noun in the construct receives the *of* marker of possession. For example:

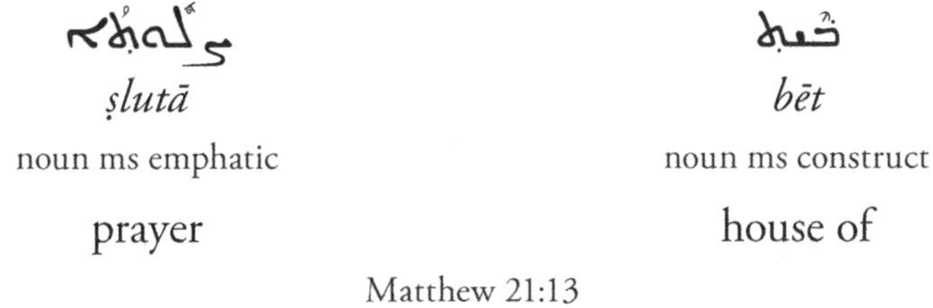

Matthew 21:13

Note that this word looks identical to the preposition ܒܝܬ (*bēt*, "between"), so care must be used when translating. For example, the term ܒܝܬ ܢܗܪܝܢ (*bēt nahrēn*) is the term used to identify Mesopotamia, which translates to "[the land] between the rivers," or ܒܝܬ ܬܚܘܡܐ (*bēt tyume*), which literally translates to "between the borders," signifying a location.

---

2. Biblical Aramaic attests a similar particle (דִּי) that can also function in this manner.

The noun endings for the construct state are as follows:

	Masculine		Feminine	
	Singular	Plural	Singular	Plural
Construct	–	◌ܰܝ	◌ܰܬ	◌ܳܬ
	–	-ay	-at	-āt

The Absolute State

In Imperial Aramaic,[3] the absolute state was the primary form of the noun that was used. This was replaced as time progressed by the emphatic state.[4] By the time that the language had developed into Classical Syriac, the absolute state was rarely used outside of predicate adjectives (see description below), numbers, in conjunction with the words ܟܽܠ (*kull*, "every") and ܕܠܳܐ (*dlā*, "without"), and a few standardized phrases. For example, note the use of the absolute in Matthew 4.22:

ܟܺܐܶܒ	ܟܽܠ
kib	*kull*
noun ms absolute	particle
sickness	every

Translation: Every sickness

The paradigm for the absolute state is as follows:

	Masculine		Feminine	
	Singular	Plural	Singular	Plural
Absolute	–	◌ܺܝܢ	◌ܳܐ	◌ܳܢ
	–	-in	-ā	-ān

Notice that the absolute ms ending is identical to the construct ms, and that the fs ending is similar to the ms emphatic. Because of this, determine which state is being used from *context*. If the form is a number, or in a predicate-adjective relationship, then it can be assumed that the word is in the absolute state.

3. Imperial Aramaic is a predecessor to Classical Syriac and the Aramaic that is found in parts of the Old Testament.
4. The emphatic state in Imperial Aramaic used to be indicative of definiteness. Later the state was nuanced to indicate either a definite or indefinite noun.

The Full Paradigm

Since the three states that are present in Syriac have all been examined, it is helpful to put everything into a single chart for review. This paradigm is a good one to have memorized, but the endings will soon become easy to identify just from the repetition of the grammar.

	Masculine		Feminine	
	Singular	Plural	Singular	Plural
Emphatic	◌ܳܐ	◌ܶ̈ܐ	◌ܬܳܐ	◌ܳܬ̈ܳܐ
Construct	–	◌ܰ̈ܝ	◌ܰܬ	◌ܳܬ̈
Absolute	–	◌ܺܝܢ	◌ܳܐ	◌ܳܢ

Adjectives

Adjectives have the same basic classifications that nouns do: state, gender, and number; they also have the same endings that were described above, so there is no need to memorize additional charts. What does need to be learned is how they function in a sentence. There are three main uses for adjectives: attributive, predicative, or substantive.

Attributive

When an adjective is in the attributive position, it modifies the noun, attributing the characteristic of the adjective to the noun, for example, "the good surfer"; *good* is an attributive adjective because it attributes the quality of *good* to the noun, *the surfer*.

Attributive adjectives are easily recognized in Syriac because the adjective will follow the noun that it modifies, and it will agree in state, number, and gender. These adjectives are also generally in the emphatic state. For example:

Translation: good teacher

Luke 18:18

Predicative

A predicate adjective will assert a quality about the noun it modifies, typically using a supplied *to be* verb that is not apparent in the Syriac. The grammar behind the predicate adjective is leftover from the older days of the language when the emphatic state was actually the determined state, which signified a definite noun. The predicate adjective would then have to disagree with the noun in definiteness, which means that the adjective was typically in the absolute state. In Classical Syriac this is still the case, as the predicate adjective is identified by the adjective being in the absolute state, and agreeing with the noun in only number and gender.[5] As far as ordering goes, predicate adjectives tend to have the adjective come first, but this is not a hard and fast rule. For example:[6]

ܓܰܒܪܳܐ	ܛܳܒ
gabrā	*ṭāb*
noun ms emphatic	adjective ms absolute
man	good

Translation: The man [is] good.

The use of the absolute state is very helpful in determining how an adjective is functioning, whether as a predicate or an attributive. Generally, if the adjective is in the absolute state, then it is a predicate adjective. If it is in the emphatic (with an *-ā* ending), then it is typically an attributive. Also, when there is a predicate adjective in a sentence, it is usually found near the beginning of the sentence.

Substantive

An adjective can function as a substantive in the emphatic state when there is no given noun that the adjective modifies. When this happens, the translator may need to supply a generic noun for a smooth rendering. For example, note Jude 14:

ܕܩܰܕܺܝܫܶܐ	ܒܪܶܒܘܳܬܳܐ
d-qadiše	*b-rebwātā*
dālat + adjective mp emphatic	*bēth* + noun fp emphatic
of holy	with thousands

Translation: With thousands of holy [ones].

5. As the Syriac language continued to develop, predicate-adjective constructions became less and less popular in use.
6. Translations with brackets indicate that the word is being supplied by the author.

Summary of Function

The following chart summarizes the three different ways that adjectives can be used in Syriac. The one item to remember when looking at adjectives is not to overcomplicate the issue. If the translator pays attention to the state of the adjective first, and then the ordering if necessary, the function of the adjective will be easy to distinguish.

Attributive: "the good king"
- adjective follows the noun
- agrees in gender, number, and state

Predicate: "the king is good".
- adjective in the absolute state
- agrees in number and gender
- adjective tends to come first

Substantive: "the good [one]"
- adjective in the emphatic state, but with nothing to modify
- subject must be supplied

Vocabulary

Nouns

ܐܰܒܳܐ	*abā*	father
ܐܰܠܳܗܳܐ	*alāhā*	God
ܒܪܳܐ	*brā*	son
ܡܫܺܝܚܳܐ	*mšiḥā*	Christ, Messiah
ܥܳܠܡܳܐ	*ʿalmā*	age, world, eternity
ܪܘܽܚܳܐ	*ruḥā*	Spirit, breath, wind

Adjectives

ܐ̱ܚܪܺܢܳܐ	*ḥrinā*[7]	other, another
ܒܺܝܫܳܐ	*bišā*	evil, wrong
ܩܰܕܺܝܫܳܐ	*qadišā*	holy
ܪܰܒܳܐ	*rabā*	great, master[8]

7. Notice that the *ālap* is not transliterated and that it has a line beneath it. This is called the *linea occultans* (literally "the line that hides"); it can appear above or below a letter and simply means that the letter has fallen silent and is not pronounced.
8. Also *rāb* = big, great.

Other

ܓܹܝܪ	*gēr*	for (Gk. γάρ)
ܟܽܘܠ / ܟܽܠ	*kull*	all, every
ܟܰܕ	*kad*	when, while, after, as
ܥܰܡ	*ʿam*	with

Exercises

Parse the following Syriac nouns.

	Noun	State	Number	Gender	Translation	Verse
(1)	ܐܰܒܳܐ					Matt 10:37
(2)	ܐܰܠܳܗܶܐ					Acts 7:40
(3)	ܥܳܠܰܡ					Matt 6:13
(4)	ܥܳܠܡܺܝܢ					Matt 6:13
(5)	ܪ̈ܽܘܚܶܐ					Matt 7:25
(6)	ܡܫܺܝܚܳܐ					Matt 1:1
(7)	ܫܶܡ					Matt 10:41
(8)	ܡܰܠܟܬܳܐ					Matt 12:42
(9)	ܡܰܠܟܽܘܬܳܐ					Matt 3:2
(10)	ܬܰܠܡܺܝ̈ܕܶܐ					Matt 14:19

Practice reading and writing the following Syriac passage from John 1:1–5.

ܒܪܫܝܬ ܐܝܬܘܗܝ ܗܘܐ ܡܠܬܐ ܘܗܘ ܡܠܬܐ ܐܝܬܘܗܝ ܗܘܐ ܠܘܬ v.1

ܐܠܗܐ ܘܐܠܗܐ ܐܝܬܘܗܝ ܗܘܐ ܗܘ ܡܠܬܐ

ܗܢܐ ܐܝܬܘܗܝ ܗܘܐ ܒܪܫܝܬ ܠܘܬ ܐܠܗܐ v.2

ܟܠ ܒܐܝܕܗ ܗܘܐ ܘܒܠܥܕܘܗܝ ܐܦܠܐ ܚܕܐ ܗܘܬ ܡܕܡ ܕܗܘܐ v.3

ܒܗ ܚ̈ܝܐ ܗܘܐ ܘܚ̈ܝܐ ܐܝܬܝܗܘܢ ܢܘܗܪܐ ܕܒܢ̈ܝܢܫܐ v.4

ܘܗܘ ܢܘܗܪܐ ܒܚܫܘܟܐ ܡܢܗܪ ܘܚܫܘܟܐ ܠܐ ܐܕܪܟܗ v.5

Translate the following short phrases from Syriac to English.

Luke 1:49 (1)

ܘܩܕܝܫ ܫܡܗ[9]

Matthew 5:35 (2)

ܡܠܟܐ ܪܒܐ

1 Corinthians 3:17 (3)

ܐܠܗܐ ܩܕܝܫ

Luke 1:44 (4)

ܒܚܕܘܬܐ ܪܒܬܐ

9. ܫܡܗ = his name.

Acts 21:28 (5)

ܗܳܢܳܐ[10] ܩܰܕ݁ܺܝܫܳܐ

Matthew 26:3 (6)

ܪܰܒ݁ܰܝ ܟ݁ܳܗܢܶ̈ܐ[11]

Matthew 9:4 (7)

ܒ݁ܺܝܫܳܬ݂ܳܐ ܒ݁ܠܶܒ݁ܟ݂ܽܘܢ[12]

Jeremiah 9:2 (8)

ܡܶܢ ܒ݁ܺܝܫܳܬ݂ܳܐ ܠܒ݂ܺܝܫܳܬ݂ܳܐ[13]

Mark 15:14 (9)

ܡܳܢܳܐ[14] ܓ݁ܶܝܪ ܕ݁ܒ݂ܺܝܫ[15] ܥܒ݂ܰܕ݂[16].

Philippians 1:1 (10)

ܠܟ݂ܽܠܗܽܘܢ[17] ܩܰܕ݁ܺܝܫܶ̈ܐ

---

10. ܗܳܢܳܐ = this.
11. ܟ݁ܳܗܢܶ̈ܐ = priests.
12. ܒ݁ܠܶܒ݁ܟ݂ܽܘܢ = in your heart.
13. The lāmad prefix is a preposition. Add "to" to your translation.
14. ܡܳܢܳܐ = what?
15. This word has a *dālat* in front of it. For now, do not include it in your translation, as these will be covered in the next chapter.
16. ܥܒ݂ܰܕ݂ = he has done.
17. ܠܟ݂ܽܠܗܽܘܢ = to all of them. Hint: the use of the adjective here is substantival.

4

Nominal Prefixes

Introduction

There are four letters that can be added to the front of a noun to modify it. They perform a variety of functions, including adding a preposition, revealing what the direct object is, showing possession, starting a relative clause, or modifying the previous word. When the prefix is ambiguous (as in the *dālat*-prefix), the context will easily determine the function.

Below is a list of the prefixes that are used in Syriac, as well as a brief, general description of how they can modify a word.

Nominal Prefixes

Letter		Translation
ܒ	*bēth*	in, at, with
ܕ	*dālat*	1. of (possession) 2. relative pronoun 3. introduce a quotation 4. alter a conjunction
ܠ	*lāmad*	1. to, for 2. direct object marker
ܘ	*waw*	and

1. *bēth*: A *bēth* affixed to the front of a noun functions as a preposition and is typically translated as "in," "at," or "with." For example:

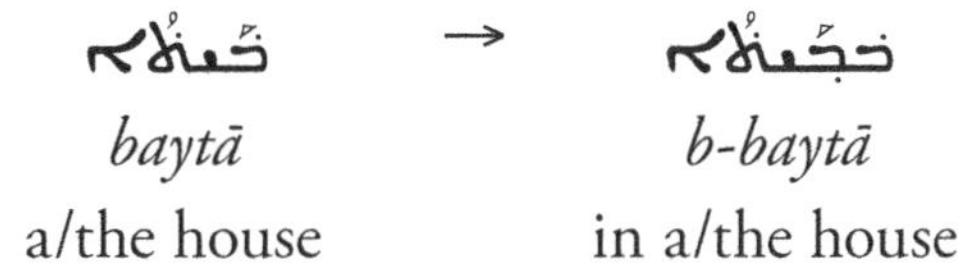

Note that the translation of the preposition above, "in a/the house," could also be rendered "at a/the house" or "with a/the house." Context best determines the meaning of this preposition.

2. *dālat*: *dālat* can serve four functions. It can (a) show possession ("of"), (b) function as a relative pronoun ("who," "whom," "which," "that," etc.), (c) introduce a quotation, much like quotation marks do in English, or (d) it can modify the translation of the word that immediately precedes it. Context will best determine which function the *dālat* is preforming. An easy place to start is this:

   - If the *dālat* is in front of a noun, then it typically shows possession.
   - If the *dālat* is in front of a word that has a verbal component (such as a participle or verb), then it is typically functioning as a relative pronoun. This is because a verb (unless it is a substantival participle) is not able to show or have possession.
   - If the *dālat* is used in a speaking context, then it can be replaced with quotation marks.

   The translation differences among the various uses of *dālat* are predictable according to their function.

   a. When the *dālat* is showing possession, add "of" to the beginning of the word with the prefix particle.[1] An alternative translation would be to add an apostrophe "s," to the end of the word. For example:

ܕܐܠܗܐ	ܡܠܬܐ
d-alāhā	*meltā*
of God	word

Translation: word of God or God's word

   b. When the *dālat* is starting a relative clause, insert a relative pronoun before the word and then readjust your translation once you have the context. "Who" and "that" are typically good places to start.

   As a brief review, a relative clause is a clause that is dependent on and modifies its antecedent. For example: Steve, *who is a surfer*, likes to surf. The relative clause is *who is a surfer*, because it modifies the subject *Steve*. In Syriac, relative clauses function the same way. For example:

ܐܠܗܐ	ܡܢ	ܕܐܫܬܕܪ	ܒܪܢܫܐ
alāhā	*men*	*d-eštadar*	*barnāšā*
God	from	who was sent	a man

Translation: A man who was sent from God.

John 1:6

1. Keep in mind that this is not the only way that possession can be shown in Syriac; the construct state can be used as well. However, the *dālat* prefix is by far the most common way to show possession.

c. When *dālat* is used for marking the beginning of a quotation it remains untranslated, and quotation marks are to be inserted within the translation.

ܐܠܗܟ	ܕܠܡܪܝܐ	ܗܘ	ܟܬܝܒ
alāhāk	*da-l-māryā*	*-aw*	*ktib*
noun ms emphatic + 2 ms pronoun	*dālat* + *lāmad* + noun ms emphatic	3 ms pronoun	peal passive participle ms
your God	to the lord	it (is)	written

Translation: It is written, "To the Lord your God . . ."
Luke 4:8

d. With certain words a *dālat* can combine with the word that comes before it in order to alter the meaning of the word slightly. One of the more common modifiers is the *dālat* after *aykanā* and *ayk*:

ܐܝܟܢܐ	→	ܐܝܟܢܐ ܕ
aykanā		*aykanā d-*
as		how

ܐܝܟ	→	ܐܝܟ ܕ
ayk		*ayk d-*
like		how

Other common modifiers include: ܐܝܠܝܢ (*aylēn*, "which") → ܐܝܠܝܢ ܕ (*aylēn d-*, "those who"); ܐܝܢܐ (*aynā*, "which") → ܐܝܢܐ ܕ (*aynā d-*, "he who"). Also note that the addition of a *dālat* in some cases doesn't necessarily change the meaning of the word substantially. For example, ܡܛܠ (*meṭṭul*, "because [of]") changes to (*meṭṭul d-*, "because"):

ܗܘܐ	ܡܥܒܝ	ܕܠܒܗܘܢ	ܡܛܠ
-wā	*mʿabay*	*d-lebhun*	*meṭṭul*
peal perfect 3ms	pael passive participle ms	*dālat*+ noun + 3mp	conjunction
it was	hardened	their heart	because

Translation: Because their heart was hardened.
Mark 6:52

3. *lāmad*: A *lāmad* at the beginning of a word can also serve multiple functions. It can either function as the preposition "to" or "for," or it can signal the direct object of a word (similar to the use of *lamed* in Biblical Aramaic). Once again, context will be enough to determine which one to use.

a. Adding the *lāmad* preposition to a word is the same as affixing the *bēth* to a word (discussed above). The preposition goes in front of the word that it is modifying and is typically translated with "to" or "for." For example:

ܐܘܪܫܠܡ	→	ܠܐܘܪܫܠܡ
urišlem		*l-urišlem*
Jerusalem		to Jerusalem

b. If the *lāmad* functions as a direct object marker, it will delineate which word is the direct object of the sentence. This is often added for clarity in cases of ambiguity.

To review, the direct object of a sentence is the thing that is receiving the action of the verb. Stated differently, it is the noun in the sentence that is not the subject. Take the following sentence, for example:

ܠܝܫܘܥ	ܚܙܐ	ܓܒܪܐ
l-yešuʿ	*ḥzā*	*gabrā*
lāmad + Jesus	he saw	man

Translation: The man saw Jesus.
Not: Jesus saw the man.
Luke 5:12

In this sentence, we can ascertain that "a/the man saw Jesus" because the *lāmad* prefix on "Jesus" reveals that he is the direct object (receives the action) of the sentence. If it were not for the *lāmad* prefix, then the sentence could be translated either "Jesus saw the man," or "the man saw Jesus." The *lāmad* prefix clears up the ambiguity so that the reader can distinguish between the subject and the direct object.

4. *waw*: An affixed *waw* functions as a conjunction to show where clauses are connected. This is typically done by adding "and" before the word to which it is attached. For example:

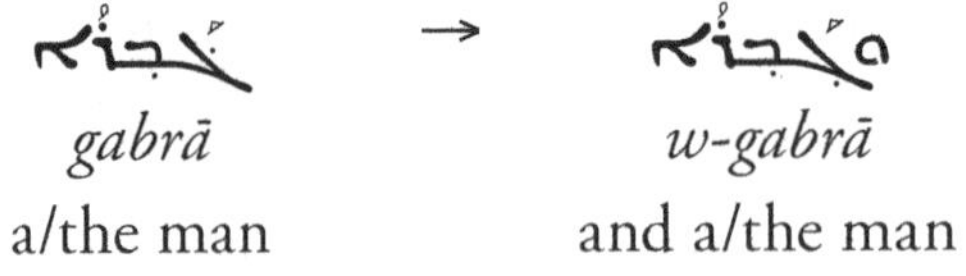

gabrā		*w-gabrā*
a/the man		and a/the man

Vowels with bēth, dālat, lāmad, waw Prefixes

Sometimes proclitic letters will have an additional *a*-vowel added to them. For example, note *waw* in the following two examples:

ܘܲܩܪܸܒ	ܘܚܵܕ
wa-qreb	*w-ḥād*
and he drew near	and one

In the example on the left, note that there is an *a* that appears above the *waw*. The reason for this addition is to break a consonantal cluster. Note that the consonant before the prefix (*qop*) does not have a vowel attached to it. Instead of trying to string a lot of consonants together without a vocalic break, the vowel is added to ease pronunciation. In the second example there is no *a* added to the *waw*. Because the initial consonant in the word is accompanied by a vowel (*ā*), there is no need to break up a consonantal cluster with an additional *a*.

One other element to note is that when the initial consonant is an *ālap*, the vowel will be transferred to the prefix. Since the *ālap* is quiescent, the vowel is paired with the consonant that preceeds it. Note that in the following example the *a*-vowel in the root word on the left is located above the *ālap*. When the *waw* is added the *a*-vowel moves to above the prefix, leaving the *ālap* with nothing above it.

ܐܲܠܵܗܵܐ	→	ܘܲܐܠܵܗܵܐ
alāhā		*w- alāhā*
God		and God

Vocabulary

Nouns

ܢܵܫܵܐ	*nāšā*	man, mankind, people
ܒܲܝܬܵܐ	*baytā*	house
ܡܵܪܝܵܐ	*māryā*	lord, master
ܢܲܦܫܵܐ	*napšā*	soul, self

Adjectives

ܚܲܕ	*ḥad*	one, a
ܛܵܒܵܐ	*ṭābā*	good
ܝܼܗܘܼܕܵܝܵܐ	*ihudāyā*	Jew
ܣܲܓܝܼܐܵܐ	*saggiā*	many, much, very[2]

2. Also *saggi*.

Other

ܐܝܟ	*ayk*	like, according to, as
ܐܠܐ	*ellā*	but
ܐܦ	*āp*	also, even
ܒ-	*b-*	in, at, with
ܕ-	*d-*	of (possession), relative clause marker
ܠ	*l-*	to, for
ܘ-	*w-*	and
ܡܛܠ	*meṭṭul*	because

Exercises

Starting with this chapter, there will be a second set of additional exercises at the end of each chapter. These will include passages from the Old Testament, as well as various other historical Syriac writings. Their main use is to gain experience in translating an unpointed text, and to additionally explore the world of Syriac literature.

Translate the following Syriac phrases into English. Words and grammatical principles that have not been covered up to this point will be translated in the footnotes.

Matthew 3:16 (1)

ܪܘܚܐ ܕܐܠܗܐ

Matthew 10:6 (2)

ܒܝܬ ܐܝܣܪܝܠ

Matthew 12:4 (3)

ܠܒܝܬܐ ܕܐܠܗܐ

Luke 20:25 (4)

ܕܩܶܣܰܪ ܠܩܶܣܰܪ ܘܰܕ݁ܐܠܳܗܳܐ ܠܰܐܠܳܗܳܐ

Matthew 15:6 (5)

ܡܶܠܬ݂ܳܐ ܕܰܐܠܳܗܳܐ

Ephesians 3:15 (6)

ܒ݁ܰܫܡܰܝܳܐ ܘܰܒ݂ܐܰܪܥܳܐ

Mark 14:4 (7)

ܕ݁ܶܝܢ ܐ̱ܢܳܫܳܐ ܡ̣ܢ ܬ݁ܰܠܡܺܝܕ݂ܶ̈ܐ

John 20:22 (8)

ܪܽܘܚܳܐ ܕܩܽܘܕ݂ܫܳܐ

Acts 19:27 (9)

ܐܰܠܳܗܬ݂ܳܐ ܪܰܒ݁ܬ݂ܳܐ

Matthew 5:45 (10)

ܥܰܠ ܛܳ̈ܒܶܐ ܘܥܰܠ ܒ̈ܺܝܫܶܐ

Jeremiah 1:16 (11)

ܠܰܐܠܳܗ̈ܐ ܢܽܘܟ݂ܪ̈ܳܝܶܐ

Matthew 8:11 (12)

ܥܡ ܐܒܪܗܡ ܘܐܝܣܚܩ ܘܝܥܩܘܒ ܒܡܠܟܘܬܐ ܕܫܡܝܐ

Matthew 24:7 (13)

ܢܩܘܡ[3] ܓܝܪ ܥܡܐ ܥܠ ܥܡܐ ܘܡܠܟܘܬܐ ܥܠ ܡܠܟܘܬܐ

Luke 5:15 (14)

ܟܢܫܐ ܣܓܝܐܐ

John 19:19 (15)

ܡܠܟܐ ܕܝܗܘܕܝܐ

John 3:25 (16)

ܥܡ ܝܗܘܕܝܐ ܚܕ

John 11:19 (17)

ܘܣܓܝܐܐ ܡܢ ܝܗܘܕܝܐ

Romans 1:4 (18)

ܒܪܐ ܕܐܠܗܐ

Ephesians 6:23 (19)

ܥܡ ܗܝܡܢܘܬܐ ܡܢ ܐܠܗܐ ܐܒܐ

---

3. ܢܩܘܡ = it will rise.

2 Thessalonians 3:6 (20)

ܡܶܢ ܟܽܠ ܐܰܚܳܐ

Additional Exercises

Genesis 1:11 (21)

ܟܠ ܐܝܠܢܐ

Ezekiel 26:7 (22)

ܡܠܟ ܡ̈ܠܟܐ[4]

Genesis 2:9 (23)

ܕܛܒܬܐ ܘܕܒܝܫܬܐ

Genesis 6:5 (24)

ܒܝܫ ܒܟܠ ܝܘܡ

Exodus 19:6 (25)

ܘܥܡܐ ܩܕܝܫܐ

1 Samuel 25:21 (26)

ܒܝܫܬܐ ܚܠܦ[5] ܛܒܬܐ

4. Note the two dots above the noun. This is to signify that this word is plural.
5. ܚܠܦ = for.

5

Pronouns

Introduction

A pronoun is a word that functions as a noun in a sentence and refers to, or takes the place of, another specific noun. This can take many forms, including personal pronouns (I, you, he, she, it, etc), demonstrative pronouns (this, these, that, those), or interrogative pronouns (who, which, etc.).

Independent Personal Pronouns

Independent personal pronouns are used to signify a person that is being represented. For example, first person addresses the speaker (I, me, my, etc.), second person refers to someone or thing who is being directly addressed by the speaker (you, your, etc.), and third person is another person or thing that is not being directly addressed (he, him, her, they, etc.). In Syriac, the third and second person pronouns attest both a masculine and a feminine pronoun form. This is different from many Indo-European languages such as Greek. See the forms below.

Person	Singular	Translation	Plural	Translation
3m	ܗܘ	*hu* he	ܗܢܘܢ ܗܢܘܢ	*hennon* *hennun* they
3f	ܗܝ	*hi* she	ܗܢܝܢ	*hennēn* they
2m	ܐܢܬ	*att* you (m)	ܐܢܬܘܢ ܐܢܬܘܢ	*atton* *attun* you (pl)
2f	ܐܢܬܝ	*att* you (f)	ܐܢܬܝܢ	*attēn* you (pl)
1c	ܐܢܐ	*enā* I	ܚܢܢ ܐܢܚܢܢ	*ḥnan* *naḥnan* us

Sometimes the masculine plural pronouns will appear with a dot above the *waw*. This is pronounced as *-on*. The two are phonetically similar, and the *u* pronunciation is found predominately in the Western Syriac tradition. Notice the *linea occultans* beneath the 2ms and 2fs personal pronouns; this line tells the reader that the letter is not pronounced. Therefore, these pronouns are pronounced *att*, *att*, *atton,* and *attēn* instead of *antt*, *ant*, etc.[1] Also note that the *yūd* at the end of the second feminine singular pronoun is typically left silent. As the language developed, the tendency was for the letter to fall silent, but both pronunciations are valid.

This is also a good time to highlight the second and third plural endings because they will show up again and again in various forms. In general, if you see the following endings, a loose association can be formed:

ܘܼܢ / ܘ̇ܢ	Masculine Plural
ܶܢ	Feminine Plural

Uses of the Independent Personal Pronouns

Independent personal pronouns have many uses in Syriac. It is a flexible grammatical construction that follows a logical pattern. Here are some of the more common uses:

1. Simple Use: Pronouns can be used as stand-alone nouns in a sentence. This is the simplest use of the personal pronouns.

ܒܰܒܥܶܠܙܒܽܘܒ	ܐܶܢܳܐ	ܘܶܐܢ
ba-bʿelzbub	*enā*	*w-en*
bēth + name	pronoun 1cs	*waw* + particle
in Beelzebub	I	and if

Translation: And if I, in Beelzebub...
Matthew 12:27

1. This is a characteristic that is shared with other Semitic langauges.

2. Simple Sentences: Pronouns can be used in a simple equative or linking sense, such as in "he is good." In these instances, the linking verb must be supplied by the translator, which is normally "to be" in the appropriate tense.

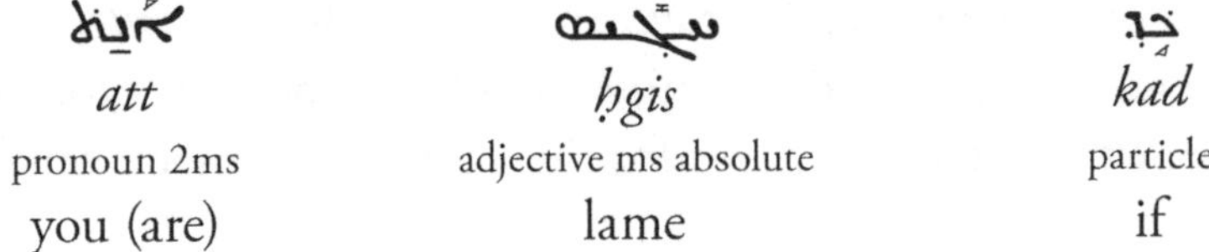

ܐܢ݁ܬ݁	ܚܓܝܣ	ܟܕ
att	*ḥgis*	*kad*
pronoun 2ms	adjective ms absolute	particle
you (are)	lame	if

Translation: If you (are) lame…
Matthew 18:8

3. Enclitic/Copulas: Pronouns can also follow nouns in an abbreviated form. The prolific use of pronouns in Syriac (and Aramaic) gave way to an abbreviated, shorthand way to say "he/she/it is ____." In doing this, the first consonant of the pronoun is not pronounced, and the two words are spoken together to make a single word. In the example below, the first two words would be pronounced as a single word: *melle-w*:

ܕܐܠܗܐ	ܗ̱ܘ	ܡܠܠܐ
d-alāhā	*-w*	*melle*
dālat + noun ms emphatic	enclitic pronoun ms	noun fp emphatic
of God	he	words

Translation: He (is) the words of God.
John 3:34

The enclitic forms include:

Person	Singular	Translation	Plural	Translation
3m	ܗ̱ܘ ܗ̱ܘ	*-u* *-w* he	ܐܢܘܢ ܐܢܘܢ	*ennon* *ennun* they
3f	ܗ̱ܝ ܗ̱ܝ	*-i* *-y* she	ܐܢܝܢ	*ennēn* they
1c	ܐ̱ܢܐ	*-na* I	ܚ̱ܢܢ	*-nan* us

Note that the 3mp and 3fp forms are not enclitic but are shortened forms (when pronounced) of the independent pronouns. Also, notice that the 3 singular forms either attest a vowel, when combined with a word ending in a consonant, or not, when combined with a word ending in a vowel.

4. As the subject of a participle: One of the most popular uses of the pronoun is to follow a participle in a sentence. (Participles will be covered later in the grammar, but this grammatical feature is so prominent that it warrants mention here). These can be either enclitic or stand-alone usages.

   Note: One other point to mention is that the participle without vowel pointing looks extremely similar to the peal perfect verb. One of the ways to distinguish a participle is that it will typically have a pronoun after it in order to indicate the subject of the participle, for example:

ܠܟܘܢ	ܐܢܐ	ܐܡܪ
l-kun	*nā*	*āmar*
lāmad + 3mp	pronoun 1cs	participle
to you	I	saying

Translation: I (am) saying to you.
Matthew 6:25

5. Emphatic: This category is not used often in Syriac, but sometimes an unnecessary pronoun can be added to a sentence for emphasis. In these cases, the subject is supplied by the verb, but the author chooses to add emphasis to what is being said by accentuating the subject of the sentence.

ܐܢܬܘܢ	ܐܦ	ܬܬܒܘܢ
attun	*āp*	*tetbun*
pronoun 2mp	particle	peal imperfect 2mp
you	also	you will sit

Translation: You (emphatic) will also sit...
Matthew 19:28

Demonstrative Pronouns

Demonstrative pronouns come in two categories, near (this, these) and far (that, those). The function of a demonstrative pronoun is to replace a noun that is understood in context. These operate the same way in English as they do in Syriac, and can be easily translated.

	Masculine		Feminine	
Near (singular)	ܗܳܢܳܐ	*hānā* this	ܗܳܕܶܐ	*hāde* this
Near (plural)	ܗܳܠܶܝܢ	*hālēn* these	ܗܳܠܶܝܢ	*hālēn* these
Far (singular)	ܗܰܘ	*haw* that	ܗܳܝ	*hāy* that
Far (plural)	ܗܳܢܽܘܢ ܗܳܢܘܿܢ	*hānun* *hānon* those	ܗܳܢܶܝܢ	*hānēn* those

Note that some of the personal pronouns and demonstrative pronouns are comprised of the same letters. This can be tricky to discern which is which when there is no vowel pointing. In this case, dots are often added as aids for the reader. If the dot is placed above the word, it is a personal pronoun, and if it is below then it is a demonstrative pronoun. For example:

ܗܢܘܢ	Demonstrative Pronoun: Those
ܗܢܘܢ	Personal Pronoun: They

Demonstrative pronouns can function either (1) independently: "That was good," (2) as an adjective: "That man is a surfer," or (3) as a substantive: "That (man) surfs."

1. Independent Demonstrative Pronouns: For these types of pronouns, the translation procedure is fairly straightforward. The demonstrative pronoun can be translated according to its parsing, and it does not modify another word in the sentence.

ܐܶܢܳܐ	ܐܶܬ݂ܺܝܬ݂	ܗܳܢܳܐ	ܡܶܛܽܠ
enā	*etit*	*hānā*	*meṭṭul*
pronoun 1cs	peal perfect 1ms	demonstrative pronoun ms	conjunction
I	I came	this	because

Translation: Because (of) this I (emphatic) came.

John 1:31

2. Adjectival Demonstrative Pronoun: When a demonstrative pronoun is used as an adjective, it modifies a noun in the sentence. These are structured the same way as adjectives and they work the same way in a sentence.

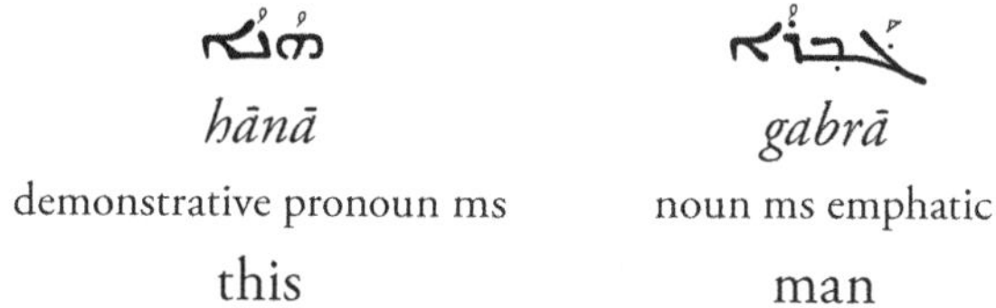

ܗܳܢܳܐ	ܓܰܒ݂ܪܳܐ
hānā	*gabrā*
demonstrative pronoun ms	noun ms emphatic
this	man

Translation: This man.
John 7:46

3. Substantival Demonstrative Pronouns: Sometimes, a demonstrative pronoun will require that the subject of the sentence be associated with it, even though it is not explicitly mentioned. These are called substantival because they represent a physical entity, but the referent is not overtly mentioned in the sentence. In these cases, a subject must be provided.

ܝܶܫܽܘܥ	ܠܘܳܬ݂	ܐܶܬ݂ܳܐ	ܗܳܢܳܐ
yešuʿ	*lwot*	*etā*	*hānā*
name	preposition	peal perfect 3ms	demonstrative pronoum ms
Jesus	toward	he came	this

Translation: This (man) came to Jesus.
John 3:2

Interrogative Pronouns

Interrogative pronouns ask a question. They can be used in several different contexts, but their general usage is very similar to that of English. The two main interrogative pronouns used are:

ܡܰܢ	ܡܳܢܳܐ
man	*mānā*
Who?	What?

When there is no vowel pointing in a text, the interrogative pronoun is distinguished from the preposition by the placement of a dot either above or below the word:

ܡܰܢ	ܡܶܢ
man	*men*
who?	from

Interrogative pronouns can take an enclitic pronoun in order to modify them into a complete sentence that is asking a question. For example, if the third masculine singular ending is added to ܡܳܢܳܐ (*mānā*), forming ܡܳܢܳܐ ܗܘ (*mānāw*), then the translation is modified to:

ܡܳܢܳܐ ܗܘ	What is it?
ܡܰܢ ܗܘ	Who is it?

These can also appear as a single word, as in:

ܡܰܢܘ	Who is it?

As with the demonstrative and personal pronouns, a dot above and below is used to distinguish between words when there is no vowel pointing:

ܡܢܘ	ܡܢܘ
manu	*mānu*
Who is it?	What is it?

Sometimes there will be varying forms of interrogative pronouns depending on what they are modifying. In certain cases, they can be inflected according to gender. Note the following examples:

Which?

Masculine	ܐܰܝܢܳܐ *aynā*
Feminine	ܐܰܝܕܳܐ *aydā*[2]
Plural	ܐܰܝܠܶܝܢ *aylēn*

2. As with other pronouns, this word is identical with another when there is no vowel pointing. Note the dot placement in: ܐܝܕܐ (*aydā*, "which?") and ܐܝܕܐ (*iydā*, "hand").

The way in which interrogative pronouns are used will become second nature as the language becomes familiar. At this point, it is necessary only to review one example in order to become familiar with a typical use.

ܐ̱ܢܳܐ	ܚܣܺܝܪ	ܡܳܢܳܐ
-nā	*ḥsir*	*mānā*
pronoun 1cs	adjective ms absolute	interrogative pronoun
I	lacking	what?

Translation: What (am) I lacking?
Matthew 19:20

Vocabulary

Nouns

ܐܰܢ̱ܬܬܳܐ	*attā*	woman, wife
ܒܰܪܢܳܫܳܐ	*barnāšā*	human, person (*bar* + *nāšā*, son of man)
ܙܰܒܢܳܐ	*zabnā*	time, season
ܚܰܝ̈ܶܐ	*ḥayye*	life, salvation
ܟܶܢܫܳܐ	*kenšā*	crowd
ܡܕܺܝܢ̱ܬܳܐ	*mdittā*	city, town
ܡܰܠܰܐܟ݂ܳܐ	*malakā*	angel, messenger
ܢܳܡܽܘܣܳܐ	*nāmusā*	law (Gk. νόμος)
ܥܒ݂ܳܕܳܐ	*ʿbādā*	deed, work
ܪܺܫܳܐ	*rišā*	beginning, head

Verbs

ܐܶܙܰܠ	*ezal*	to go, depart
ܐܶܡܰܪ	*emar*	to say, speak
ܗܘܳܐ	*hwā*	to be
ܟܬܰܒ	*ktab*	to write
ܥܒܰܕ	*ʿbad*	to do, make

ܩܪܶܒ	*qreb*	to draw near
ܫܟܰܚ	*škaḥ*	to be able, find, happen[3]
ܫܡܰܥ	*šmaʿ*	to hear, obey

Other

ܐܰܘ	*aw*	or, else
ܐܰܝܟܰܢܳܐ	*aykanā*	how? ("as" with *dālat*)
ܐܶܢ	*en*	if
ܠܘܳܬ	*lwāt*	to, towards, with

Exercises:

Matthew 11:23 (1)

ܘܰܐܢ̱ܬܝ ܟܦܰܪܢܰܚܘܡ

Mark 15:23 (2)

ܗܽܘ ܕܶܝܢ ܠܳܐ ܢܣܰܒ[4]

John 7:49 (3)

ܐܶܠܳܐ ܐܶܢ ܥܰܡܳܐ ܗܳܢܳܐ ܕܠܳܐ ܝܳܕܰܥ[5] ܢܳܡܽܘܣܳܐ

Matthew 9:14 (4)

ܠܡܳܢܳܐ ܚܢܰܢ ܘܦܪ̈ܝܫܶܐ ܨܳܝܡܺܝܢ ܚܢܰܢ[6] ܣܰܓܺܝ

---

3. The verb ܫܟܰܚ will often appear with an *ālap* in front of the word: ܐܶܫܟܰܚ. Also, the peal participle of the word appears with a *mīm* in the front. This is a common form of this verb and is worth committing to memory. ܡܶܫܟܰܚ = peal participle, "being able."
4. ܢܣܰܒ = he received.
5. ܝܳܕܰܥ = knowing.
6. ܨܳܝܡܺܝܢ ܚܢܰܢ = we are fasting.

John 7:39 (5)

ܗܳܕܶܐ ܕܶܝܢ ܐܶܡܰܪ[7] ܥܰܠ ܪܽܘܚܳܐ

Acts 16:24 (6)

ܗܽܘ ܕܶܝܢ ܟܰܕ ܩܰܒܶܠ[8] ܗܳܢܳܐ ܦܽܘܩܕܳܢܳܐ[9]

Matthew 5:15 (7)

ܕܒܰܝܬܳܐ ܐܶܢܽܘܢ

Matthew 10:14 (8)

ܟܰܕ ܢܳܦܩܺܝܢ[10] ܐܢ݇ܬܽܘܢ ܡܶܢ ܒܰܝܬܳܐ

Matthew 21:10 (9)

ܡܰܢܽܘ ܗܳܢܳܐ

Matthew 7:12 (10)

ܗܳܢܽܘ[11] ܓܶܝܪ ܢܳܡܽܘܣܳܐ ܘܰܢܒ݂ܺܝܶܐ

Matthew 7:28 (11)

ܘܰܗܘܳܐ[12] ܕܟܰܕ ܫܰܠܶܡ[13] ܝܶܫܽܘܥ ܡܶܠܶܐ ܗܳܠܶܝܢ

---

7. ܐܶܡܰܪ = he said.
8. ܩܰܒܶܠ = receiving.
9. ܦܽܘܩܕܳܢܳܐ = commandment.
10. ܢܳܦܩܺܝܢ = going.
11. Note how the pronouns contract (ܗܳܢܳܐ + ܗܽܘ).
12. ܘܰܗܘܳܐ = and he was.
13. ܫܰܠܶܡ = completed.

Matthew 22:32 (12)

ܕܐܢܐ ܐܢܐ ܐܠܗܗ[14] ܕܐܒܪܗܡ ܐܠܗܗ ܕܐܝܣܚܩ ܐܠܗܗ ܕܝܥܩܘܒ

John 7:39 (13)

ܗܕܐ ܕܝܢ ܐܡܪ[15] ܥܠ ܪܘܚܐ

Luke 20:2 (14)

ܒܐܝܢܐ ܫܘܠܛܢܐ[16] ܗܠܝܢ ܥܒܕ[17] ܐܢܬ

Matthew 23:17 (15)

ܡܢܘ ܓܝܪ ܪܒ

John 8:46 (16)

ܠܡܢܐ ܠܐ ܡܗܝܡܢܝܢ[18] ܐܢܬܘܢ

Matthew 22:36 (17)

ܐܝܢܐ ܦܘܩܕܢܐ[19] ܪܒ ܒܢܡܘܣܐ

Matthew 22:30 (18)

ܐܠܐ ܐܝܟ ܡܠܐܟܐ ܕܐܠܗܐ ܒܫܡܝܐ

---

14. ܐܠܗܗ = the god of him (x3). Note the additional *hē* on the end of ܐܠܗܐ. This is what is known as a pronominal suffix and will be covered in the next chapter.
15. ܐܡܪ = he said.
16. ܫܘܠܛܢܐ = authority.
17. ܥܒܕ = doing.
18. ܡܗܝܡܢܝܢ = believing.
19. ܦܘܩܕܢܐ = commandment.

Acts 4:17 (19)

ܢܦܘܩ[20] ܒܥܡܐ ܛܒܐ[21] ܗܢܐ

Matthew 5:14 (20)

ܐܢܬܘܢ ܐܢܘܢ ܢܘܗܪܗ[22] ܕܥܠܡܐ

Additional Exercises

Genesis 15:7 (21)

ܐܢܐ ܐܢܐ ܡܪܝܐ

Exodus 3:11 (22)

ܘܐܡܪ[23] ܡܘܫܐ ܠܐܠܗܐ ܡܢ ܐܢܐ

Exodus 19:6 (23)

ܘܐܢܬܘܢ ܬܗܘܘܢ[24] … ܥܡܐ ܩܕܝܫܐ

Exodus 32:10 (24)

ܘܐܥܒܕܟ[25] ܠܥܡܐ ܪܒܐ

Proverbs 16:14 (25)

ܚܡܬܗ[26] ܕܡܠܟܐ ܡܠܐܟܐ ܐܢܘܢ ܕܡܘܬܐ[27]

1 Samuel 20:12 (26)

---

20. ܢܦܘܩ = he will go out.
21. ܛܒܐ = fame, reputation.
22. ܢܘܗܪܗ = light of it.
23. ܘܐܡܪ = and he said.
24. ܬܗܘܘܢ = you will be.
25. ܘܐܥܒܕܟ = and I will make you.
26. ܚܡܬܗ = his anger.
27. ܕܡܘܬܐ = of death.

ܐܝܟ ܕܟܠܐ ܗܠܐ ܡܚܪ[1]

6

Pronominal Suffixes

Introduction

In Syriac, as with many other Semitic languages, a suffix can be added to the end of various words in order to show a variety of different functions. The five main functions are:

1. When attached to the end of a noun, suffixes show possession ("*his* house").
2. When attached to the end of a preposition, suffixes show what the object of the preposition is ("to *him*").
3. When attached to the end of a verb, suffixes reveal the direct object of the verb ("he ate *it*"). These will be discussed later in the grammar.
4. When attached to the particles ܐܝܬ/ ܠܝܬ (*it* / *layt*), suffixes act as a linking verb ("*you are* the teacher").
5. Suffixes can be used with various particles as a means to associate the particle with an object ("all *of it*" or "belonging *to you*").

These are general categories, as the flexibility of the pronominal suffix in Syriac is truly impressive. Therefore, while this may seem like a dizzying amount of information for an introduction, just know that the bottom line is that pronouns are very flexible in their usage and at the same time very predictable in their interpretation.

25. ܡܚܪ = tomorrow.

The Pronominal Suffix Paradigms

Before diving deeper into the uses of pronominal suffixes, it is important to become familiar with the following two paradigms. While there are two paradigms to learn, they are both very similar. The guidelines for when a certain set is used over another are not uniform, but the general pattern is that the first set of pronominal suffixes is used with all nouns except for those that are masculine plural.

Type 1: Masculine Singular, Feminine Singular, and Feminine Plural

	Singular	Plural
3m	◌ܶܗ *-eh*	ܗܘܿܢ / ܗܽܘܢ *-hon/hun*
3f	◌ܳܗ̇ *-āh*	ܗܶܝܢ *-hēn*
2m	◌ܳܟ *-āk*	ܟܘܿܢ / ܟܽܘܢ *-kon/kun*
2f	◌ܶܟܝ *-ek*	ܟܶܝܢ *-kēn*
1c	ܝ -	◌ܰܢ *-an*

Type 2: Masculine Plural

	Singular	Plural
3m	◌ܰܘܗܝ *-aw*	◌ܰܝܗܘܿܢ / ◌ܰܝܗܽܘܢ *-awhon/-awhun*
3f	◌ܶܝܗ̇ *-ēh*	◌ܰܝܗܶܝܢ *-ayhēn*
2m	◌ܰܝܟ *-ayk*	◌ܰܝܟܘܿܢ / ◌ܰܝܟܽܘܢ *-aykon/-aykun*
2f	◌ܰܝܟܝ *-ayk*	◌ܰܝܟܶܝܢ *-aykēn*
1c	◌ܰܝ *-ay*	◌ܰܝܢ *-ayn*

Note that the primary difference between the two paradigms is a *yūd* placed in the suffix. Because of this, it is recommended that the first paradigm be memorized, and then the second be recognized by where the *yūd* is placed.

Also, if a word ends in an *ālap* and there is a pronominal suffix attached to it, the *ālap* will assimilate into the pronominal suffix and linking vowel.

ܟܬܳܒܳܐ	→	ܟܬܳܒܶܗ	not	ܟܬܳܒܐܶܗ
ktābā		*ktābeh*		
book		his book		

Below is an example of the pronominal suffixes attached to the noun ܒܰܝܬܳܐ (*baytā*, "house").

Masculine Singular

	Singular	Plural
3m	ܒܰܝܬܶܗ *bayteh* his house	ܒܰܝܬܗܘܿܢ / ܒܰܝܬܗܽܘܢ *baython/baythun* their house
3f	ܒܰܝܬܳܗ̇ *baytāh* her house	ܒܰܝܬܗܶܝܢ *baythēn* their house
2m	ܒܰܝܬܳܟ݂ *baytāk* your house	ܒܰܝܬܟ݂ܘܿܢ / ܒܰܝܬܟ݂ܽܘܢ *baytkon/baytkun* your house
2f	ܒܰܝܬܶܟ݂ܝ *baytek* your house	ܒܰܝܬܟ݂ܶܝܢ *baytkēn* your house
1c	ܒܰܝܬܝ *bayt* my house	ܒܰܝܬܰܢ *baytan* our house

Masculine Plural

	Singular	Plural
3m	ܒ̈ܳܬܰܘܗ̱ܝ *baytaw* his houses	ܒ̈ܳܬܰܝܗܘܿܢ / ܒ̈ܳܬܰܝܗܽܘܢ *baytayhun / baytayhon* their houses
3f	ܒ̈ܳܬܶܝܗ̇ *bayteh* her houses	ܒ̈ܳܬܰܝܗܶܝܢ *baytayhēn* their houses
2m	ܒ̈ܳܬܰܝܟ *baytayk* your houses	ܒ̈ܳܬܰܝܟܘܿܢ / ܒ̈ܳܬܰܝܟܽܘܢ *baytaykon/baytaykun*
2f	ܒ̈ܳܬܰܝܟܝ *baytayk* your houses	ܒ̈ܳܬܰܝܟܶܝܢ *baytaykēn* your houses
1c	ܒ̈ܳܬܰܝ *baytay* his houses	ܒ̈ܳܬܰܝܢ *baytayn* our houses

The feminine verbs are formed regularly after the same pattern as the masculine. For example, note Matthew 1:6:

ܐܰܢ̱ܬ݁ܬ݂ܳܐ	+	◌ܗ̇	not	ܐܰܢ̱ܬ݁ܬ݂ܶܗ
attā		*ktābeh*	*-eh*	*atteh*
wife		3 ms		his wife

Uses of Pronominal Suffixes

1. Nouns: A pronominal suffix can be added to the end of a noun in order to show possession of an object. For example, when you add the third masculine singular pronominal suffix to "house," it becomes "his house."

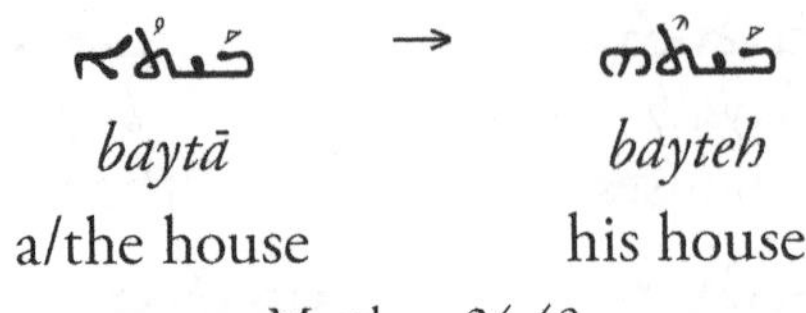

baytā → *bayteh*

a/the house → his house

Matthew 24:43

Note that pronominal suffixes can also be redundant. These are technically called pleonastic datives. For example, consider the use in "the son of man."

ܕܐܢܳܫܳܐ	ܒܪܶܗ
d-nāšā	*breh*
dālat + noun ms emphatic	noun ms emphatic + 3ms
of man	his son

Literal Translation: Son of him of the man

Translation: Son of Man

Matthew 24:44

2. Prepositions: A pronominal suffix can be added to the end of a preposition in order to show the object of the preposition. This is seen in its simplest form with the *lāmad* and *bēth* prefixes. For example:

ܠ- → ܠܶܗ

l- → *leh*

to/for → to / for him

Matthew 25:26

One of the most common phrases used to introduce a speaking quotation in the New Testament often makes use of the pronominal suffix attached to a preposition:

ܝܫܘܥ	ܠܗܘܢ	ܐܡܪ
yešuʿ	*lhun*	*āmar*
name	*lāmad* + 3mp	peal participle ms
Jesus	to them	saying

Translation: Jesus (was) saying to them.
John 6:35

These can also be attached to stand-alone prepositions, and their function is similar.

ܠܘܬܗ	ܘܩܪܒܘ
lwāteh	*wa-qreb*
preposition + 3ms	peal perfect 3mp
toward him	they approached

Translation: They approached toward/near him.
Matthew 13:36

Different prepositions or particles can have either type 1 or type 2 pronominal suffixes attached to them. Here is a short list of some of the most often used stand-alone words and their associated pronominal suffixes. This is just for reference, and it is not necessarily recommended that this chart be memorized.

Type 1 Suffixes

ܡܢ	*men*	from
ܡܛܠ	*meṭṭul*	because of, for the sake of
ܒܝܢܬ	*baynāt*	among, between
ܠܘܬ	*lwāt*	at, near, with, to toward
ܐܝܟ	*ayk*	like, as

Type 2 Suffixes

ܥܠ	*ʿal*	on, upon, over
ܬܚܝܬ	*tḥeyt*	under
ܩܕܡ	*qdām*	before
ܒܝܢܝ	*baynay*	among, between

Note: The terms *baynāt* and *baynay* both mean the same thing, but their spelling can differ depending on which ending they take.

3. Verbs: Verbs can have pronominal suffixes added to them in order to introduce the object of the verb. These will be covered later in the grammar.
4. ܐܝܬ/ ܠܝܬ (*it*, *layt*): Pronominal suffixes can also attach themselves to the ends of particles in order to modify them. Two of the most common in the language are the particles ܐܝܬ (*it*, "there is") and ܠܝܬ (*layt*, "there is not"):

ܐܝܬ	ܠܐܝܬ (ܐܝܬ + ܠܐ)
it	*layt*
there is	there is not

The words ܐܝܬ/ ܠܝܬ (*it* / *layt*) are very important in Syriac for showing a predication of existence. These constructions are formulated by using ܐܝܬ/ ܠܝܬ (*it* / *layt*) + prepositional phrase + subject. When translating, ܐܝܬ/ ܠܝܬ *it* / *layt* may be read literally, for example: "There is, in the house, food" = "There is food in the house."

ܐܒܪܗܡ	ܠܢ	ܐܝܬ	ܐܒܐ
abrāhām	*lan*	*it*	*abā*
name	*lāmad* + 1cp	particle	noun ms emphatic
Abraham	to us	there is	father

Translation: Our father is Abraham.

Matthew 3:9

However, when a pronominal suffix is attached to the word, it functions as a linking verb (to be). These will literally be read, for example, as: "there is you, a father" = "you are a father."

ܕܐܢܫܐ	ܒܪܗ	ܐܝܬܘܗܝ
d-nāšā	*breh*	*itaw*
dālat + noun ms emphatic	noun+ 3 ms	particle
of the man	son of him	there is him

Translation: He is the Son of Man.

Matthew 12:8

5. Other Particles: When a pronominal suffix is added to other specific particles, it can point to the object of the particle. This can be seen simply as the possessive element of the suffix. For example, the particle ܟܽܠ (*kull*) means "everything," and when a pronominal suffix is attached to the word it makes that the object of the particle.

ܦܰܓ݂ܪܳܟ݂	ܟܽܠܶܗ
pagrāk	*kulleh*
noun ms emphatic + 2ms	particle + 3ms
your body	all of it

Translation: All of your body.
Matthew 5:30

The same thing happens with the particle ܕܺܝܠ (*dill*), which means "belonging to." This is generally used to show possession.

ܕܺܝܠܝ	ܙܰܒܢܝ
dill	*zabn*
particle + 1cs	noun ms emphatic + 1cs
belonging to me	my time

Translation: My time.
John 7:6

Postpositive Conjunctions

One element to note from a translation standpoint is that often a conjunction appears as the second word of a sentence; this reflects the pattern of Greek grammar. Simply translate the conjunction as the first word in the sentence, even though it appears as the second word.

ܐܶܡܰܪ	ܕܶܝܢ	ܝܶܫܘܥ
emar	*dēn*	*yešuʿ*
peal perfect 3ms	conjunction	name
he said	but	Jesus

Translation: But Jesus said.
Luke 18:27

Vocabulary

Nouns

ܐܦܐ	*appe*	face[1]
ܚܝܠܐ	*ḥaylā*	power, strength, might
ܠܒܐ	*lebbā*	heart
ܢܒܝܐ	*nbiyā*	prophet
ܥܝܢܐ	*ʿaynā*	eye
ܦܓܪܐ	*pagrā*	body
ܩܠܐ	*qālā*	voice
ܫܠܡܐ	*šlāmā*	peace
ܫܥܬܐ	*šāʿtā*	hour
ܬܝܒܘܬܐ	*taybutā*	repentance

Verbs

ܢܣܒ	*nsab*	to take, receive
ܩܒܠ	*qbal*	to receive, accuse, appeal
ܫܒܩ	*šbaq*	to forgive, leave
ܫܠܡ	*šlem*	to complete, be full

Other

ܐܝܬ / ܠܝܬ	*it / layt*	there is / there is not
ܗܐ	*hā*	lo, behold
ܗܟܢܐ	*hākannā*	thus
ܥܕܡܐ	*ʿadmā*	until
ܩܕܡ	*qdām*	before
ܬܡܢ	*tammān*	there

1. When ܐܦܐ is used with ܢܣܒ, it means “hypocrite”: ܢܣܒ ܒܐܦܐ.

Exercises

Mark 12:36 (1)

ܕܶܐܡܰܪ[2] ܡܳܪܝܳܐ ܠܡܳܪܝ

Mark 12:43 (2)

ܘܶܐܡܰܪ[3] ܠܗܽܘܢ ܐܰܡܺܝܢ[4]

Acts 5:11 (3)

ܘܰܠܟܽܠܗܽܘܢ ܗܳܢܽܘܢ ܕܫܡܰܥܘ[5]

Matthew 9:31 (4)

ܗܶܢܽܘܢ ܕܶܝܢ ܢܦܰܩܘ[6]... ܒܟܽܠܳܗ ܐܰܪܥܳܐ ܗܳܝ

Matthew 12:11 (5)

ܗܽܘ ܕܶܝܢ ܐܶܡܰܪ[7] ܠܗܽܘܢ ܡܰܢܽܘ ܡܶܢܟܽܘܢ ܓܰܒܪܳܐ ܕܐܺܝܬ ܠܶܗ ܥܶܪܒܳܐ[8] ܚܰܕ

Matthew 6:1 (6)

ܘܶܐܠܳܐ ܐܰܓܪܳܐ[9] ܠܰܝܬ ܠܟܽܘܢ ܠܘܳܬ ܐܰܒܽܘܟܽܘܢ ܕܒܰܫܡܰܝܳܐ

---

2. ܕܶܐܡܰܪ = he said.
3. ܘܶܐܡܰܪ = and he said.
4. Sound this one out.
5. ܕܫܡܰܥܘ = who heard.
6. ܢܦܰܩܘ = they went out.
7. ܐܶܡܰܪ = he said.
8. ܥܶܪܒܳܐ = sheep.
9. ܐܰܓܪܳܐ = reward.

John 3:6 (7)

ܡܶܕܶܡ ܕܺܝܠܺܝܕ[10] ܡܶܢ ܒܶܣܪܳܐ[11] ܒܶܣܪܳܐ ܗܽܘ ܘܡܶܕܶܡ ܕܺܝܠܺܝܕ[12] ܡܶܢ ܪܽܘܚܳܐ
ܪܽܘܚܳܐ ܗܽܘ

Matthew 4:9 (8)

ܘܶܐܡܰܪ[13] ܠܶܗ ܗܳܠܶܝܢ ܟܽܠܗܶܝܢ ܠܳܟ ܐܶܬܶܠ[14]

Luke 18:31 (9)

ܟܽܠܗܶܝܢ ܕܰܟܬܺܝܒܳܢ[15] ܒܰܢܒ݂ܺܝܳܐ ܥܰܠ ܒܪܶܗ ܕܐ݈ܢܳܫܳܐ

John 10:17 (10)

ܡܶܛܽܠ ܗܳܢܳܐ ܐܳܒ݂ܝ ܪܳܚܶܡ[16] ܠܝ

Mark 7:15 (11)

ܠܰܝܬ ܡܶܕܶܡ ܕܠܒܰܪ[17] ܡܶܢ ܒܰܪܢܳܫܳܐ

John 12:34 (12)

ܡܰܢܽܘ ܗܳܢܳܐ ܒܪܶܗ ܕܐ݈ܢܳܫܳܐ

Matthew 5:1 (13)

ܩܪܶܒ݂ܘ[18] ܠܘܳܬܶܗ ܬܰܠܡܺܝܕܰܘܗ̱ܝ

---

10. ܕܺܝܠܺܝܕ = that is born.
11. ܒܶܣܪܳܐ = flesh
12. ܕܺܝܠܺܝܕ = that is born.
13. ܘܶܐܡܰܪ = and he said.
14. ܐܶܬܶܠ = I give.
15. ܕܰܟܬܺܝܒܳܢ = that is/are written.
16. ܪܳܚܶܡ = he loves
17. ܕܠܒܰܪ = outside.
18. ܩܪܶܒ݂ܘ = they drew near.

Romans 1:1 (14)

ܦܘܠܘܣ ܥܒܕܐ ܕܝܫܘܥ ܡܫܝܚܐ

John 1:1 (15)

ܒܪܫܝܬ[19] ܐܝܬܘܗܝ ܗܘܐ[20] ܡܠܬܐ ܘܗܘ ܡܠܬܐ ܐܝܬܘܗܝ ܗܘܐ ܠܘܬ
ܐܠܗܐ ܘܐܠܗܐ ܐܝܬܘܗܝ ܗܘܐ ܗܘ ܡܠܬܐ

John 3:17 (16)

ܠܐ ܓܝܪ ܫܕܪ[21] ܐܠܗܐ ܠܒܪܗ ܠܥܠܡܐ ܕܢܕܘܢܝܗܝ[22] ܠܥܠܡܐ ܐܠܐ
ܕܢܚܐ[23] ܠܥܠܡܐ ܒܐܝܕܗ

Matthew 28:11 (17)

ܘܐܡܪܘ[24] ܠܪܒܝ ܟܗܢܐ[25] ܟܠ ܡܕܡ ܕܗܘܐ[26]

John 11:37 (18)

ܐܢܫܝܢ[27] ܕܝܢ ܡܢܗܘܢ ܐܡܪܘ[28] ܠܐ ܡܫܟܚ ܗܘܐ[29] ܗܢܐ

Matthew 13:1 (19)

ܒܗܘ ܕܝܢ ܝܘܡܐ ܢܦܩ[30] ܝܫܘܥ ܡܢ ܒܝܬܐ

---

19. ܒܪܫܝܬ = in the beginning (see also Gen 1:1).
20. ܗܘܐ = he was (x3).
21. ܫܕܪ = he sent.
22. ܕܢܕܘܢܝܗܝ = to judge it.
23. ܕܢܚܐ = that he would save.
24. ܘܐܡܪܘ = and they said.
25. ܟܗܢܐ = priests.
26. ܕܗܘܐ = which were.
27. Note that the *ālap* at the end of this word disappears when the ending is added.
28. ܐܡܪܘ = they said.
29. ܡܫܟܚ ܗܘܐ = he is able.
30. ܢܦܩ = he went out.

1 Corinthians 15:10 (20)

ܒܛܰܝܒܽܘܬܶܗ[31] ܕܶܝܢ ܕܰܐܠܳܗܳܐ ܐܺܝܬܰܝ ܡܶܕܶܡ ܕܺܐܝܬܰܝ ܘܛܰܝܒܽܘܬܶܗ ܕܒܺܝ

Additional Exercises

Exodus 32:12 (21)

ܘܕܚܘܪܒ[32] ܐܢܘܢ ܡܢ ܐ̈ܦܝ ܐܪܥܐ

Exodus 6:14 (22)

ܘܗܠܝܢ ܪ̈ܫܝܐ ܕܒܝܬ ܐ̈ܒܗܝܗܘܢ

Genesis 47:6 (23)

ܐܝܬ ܕܐܝܬ ܒܗܘܢ ܓܒܪ̈ܐ ܒܢ̈ܝ ܚܝܠܐ

Genesis 27:38 (24)

ܘܐܡܰܪ[33] ܥܣܘ[34] ܠܐܒܘܗܝ ܒܘܪܟܬܐ[35] ܚܕܐ ܗܝ ܠܟ ܐܒܝ

2 Chronicles 29:25 (25)

ܕܗܟܢܐ ܐܠܗܗ ܐܡܪ ܕܡܢ ܦܘܡܐ[36] ܕܢܒܝܐ

Genesis 24:26 (26)

ܘܒܪܟ[37] ܓܒܪܐ ܥܠ ܐܪܥܐ

---

31. ܛܝܒܘܬܐ = grace (x2).
32. ܘܕܚܘܪܒ = and destroy.
33. ܘܐܡܪ = and he said.
34. This is a name.
35. ܒܘܪܟܬܐ = blessing.
36. ܦܘܡܐ = mouth.
37. ܒܪܟ= he bowed.

7

Introduction to Syriac Verbs

Introduction

With a basic understanding of the nominal system, it is now appropriate to direct the attention of the rest of the grammar to the verbal system. This chapter will serve as a very brief overview of the different features of Syriac verbs, and then the subsequent chapters will cover each conjugation and stem in greater depth.

Like nouns, the verb is formed from a triconsonantal root. Many times, a root will form the basis of understanding in all parts of speech. For example, the root ܡܠܟ (*mlk*) forms the basis for:

ܡܲܠܟܵܐ	ܡܲܠܟܘܼܬܵܐ	ܡܠܲܟ	ܡܲܠܟܵܝ
malkā	*malkutā*	*mlak*	*malkāy*
king	kingdom	to rule, reign	royal, regal

This is one of the advantages of learning Semitic languages—you can often master multiple vocabulary words simply by knowing the root.

Verbal Stems

The stem of the verb tells the translator what type of action is being performed. There are three basic categories that Syriac stems can fall into.

Simple (Peal and Ethpeel): This is the most basic form of the action.

Intensive (Pael and Ethpaal): This conjugation is hard to simplify because of its complexity, but it is generally classified by an intensity in the action that is being performed. For example, this would be the difference between looking for a pencil (simple), and looking for a lost paycheck (intensive).

Causative (Aphel and Ettaphal): At the risk of again oversimplifying things, these stems generally can be translated with a causative element. For example, the difference between "he wrote" and "he caused to write."

It is best practice when dealing with multiple stems of a particular root to have a good lexicon available. Especially with intensive and causative stems, the change in stem can often cause changes in lexical meaning that are unpredictable.

Voice

The categories above (simple, intensive, causative) can be broken down further by denoting the voice of the stem, whether active or passive. An active verb is one in which the subject of the sentence is performing the action, and a passive verb is one where the subject is receiving the action. For example:

Steve is eating.	Steve is being eaten.
Active	Passive

The passive voice in Classical Syriac is easy enough to distinguish, with an–ܐܶܬ (*et-*) prefix. The active voice does not attest this prefix. Note the chart below for further explanation, organized by both verbal voice and type of verbal action.

Active Form of the Verb			**Passive Form of the Verb**	
Peal	Basic Action	→	*Ethpeel*	Passive Basic
Pael	Intensive Action	→	*Ethpaal*	Passive Intensive
Aphel	Causative Action	→	*Ettaphal*	Passive Causative

Naming the Stems

To the new student of Semitic languages, it might seem odd to name certain stems like peal, pael, ettaphal, etc. This comes from the root form of the verb ܦܥܠ ("to work"), and it is a handy way to see the stem vowel of the conjugation that is being examined. The stem vowel is the vowel that appears over the middle consonant of the root of the verb. For example, note the following verb:

ܦܬܰܚ

ptaḥ

to open

The stem vowel in this example would be an *a* because it is the vowel that is above the middle consonant. The six stems that will be covered in this grammar are listed below. Note how the vowels roughly correspond with the vowels in the stem names:

Active		Passive	
ܟܬܰܒ *ktab*	Peal	ܐܶܬܟܬܶܒ *etkteb*	Ethpeel
ܟܰܬܶܒ *katteb*	Pael	ܐܶܬܟܰܬܰܒ *etkattab*	Ethpaal
ܐܰܟܬܶܒ *akteb*	Aphel	ܐܶܬܬܰܟܬܰܒ *ettkatab*	Ettaphal

Be careful when looking at other grammars or parsing because there is no standardization for the spelling of these words, being that they are transliterations of the Syriac. For example, some grammars will call the Ethpeel the Ethpeal, some will transliterate the *ʿē* with apostrophes, as in Ethpe'el, and others will use the transliterated symbols for the guttural: Ethpeʿel. So, while this naming designation can be helpful in determining the stem vowel, it can also be a detriment when trying to standardize nomenclature across multiple resources.

A newer method of determining the classifications of various stems is to use Latin/Roman alphabetic abbreviations instead of transliterations. Doing this has introduced a little bit more stability in the naming of the stems. The G stands for *Grundstamm* and is the basic form of the verb. The lowercase p after the designation stands for passive. The D for the *Pael* and *Ethpaal* stands for doubled, as the middle consonant is doubled in this stem. The A stands for the prefix associated with the Aphel stem, but can also be represented with an H.[1]

Active Form of the Verb			Passive Form of the Verb	
Peal	G	→	*Ethpeel*	Gp
Pael	D	→	*Ethpaal*	Dp
Aphel	A / H	→	*Ettaphal*	Ap / Hp

Conjugations

In addition to the type of verbal action (simple, intensive, causative) and its voice (active, passive), Classical Syriac attests five basic conjugations that denote generally when an action takes place. These conjugations include the Perfect, Imperfect, Participle, Imperative, and Infinitive. Please keep in mind that the descriptions below are generalizations and further elaboration will occur within the following chapters.

Perfect: The perfect conjugation describes an action that is completed. Due to this, it can be understood generally as an equivalent to the English past tense. An example of English verbs in the perfect tense would be: he studied, she ran, he walked. These are all actions that have been completed. The perfect is characterized by only adding afformatives (letters to the end) to the word.

1. The H is used when comparing with Aramaic, which uses a *he* to signify the causative (*haphel*, *hophal*).

Participles: The participle is a verbal adjective and is usually equated with the English present tense, typically translated using the "-ing" ending. Participles will often be accompanied with a linking verb: I am studying, she is running, he is eating. Participles can also function as a *nomen agentis* (agent-noun), in which the noun part of the participle is emphasized. These are translated by adding an "-er" to the end of the word. Some examples of this include: studier, runner, walker. Participles have nominal endings attached as an afformative.

Imperfect: The imperfect conjugation describes an action that is not yet completed. Therefore, it can be generalized as an equivalent to the English future tense. Examples of this would be: he will study, she will run, he will walk. In the imperfect, there is a combination of preformatives (*nūn*, *taw* or *ālap*) and afformatives.

To summarize the basic English tense equivalents, the following chart is helpful:

Syriac		English Tense
Perfect Tense	→	Past Tense "He studied."
Participles	→	Present Tense "He is studying"
Imperfect Tense	→	Future Tense "He will study."

Imperative: The imperative is used in a direct address. Some examples include: Study! Run! Walk! It is formed simply by dropping the preformative of the imperfect tense, and keeping the rest of the verb the same.

Infinitive: Infinitives are verbal nouns and are typically translated by adding a "to" to the front of the verb: to study, to run, to walk. Syriac also attests infinitive absolutes; and their specific function which will be covered later in the grammar. Infinitives are recognizable by the addition of a *mīm* to the front of the vowel. The form is also sometimes accompanied by a *lāmad*, but it is not necessary for the construction.

When parsing a verb in Syriac, first identify its stem and conjugation. Next list the person, gender, and number when applicable.

Stem	Conjugation	Person	Gender	Number
Peal	Perfect	3	Masculine	Singular
Pael	Participle	2	Feminine	Plural
Aphel	Imperfect	1		
Ethpeel	Imperative			
Ethpaal	Inifnitive			
Ettaphal				

Note that when parsing a participle, one must also identify whether or not it is active or passive.

Weak Verbs

Like other Semitic languages, verbs in Syriac are classified as either strong or weak. Strong verbs have no weak consonants and conjugate normally. Weak verbs do not conjugate normally and attest at least one weak consonant. Such consonants are those that are often overpowered by other consonants around them. This is because when spoken, the speaker has a natural tendency to shorten them when he/she is speaking, and therefore the typical conjugations are modified. The weak consonants in Syriac are below.

Weak Consonants

ܐ	Alaph
ܘ	Waw
ܝ	Yod

Roman numerals I, II, and III are used to describe the first, second, and third consonants of a root. Keep in mind that this refers to the first, second, and third consonants in the order that they are read in Syriac—right to left. If a verb is labeled a I-Weak verb, then the first letter in the root is a weak consonant (as in ܐܶܟ݂ܰܠ, *ekal*), if it is labeled a III-Weak verb, then the third consonant would be weak (as in ܒܢܳܐ, *bnā*), and so on. Note how the conjugation would be constructed in the peal perfect third feminine singular.

ܒܢܳܐ	+	ܬ	→	ܒܢܳܐܬ	→	ܒܢܳܬ
bnā		*t*		*bnāt*		*bnāt*
root		feminie ending		full hypothetical conjugation		actual form

Notice how the pronunciation of the full hypothetical conjugation would be identical to that of the actual form of the word that occurs. This is the idea behind why the weak consonants often disappear—they are not necessary in pronunciation of the word.

The weak verbs that will be covered in this grammar are: I-*ālap*, III-Weak, I-*yūd*, I-*nūn*, geminate (verbs with two identical final consonants), hollow (verbs with a *waw* or *yūd* in the middle), and II-*ālap*.[2]

2. Not all of the weak verbs noted here attest specifically weak letters (such as I-*nūn*). Rather, the weak categories indicate that the verb doesn't conjugate as we might expect.

Lexical Forms

The lexical form for Syriac verbs is the peal active 3ms. For example, if one were to look up the verb "to write" in a lexicon, it would be found under the entry for:

ܟܬܰܒ — to write (verb)

The exception to this is hollow verbs. Often, lexicons will print these with the root of the word instead because its conjugations alter the spelling. For example:

Root	Peal Perfect 3ms	→	Lexical Entry
ܡܘܬ	ܡܺܝܬ		ܡܘܬ

With geminate verbs, note that what is often printed is the standard peal perfect 3ms form, but there is a doubled letter that is in the root. For example:

Root	Peal Perfect 3ms	→	Lexical Entry
ܚܠܠ	ܚܰܠ		ܚܰܠ

Word Order

This is a good time to make a few comments regarding word order. As has been seen in the examples in the grammar, word order in Syriac differs from word order in English. The order of appearance of words doesn't necessarily matter when it comes to translation, with the slight exception of adjectives, where the order helps to determine if it is an attributive or a predicative adjective. Additionally, pronouns are often paired with participles that they modify, and construct states must be paired with their respective words.

For verbs, Syriac will sometimes follow the Semitic pattern of verb-subject-object in its sentences. However, it is far less rigorous in this respect than Hebrew. When translating, if the direct object is not apparent from context or marked with a *lāmad*, then the translator may wish to follow the v-s-o pattern. Just be aware that it is often not consistent in every situation and word order alone is not a reliable guide for translation.

Comparative Charts for Verbs

Strong Verb

Below is a comparative chart of verbal patterns for the 3ms strong verb ܟܬܰܒ (*ktab*, to read). Use this chart as a reference when leaning each verb conjugation so that quick comparisons can be made between the different stems.

	Perfect	Participle	Imperfect	Imperative	Infinitive
Peal	ܟܬܰܒ *ktab*	ܟܳܬܶܒ *kāteb*	ܢܶܟܬܘܽܒ *nektob*	ܟܬܘܽܒ *ktob*	ܡܶܟܬܰܒ *mektab*
Pael	ܟܰܬܶܒ *katteb*	ܡܟܰܬܶܒ *mkatteb*	ܢܟܰܬܶܒ *nkatteb*	ܟܰܬܶܒ *katteb*	ܡܟܰܬܳܒܘܽ *mkattābu*
Aphel	ܐܰܟܬܶܒ *akteb*	ܡܰܟܬܶܒ *makteb*	ܢܰܟܬܶܒ *nakteb*	ܐܰܟܬܶܒ *akteb*	ܡܰܟܬܳܒܘܽ *maktābu*
Ethpeel	ܐܶܬܟܬܶܒ *etkteb*	ܡܶܬܟܬܶܒ *metkteb*	ܢܶܬܟܬܶܒ *netkteb*	ܐܶܬܟܰܬܒ *etkatb*	ܡܶܬܟܬܳܒܘܽ *metktābu*
Ethpaal	ܐܶܬܟܰܬܰܒ *etkattab*	ܡܶܬܟܰܬܰܒ *metkattab*	ܢܶܬܟܰܬܰܒ *netkattab*	ܐܶܬܟܰܬܰܒ *etkattab*	ܡܶܬܟܰܬܳܒܘܽ *metkattābu*
Ettaphal	ܐܶܬܬܰܟܬܰܒ *ettaktab*	ܡܶܬܬܰܟܬܰܒ *mettaktab*	ܢܶܬܬܰܟܬܰܒ *nettaktab*	ܐܶܬܬܰܟܬܰܒ *ettaktab*	ܡܶܬܬܰܟܬܳܒܘܽ *mettaktābu*

Note: If the root attests a guttural as the final letter (*ālap, hē, ḥēt, ʿē*) or a *rīš* then the final vowel will always be an a.

Weak Verbs

	Perfect	Participle	Imperfect	Imperative	Infinitive
I-*ālap*	ܐܶܟ݂ܰܠ *ekal*	ܐܳܟ݂ܶܠ *ākel*	ܢܶܐܟ݂ܽܘܠ *nekul*	ܐܶܟ݂ܽܘܠ *Akul*	ܡܶܐܟ݂ܰܠ *mekal*
III-Weak	ܒܢܳܐ *bnā*	ܒܳܢܶܐ *bāne*	ܢܶܒܢܶܐ *nebne*	ܒܢܺܝ *bni*	ܡܶܒܢܳܐ *mebnā*
I-*yūd*	ܝܺܠܶܕ *iled*	ܝܳܠܶܕ *yāled*	ܢܺܐܠܰܕ *nilad*	ܝܺܠܰܕ *ilad*	ܡܺܐܠܰܕ *milad*
I-*nūn*	ܢܦܰܩ *npaq*	ܢܳܦܶܩ *nāpeq*	ܢܶܦܽܘܩ *neppuq*	ܦܽܘܩ *puq*	ܡܶܦܰܩ *mepaq*
Geminate	ܥܰܠ *ʿal*	ܥܳܐܶܠ *ʿāel*	ܢܶܥܽܘܠ *neʿʿol*	ܥܽܘܠ *ʿul*	ܡܶܥܰܠ *meʿʿal*
Hollow	ܩܳܡ *qām*	ܩܳܐܶܡ *qāem*	ܢܩܽܘܡ *nqum*	ܩܽܘܡ *qum*	ܡܩܳܡ *mqām*
II-*ālap*	ܫܶܐܶܠ *šel*	ܫܳܐܶܠ *šāel*	ܢܶܫܐܰܠ *nešal*	ܫܐܰܠ *šal*	ܡܶܫܐܰܠ *mešal*

Vocabulary

Nouns

ܐܰܬ݂ܪܳܐ	*atrā*	country, place
ܒܶܣܪܳܐ	*besrā*	flesh
ܗܰܝܟ݁ܠܳܐ	*hayklā*	temple
ܚܽܘܒܳܐ	*ḥubā*	love, loving-kindness
ܝܰܡܳܐ	*yammā*	sea
ܟ݁ܳܗܢܳܐ	*kāhnā*	priest
ܡܰܘܬ݁ܳܐ	*mawtā*	death
ܥܰܒ݂ܕ݁ܳܐ	*ʿabdā*	servant
ܥܺܕ݁ܬ݂ܳܐ	*ʿidtā*	church, assembly
ܥܰܝܢܳܐ	*ʿaynā*	eye

Verbs

ܐܶܬ݂ܳܐ	*etā*	to come
ܚܙܳܐ	*ḥzā*	to see, behold
ܝܺܕܰܥ	*ida'*	to know
ܝܰܗ݈ܒ	*yab*	to give[3]
ܢܦܰܩ	*npaq*	to go out, go forth
ܩܪܳܐ	*qrā*	to call

Other

ܒܳܬ݂ܰܪ	*bātar*	after, behind
ܗܳܟ݂ܺܝܠ	*hākil*	thus, hence, therefore
ܗܰܝܕܶܝܢ	*haydēn*	then, afterwards, next
ܗܳܫܳܐ	*hāšā*	now
ܬܽܘܒ	*tub*	again

Homework

There are no translation exercises for this chapter. However, it is highly recommended that the student take extra care to become familiar with the concepts, labels, and structures of the verbal system in this chapter before moving on. Now is also a good time to review the nominal system as well as the vocabulary introduced so far.

---

3. The verb ܝܰܗ݈ܒ (*yab*, to give) appears in this form only in the perfect and imperative. In the other conjugations it takes the form ܢܶܬܶܒ (*neteb*). In all but the 3fs and 1cs forms, the vowel that typically appears above the middle consonant is shifted to the *yūd* and the *hē* is not pronounced.

8

Peal (G) Perfect and ܗܘܳܐ (*hwā*)

	Perfect
Peal	ܟܬܰܒ *ktab*

Introduction

The peal stem represents the basic action of the verb. It is active in the sense that the subject is performing the action of the verb, and the perfect tense shows that it is an action that is completed. For now simply translate the peal perfect verbs as an action that is already complete, as in: "I studied," "he said," "we went up," etc. One important element to note is that while the verb often presents itself in the past tense, it can also be translated in the present or future English tenses. As in all things, context will guide your translation.

The peal verb is frequently formed by adding either an *a* (*ptāḥā*) or an *e* (*rbāṣā*) after the second consonant (CCaC or CCeC).[1] For example, note the different vowels that are used below:

ܩܛܰܠ	*qṭal*	to kill
ܩܪܶܒ	*qreb*	to draw near

Peal Perfect Paradigm

A-Class Verbs

When learning any language, verbal paradigms are inevitable. They can be intimidating at first because of all of the information that they display. The peal perfect paradigm is

1. The designation CCaC / CCeC and its variations will be used throughout the grammar in order to show the formation of a particular verb. The C's represent the consonants that are found in the root, as in: ܟܬܒ= *ktb*, CCaC = ܟܬܰܒ. This method of identifying vowels and consonants was borrowed from W. M. Thackston, *Introduction to Syriac: An Elementary Grammar with Readings from Syriac Literature*, Bethesda, Maryland: Ibex, 1999.

one that the student should commit to memory, due to its prominence in Syriac. In doing so, look for patterns within the paradigm in order to help. As the book progresses, it will become easier and easier to distinguish the various differences and similarities among the different conjugations of the verb.

ܟܬܰܒ = to read

	Singular		Plural	
3m	ܟܬܰܒ	*ktab* he wrote	ܟܬܰܒܘ ܟܬܰܒܘܢ	*ktab* *ktabun* they wrote
3f	ܟܶܬܒܰܬ	*ketbat* she wrote	ܟܬܰܒ ܟܬܰܒ̈ܝ ܟܬܰܒܶܝܢ	*ktab* *ktab* *ktabēn* they wrote
2m	ܟܬܰܒܬ	*ktabt* you wrote	ܟܬܰܒܬܘܢ ܟܬܰܒܬܘܢ	*ktabton* *ktabtun* you wrote
2f	ܟܬܰܒܬܝ	*ktabt* you wrote	ܟܬܰܒܬܶܝܢ	*ktabtēn* you wrote
1c	ܟܶܬܒܶܬ	*ketbet* I wrote	ܟܬܰܒܢ ܟܬܰܒܢܰܢ	*ktabn* *ktabnan* we wrote

Note: The 3fp conjugation of the verb looks identical to the 3ms form of the verb. In order to distinguish the two, a *seyame* is often added to the end of the word, with a silent *yod*. However, this is not always the case, and sometimes what might look like a 3ms verb is actually a 3fp.

E-Class Verbs

The verbs above have an *a* as the stem vowel. The stem vowel is simply the vowel that appears (typically) above the second consonant in the root. For example, the vowel that appears above the *taw* in ܟܬܰܒ is an *a*. This is the stem vowel. In the perfect, the verb will sometimes take an *e* instead of an *a* for the stem vowel. The actual placement of the vowel is not effected, and the paradigm looks identical to the one above in all aspects except that the vowel is changed. For reference, the verb *qreb* (to draw near) will be used.

	Singular		Plural	
3m	ܩܪܶܒ	*qreb* he drew near	ܩܪܶܒܘ ܩܪܶܒܘܢ	*qreb* *qrebun* they drew near
3f	ܩܶܪܒܰܬ	*qerbat* she drew near	ܩܪܶܒ ܩܪܶܒܝ ܩܪܶܒܶܝܢ	*qreb* *qreb* *qrebēn* they drew near
2m	ܩܪܶܒܬ	*qrebt* you drew near	ܩܪܶܒܬܘܢ ܩܪܶܒܬܘܢ	*qrebton* *qrebtun* you drew near
2f	ܩܪܶܒܬܝ	*qrebt* you drew near	ܩܪܶܒܬܶܝܢ	*qrebtēn* you drew near
1c	ܩܶܪܒܶܬ	*qerbet* I drew near	ܩܪܶܒܢ ܩܪܶܒܢܰܢ	*qrebn* *qrebnan* we drew near

Examples

In order to get a feel for how verbs present themselves in Syriac, here are a few examples from the *Peshitta*.

ܠܟܺܐܦܳܐ	ܝܶܫܘܥ	ܘܶܐܡܰܪ
l-kipā	*yešuʿ*	*w-emar*
lāmad + name	name	peal perfect 3ms
to Cephas	Jesus	and he said

Translation: And Jesus said to Peter.

John 18:11

Note: This is a good example of the v-s-o pattern that occasionally appears in Syriac. Additionally, notice that the verb attests an *ālap* as the first letter of the root. Since *ālap* is quiescent, it requires that a vowel be placed with the letter. For ܐܶܡܰܪ (*emar*, "to say, speak"), the *ālap* takes an *e*-vowel. Also, since the verb is paired with a *waw*, the *waw* "steals" the vowel and it appears above the initial letter.

The verb ܐܶܡܰܪ (*emar*, to say / speak) is used widely in the exercises and is worth addressing here. It is a weak verb, and since it begins with an *ālap*, it takes an additional vowel. In order to avoid copious footnotes, it is best to simply note the vowels that accompany the *ālap* in these conjugations.

ܐܶܡܰܪ	ܢܺܐܡܰܪ	ܐܶܡܰܪ	ܡܺܐܡܰܪ	ܐܳܡܰܪ	ܐܡܺܝܪ
emar	*nimar*	*āmar*	*mimar*	*mawkālu*	*emir*
Perfect	Imperfect	Imperative	Infinitive	Active Participle	Passive Participle

Also note that there are two different types of I-*ālap* verbs. For more information about I-*ālap* verbs, see chapter 17.

The Verb "To Be" (*hwā*)

Like any language, Syriac has its fair share of irregular verbs. Not all of the irregular verb paradigms will be covered in this grammar, but there is one that will need to be known early in one's learning of Syriac: "to be." This verb is extremely common in Syriac.

	Singular		Plural	
3m	ܗܘܳܐ	*hwā* he is	ܗܘܰܘ	*hwaw* they are
3f	ܗܘܳܬ	*hwāt* she is	ܗܘܳܝ̈	*hwāy* they are
2m	ܗܘܰܝܬ	*hwayt* you are	ܗܘܰܝܬܘܿܢ ܗܘܰܝܬܽܘܢ	*hwayton* *hwaytun* you are
2f	ܗܘܰܝܬܝ	*hwayt* you are	ܗܘܰܝ̈ܬܶܝܢ	*hwaytēn* you are
1c	ܗܘܺܝܬ	*hwit* I am	ܗܘܰܝܢ	*hwayn* we are

The verb "to be" has many uses in Syriac; for now we will mention the two most common ones: (1) as a normal verb and (2) as an enclitic.

1. In the example below *hwā* functions as a normal verb.

ܗܘܳܐ	ܘܰܐܒܺܝܕܳܐ	ܘܰܚܝܳܐ	ܗܘܳܐ	ܡܺܝܬܳܐ	ܒܶܪܝ
hwā	*wabidā*	*waḥyā*	*hwā*	*mitā*	*ber*
peal perfect 3ms	waw + adjective ms emphatic	waw + peal perfect 3ms	peal perfect 3ms	adjective ms emphatic	noun + 1cs ms emphatic
he was	and was lost	and he is alive	he was	dead	my son

Translation: My son was dead, and he is alive, and he was lost...
Luke 15:21

2. In the Semitic family of languages, some of the more common phrases are shortened and abbreviated. In the case of ܗܘܳܐ (*hwā*), it is often seen attached to the end of various words in an abridged manner. When this happens, the *hē* becomes silent (note the *linea occultans*, the line beneath the *hē*) and the two words are pronounced as a single word. The technical term for this is enclitic. For example, note the usage and pronunciation of ܗܘܳܐ (*hwā*) in the following sentence. The word would be pronounced as one word: *kināwā*, instead of two: *kinā hwā*.

ܗ̱ܘܳܐ	ܟܺܐܢܳܐ
-wā	*kinā*
peal perfect 3ms	adjective ms emphatic
he was	righteous

Translation: He was righteous.
Matthew 1:19

Note: Sometimes, 3rd person enclitics can show up with 2nd person objects (such as pronouns). In these instances, translate the enclitic pronoun as appropriate.

ܗ̱ܽܘ	ܐܰܢ̱ܬ
-u	*att*
3ms pronoun	2ms pronoun
he (is)	you

Literal Translation: You is...
Actual translation: You are...
Matthew 11:3

Below is the full paradigm for the enclitic ܗܘܳܐ (*hwā*). Note the *linea occultans* that appears in every word. Keep in mind that these attach themselves to the end of the previous word in order to form a single compound, even though they are written with a space in between them.

	Singular		Plural	
3m	ܗܘܳܐ	*-wā* he is	ܗܘܰܘ	*-waw* they are
3f	ܗܘܳܬ	*-wāt* she is	ܗܘܳܝ	*-wāy* they are
2m	ܗܘܰܝܬ	*-wayt* you are	ܗܘܰܝܬܘܢ ܗܘܰܝܬܽܘܢ	*-wayton* *-waytun* you are
2f	ܗܘܰܝܬܝ	*-wayt* you are	ܗܘܰܝܬܶܝܢ	*-waytēn* you are
1c	ܗܘܺܝܬ	*-wit* I am	ܗܘܰܝܢ	*-wayn* we are

The verb "to be" can be attached to the end of participles, adjectives, and several other parts of speech in order to serve various functions; these will be covered later in the grammar. For now, it is only important to memorize the paradigm and keep in mind that it can serve a number of purposes.

Pronominal Suffixes

Verbs can have pronominal suffixes added to them in order to introduce an object of the verb. To review, the object of the verb in simple terminology is what is associated with the verb, but not the subject. For example, Steve went *home*. These pronominal objects are similar to nouns and prepositions, but they differ slightly in how they are spelled. One of the good things about these suffixes attached to verbs is that they generally follow the same patterns as the pronominal suffixes examined above. That combined with the fact that they make verbs into very long words makes these easy to identify when translating.

	Singular	Plural
3m	ܗ / ܗܝ / ܝܗܝ / ܘܗܝ	–
3f	ܗ̇	–
2m	ܟ	ܟܘܢ / ܟ݁ܘܢ
2f	ܟܝ	ܟܶܝܢ
1c	ܢܝ	ܢ

In addition to these endings, each verb will have an accompanying connecting vowel. Each verb, in each form, will vary in its connecting vowel according to its structure and endings. Trying to memorize every tense and ending can get complicated very quickly. For the beginner, the best advice is simply to recognize the endings in addition to the verbs and then parse the verbs according to their *general* form. The general pattern for the peal perfect is as follows.

	Singular	Plural
3m	ܟܰܬܒ– *katb-*	◌–ܟܰܬܒܘ *katbu-*
3f	ܟܬܰܒܬ– *ktabt-*	◌–ܟܰܬܒ *katbā-*
2m	◌–ܟܬܰܒܬ *ktabtā-*	◌–ܟܬܰܒܬܘܢ *ktabtonā-*
2f	◌–ܟܬܰܒܬܝ *ktabti-*	◌–ܟܬܰܒܬܶܝܢ *ktabtenā-*
1c	ܟܬܰܒܬ– *ktabt-*	◌–ܟܬܰܒܢ *ktabnā-*

For example:

ܝܺܕܰܥ *idaʿ* to know lexical form	→	ܝܶܕܥܶܬ *yedʿet* I know peal perfect 1cs (Luke 16:4)	→	ܝܺܕܰܥܬܟ݂ܽܘܢ *idaʿtkun* I know you peal perfect 1cs + 2mp suffix (Matthew 7:23)

Appendix 6 has the complete chart for all of the peal perfect conjugation. Other conjugations can be inferred from similar patterns. It is recommended to look over that chart in order to note the general patterns that emerge when a pronominal suffix is added to the end of a verb.

The good news is that, while there may seem like an overabundant amount of information to learn when it comes to adding pronominal suffixes to verbs, their use is relatively limited. Because of this, all the occurrences of a pronominal suffix with a verb in the exercises will be noted in a footnote, complete with parsing information. At this stage, it is more important to pay attention to how the verb functions and is altered with these pronominal suffixes, than to memorize all the paradigms.

Texts with No Vowel Pointing

In older texts, forms of the perfect will often be designated with a dot beneath (or above in the case of the 1cs) the verb in order to distinguish it from other similar verb forms. This is especially important in the 2ms, 3fs, and 1cs forms, where the consonants are identical. In the chart below, notice also how the *seyame* appear above the 3fp forms, a common feature for feminine plural forms.

	Singular		Plural	
3m	ܟܬܒ݂	*ktab* he wrote	ܟܬܒܘ ܟܬܒܘܢ	*ktab* *ktabun* they wrote
3f	ܟܬܒܬ݂	*ketab* she wrote	ܟܬܒ ܟܬܒ̈ܝ ܟܬܒ̈ܢ	*ktab* *ktab* *ktabēn* they wrote
2m	ܟܬܒܬ݂	*ktabt* you wrote	ܟܬܒܬܘܢ	*ktabton* you wrote
2f	ܟܬܒܬ݂ܝ	*ktabt* you wrote	ܟܬܒܬܝܢ	*ktabten* you wrote
1c	ܟܬܒܬ݁	*ketbet* I wrote	ܟܬܒܢ ܟܬܒܢܢ	*ktabn* *ktabnan* we wrote

Vocabulary

Nouns

ܐܽܘܪܚܳܐ	*urḥā*	road, way
ܪܶܓܠܳܐ	*reglā*	foot
ܕܺܝܢܳܐ	*dinā*	judgment
ܕܡܳܐ	*dmā*	blood
ܚܛܳܗܳܐ	*ḥṭāhā*	sin
ܟܬܳܒܳܐ	*ktābā*	book
ܠܰܚܡܳܐ	*laḥmā*	bread
ܡܰܝ̈ܳܐ	*mayyā*	water
ܨܶܒܝܳܢܳܐ	*ṣebyānā*	will, desire
ܩܘܽܕܫܳܐ	*qudšā*	holiness, sanctuary
ܬܶܫܒܽܘܚܬܳܐ	*tešbuḥtā*	glory, praise

Verbs

ܐܶܟܰܠ	*ekal*	to eat
ܒܥܳܐ	*bʿā*	to seek, search for
ܗܰܝܡܶܢ	*haymen*	to believe, trust in
ܡܰܠܶܠ	*mallel*	to speak
ܣܳܡ	*sām*	to put, place
ܥܰܠ	*ʿal*	to enter
ܨܒܳܐ	*ṣbā*	to want, will, desire
ܫܶܐܠ	*šel*	to ask, seek, inquire
ܫܰܕܰܪ	*šadar*	to send
ܫܪܳܐ	*šrā*	to loosen, begin, stop, camp

Other

ܐܰܝܟܳܐ	*aykā*	where?
ܐܰܡܺܝܢ	*amin*	amen, verily
ܒܰܠܚܽܘܕ	*balḥud*	alone, only
ܚܰܝܳܐ	*ḥayyā*	alive, living
ܚܠܳܦ	*ḥlāp*	for, instead of, on account of
ܝܰܬܺܝܪܳܐ	*yatirā*	better, greater
ܡܺܝܬܳܐ	*mitā*	dead
ܩܰܕܡܳܝ	*qadmāy*	first
ܫܰܦܺܝܪܳܐ	*šapirā*	beautiful, good

Exercises

Matthew 2:9 (1)

ܕܝܢ ܟܕ ܫܡܥܘ ܡܢ ܡܠܟܐ

Matthew 3:2 (2)

ܩܪܒܬ ... ܡܠܟܘܬܐ ܕܫܡܝܐ

Mark 5:27 (3)

ܟܕ ܫܡܥܬ ܥܠ ܝܫܘܥ

Matthew 13:46 (4)

ܟܕ ܕܝܢ ܐܫܟܚ[2] ܡܪܓܢܝܬܐ[3] ܚܕܐ

John 8:40 (5)

ܫܡܥܬ ܡܢ ܐܠܗܐ

Matthew 21:1 (6)

ܘܟܕ ܩܪܒ ܠܐܘܪܫܠܡ

Matthew 15:1 (7)

ܩܪܒܘ ܠܘܬ ܝܫܘܥ ܦܪܝܫܐ ܘܣܦܪܐ[4] ܕܡܢ ܐܘܪܫܠܡ

---

2. This verb will typically attest an *ālap* and an *e*-vowel in the front of the verb. Look for the stem vowel to help in conjugating this verb.
3. ܡܪܓܢܝܬܐ = a pearl.
4. ܘܣܦܪܐ = and scribes.

Mark 5:36 (8)

ܝܶܫܽܘܥ ܕܶܝܢ ܫܡܰܥ ܠܡܶܠܬ݂ܳܐ ܕܶܐܡܰܪܘ

Matthew 2:22 (9)

ܟܰܕ ܕܶܝܢ ܫܡܰܥ ܕܰܐܪܟܶܠܰܐܘܣ[5] ܗ̱ܘܳܐ ܡܰܠܟܳܐ ܒܺܝܗܽܘܕ.

Luke 6:39 (10)

ܘܶܐܡܰܪ ܗ̱ܘܳܐ ܠܗܽܘܢ ܡܰܬ݂ܠܳܐ[6]

Matthew 8:3 (11)

ܝܶܫܽܘܥ ܩܪܶܒ ܠܶܗ ܘܶܐܡܰܪ

Luke 3:2 (12)

ܗܘܳܬ݂ ܡܶܠܬ݂ܳܐ ܕܰܐܠܳܗܳܐ ܥܰܠ ܝܽܘܚܰܢܳܢ

Mark 6:18 (13)

ܐܳܡܰܪ ܗ̱ܘܳܐ ܓܶܝܪ ܝܽܘܚܰܢܳܢ ܠܗܶܪܳܘܕܶܣ

Matthew 26:17 (14)

ܩܪܶܒܘ ܬܰܠܡܺܝܕܶܐ ܠܘܳܬ݂ ܝܶܫܽܘܥ ܘܶܐܡܰܪܘ

---

5. ܕܰܐܪܟܶܠܰܐܘܣ = that Archelaus.
6. ܡܰܬ݂ܠܳܐ = parable.

Luke 15:25 (15)

ܘܩܪܶܒ ܠܘܳܬ ܒܰܝܬܳܐ ܫܡܰܥ ܩܳܠ

Luke 2:22 (16)

ܐܰܝܟ ܢܳܡܽܘܣܳܐ ܕܡܽܘܫܶܐ

Matthew 2:9 (17)

ܕܶܝܢ ܟܰܕ ܫܡܰܥܘ ܡܶܢ ܡܰܠܟܳܐ ܐܶܙܰܠܘ

Revelation 1:3 (18)

ܙܰܒܢܳܐ ܓܶܝܪ ܩܪܶܒ

Matthew 14:13 (19)

ܘܟܰܕ ܫܡܰܥܘ ܟܶܢܫܶ̈ܐ

Luke 2:15 (20)

ܐܰܝܟ ܚܢܰܢ ܫܒܰܩܢ ܠܚܰܝܳܒܰܝܢ[7]

Additional Exercises

Joshua 15:15 (21)

ܘܣܠܩ ܡܢ ܬܡܢ

Proverbs 22:20 (22)

ܘܗܐ ܟܬܒܬ ܐܢ̈ܝܢ ܠܟ ܟܠ ܬܠܬ ܙܒ̈ܢܝܢ

---

7. ܠܚܰܝܳܒܰܝܢ = our debts.

Exodus 34:32 (23)

ܘܩܪܒܝܢ ܗܘܘ ܠܘܬܗ ܟܠܗܘܢ ܒܢܝ̈ ܐܝܣܪܝܠ

Genesis 21:26 (24)

ܘܐܦ ܐܢܐ ܠܐ ܫܡܥܬ ܐܠܐ ܐܢ ܝܘܡܢܐ

Genesis 24:52 (25)

ܘܟܕ ܫܡܥ ܥܒܕܐ ܕܐܒܪܗܡ ܡ̈ܠܝܗܘܢ ܣܓܕ[8] ܥܠ ܐܪܥܐ ܩܕܡ ܡܪܝܐ.

1 Samuel 14:38 (26)

ܘܐܡܪ ܫܐܘܠ ܩܪܒܘ ܠܝ ܗܪܟܐ[9] ܟܠܗܘܢ

---

8. ܣܓܕ = he worshiped.
9. ܗܪܟܐ = here.

9

Peal Participle

	Perfect	Participle
Peal	ܟܬܰܒ *ktab*	ܟܳܬܶܒ *kāteb*

Introduction

Participles can function as either nouns, adjectives, or verbs. The most basic way to translate a participle is to add *-ing* or *-er* to the end of the word, as in "reading" or "reader." However this is not always guaranteed, so make sure to let context guide the translation.

Active and Passive Participle Forms

The active participle is recognized by the vocalization pattern of CaCeC, as in KaTeB, instead of the peal perfect KTaB. In the passive, the participle takes the pronunciation of CCiC, as in KTiB.

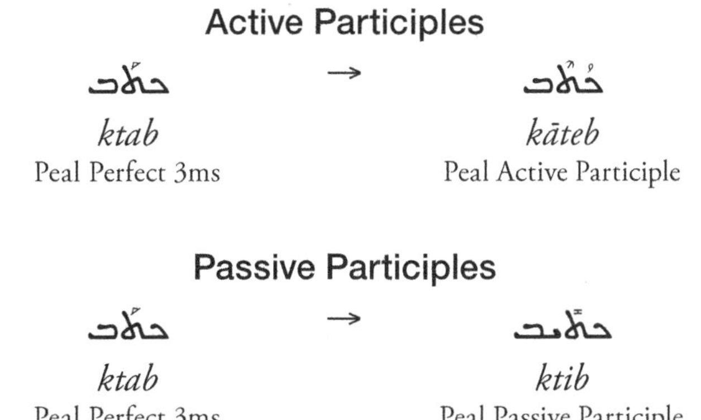

When there is no vowel pointing present the participle is distinguished by a dot on top of the word.

ܟܬܒ

kāteb

reading

Since participles have both verbal and nominal characteristics, the participle will inflect depending on gender, number, and state (just like a noun). The good news is that these endings are predictable and similar to the noun endings that were learned earlier in the grammar. Therefore, the paradigm logically follows what is already familiar (see ch. 3 for a review of the noun endings if necessary). The endings, for the most part, form regularly on the ends of the participles.

Active Participles

Masculine		Feminine	
Singular	Plural	Singular	Plural
ܟܳܬܶܒ	ܟܳܬܒܺܝܢ	ܟܳܬܒܳܐ	ܟܳܬܒ̈ܳܢ
kāteb	*kātbin*	*kātbā*	*kātbān*

Passive Participles

Masculine		Feminine	
Singular	Plural	Singular	Plural
ܟܬܺܝܒ	ܟܬܺܝܒܺܝܢ	ܟܬܺܝܒܳܐ	ܟܬܺܝܒ̈ܳܢ
ktib	*ktibin*	*ktibā*	*ktibān*

Note the *seyame* (two dots) above the fp participles.

It not recommended to memorize these paradigms as they appear here, but rather focus on knowing the endings of the noun and then apply these to the end of the basic forms of the participle. This will save a lot of work memorizing a new paradigm for each new participle form that is learned later in the grammar.

The peal participle is by far the most commonly used in Syriac. It is important to be able to readily recognize the peal participle in order to make translation a much easier process.

Variable Vowels

One important element to mention is that if the final consonant is a guttural (*ālap*, *hē*, *ḥēt*, *ʿē*) or a *rīš*, then the final vowel will always be an *a*. For example, note how the verb ܫܡܥ *šmʿ* ("to hear") has an *ʿē* as the third root letter. In this case, the vowel changes from what should be an *e* to an *a*.

ܫܡܰܥ	→	ܫܳܡܰܥ	NOT	ܫܳܡܶܥ
šmaʿ		*šāmaʿ*		*šāmeʿ*
to hear		hearing		

This should be kept in mind, as sometimes the vowel will not align with the paradigm exactly. In these cases check to see if the final consonant is a guttural.

Participles and Pronouns

As was introduced in chapter 5, participles will often be accompanied by a pronoun, sometimes in the abbreviated form (also known as pronominal enclitics). These can be translated literally, as they supply the subject of the action.

ܠܟ݂ܽܘܢ	ܐ̱ܢܳܐ	ܐܳܡܰܪ
l-kun	*-nā*	*āmar*
lāmad + pronoun 3mp	pronoun 1cs	peal active participle
to you	I (am)	saying

Translation: I (am) saying to you.
Matthew 3:9

Note: As with other pronominal enclitics, the pronoun is pronounced as a single word. For example, the above is pronounced *āmar-nā*.

Typically, the third person singular and plural forms do not appear with these pronominal enclitics; they are more common in the second and first person forms.

	Singular	Plural
2m	ܟܳܬ݂ܶܒ ܐܢ̱ܬ ܟܳܬ݂ܶܒܬ you are reading *kāteb-att*	ܟܳܬ݂ܒܻܝܢ ܐܢ̱ܬܘܢ ܟܳܬ݂ܒܻܝܢ ܐܢ̱ܬܽܘܢ ܟܳܬ݂ܒܻܝܬܘܢ ܟܳܬ݂ܒܻܝܬܽܘܢ you are reading *kātbi-tton* *kātbi-ttun*
2f	ܟܳܬ݂ܒܳܐ ܐܢ̱ܬܝ ܟܳܬ݂ܒܳܬܝ you are reading *kātbā-att*	ܟܳܬ݂ܒܳܢ ܐܢ̱ܬܶܝܢ ܟܳܬ݂ܒܳܬܶܝܢ you are reading *kātbā-ttēn*
1m	ܟܳܬ݂ܶܒ ܐ̱ܢܳܐ ܟܳܬ݂ܶܒܢܳܐ I am reading *kāteb-nā*	ܟܳܬ݂ܒܻܝܢ ܚ̱ܢܰܢ ܟܳܬ݂ܒܻܝܢܰܢ we are reading *kātbin-nan*
1f	ܟܳܬ݂ܒܳܐ ܐ̱ܢܳܐ ܟܳܬ݂ܒܳܐܢܳܐ I am reading *kātbā-nā*	ܟܳܬ݂ܒܳܢ ܚ̱ܢܰܢ ܟܳܬ݂ܒܳܢܰܢ we are reading *kātbā-nan*

Participles with the Verb *hwā*

Where the pronouns are often used in the first and second person with participles, the verb *hwā* (to be) is typically used with third person designations. The verb will appear immediately after the participle and will often be enclitic (pronounced as a single word with the participle).

ܗܘܐ	ܘܐܡܪ
-wā	*w-āmar*
peal perfect 3ms	peal active participle ms
he was	and saying

Translation: He was saying...

Matthew 11:21

Note that the participle has to agree with the verb in terms of number, so the plural forms of *hwā* will be paired with the plural forms of the participle.

ܗܘܘ	ܐܡܪܝܢ	ܕܝܢ	ܟܢܫ̈ܐ
-waw	*āmrin*	*den*	*kenše*
peal perfect 3mp	peal participle mp	conjunction	noun mp emphatic
they were	saying	but	the crowds

Translation: But the crowds were saying...

Matthew 21:11

Therefore, the full paradigm looks as follows:

	Singular	**Plural**
3m	ܟܬܒ ܗܘܐ he/it is reading *kāteb-wā*	ܟܬܒܝܢ ܗܘܘ they are reading *kātbin-waw*
3f	ܟܬܒܐ ܗܘܬ she/it is reading *kātbā-wāt*	ܟܬ̈ܒܢ ܗܘܝ they are reading *kātbān-way*

Uses of Participles

1. Participles as Nouns: A participle can function as a noun/substantive within a sentence. In these cases, the noun aspect of the participle is emphasized. These can be translated as either substantives ("the [ones] eating"), where the subject is supplied, or as simple nouns ("the eaters"). Note the paiel participle in the following example. The paiel stem functions and is formed in the same manner as the pael stem but attests an additional *yūd* in the middle of the word (ܗܝܡܢ, "hymn, to believe"). The student should become comfortable with the appearance of the paiel stem and recognize it based on its similarity to the pael.

ܡܗܝܡܢܝܢ	ܠܐ
mhaymnin	*lā*
paiel active particicple mp	negative particle
believing	not

Translation: Unbelievers

or

(The ones) not believing

Luke 12:46

2. Participles as Adjectives: Participles can function in both predicate and attributive roles (see ch. 3 for a review on the difference between predicate and attributive adjectives). When used in the attributive sense, they often appear in a relative clause with a *dālat* prefix.

ܒܐܘܪܫܠܡ	ܕܥܡܪܝܢ	ܘܟܠܗܘܢ
b-uwrišlem	*d-ʿāmrin*	*w-kulhun*
bēth + name	*dālat* + peal active participle mp	*waw* + particle + 3mp
in Jerusalem	dwelling	and all of them

Translation: And all of them who are dwelling in Jerusalem...

Acts 2:14

3. Participles as Verbs: In addition, participles can function as verbs. These forms will typically take enclitics or be paired with a linking verb, but as the example below illustrates, this is not always the case.

ܡܠܟܐ	ܐܝܟܘ	ܘܐܡܪܝܢ
malkā	*aykaw*	*w-āmrin*
noun ms emphatic	interrogative particle	*waw* + peal active participle mp
the king	where	and saying

Translation: And saying, "Where (is) the king . . ."
Matthew 2:2

4. Passive Participles: Passive participles can act in the same way that active participles do (as nouns, adjectives, or verbs), but the action is being performed *on* the subject of the sentence rather than *by* the subject.

ܚܛܗ̈ܝܟ	ܠܟ	ܫܒܝܩܝܢ
ḥṭāhayk	*lāk*	*šbiqin*
noun mp emphatic + 2 MS	*lāmad* + 2ms	peal passive participle mp.
your sins	to you	they are forgiven

Translation: Your sins are forgiven.
Luke 5:20

Vocabulary

Nouns

ܐܡܐ	*emmā*	mother
ܐܬܐ	*ātā*	miraculous sign
ܕܚܠܬܐ	*dḥeltā*	fear
ܚܛܝܬܐ	*ḥṭitā*	sin
ܦܘܡܐ	*pumā*	mouth, edge
ܦܘܩܕܢܐ	*puqdānā*	commandment
ܩܫܝܫܐ	*qašišā*	elder
ܫܘܒܚܐ	*šubḥā*	glory, praise
ܫܠܝܚܐ	*šliḥā*	apostle
ܫܪܪܐ	*šrārā*	truth

Verbs

ܐܚܕ	*eḥad*	to take, seize, apprehend
ܚܝܐ	*ḥyā*	to live
ܝܠܦ	*ilep*	to learn
ܝܬܒ	*iteb*	to sit
ܡܝܬ	*mit*	to die
ܡܠܐ	*mlā*	to complete, be full
ܢܦܠ	*npal*	to fall
ܣܠܩ	*sleq*	to ascend, go up
ܥܢܐ	*ʿnā*	to answer
ܫܩܠ	*šqal*	to remove, take up

Other

ܐܦܠܐ	*āplā*	not even (*ap+la*)
ܕܠܡܐ	*dalmā*	lest
ܘܠܐ	*wāle*	it is necessary for, right
ܙܥܘܪܐ	*zʿurā*	least, little
ܝܬܝܪܐܝܬ	*yattirāit*	abundantly, especially
ܟܠܡܕܡ	*kullmeddem*	everything
ܟܠܢܫ	*kullnāš*	every one (man)
ܟܡܐ	*kmā*	how many/much?
ܠܒܪ	*lbar*	outside

Exercises

Matthew 13:22 (1)

ܗܽܘ ܗ̱ܘ ܕܫܳܡܰܥ[1] ܡܶܠܬ݂ܳܐ

John 3:3 (2)

ܘܶܐܡܰܪ ܠܶܗ ܐܰܡܺܝܢ ܐܰܡܺܝܢ ܐܳܡܰܪ[2] ܐ̱ܢܳܐ ܠܳܟ݂

Luke 8:12 (3)

ܐܺܝܬܰܝܗܽܘܢ ܗܳܢܽܘܢ ܕܫܳܡܥܺܝܢ ܡܶܠܬ݂ܳܐ

Matthew 5:46 (4)

ܠܳܐ ܗܳܐ ܐܳܦ ܡܳܟ݂ܣܶܐ[3] ܗ̄ܝ ܗܳܕܶܐ ܥܳܒ݂ܕܺܝܢ

Matthew 21:29 (5)

ܗܽܘ ܕܶܝܢ ܥܢܳܐ ܘܶܐܡܰܪ ܠܳܐ ܨܳܒܶܐ ܐ̱ܢܳܐ

Mark 14:71 (6)

ܕܠܳܐ ܝܳܕܰܥ[4] ܐ̱ܢܳܐ ܠܓܰܒ݂ܪܳܐ ܗܳܢܳܐ ܕܳܐܡܪܺܝܢ ܐܢ̱ܬܽܘܢ

Matthew 4:4 (7)

ܗܽܘ ܕܶܝܢ ܥܢܳܐ ܘܶܐܡܰܪ ܟܬ݂ܺܝܒ݂ ܕܠܳܐ ܗ̱ܘܳܐ ܒܰܠܚܡܳܐ ܒܰܠܚܽܘܕ݂ܰܘܗ݈ܝ ܚܳܝܶܐ
ܒܰܪܢܳܫܳܐ

---

1. Note the variable vowel from the guttural.
2. This is another common participle. Note the variable vowel because of the *rīš*.
3. ܡܳܟ݂ܣܶܐ = tax collectors.
4. Again, note the variable vowel.

Matthew 13:13 (8)

ܡܛܠ ܕܚܙܝܢ[5] ܘܠܐ ܚܙܝܢ ܘܫܡܥܝܢ ܘܠܐ ܫܡܥܝܢ

Acts 11:16 (9)

ܘܐܬܕܟܪܬ[6] ܡܠܬܗ ܕܡܪܢ ܕܐܡܪ ܗܘܐ ܕܝܘܚܢܢ ܐܥܡܕ[7] ܒܡܝܐ
ܐܢܬܘܢ ܕܝܢ ܬܬܥܡܕܘܢ[8] ܒܪܘܚܐ ܕܩܘܕܫܐ

John 6:32 (10)

ܐܡܪ ܠܗܘܢ ܝܫܘܥ ܐܡܝܢ ܐܡܝܢ ܐܡܪ ܐܢܐ ܠܟܘܢ ܕܠܐ ܗܘܐ
ܡܘܫܐ ܝܗܒ ܠܟܘܢ ܠܚܡܐ ܡܢ ܫܡܝܐ ܐܠܐ ܐܒܝ ܝܗܒ ܠܟܘܢ
ܠܚܡܐ ܕܩܘܫܬܐ[9] ܡܢ ܫܡܝܐ

Matthew 13:11 (11)

ܘܐܡܪ ܠܗܘܢ ܕܠܟܘܢ ܗܘ ܝܗܝܒ[10] ܠܡܕܥ ܐܪ̈ܙܐ[11] ܕܡܠܟܘܬܐ
ܕܫܡܝܐ ܠܗܢܘܢ ܕܝܢ ܠܐ ܝܗܝܒ

Matthew 13:36 (12)

ܗܝܕܝܢ ܝܫܘܥ ܫܒܩ ܠܟܢܫܐ ܘܐܬܐ[12] ܠܒܝܬܐ ܘܩܪܒܘ ܠܘܬܗ ܬܠܡܝܕܘܗܝ

---

5. This is a participle with the root ܚܙܐ. Note what happens to the *ālap* at the end (x2).
6. ܘܐܬܕܟܪܬ = I remembered.
7. ܐܥܡܕ = baptized.
8. ܬܬܥܡܕܘܢ = you will be baptized.
9. ܩܘܫܬܐ = truth, true.
10. This is a passive participle. Note what happens with the vowel on the first letter when it is a *yūd*.
11. ܠܡܕܥ ܐܪ̈ܙܐ = to know the mysteries.
12. This form is not a participle but a peal perfect 3ms verb. Note that words starting with an *ālap* can sometimes look like a participle.

1 Cor. 15:50 (13)

ܗܳܕܶܐ ܕܶܝܢ ܐܳܡܰܪ ܐ̱ܢܳܐ ܐܰܚܰܝ ܕܒܶܣܪܳܐ ܘܰܕܡܳܐ ܡܰܠܟܽܘܬܳܐ ܕܰܫܡܰܝܳܐ

ܠܡܺܐܪܰܬ[13] ܠܳܐ ܡܶܫܟܚܺܝܢ[14]

Luke 7:49 (14)

ܐܳܡܪܺܝܢ ܒܢܰܦܫܗܽܘܢ ܡܰܢܽܘ ܗܳܢܳܐ ܕܰܐܦ ܚܛܳܗ̈ܶܐ ܫܳܒܶܩ

Acts 15:18 (15)

ܝܺܕ̈ܥܺܝܢ[15] ܡܶܢ ܥܳܠܰܡ ܥܒ̈ܳܕܰܘܗ̱ܝ ܕܰܐܠܳܗܳܐ

Matthew 21:31 (16)

ܡܰܢܽܘ ܡܶܢ ܗܳܠܶܝܢ ܬܪ̈ܰܝܗܽܘܢ[16] ܥܒܰܕ ܨܶܒܝܳܢܶܗ ܕܰܐܒܽܘܗ̱ܝ ܐܳܡܪܺܝܢ ܠܶܗ ܗܰܘ

ܩܰܕܡܳܝܳܐ ܐܳܡܰܪ ܠܗܽܘܢ ܝܶܫܽܘܥ ܐܰܡܺܝܢ ܐܳܡܰܪ ܐ̱ܢܳܐ ܠܟܽܘܢ

Matthew 7:21 (17)

ܠܳܐ ܗ̱ܘܳܐ ܟܽܠ ܕܳܐܡܰܪ ܠܝ ܡܳܪܝ ܡܳܪܝ ܥܳܐܶܠ[17] ܠܡܰܠܟܽܘܬܳܐ ܕܰܫܡܰܝܳܐ ܐܶܠܳܐ

ܡܰܢ ܕܥܳܒܶܕ ܨܶܒܝܳܢܶܗ ܕܳܐܒܝ ܕܒܰܫܡܰܝܳܐ

Luke 7:47 (18)

ܚܠܳܦ ܗܳܕܶܐ ܐܳܡܰܪ ܐ̱ܢܳܐ ܠܳܟ ܕܶܫܒܺܝܩܺܝܢ ܠܳܗ ܚܛܳܗ̈ܶܝܗ ܣܰܓ̈ܺܝܐܳܐ

---

13. ܠܡܺܐܪܰܬ = to inherit.
14. ܡܶܫܟܚܺܝܢ = to be able.
15. Note the vowel above the initial *yūd*. This is a common characteristic of verbs that start with a *yūd*.
16. ܬܪ̈ܰܝܗܽܘܢ = two (with 3ms suffix).
17. This is the active participle of ܥܰܠ, to enter.

John 6:35 (19)

ܐܶܡܰܪ ܠܗܽܘܢ ܝܶܫܽܘܥ ܐܶܢܳܐ ܐܶܢܳܐ ܠܰܚܡܳܐ ܕܚܰܝ̈ܶܐ ܡܰܢ ܕܐܳܬܶܐ ܠܘܳܬܝ ܠܳܐ
ܢܶܟܦܰܢ[18]

Romans 11:36 (20)

ܡܶܛܽܠ ܕܟܽܠ ܡܶܢܶܗ ܘܟܽܠ ܒܶܗ ܘܟܽܠ ܒܺܐܝܕܶܗ[19] ܕܠܶܗ ܬܶܫܒ̈ܚܳܢ ܘܒܽܘܪ̈ܟܳܢ[20]
ܠܥܳܠܰܡ ܥܳܠܡܺܝܢ ܐܰܡܺܝܢ

Additional Exercises

Jeremiah 36:18 (21)

ܘܐܡܪ ܠܗܘܢ ܒܪܘܟ[21] ܡܢ ܦܘܡܗ ܐܡܪ ܗܘܐ ܠܝ

Genesis 9:25 (22)

ܥܒܕ ܥܒ̈ܕܝܢ ܢܗܘܐ ܠܐܚܘܗܝ

Esther 3:11 (23)

ܘܐܡܪ ܡܰܠܟܐ ܟܣܦܟ[22] ܝܗܝܒ ܠܟ

2 Chronicles 25:4 (24)

ܡܛܠ ܕܗܟܢܐ ܟܬܝܒ ܒܣܦܪܐ[23] ܕܢܡܘܣܗ ܕܡܘܫܐ ܕܦܩܕ ܡܪܝܐ

---

18. ܢܶܟܦܰܢ = he will be hungry.
19. ܒܺܐܝܕܶܗ = through him (it is the word "hand" with a *bēth* prefix and 3ms ending).
20. ܘܒܽܘܪ̈ܟܳܢ = blessing.
21. Hint: This is a name.
22. ܟܣܦܟ = your silver.
23. ܣܦܪܐ = scribe.

1 Samuel 2:15 (25)

ܠܐ ܢܣܒ ܐܢܐ ܡܢܟ

Genesis 3:22 (26)

ܘܐܡܪ ܡܪܝܐ ܐܠܗܐ ܗܐ ܐܕܡ ܗܘܐ ܐܝܟ ܚܕ ܡܢܢ

10

Peal Imperfect

	Perfect	Participle	Imperfect
Peal	ܟܬܰܒ	ܟܳܬܶܒ	ܢܶܟܬܘܿܒ
	ktab	*kāteb*	*nektob*

Introduction

Where the perfect tense is used to describe an event that is typically in the past (think: an action that is completed), the imperfect tense is used to describe an event that is often in the future (think: an action that is incomplete) from the standpoint of the author.

In the perfect tense, various endings were added to a word to show its inflection. The imperfect tense is formed with both a preformative as well as a suffix. The imperfect tense is most often formed with an *o/u*-vowel (neCCoC), as in ܢܶܟܬܘܿܒ (*nektob*) but can also be formed with *a*- and *e*-vowels as well (see below).[1] In the case of the former, the addition of the *o/u* sound necessitates that an additional letter *waw* be added to the middle of some of the conjugations to make this sound. For example, note the paradigm of the verb *ktab* (to read):

	Singular		Plural	
3m	ܢܶܟܬܘܿܒ ܢܶܟܬܽܘܒ	*nektob, nektub* he, will write	ܢܶܟܬܒܽܘܢ	*nektbun* they, will write
3f	ܬܶܟܬܘܿܒ ܬܶܟܬܘܿܒ݂ ܬܶܟܬܽܘܒ ܬܶܟܬܽܘܒ݂	*tektob* *tektub* she, will write	ܢܶܟܬܒܳܢ	*nektbān* they, will write
2m	ܬܶܟܬܘܿܒ ܬܶܟܬܽܘܒ	*tektob, tektub* you, will write	ܬܶܟܬܒܽܘܢ	*tektbun* you, will write
2f	ܬܶܟܬܒܺܝܢ	*tektbin* you, will write	ܬܶܟܬܒܳܢ	*tektbān* you, will write
1c	ܐܶܟܬܘܿܒ ܐܶܟܬܽܘܒ	*ektob, ektub* I, will write	ܢܶܟܬܘܿܒ ܢܶܟܬܽܘܒ	*nektob, nektub* we, will write

1. As with other cases, the Western tradition uses a *u* to represent the *o* sounds. Both conventions are represented in the paradigm.

Note: There are a few similarities within the paradigm that are important to note. First, the 3fs and the 2fs forms are identical, as well as the 3ms and the 1cp. Context will guide the selection of these, which is generally obvious.

A- or *E*- Stem Vowels

In the perfect tense, there is the option of having an *a*-vowel or an *e*-vowel as the stem vowel. For example, *ktab* (to read) takes an *a*-vowel, and *rhet* (to run) takes an *e*-vowel. Whichever stem vowel a verb has in the perfect will guide the stem vowel that the verb has in the imperfect.

Perfect		Imperfect
a-stem vowel	→	*o/u*-stem vowel
e-stem vowel	→	*a*-stem vowel

In these instances, the stem vowels will behave very predictably. The paradigm for the *a*-stem vowel in the imperfect is identical to that of the *o/u*-stem vowel in the imperfect, simply replacing the *o/u* with the *a*. However, in this change, it also means that some conjugations do not have the additional *waw* that is necessary to make the *o/u* sound.

	Singular		Plural	
3m	ܢܶܪܗܰܛ	*nerhaṭ* he will run	ܢܶܪܗܛܽܘܢ	*nerhṭun* they will run
3f	ܬܶܪܗܰܛ ܬܶܪܗܰܛ	*terhaṭ* she will run	ܢܶܪ̈ܗܛܳܢ	*nerhṭān* they will run
2m	ܬܶܪܗܰܛ	*terhaṭ* you will run	ܬܶܪܗܛܽܘܢ	*terhṭun* you will run
2f	ܬܶܪܗܛܺܝܢ	*terhṭin* you will run	ܬܶܪ̈ܗܛܳܢ	*terhṭān* you will run
1c	ܐܶܪܗܰܛ	*erhaṭ* I will run	ܢܶܪ̈ܗܰܛ	*nerhaṭ* we will run

There is one more possible ending that some verbs can have in the imperfect: an *e*-stem vowel. In these instances, the paradigm is identical to the one above, with the *e* as the stem vowel instead of an *a*.

One additional element to mention is that words whose root begins with an *ālap* (I-*ālap*) will not double the initial vowel in the 1cs form. Rather, the two *ālaps* will assimilate into one. See chapter 17 for futher discussion on I-*ālap* verb forms.

Uses of the Imperfect Tense

1. The most basic form of the imperfect is simply to represent an action that is not yet complete. In these occurrences, a simple future tense will suffice for translation:

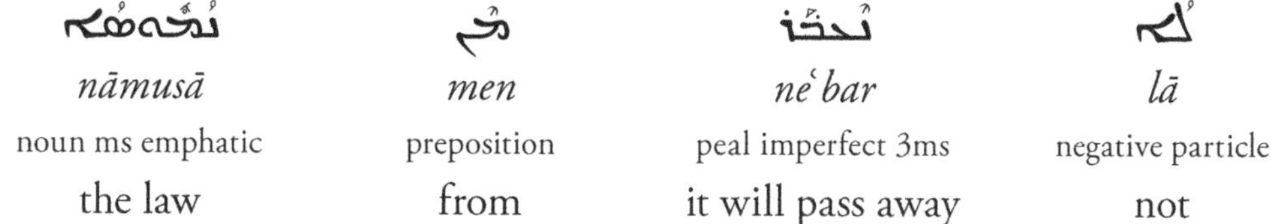

Translation: It will not pass away from the law.
Matthew 5:18

2. Prohibitive Actions/Negative Imperative: As will be discussed later in the grammar, the imperative (for now, simply equate this to a command) is never used with the negative particle, ܠܳܐ (*lā*). Due to this, if the author wished to express a prohibitive command in Syriac with a negative particle, it had to be done using the imperfect tense. Since this takes the place of the imperative, they are most often in the second person.

ܬܶܕܚܰܠ	ܠܳܐ
tedḥal	*lā*
peal imperfect 2ms	negative particle
you will be afraid	not

Translation: Do not be afraid!
Luke 8:50

3. Purpose Clause: Oftentimes an imperfect will be used to express the purpose of an action. This is seen in a subordinate clause that is predicated by the relative pronoun *dālat*. These clauses can either be preceded by ܐܰܝܟܰܢܳܐ ܕ / ܐܰܝܟ ܕ *ayk d- / aykanā d-* ("as") or it can be implied. For example, with the explicit particle:

ܒܢܰܘ̈ܗܝ	ܕܬܶܗܘܽܘܢ	ܐܰܝܟܰܢܳܐ
bnawi	*d-tehun*	*aykanā*
noun mp emphatic + 3ms	*dālat* + peal imperfect 2mp	particle
his sons	that you will be	as

Translation: In order that you will be his sons.
Matthew 5:45

And without the explicit particle:

ܗܽܘ	ܕܰܫܠܺܝܛ	ܕܶܝܢ	ܕܬܶܕܥܽܘܢ
-u	*dšaliṭ*	*den*	*d-tedʿun*
pronoun 3ms	adjective ms absolute	conjunction	*dālat* + peal imperfect 2mp
he is	permitted	but	that you will know

Translation: But (so/in order) that you may know he is permitted.
Mark 2:10

The verb in the above example is ܝܺܕܰܥ ("to know"), a weak verb with an initial *yūd*. In this particular form the *yūd* consonant disappears. I-*yūd* verbs and their expected forms will be covered further in chapter 18 but for now simply note the usage.

4. Jussive: Much like negative commands, the imperfect can also be used to represent the jussive mood. The jussive is used when a command is being expressed by the author. In these instances, it might be necessary to add an additional word in the translation to communicate this idea.[2]

ܩܪܶܒ	ܗܳܐ	ܢܺܐܙܰܠ
qreb	*hā*	*nizal*
peal perfect 3ms	particle	peal imperfect 1cp
he has drawn near	behold	we will go

Let us be going! Behold, he has drawn near.
Mark 14:42

Note that the vowel over the prefix of the imperfect verb changes when the initial letter of the root is an *ālap*. I-*ālap* verbs will be discussed in chapter 17 but the general idea is that an *a*-class, I-*ālap* verb will change its prefix vowel to an *i*. In other cases (*o*-class verbs) it remains an *e*.

Adding Pronominal Suffixes to the Imperfect Tense

As with the perfect tense, the imperfect can also take a pronominal suffix that reveals the object of the verb. These inflect in patterns very similar to the perfect tense verbs, with one exception. The stem vowels are often removed when there is an enclitic object attached to the verb (with the exception of the 2mp and 2fp endings, in which the stem vowel is kept). Therefore, there is not typically a *waw* that appears in the middle of the imperfect verb if a pronominal suffix attaches to it. For example:

---

2 Note that there is no designation between the jussive and the cohortative in Syriac (as in Hebrew, where the jussive is third person and the cohortative is first person). In the sense used here the jussive is used to suggest a mild command.

ܢܶܟܬܽܘܒ / ܢܶܟܬܘܿܒ → ܢܶܟܬܒܶܗ / ܢܶܟܬܒܺܝܘܗܝ

nektub / nektob — peal imperfect 3ms → *nektbeh / nektbiw* — peal imperfect 3ms + 3ms pronominal suffix

Translation: He will write it.

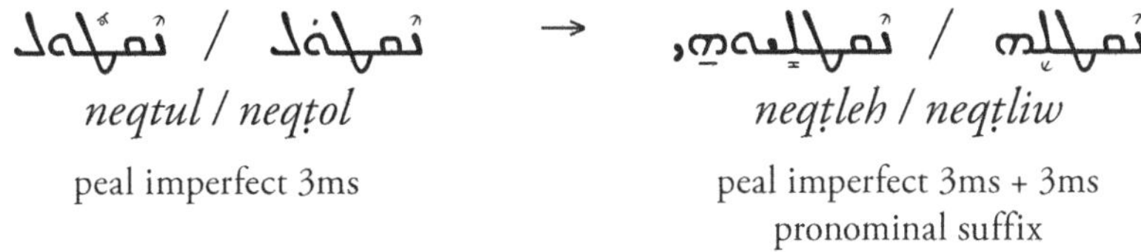

neqtul / neqṭol — peal imperfect 3ms → *neqṭleh / neqṭliw* — peal imperfect 3ms + 3ms pronominal suffix

Translation: He will kill him.

Note that both the *-eh* and *-iw* forms of the suffix are viable options for the 3ms enclitic object

Vocabulary

Nouns

ܛܰܠܝܳܐ	*ṭalyā*	youth, child
ܟܢܽܘܫܬܳܐ	*knuštā*	council, synagogue
ܢܽܘܪܳܐ	*nurā*	fire
ܣܳܦܪܳܐ	*sāprā*	scribe, lawyer
ܦܺܐܪܳܐ	*pirā*	fruit
ܪܶܥܝܳܢܳܐ	*reʿyānā*	mind, idea
ܫܽܘܠܛܳܢܳܐ	*šulṭānā*	authority, dominion, power
ܫܰܢ̱ܬܳܐ	*šatā*	year
ܫܰܪܒܬܳܐ	*šarbtā*	family, generation
ܬܰܪܥܳܐ	*tarʿā*	door, gate

Verbs

ܕܚܠ	*dḥel*	to fear
ܝܠܕ	*iled*	to give birth to
ܢܛܪ	*nṭar*	to keep, guard
ܣܒܪ	*sbar*	to preach, declare
ܣܗܕ	*sed*	to testify, witness
ܥܬܕ	*ʿtad*	to prepare
ܦܩܕ	*pqad*	to command
ܩܛܠ	*qṭal*	to kill
ܪܚܡ	*rḥem*	to love
ܪܡܐ	*rmā*	to cast, put, place

Other

ܐܠܘ	*ellu*	if
ܐܡܬܝ	*emat*	when
ܚܒܝܒܐ	*ḥbibā*	beloved
ܚܕܬܐ	*ḥadtā*	new
ܠܘܩܒܠ	*luqbal*	against, near
ܠܡܐ	*lmā*	why?
ܡܚܕܐ	*meḥdā*	at once, immediately
ܦܪܝܫܐ	*prišā*	Pharisee
ܩܠܝܠܐ	*qalilā*	little
ܫܪܝܪܐ	*šarirā*	steadfast, true

Exercises

Matthew 5:18 (1)

ܠܐ ܢܥܒܪ ܡܢ ܢܡܘܣܐ ܥܕܡܐ ܕܟܠ ܢܗܘܐ

Matthew 13:9 (2)

ܡܢ ܕܐܝܬ ܠܗ ܐܕܢܐ[3] ܕܢܫܡܥ ܢܫܡܥ

Matthew 19:5 (3)

ܘܐܡܪ ܡܛܠ ܗܢܐ ܢܫܒܘܩ ܓܒܪܐ ܠܐܒܘܗܝ ܘܠܐܡܗ ܘܢܩܦ[4] ܠܐܢܬܬܗ

John 8:12 (4)

ܐܠܐ ܢܫܟܚ ܠܗ ܢܘܗܪܐ ܕܚܝܐ

Matthew 12:32 (5)

ܘܟܠ ܡܢ ܕܢܐܡܪ[5] ܡܠܬܐ ܥܠ ܒܪܗ ܕܐܢܫܐ ܢܫܬܒܩ[6] ܠܗ ܟܠ ܕܝܢ
ܕܥܠ ܪܘܚܐ ܕܩܘܕܫܐ ܢܐܡܪ ܠܐ ܢܫܬܒܩ ܠܗ ܠܐ ܒܥܠܡܐ ܗܢܐ ܘܠܐ
ܒܥܠܡܐ ܕܥܬܝܕ[7]

3. ܐܕܢܐ = ears.
4. ܢܩܦ = he will cleave.
5. This is an imperfect verb that starts with *ālap*. Note the vowel above the *ālap*. (x2)
6. ܢܫܬܒܩ = he will be forgiven (x2).
7. ܥܬܝܕ = being prepared.

Mark 10:15 (6)

ܐܡܝܢ ܐܡܪ ܐܢܐ ܠܟܘܢ ܕܟܠ ܕܠܐ ܢܩܒܠ[8] ܡܠܟܘܬܐ ܕܐܠܗܐ ܐܝܟ
ܛܠܝܐ

Matthew 6:14–15 (7)

ܐܢ ܓܝܪ ܬܫܒܩܘܢ ܠܒܢܝܢܫܐ[9] ܣܟܠܘܬܗܘܢ[10] ܢܫܒܘܩ ܐܦ ܠܟܘܢ
ܐܒܘܟܘܢ ܕܒܫܡܝܐ ܐܢ ܕܝܢ ܠܐ ܬܫܒܩܘܢ ܠܒܢܝܢܫܐ ܐܦܠܐ
ܐܒܘܟܘܢ ܫܒܩ ܠܟܘܢ ܣܟܠܘܬܟܘܢ

Matthew 18:17 (8)

ܐܢ ܕܝܢ ܐܦ ܠܐ ܠܗܘܢ ܢܫܡܥ ܐܡܪ[11] ܠܥܕܬܐ ܐܢ ܕܝܢ ܐܦ ܠܐ
ܠܥܕܬܐ ܢܫܡܥ

Matthew 18:21 (9)

ܗܝܕܝܢ ܩܪܒ ܠܘܬܗ ܟܐܦܐ ܘܐܡܪ ܡܪܝ ܟܡܐ ܙܒܢܝܢ ܐܢ ܢܣܟܠ[12] ܒܝ
ܐܚܝ ܐܫܒܘܩ ܠܗ ܥܕܡܐ ܠܫܒܥ[13] ܙܒܢܝܢ

---

8. This is the pael stem (3ms) but resembles the peal stem closely. The difference is in the vowel pointing. The pael stem will be covered later, but note the distinction here.
9. A variation on ܒܪܢܫܐ.
10. ܣܟܠܘܬܗܘܢ = your trespasses (x2).
11. ܐܡܪ = tell (imperative).
12. This is an aphel imperfect. It has the same consonants as the peal imperfect but with different vowels. It translates "if he offends."
13. ܠܫܒܥ = seven.

Luke 18:19 (10)

ܐܶܡܰܪ ܠܶܗ ܝܶܫܽܘܥ ܡܳܢܳܐ ܩܳܪܶܐ ܐܢ̱ܬ ܠܺܝ ܛܳܒ݂ܳܐ ܠܰܝܬ ܛܳܒ݂ܳܐ ܐܶܠܳܐ ܐܶܢ

ܚܰܕ ܐܰܠܳܗܳܐ

Matthew 18:35 (11)

ܗܳܟ݂ܰܢܳܐ ܢܶܥܒܶܕ ܠܟ݂ܽܘܢ ܐܳܦ ܐܳܒ݂ܝ ܕܒ݂ܰܫܡܰܝܳܐ ܐܶܢ ܠܳܐ ܬܶܫܒ݁ܩܽܘܢ ܐ̱ܢܳܫ ܠܰܐܚܽܘܗ̱ܝ

ܡܶܢ ܠܶܒ݁ܟ݂ܽܘܢ ܣܰܟ݂ܠܘܳܬ݂ܶܗ[14]

Luke 16:29 (12)

ܐܶܡܰܪ ܠܶܗ ܐܰܒ݂ܪܳܗܳܡ ܐܺܝܬ ܠܗܽܘܢ ܡܽܘܫܶܐ ܘܰܢܒ݂ܺܝܶܐ ܢܶܫܡܥܽܘܢ ܐܶܢܽܘܢ

Acts 16:28 (13)

ܘܶܐܡܰܪ ܠܶܗ ܠܳܐ ܬܶܥܒܶܕ ܠܢܰܦ݂ܫܳܟ ܡܶܕܶܡ ܕܒ݂ܺܝܫ ܕܟ݂ܽܠܰܢ ܗܳܪܟܳܐ[15] ܚܢܰܢ

Matthew 11:15 (14)

ܡܰܢ ܕܐܺܝܬ ܠܶܗ ܐܶܕ݂ܢܶܐ[16] ܕܢܶܫܡܰܥ ܢܶܫܡܰܥ

Mark 4:41 (15)

ܕܶܐܬ݂ܳܬ݂[17] ܡܶܢ ܥܶܒ݂ܪܰܝܗ̇[18] ܕܰܐܪܥܳܐ ܕܬ݂ܶܫܡܰܥ ܚܶܟ݂ܡܬ݂ܶܗ ܕܫܠܶܝܡܽܘܢ

---

14. ܣܰܟ݂ܠܘܳܬ݂ܶܗ = his sins.
15. ܗܳܪܟܳܐ = here.
16. ܐܶܕ݂ܢܶܐ = ears
17. This is a peal perfect 3fs from ܐܶܬ݂ܳܐ, to come.
18. ܥܶܒ݂ܪܰܝܗ̇= crossing it (note the feminine pronominal suffix).

Matthew 19:16 (16)

ܘܶܐܬ݂ܳܐ ܚܰܕ݂ ܩܪܶܒ݂ ܘܶܐܡܰܪ ܠܶܗ ܡܰܠܦܳܢܳܐ[19] ܛܳܒ݂ܳܐ ܡܳܢܳܐ ܕܛܳܒ݂ ܐܶܥܒܶܕ݂.
ܕܢܶܗܘܽܘܢ ܠܺܝ ܚܰܝ̈ܶܐ ܕܰܠܥܳܠܰܡ

James 4:15 (17)

ܚܠܳܦ ܕܢܺܐܡܪܽܘܢ[20] ܕܶܐܢ ܡܳܪܝܳܐ ܢܶܨܒܶܐ ܘܢܺܚܶܐ[21] ܥܳܒ݂ܕܺܝܢܰܢ[22] ܗܳܕܶܐ ܐܳܘ
ܗܳܝ

John 8:12 (18)

ܐܶܠܳܐ ܢܶܫܟܰܚ ܠܶܗ ܢܽܘܗܪܳܐ ܕܚܰܝ̈ܶܐ

Mark 9:5 (19)

ܘܶܐܡܰܪ ܠܶܗ ܟܺܐܦܳܐ ܪܰܒܝ ܫܰܦܺܝܪ ܗܽܘ ܠܰܢ ܕܗܳܪܟܳܐ ܢܶܗܘܶܐ ܘܢܶܥܒܶܕ݂ ܬܠܳܬ݂[23]
ܡܰܛ̈ܠܶܢ[24] ܠܳܟ ܚܕܳܐ ܘܠܡܽܘܫܶܐ ܚܕܳܐ ܘܠܶܐܠܺܝܳܐ ܚܕܳܐ

John 6:45 (20)

ܟܬܺܝܒ݂ ܓܶܝܪ ܒܰܢܒ݂ܺܝ̈ܶܐ ܕܢܶܗܘܽܘܢ ܟܽܠܗܽܘܢ ܡܰܠ̈ܦܶܐ[25] ܕܰܐܠܳܗܳܐ ܟܽܠ ܡܰܢ
ܕܫܡܰܥ ܗܳܟܺܝܠ ܡܶܢ ܐܰܒ݂ܳܐ

19. ܡܰܠܦܳܢܳܐ = teacher.
20. Note the additional vowel above the *ālap*. The parsing is apparent from the ending.
21. ܘܢܺܚܶܐ = we will live.
22. This is a participle with a pronominal suffix: peal active mp + 1cp.
23. ܬܠܳܬ݂ = three
24. ܡܰܛ̈ܠܶܢ = shelters
25. ܡܰܠ̈ܦܶܐ = taught

Additional Exercises

Tobit 11:3 (21)

ܢܪܗܛ ܩܕܡ ܐܢܬܬܐ ܕܝܠܟ ܘܢܛܝܒ[26] ܒܝܬܐ

Genesis 26:24 (22)

ܠܐ ܬܕܚܠ ܡܛܠ ܕܥܡܟ ܐܢܐ

Exodus 14:14 (23)

ܡܪܝܐ ܢܬܟܬܫ[27] ܥܠ ܐ̈ܦܝܟܘܢ. ܟܕ ܐܢܬܘܢ ܬܗܘܘܢ ܫܠܝܢ[28] ܘܨܠܘ[29]

ܗܫܐ ܩܕܡ ܡܪܝܐ

Jeremiah 7:23 (24)

ܐܠܐ ܐܢܐ ܗܢܐ ܦܬܓܡܐ[30] ܦܩܕܬ ܐܢܘܢ ܘܐܡܪܬ ܫܡܥܘ ܒܩܠܝ[31]

ܘܐܗܘܐ ܠܟܘܢ ܐܠܗܐ ܘܐܢܬܘܢ ܬܗܘܘܢ ܠܝ ܥܡܐ

Exodus 24:7 (25)

ܟܠ ܡܕܡ ܕܐܡܪ ܡܪܝܐ ܢܥܒܕ ܘܢܫܡܥ.

Jonah 1:11 (26)

ܐܡܪܘ ܠܗ ܡܢܐ ܢܥܒܕ ܠܟ

---

26. ܘܢܛܝܒ = and prepare.
27. ܢܬܟܬܫ = he will fight.
28. ܫܠܝܢ = be silent.
29. ܨܠܘ = pray.
30. ܦܬܓܡܐ = word.
31. Note the *ālap* disappears with the presence of the pronominal suffix.

11

Peal Imperative and Infinitive

	Perfect	Participle	Imperfect	Imperative	Infinitive
Peal	ܟܬܰܒ	ܟܳܬܶܒ	ܢܶܟܬܘܿܒ	ܟܬܘܿܒ	ܡܶܟܬܰܒ
	ktab	*kāteb*	*nektob*	*ktub*	*mektab*

Peal Imperative Introduction

The imperative is used in direct address, thus the second person is implied. The forms will be classified according to their stem vowels—either *o/u* or *a/e*. As a review, the stem vowel is the vowel that appears over the middle consonant.

O/U-Stem Vowels

The initial structure of the imperative (the masculine singular form) is derived by simply dropping the preformative of the imperfect tense (CCoC).

ܢܶܟܬܽܘܒ / ܢܶܟܬܘܿܒ	→	ܟܬܽܘܒ / ܟܬܘܿܒ
nektub / nektob		*ktub / ktob*
Imperfect		Imperative

The other forms are made by adding either a *yūd* (fs and fp) or a *waw* (mp) to this basic structure (see chart below). Neither the *yūd* nor the *waw* are pronounced, but are only for recognition of the masculine or feminine gender. As the language developed, a *nūn* was added to these plural endings to distinguish the two phonetically. This distinction is marked with the Roman numerals I and II below. The Western vocalization is included in the paradigm for reference.

	Singular	Plural I	Plural II
Masculine	ܟܬܘܿܒ ܟܬܘܼܒ *ktob* *ktub* Write!	ܟܬܘܿܒܘ ܟܬܘܼܒܘ *ktob* *ktub* Write!	ܟܬܘܿܒܘܿܢ ܟܬܘܼܒܘܿܢ *ktobun* *ktubun* Write!
Feminine	ܟܬܘܿܒܝ ܟܬܘܼܒܝ *ktob* *ktub* Write!	ܟܬܘܿܒܝ̈ ܟܬܘܼܒܝ̈ *ktob* *ktub* Write!	ܟܬܘܿܒܹܝܢ ܟܬܘܼܒܹܝܢ *ktobēn* *ktubēn* Write!

A- and *E*-Stem Vowels

Verbs that have *a*- or *e*-stem vowels in the imperfect will behave the exact same way, with the preformative of the imperfect dropped in order to make the masculine singular form (CCaC).

ܢܸܪܗܲܛ	→	ܪܗܲܛ
nerhaṭ		*rhaṭ*
Imperfect		Imperative

Note the similarities with the *o/u*-stem vowel conjugations. As with the imperfect tense, the imperative forms with an *a*- or *e*-stem vowel do not have the accompanying *waw* in the middle of the root.

	Singular	Plural I	Plural II
Masculine	ܪܗܲܛ *rhaṭ* Run!	ܪܗܲܛܘ *rhaṭ* Run!	ܪܗܲܛܘܿܢ *rhaṭun* Run!
Feminine	ܪܗܲܛܝ *rhaṭ* Run!	ܪܗܲܛܝ̈ *rhaṭ* Run!	ܪܗܲܛܹܝܢ *rhaṭēn* Run!

The full paradigm for the words with the *a*-stem vowel and *e*-stem vowel are again similar; the only difference is that the stem vowel is either an *a* or an *e*.

Uses of the Imperative

1. Direct Commands: The usage of the imperative is not as diverse as other verb forms in Syriac. For the most part, it is limited to direct commands.

ܦܘܡܗ	ܦܬܚ
pumeh	*ptaḥ*
noun ms emphatic + 3 ms suffix	peal imperative ms
its mouth	open!

Translation: Open its mouth!
Matthew 17:21

ܦܘܡܟ	ܣܟܘܪ
pumāk	*skur*
noun ms emphatic + 2ms suffix	peal imperative ms
your mouth	shut!

Translation: Shut your mouth!
Mark 1:25

2. Negative Imperative: Remember that there is no way to express a negative by using the imperative. This must be done by using the negative particle *lā* + the imperfect tense. See the previous chapter for more examples.

ܬܟܠܘܢ	ܠܐ
teklun	*lā*
peal imperfect 2ms	negative particle
you will hinder	not

Translation: Do not hinder!
Luke 9:50

The verb used here attests an *ālap* as the final vowel in the root, ܟܠܐ ("to hinder'). Note when the ending is added the *ālap* disappears. III-*ālap* verbs will be covered later in the grammar.

Peal Infinitive Introduction

An infinitive can be preliminarily translated by adding a "to" in front of the verb. However, there are additional uses of the infinitive, and context always needs to have the final say when translating.

Infinitives are given a *mīm* prefix and an *a*-stem vowel. The pattern follows suit regardless of the original stem vowel that is used for the word (meCCaC).

ܟܬܒ	→	ܡܟܬܒ
ktab		*mektab*
		to write

In the case of the infinitive, it does not matter whether the stem vowel is an *a* or an *e*. Both will revert to an *a*-stem vowel regardless. For example:

ܪܗܛ	→	ܡܪܗܛ
rheṭ		*merhaṭ*
		to run

Translating Infinitives

1. *lāmad* Prefix: Infinitives will often take a *lāmad* prefix (sometimes to show purpose). This is a convenient reminder of the translation of the infinitive because the *lāmad* prefix is the same as adding "to" to the front of a word. In the New Testament, this is the most often used prefix for the infinitive, so if there is a *lāmad-mīm* prefixed to a word, there is a good likelihood that it is an infinitive.

ܠܟܘܢ	ܠܡܐܡܪ	ܠܝ	ܐܝܬ	ܣܓܝ
l-kun	*l-mimar*	*li*	*it*	*saggi*
lāmad + 3 mp	*lāmad* + peal infinitive	*lāmad* + 1cp	particle	adjective ms absolute
to you (pl.)	to say	for me	there is	much/many

Literal Translation: There is much for me to say to you.

Contextual Translation: I have much to say to you.

John 16:12

In the above example, note what happens when the initial letter is an *ālap*. The vowel over the *mīm* changes to an *i* for verbs with an *a*-stem vowel.

2. Infinitive Absolute: Infinitives will sometimes join other verb forms of the same root in order to add prominence to what is being said. The infinitive absolute is typically used either to point out a contrast between two differing things, or to add emphasis by intensifying the action. Both are slight. Note the example:

ܬܕܥܘܢ	ܘܠܐ	ܡܚܙܐ	ܘܚܙܘ
tedʿun	*w-la*	*meḥza*	*w-ḥazu*
peal imperfect 2mp	*waw* + negative particle	peal infinitive	waw + peal imperative 2mp
they will know	and not	to see	they will see

Translation: They will see and not know.

Isaiah 6:9

Adding Pronominal Suffixes to Imperatives and Infinitives

While in the imperfect form the stem vowel typically dropped out if a pronominal suffix was added, it will be retained when the imperative form is used.

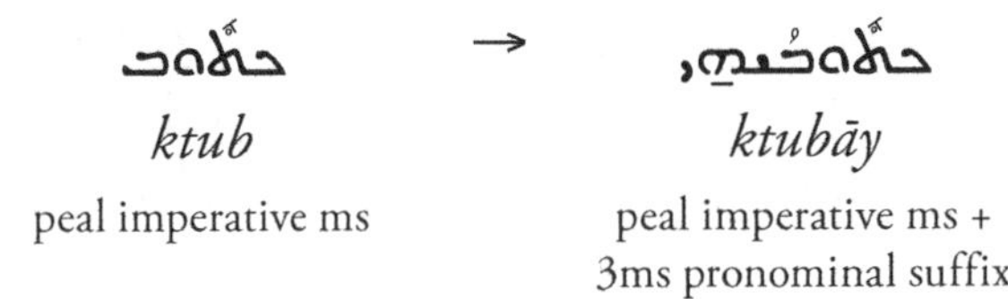

ktub → *ktubāy*

peal imperative ms → peal imperative ms + 3ms pronominal suffix

Translation: Write him!

As we might expect, infinitives conjugate according to the rules of adding pronominal suffixes to nouns. One element to note is that the stem vowel will typically be dropped when a suffix is added (except for the 2mp and 2fp conjugations).

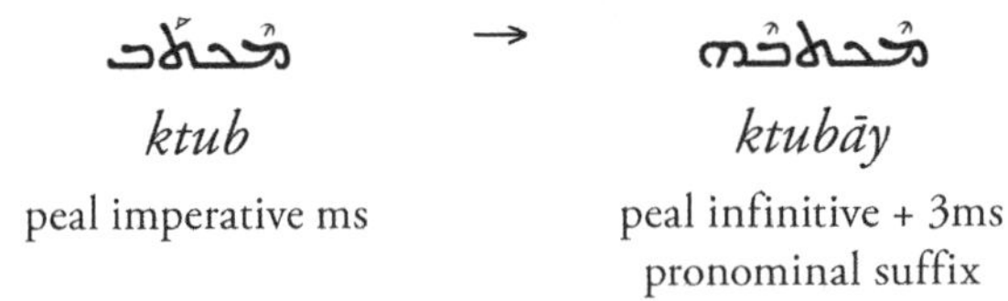

ktub → *ktubāy*

peal imperative ms → peal infinitive + 3ms pronominal suffix

Translation: To write it.

Vocabulary

Nouns

ܕܽܘܟܬܳܐ *dukktā* place
ܚܰܝܽܘܬܳܐ *ḥayutā* animal
ܛܽܘܪܳܐ *ṭurā* mountain
ܟܺܐܢܽܘܬܳܐ *kinutā* righteousness, justice
ܟܺܐܦܳܐ *kipā* rock, stone
ܠܺܠܝܳܐ *lilyā* night
ܢܽܘܗܪܳܐ *nuhrā* light
ܣܳܗܕܽܘܬܳܐ *sahdutā* testimony, martyrdom
ܩܪܺܝܬܳܐ *qritā* village
ܫܰܒܬܳܐ *šabtā* Sabbath

Verbs

ܓܠܳܐ *glā* to reveal
ܗܰܠܶܟ *hallek* to walk
ܚܰܒ *ḥab* to be loving, kindled
ܚܰܘܳܐ *ḥwwā* to show
ܟܢܰܫ *knaš* to assemble
ܢܚܶܬ *nḥet* to descend
ܣܒܰܪ *sbar* to think, consider
ܥܒܰܪ *ʿbar* to cross over (with ܥܰܠ = to transgress)
ܨܠܳܐ *ṣlā* to incline toward, pray
ܩܳܡ *qām* to stand, arise

Other

ܐܚܪܝܐ	*ḥrāyā*	last, extreme
ܒܝܢܬ	*baynāt*	between, among
ܗܪܟܐ	*harkā*	here
ܚܫܘܟܐ	*ḥešukā*	darkness
ܟܠܙܒܢ	*kullzban*	always
ܠܘܩܕܡ	*luqdam*	before, formerly
ܠܡܢܐ	*lmānā*	why?
ܡܟܝܠ	*mekkil*	now, therefore, henceforth
ܩܪܝܒܐ	*qaribā*	neighbor, near, at hand
ܫܠܝܛܐ	*šaliṭā*	lawful, permitted (pl. rulers)

Exercises

Note: Exercises 1 – 10 deal with imperatives, 11 – 20 deal with infinitives.

Matthew 3:15 (1)

ܗܘ ܕܝܢ ܝܫܘܥ ܥܢܐ ܘܐܡܪ ܠܗ ܫܒܘܩ ܗܫܐ

Matthew 14:28 (2)

ܥܢܐ ܟܐܦܐ ܘܐܡܪ ܠܗ ܡܪܝ ܐܢ ܐܢܬ ܗܘ ܦܩܘܕ ܠܝ ܐܬܐ[1]

ܠܘܬܟ ܥܠ ܡܝܐ

Luke 7:40 (3)

ܥܢܐ ܕܝܢ ܝܫܘܥ ܘܐܡܪ ܠܗ ܫܡܥܘܢ ܡܕܡ ܐܝܬ ܠܝ ܠܡܐܡܪ ܠܟ ܗܘ

ܕܝܢ ܐܡܪ ܠܗ ܐܡܪ ܪܒܝ[2]

1. ܐܬܐ = I will come.
2. ܪܒܝ = teacher.

Romans 13:4 (4)

ܡܫܡܫܢܐ[3] ܗܘ ܓܝܪ ܕܐܠܗܐ ܐܠܐ ܠܟ ܠܛܒܬܐ ܘܐܢ ܒܝܫܬܐ

ܥܒܕ ܐܢܬ ܕܚܠ[4]

Revelation 2:1 (5)

ܘܠܡܠܐܟܐ ܕܒܥܕܬܐ ܕܐܦܣܘܣ ܟܬܘܒ

Mathew 8:9 (6)

ܘܠܥܒܕܝ ܕܥܒܕ[5] ܗܕܐ ܘܥܒܕ

Matthew 11:29 (7)

ܫܩܘܠܘ ܢܝܪܝ[6] ܥܠܝܟܘܢ ܘܐܠܦܘ ܡܢܝ

Luke 4:23 (8)

ܘܟܠ ܕܫܡܥܢ ܕܥܒܕܬ ܒܟܦܪܢܚܘܡ ܥܒܕ[7] ܐܦ ܗܪܟܐ ܒܡܕܝܢܬܟ

Luke 9:60 (9)

ܐܡܪ ܠܗ ܝܫܘܥ ܫܒܘܩ ܡܝܬܐ ܩܒܪܝܢ[8] ܡܝܬܝܗܘܢ ܘܐܢܬ ܙܠ[9] ܣܒܪ[10]

ܡܠܟܘܬܗ ܕܐܠܗܐ

---

3. ܡܫܡܫܢܐ = minister.
4. This is a hard word to parse. The key to understanding is in the vowel, which will differ between the peal perfect (*e*) and imperative (*a*).
5. Look for the vowel as a key for parsing (*e* in the imperative and *a* in the perfect).
6. ܢܝܪܝ = my yoke.
7. Look at the vowel for a clue. The same word is in (6).
8. ܩܒܪܝܢ = burying.
9. ܙܠ = go! (imperative).
10. ܣܒܪ = proclaim.

Luke 5:8 (10)

ܟܕ ܚܙܐ ܕܝܢ ܫܡܥܘܢ ܟܐܦܐ ܢܦܠ ܩܕܡ ܪ̈ܓܠܘܗܝ[11] ܕܝܫܘܥ ܘܐܡܪ
ܠܗ ܒܥܐ ܐܢܐ ܡܢܟ ܡܪܝ، ܦܘܩ ܠܟ ܡܢܝ ܕܓܒܪܐ ܐܢܐ ܚܛܝܐ

Matthew 7:18 (11)

ܠܐ ܡܫܟܚ[12] ܐܝܠܢܐ[13] ܛܒܐ ܦܐܪ̈ܐ ܒܝ̈ܫܐ ܠܡܥܒܕ. ܘܠܐ ܐܝܠܢܐ
ܒܝܫܐ ܦܐܪ̈ܐ ܛܒ̈ܐ ܠܡܥܒܕ.

Matthew 9:5 (12)

ܡܢܐ ܓܝܪ ܦܫܝܩ[14] ܠܡܐܡܪ[15] ܕܫܒܝܩܝܢ ܠܟ ܚܛܗ̈ܝܟ ܐܘ ܠܡܐܡܪ
ܩܘܡ ܗܠܟ[16]

Matthew 14:16 (13)

ܗܘ ܕܝܢ ܐܡܪ ܠܗܘܢ ܠܐ ܡܬܒܥܝܐ[17] ܠܗܘܢ ܠܡܐܙܠ[18] ܗܒܘ[19] ܠܗܘܢ
ܐܢܬܘܢ ܠܡܐܟܠ

3 John 13 (14)

ܣܓܝ̈ܐܬܐ ܐܝܬ ܗܘܐ ܠܝ ܠܡܟܬܒ ܠܟ

---

11. ܪ̈ܓܠܘܗܝ = his feet.
12. ܡܫܟܚ = being able (participle).
13. ܐܝܠܢܐ = tree (x2 in this verse).
14. ܦܫܝܩ = easier (in context).
15. This is an infinitive. Note the vowel that is used over the *ālap* (x2).
16. ܩܘܡ ܗܠܟ = Get up! Walk! (imperatives).
17. ܡܬܒܥܝܐ = require.
18. This is an infinitive. Note the vowel that goes with the *ālap*.
19. ܗܒܘ = Give! (imperative).

Mark 6:36 (15)

ܠܝܬ ܠܗܘܢ ܓܝܪ ܡܕܡ ܠܡܐܟܠ[20]

John 5:16 (16)

ܘܡܛܠ ܗܕܐ ܪܕܦܝܢ[21] ܗܘܘ ܝܗܘܕܝܐ ܠܝܫܘܥ ܘܒܥܝܢ[22] ܗܘܘ ܠܡܩܛܠܗ[23]

Acts 13:44 (17)

ܟܢܫܬ[24] ܟܠܗ ܡܕܝܢܬܐ ܠܡܫܡܥ ܡܠܬܗ ܕܐܠܗܐ

Mark 2:7 (18)

ܡܢܘ ܡܫܟܚ[25] ܠܡܫܒܩ ܚܛܗܐ ܐܠܐ ܐܢ ܚܕ ܐܠܗܐ

Luke 24:41 (19)

ܐܡܪ ܠܗܘܢ ܐܝܬ ܠܟܘܢ ܗܪܟܐ[26] ܡܕܡ ܠܡܐܟܠ[27]

Mark 4:33 (20)

ܒܡܬܠܐ[28] ܕܐܝܟ ܗܠܝܢ ܡܡܠܠ[29] ܗܘܐ ܝܫܘܥ ܥܡܗܘܢ ܡܠܬܐ ܐܝܟ

ܕܡܫܟܚܝܢ[30] ܗܘܘ ܠܡܫܡܥ

---

20. This is a I-*ālap* infinitive.
21. ܪܕܦܝܢ = persecuting.
22. ܒܥܝܢ = seeking.
23. This is an infinitive with a 3ms pronominal suffix.
24. ܟܢܫܬ = they gathered.
25. ܡܫܟܚ = being able (participle).
26. ܗܪܟܐ = here.
27. This is another I-*ālap* infinitive.
28. ܒܡܬܠܐ = in parables.
29. ܡܡܠܠ = speaking.
30. ܕܡܫܟܚܝܢ = were able.

Additional Exercises

Deuteronomy 15:3 (21)

ܘܡܕܡ ܕܐܝܬ ܠܟ ܠܘܬ ܐܚܘܟ ܫܒܘܩ

Psalms 68:29 (22)

ܦܩܘܕ ܐܠܗܐ ܒܥܘܫܢܟ[31]

2 Esdras 12:37 (23)

ܟܬܘܒ ܗܟܝܠ ܒܣܦܪܐ ܗܠܝܢ ܟܠܗܝܢ

Genesis 24:50 (24)

ܠܐ ܡܫܟܚܝܢ ܚܢܢ ܠܡܐܡܪ ܠܟ ܛܒܬܐ ܐܘ ܒܝܫܬܐ

Judges 20:12 (25)

ܓܒܖ̈ܐ ܠܘܬ ܟܠܗܘܢ ܕܒܝܬ ܒܢܝܡܝܢ[32] ܠܡܐܡܪ ܡܢܐ ܗܝ ܒܝܫܬܐ
ܗܕܐ ܕܗܘܬ ܒܟܘܢ

Deuteronomy 5:25 (26)

ܠܡܫܡܥ ܩܠܗ ܕܡܪܝܐ ܐܠܗܢ

31. ܒܥܘܫܢܟ = your strength.
32. This is a name.

12

Ethpeel (Gp)

	Perfect	Participle	Imperfect	Imperative	Infinitive
Ethpeel	ܐܶܬܟܬܶܒ	ܡܶܬܟܬܶܒ	ܢܶܬܟܬܶܒ	ܐܶܬܟܰܬܒ	ܡܶܬܟܬܳܒܽܘ
	etkteb	*metkteb*	*netkteb*	*etkatb*	*metktābu*

Introduction

To review, the ethpeel stem is used to describe the basic, passive action of a verb. While the nomenclature of the different conjugations might seem confusing at first, it is actually very helpful in determining what the typical stem vowel is going to be for the paradigm. In this case, the name of the passive conjugation is the ethp*ee*l conjugation, so one could expect for the stem vowels to be in the *e*-class. For example, from the peal form *ktab* (he/it wrote) comes *etkteb* (it was written) in the ethpeel.[1] However, be aware that sometimes the stem vowel will change depending on the verb, so always be flexible with an estimation of the stem vowel.

ܟܬܰܒ	+	ܐܶܬ	=	ܐܶܬܟܬܶܒ
ktab		*et-*		*etkteb*

Ethpeel Perfect

With the exception of the different stem vowels and the *et-* preformative, the ethpeel perfect paradigm is nearly identical to that of the peal perfect (etCCeC). Therefore, it is not necessary to remember the entire paradigm, but simply the stem vowel and the perfect conjugations. This should make memorizing this paradigm a lot easier. The full paradigm for the ethpeel perfect is as follows:

1. This is a good time to mention that just because the stem name attests a soft *t*, Ethpeel, does not necessarily mean that verbs in the Ethpeel conjugation will always be pronounced with a soft *t*.

	Singular		Plural	
3m	ܐܬܟܬܒ	*etkteb* he/it was written	ܐܬܟܬܒܘ ܐܬܟܬܒܘܢ	*etkateb* *etktebun* they were written
3f	ܐܬܟܬܒܬ	*etkatbat* she was written	ܐܬܟܬܒ ܐܬܟܬ̈ܒ ܐܬܟܬ̈ܒܢ	*etkteb* *etkteb* *etktebēn* they were written
2m	ܐܬܟܬܒܬ	*etktebt* you were written	ܐܬܟܬܒܬܘܢ ܐܬܟܬܒܬܘܢ	*etktebton* *etktebtun* you were written
2f	ܐܬܟܬܒܬܝ	*etktebt* you were written	ܐܬܟܬ̈ܒܬܝܢ	*etktebtēn* you were written
1c	ܐܬܟܬܒܬ	*etkatbet* I was written	ܐܬܟܬܒܢ ܐܬܟܬܒܢܢ	*etktebn* *etktebnan* we were written

The function of the ethpeel is very similar to that of the peal. Note in the example below how the passive changes the translation from "he/it wrote," to "it was written."

ܐܬܟܬܒ	ܩܕܝܡ	ܡܢ
etkteb	*qdim*	*men*
ethpeel perfect 3ms	preposition	preposition
it was written	before	from

Translation: From before it was written.

Romans 15:4

Switching the *taw* (Metathesis)

In some cases, when the first letter of the verbal root is a *šīn*, *semkat*, *zayn*, or *ṣādē*—all *s* sounds (called sibilants)—then the *taw* from the *et-* prefix will switch places with the first consonant.[2] This sounds more complicated than it really is. Note the position of the *taw* in each of the ethpeel verbs in the following two tables.

2. This is a common characteristic among Semitic languages.

1. In the case of *šīn* and *semkat*, the *taw* from *eth-* switches places with the first letter of the root.

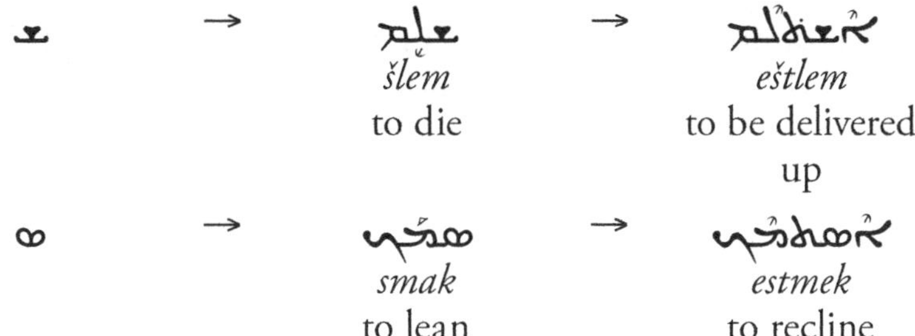

ܫ	→	ܫܠܡ *šlem* to die	→	ܐܫܬܠܡ *eštlem* to be delivered up
ܣ	→	ܣܡܟ *smak* to lean	→	ܐܣܬܡܟ *estmek* to recline

2. In the case of *zayn* and *ṣādē*, the *taw* is switched as well. In addition, with *ṣādē* the *taw* also becomes a *ṭēt*, while with *zayn* it becomes a *dālat*. In essence there are two things that are changing in this instance: the position of the letter and the letter itself.

ܙ	→	ܙܒܢ *zban* to buy	→	ܐܙܕܒܢ *ezdben* to be bought
ܨ	→	ܨܠܒ *ṣlab* to crucify	→	ܐܨܛܠܒ *eṣṭleb* to be crucified

For an example of metathesis consider the following.

ܠܝ	ܐܫܬܠܡ	ܡܕܡ	ܟܠ
li	*eštlem*	*medem*	*kull*
lāmad + 1cs	ethpeel perfect 3ms	noun	particle
to me	he has delivered	thing	every

Translation: He has delivered everything to me.
Matthew 11:27

Ethpeel Imperfect

With the ethpeel imperfect, a situation arises where to prefixes attach to the verb: the preformative for the imperfect tense (either *nūn* or *taw*) and the preformative for the ethpeel stem (*et-*). These are added by simply compounding the two and assimilating the *ālap* from the *eth-* prefix into the prefix for the imperfect. The prefix then becomes either *net-* or *tet-* (netCCeC).

ܢ	+	ܐܬ	=	ܢܬܟܬܒ
n		*et*		*netkteb*

ܬ	+	ܐܬ	=	ܬܬܟܬܒ
t		*et*		*tetkteb*

	Singular		Plural	
3m	ܢܬܟܬܒ	*netkteb* he/it will be written	ܢܬܟܬܒܘܢ	*netkatbun* they will be written
3f	ܬܬܟܬܒ	*tetkteb* she/it will be written	ܢܬܟܬܒܢ	*netkatbān* they will be written
2m	ܬܬܟܬܒ	*tetkteb* you will be written	ܬܬܟܬܒܘܢ	*tetkatbun* you will be written
2f	ܬܬܟܬܒܝܢ	*tetkatbin* you will be written	ܬܬܟܬܒܢ	*tetkatbān* you will be written
1c	ܐܬܟܬܒ	*etktbet* I will be written	ܢܬܟܬܒ	*netkteb* we will be written

Note: The ethpeel imperfect 1cp form is exactly the same as the ethpeel perfect 3ms (a very common use), and the 3fs and 2ms are identical. Context will sufficiently determine which should be used in each scenario.

The ethpeel imperfect tense should be translated as a passive action (or medio-passive), that is not yet completed. It can also include the other uses outlined previously for the imperfect tense, such as the prohibitive action (with *lā*), or the purpose clause, etc. For now, consider the following examples of the typical use of the conjugation. Note how the action is not yet complete and passive.

ܢܬܟܬܒ	ܕܬܡܢ
netkteb	*d-tamān*
ethpeel imperfect 3ms	*dālat* + particle
he would be written (registered)	that there

Translation: That there he would be registered.
Luke 2:5

Metathesis (switching the *taw*) occurs with the imperfect as it does with the perfect. Note the difference in the two ethpeel verbs below.

ܢܫܬܒܩ	ܘܚܕ	ܢܬܕܒܪ	ܚܕ
neštbeq	*w-ḥad*	*netdbar*	*ḥad*
ethpeel imperfect 3md	*waw* + number	ethpeel imperfect 3ms	number
he will be left	and one	he will be taken	one

Translation: One will be taken, and one will be left.
Matthew 24:40

In the example above, note the vowels on the first imperfect ethpeel verb. Remember the rules for variable vowels—the vowel will always be an *a* if it is followed by a guttural or a *resh*.

Ethpeel Imperative

The ethpeel imperative is formed with the typical *et-* preformative. Note that the second consonant can sometimes take a *linea occultans* (meaning that the consonant is not pronounced), but this is optional. As with the active, the pronunciation of each form of the verb is identical, despite the fact that they are spelled differently (with the exception of the plural forms with extended endings) and the only alteration is the *et-* prefix. Additionally, the stem vowel is placed above the initial consonant and is typically an *a* (etCaCC)

	Singular	Plural I	Plural II
Masculine	ܐܬܟܬܒ ܐܬܟܬܒ *etkatb* *etkab* Be written!	ܐܬܟܬܒܘ ܐܬܟܬܒܘ *etkatb* *etkab* Be written!	ܐܬܟܬܒܘܢ ܐܬܟܬܒܘܢ *etkatbun* *etkabun* Be written!
Feminine	ܐܬܟܬܒܝ ܐܬܟܬܒܝ *etkatb* *etkab* Be written!	ܐܬܟܬܒܝ ܐܬܟܬܒܝ *etkatb* *etkab* Be written!	ܐܬܟܬܒܝܢ ܐܬܟܬܒܝܢ *etkatbēn* *etkabēn* Be written!

ܒܝܡܐ	ܘܐܬܢܨܒ	ܕܐܬܥܩܪ
b-yamā	*w-etnaṣb*	*d-etʿar*
bēth + noun fs emphatic	*waw* + ethpeel imperative ms	*dalat* + ethpeel imperative ms
in the sea	and be planted	be uprooted

Translation: Be uprooted and be planted in the sea.

Luke 17:6

Ethpeel Infinitive

While the peal infinitive that was introduced earlier in the grammar follows the pattern of meCCāC (as in *mektab* "to write"), the ethpeel infinitive follows a more standard method of forming the infinitive: metCCāCu. This pattern (with the *a*- and the *u*-vowels placed between the last consonants and at the end) is the standard pattern for all of the stems of the infinitive that are not the peal.

Because the initial *mīm* and the *et*- are both at the start of the word, they will combine to form *met*-, and the *ālap* will drop out (just as in the imperfect).

ܡ	+	ܐܬ	=	ܡܬܟܬܒܘ
m		*et*		*metktābu*

In the biblical text, there are few examples of ethpeel infinitives. However, one common phrase that employs the construction is the command to put a person to death. This utilizes an infinitive absolute:

ܢܬܩܛܠ	ܡܬܩܛܠܘ
netqtel	*metqṭalu*
peal imperfect 3ms	ethpeel infinitive ms
he will kill	to be put to death

Translation: He will (surely) be put to death.

Exodus 21:12

Ethpeel Participle

The ethpeel participle is formed with a *mīm* preformative (metCCeC). Outside of the peal stem, the addition of a *mīm* to the beginning of a word is the standard way to denote a participle in the derived stems.

ܡ	+	ܐܬ	=	ܡܬܟܬܶܒ
m		*et*		*metkteb*

Masculine		Feminine	
Singular	Plural	Singular	Plural
ܡܬܟܬܶܒ	ܡܬܟܰܬܒܺܝܢ	ܡܬܟܰܬܒܳܐ	ܡܬܟܰܬܒܳܢ
metkteb	*metkatbin*	*metkatbā*	*metkatban*

Note below a typical use of the ethpeel participle.

ܟܺܐܒܳܐ	ܟܽܠ	ܗܘܳܐ	ܡܬܚܠܶܡ
kibā	*kull*	*-wā*	*metḥlem*
noun ms emphatic	particle	peal perfect 3ms	ethpeel participle ms
pain	all	he was	being cured

Translation: He was being cured of all pain.
John 5:4

Vocabulary

Nouns

ܐܘܠܨܢܐ	*ulṣānā*	affliction, oppression
ܕܡܘܬܐ	*dmutā*	form, image
ܚܕܘܬܐ	*ḥadutā*	joy, gladness
ܚܟܡܬܐ	*ḥekmtā*	wisdom
ܝܘܠܦܢܐ	*yulpānā*	teaching, learning, doctrine
ܝܡܝܢܐ	*yamminā*	right
ܟܘܪܣܝܐ	*kursyā*	seat, throne
ܠܫܢܐ	*leššānā*	language
ܡܐܢܐ	*mānā*	garment, vessel
ܣܒܪܐ	*sabrā*	hope

Verbs

ܐܒܕ	*ebad*	to perish, be lost
ܐܫܬܝ	*ešti*	to drink
ܕܒܪ	*dbar*	to lead, take
ܗܦܟ	*hpak*	to turn, return
ܚܕܝ	*ḥdi*	to rejoice, be glad
ܝܬܪ	*ittar*	to gain, prefer
ܥܡܕ	*ʿmad*	to baptize, sink
ܦܬܚ	*ptaḥ*	to open
ܩܥܐ	*qʿā*	to appeal to, cry out
ܫܘܐ	*šwā*	to be worthy, equal

Other

ܒܝܬ	*bēt*	between, among
ܒܥܠܕܒܒܐ	*bʿeldbābā*	enemy
ܕܓܠܐ	*daggālā*	liar, false
ܘܝ	*wāy*	woe!
ܙܕܝܩܐ	*zaddiqā*	righteous, just
ܚܛܝܐ	*ḥaṭāyā*	sinner
ܚܝܒܐ	*ḥayābā*	debtor
ܣܡܝܐ	*samyā*	blind (also ܣܡܐ)
ܩܕܝܡܐ	*qdimā*	before
ܪܡܐ	*rāmā*	high

Exercises

Luke 15:24 (1)

ܕܗܢܐ ܒܪܝ ܡܝܬܐ ܗܘܐ ܘܚܝܐ ܘܐܒܝܕܐ[3] ܗܘܐ ܘܐܫܬܟܚ[4]

Matthew 28:18 (2)

ܘܩܪܒ ܝܫܘܥ ܡܠܠ[5] ܥܡܗܘܢ ܘܐܡܪ ܠܗܘܢ ܐܬܝܗܒ[6] ܠܝ ܟܠ ܫܘܠܛܢ
ܒܫܡܝܐ ܘܒܐܪܥܐ

Matthew 1:16 (3)

ܕܡܢܗ ܐܬܝܠܕ[7] ܝܫܘܥ ܕܡܬܩܪܐ ܡܫܝܚܐ

---

3. ܘܐܒܝܕܐ = and lost.
4. Note the variable vowel.
5. ܡܠܠ = he spoke. This verb is in the pael stem, which will be covered in the next chapter.
6. This is a I-*yūd* verb. Note the addition of the vowel above the *taw*.
7. This is a I-*yūd* verb. Note the addition of the vowel above the *taw*.

Matthew 3:17 (4)

ܘܗܐ ܩܠܐ ܡܢ ܫܡܝܐ ܕܐܡܪ ܗܢܘ ܒܪܝ ܚܒܝܒܐ ܕܒܗ ܐܨܛܒܝܬ[8]

Matthew 10:2 (5)

ܫܡܗܘܢ ܕܬܪܬܥܣܪܐ ܫܠܝܚܐ

Matthew 21:43 (6)

ܡܛܠ ܗܢܐ ܐܡܪ ܐܢܐ ܠܟܘܢ ܕܬܫܬܩܠ ܡܢܟܘܢ ܡܠܟܘܬܐ ܕܐܠܗܐ

ܘܬܬܝܗܒ[9] ܠܥܡܐ ܕܥܒܕ ܦܐܪܐ

Acts 13:46 (7)

ܘܠܐ ܗܘܐ ܩܕܡܝܬ ܕܬܬܐܡܪ[10] ܡܠܬܗ ܕܐܠܗܐ

Matthew 2:15 (8)

ܕܐܬܐܡܪ[11] ܡܢ ܡܪܝܐ ܒܢܒܝܐ ܕܐܡܪ

Matthew 23:38 (9)

ܗܐ ܡܫܬܒܩ ܠܟܘܢ ܒܝܬܟܘܢ ܚܪܒܐ[12]

Matthew 8:27 (10)

ܘܐܡܪܝܢ ܡܢܘ ܗܢܐ ܕܪܘܚܐ ܘܝܡܐ ܡܫܬܡܥܝܢ ܠܗ

---

8. Note how the ethpeel changes here. The root is ܨܒܐ, "to will or desire."
9. This is a I-*yūd* verb. Note the addition of the vowel above the *taw*.
10. Note the guttural ending that changes the *e* to an *a*.
11. As in (7), note the variable vowel.
12. ܚܪܒܐ = desolate.

Mark 4:25 (11)

ܡܰܢ ܕܐܺܝܬ ܠܶܗ ܓܶܝܪ ܢܶܬܝܰܗܶܒ[13] ܠܶܗ ܘܡܰܢ ܕܠܰܝܬ ܠܶܗ ܐܳܦ ܗܰܘ ܕܐܺܝܬ
ܠܶܗ ܢܶܫܬܩܶܠ ܡܶܢܶܗ

Acts 10:31 (12)

ܘܶܐܡܰܪ ܠܺܝ ܩܽܘܪܢܶܠܝܳܐ ܐܶܫܬܡܰܥܰܬ ܨܠܽܘܬܳܟ

Matthew 24:40 (13)

ܗܳܝܕܶܝܢ ܬܪܶܝܢ ܢܶܗܘܽܘܢ ܒܚܰܩܠܳܐ ܚܰܕ ܢܶܬܕܒܰܪ ܘܚܰܕ ܢܶܫܬܒܶܩ

Matthew 10:19 (14)

ܡܶܬܝܰܗܒ[14] ܠܟܽܘܢ ܓܶܝܪ ܒܗܺܝ ܫܳܥܬܳܐ ܡܳܐ ܕܬܡܰܠܠܽܘܢ[15]

Matthew 26:45 (15)

ܗܳܐ ܡܛܳܬ[16] ܫܳܥܬܳܐ ܘܒܪܶܗ ܕܐܢܳܫܳܐ ܡܶܫܬܠܶܡ ܒܺܐܝܕܰܝܗܽܘܢ ܕܚܰܛܳܝܶܐ

Matthew 14:19 (16)

ܘܦܰܩܶܕ ܠܟܶܢܫܶܐ ܠܡܶܣܬܡܟܽܘ[17] ܥܰܠ ܐܰܪܥܳܐ ܘܢܶܣܰܒ ܗܳܢܽܘܢ ܚܰܡܫܳܐ[18]
ܠܰܚܡܺܝܢ ܘܬܪܶܝܢ[19] ܢܽܘܢܺܝܢ[20]

---

13. This is a I-*yūd* verb. Note the addition of the vowel above the *taw*.
14. This is a I-*yūd* verb. Note the addition of the vowel above the *taw*.
15. ܕܬܡܰܠܠܽܘܢ = you will say.
16. ܡܛܳܬ = it has arrived.
17. ܠܡܶܣܬܡܟܽܘ =The root for this word is ܣܡܟ, "recline."
18. ܚܰܡܫܳܐ = five.
19. ܘܬܪܶܝܢ = and two.
20. ܢܽܘܢܺܝܢ = fish.

Luke 15:19 (17)

ܘܠܐ ܡܟܝܠ[21] ܫܘܐ[22] ܐܢܐ ܕܐܬܩܪܐ ܒܪܟ ܥܒܕܝܢܝ[23] ܐܝܟ ܚܕ ܡܢ
ܐܓܝܪ̈ܝܟ[24]

Matthew 5:27 (18)

ܫܡܥܬܘܢ ܕܐܬܐܡܪ[25] ܕܠܐ ܬܓܘܪ[26]

Matthew 16:21 (19)

ܡܢ ܪ̈ܒܝ ܟܗܢܐ ܘܣܦܪ̈ܐ ܘܢܬܩܛܠ

Mark 11:23 (20)

ܐܡܝܢ ܓܝܪ ܐܡܪ ܐܢܐ ܠܟܘܢ ܕܡܢ ܕܢܐܡܪ[27] ܠܛܘܪܐ ܗܢܐ
ܕܐܫܬܩܠ[28] ܘܦܠ[29] ܒܝܡܐ

Additional Exercises

Esther 3:12 (21)

ܐܬܟܬܒ ܟܠܡܕܡ ܕܦܩܕ ܗܡܢ[30] ܠܘܬ ܚܝ̈ܠܐ[31] ܕܡܠܟܐ

21. ܡܟܝܠ = therefore.
22. ܫܘܐ = worthy.
23. This is a verb with a pronominal suffix: peal imperative + 1cs.
24. ܐܓܝܪ̈ܝܟ = your servants.
25. Note the vowel switches from an *e* to an *a*.
26. ܬܓܘܪ = commit adultery.
27. This is a peal imperfect of this verb.
28. Note the *linea occultans* below the second radical. This is a common characteristic of the imperative.
29. ܘܦܠ = and fall!
30. This is a name.
31. ܚܝ̈ܠܐ = mighty ones (satraps).

2 Chronicles 28:5 (22)

ܘܐܦ ܒܐܝܕܝ̈ ܡܠܟܐ ܕܐܝܣܪܝܠ ܐܫܬܠܡ ܘܚܪܒ[32] ܡܢܗ ܚܪܒܐ[33] ܪܒܬܐ

Numbers 32:5 (23)

ܬܬܝܗܒ ܐܪܥܐ ܗܕܐ ܠܥܒ̈ܕܝܟ

Sirach 26:3 (24)

ܐܢܬܬܐ ܛܒܬܐ ܬܬܝܗܒ ܠܓܒܪܐ ܕܕܚܠ ܡܢ ܡܪܝܐ

Sirach 15:10 (25)

ܒܦܘܡܐ ܕܚܟܝ̈ܡܐ ܬܬܐܡܪ ܬܫܒܘܚܬܐ[34]

Leviticus 7:15 (26)

ܒܝܘܡܐ ܕܡܩܪܒ[35] ܠܗ ܢܬܐܟܠ ܘܠܐ ܢܫܬܒܩ ܡܢܗ ܡܕܡ ܠܨܦܪܐ[36]

---

22. ܘܚܪܒ = and he inflicted / destroyed.
23. ܚܪܒܐ = casualties.
24. ܬܫܒܘܚܬܐ = praise.
25. This is in the pael, meaning "that it is offered."
26. ܨܦܪܐ = morning.

13

Pael (D)

Pael	Perfect	Participle	Imperfect	Imperative	Infinitive
	ܟܰܬܶܒ	ܡܟܰܬܶܒ	ܢܟܰܬܶܒ	ܟܰܬܶܒ	ܡܟܰܬܳܒܽܘ
	katteb	*mkatteb*	*nkatteb*	*katteb*	*mkattābu*

Introduction

The pael conjugation is more complex than the other derived stems in that its uses are far more multifaceted. Therefore, while in some uses the pael conjugation attests an intensive function, other uses indicate an alteration of the lexical definition. Others simply change the verb to a transitive, requiring a direct object, as in "Steve *rode* the bike" (versus an intransitive verb that does not require a direct object, as in "Steve *rides*.") The bottom line with all of this is that it is good practice to have a lexicon handy when dealing with pael verbs (and other stems) because using the simple "pael = intensive action" equation can sometimes lead to a poor translation. (See below for a more thorough discussion on how the pael can modify the peal meaning of a word).

The pael conjugation is recognized by the *doubling* of the middle consonant when it is pronounced, hence the abbreviation D for the stem. Where the peal stem has a vocalization of CCaC/CCeC (as in *ktab*), the pael is typically CaCCeC (as in *katteb*).

Pael Perfect

The paradigm for the pael perfect is seen below. When translating, look for the *a*-vowel after the first consonant in order to identify the pael conjugation of a verb. These forms are similar to that of the G-stem (peal) that was learned earlier and should be familiar by now.

	Singular		Plural	
3m	ܟܰܬܶܒ	*katteb* he writes	ܟܰܬܶܒܘ ܟܰܬܶܒܘܢ	*katteb* *kattebun* they write
3f	ܟܰܬܒܰܬ	*kattbat* she writes	ܟܰܬܶܒ ܟܰܬܶܒ̈ ܟܰܬܶܒܶܝܢ	*katteb* *katteb* *kattebēn* they write
2m	ܟܰܬܶܒܬ	*kattebt* you write	ܟܰܬܶܒܬܽܘܢ ܟܰܬܶܒܬܘܢ	*kattebton* *kattebtun* you write
2f	ܟܰܬܶܒܬܝ	*kattebt* you write	ܟܰܬܶܒܬܶܝܢ	*kattebtēn* you write
1c	ܟܰܬܒܶܬ	*kattbet* I write	ܟܰܬܶܒܢ ܟܰܬܶܒܢܰܢ	*kattebn* *kattebnan* we write

Note: Remember to keep an eye out for variable vowels. If the final consonant in a verb is a guttural (*ālap*, *hē*, *ḥēt*, *ʿē*) or a *rīš*, then the final vowel will be an *a*. For example, the pael perfect for ܫܕܰܪ ("to send") is:

ܫܕܰܪ	→	ܫܰܕܰܪ
peal		pael

Additionally, if there is no vowel pointing in a text, it can be difficult to distinguish between a pael and peal stem. Scribes will again employ dots to make this distinction:

ܟܬܒ	ܟܬܒ
katteb	*ktab*
Pael (D)	Peal (G)

Sometimes the pael stem can be accompanied with a change in meaning of a word. It is helpful to have a reliable lexicon handy when beginning to learn Syriac so that variations according to stem can be utilized in translation.[1] For example, the verb below changes its meaning from the peal (to appeal, accuse) to the pael (to receive, take):

---

1. Some recommendations (among others): J. Payne Smith, *A Compendius Syriac Dictionary* (Oxford: Oxford University Press, 1903), or Michael Sokoloff, *A Syriac Lexicon: A Translation from the Latin, Correction, Expansion, and Update of C. Brockelmann's Lexicon Syriacum* (Winona Lake, IN: Eisenbrauns; Piscataway, NJ: Gorgias Press, 2009).

ܐܓܪܗܘܢ	ܩܒܠܘ
agrhun	*qabbel*
noun ms emphatic + 3ms	pael perfect 3mp
their reward	they received

Translation: They received their reward.
Matthew 6:5

If this were to be translated as "They adamantly appealed/accused their reward," then the translation would be far from accurate.

Note: The pael perfect can be easily mistaken for the peal participle—the difference being the vowel above the first consonant:

ܟܬܒ	ܟܬܒ
katteb	*kāteb*
Pael Perfect	Peal Participle

Pael Imperfect

The pael imperfect doesn't have a vowel accompanying the prefix (with the exception of the *e* in the first common singular): (nCaCCeC). This is an easy way to distinguish the pael imperfect from other stems.

	Singular		Plural	
3m	ܢܟܬܒ	*nkatteb* he will write	ܢܟܬܒܘܢ	*nkattbun* they write
3f	ܬܟܬܒ ܬܟܬܒ	*tkatteb* she will write	ܢܟܬܒܢ	*nkattbān* they write
2m	ܬܟܬܒ	*tkatteb* you write	ܬܟܬܒܘܢ	*tkattbun* you write
2f	ܬܟܬܒܝܢ	*tkattbin* you write	ܬܟܬܒܢ	*tkattbān* you write
1c	ܐܟܬܒ	*ekatteb* I write	ܢܟܬܒ	*nkatteb* we write

Keep in mind that the imperfect can function as a command when the negative particle *lā* is used. Note the following verse, which would be equivalent to the imperative in translation.

ܒܡܰܘܡܳܬܳܟ݂	ܬܕܰܓܶܠ	ܠܳܐ
b-mawmātāk	*tdaggel*	*lā*
bēth + noun fp emphatic + 2 ms	pael imperfect 2ms	negative particle
with your oaths	you speak falsely	not

Translation: Do not speak falsely with your oaths.
Matthew 5:33

Pael Imperative

The pael imperative functions as expected, and is formed in the typical manner—by dropping the preformative of the imperfect (CaCCeC). In the pael conjugation, recognizing the pael imperative can be difficult because it is identical to several pael perfect forms (see above). As always, context must guide the translation.

	Singular	Plural I	Plural II
Masculine	ܟܰܬܶܒ *katteb* Write!	ܟܰܬܶܒܘ *katteb* Write!	ܟܰܬܶܒܘܢ *kattebun* Write!
Feminine	ܟܰܬܶܒܝ *katteb* Write!	ܟܰܬܶܒ̈ܝ *katteb* Write!	ܟܰܬܶܒ̈ܶܝܢ *kattebtēn* Write!

The pael imperative will often take an objective suffix (typically the 1cp in the New Testament) as a plea for help or deliverance. In the example below the verbal root is ܦܨܐ, ("to deliver") which ends in an *ālap*. Notice that the objective suffix ending and connecting vowel overpowers the *ālap* and it is lost (more on irregular verbs later on in the grammar).

ܒܺܝܫܳܐ	ܡܶܢ	ܦܰܨܳܢ	ܐܶܠܳܐ
bišā	*men*	*paṣṣān*	*ellā*
noun ms emphatic	preposition	pael imperative ms + 1cp	conjunction
evil	from	deliver us	but

Translation: But deliver us from evil.
Matthew 6:13

Pael Infinitive

The pael infinitive can be identified because there is no vowel after the initial infintival consonant—the *mīm* prefix (mCaCCāCu). This is an easy way to distinguish the pael infinitive from the peal infinitive (*mektab*). The pael infinitive also can be recognized by the *ā-u* pattern for the vowels, which is standard for infinitives that are not in the peal stem.

ܡܟܬܒܘ

mkattābu

Note the passage below. In context, this is a reflexive question, as in "are the blind able to guide the blind?" Each adjective takes the form of a substantive, and the *lāmad* prefix on the second adjective is a hint that this is the direct object of the sentence. This is paired with the pael stem, as it alludes to its transitive nature (needing a direct object).

ܠܡܕܒܪܘ	ܠܣܡܝܐ	ܣܡܝܐ	ܡܫܟܚ
la-mdabbāru	*l-samyā*	*samyā*	*meškaḥ*
lāmad + pael infinitive	*lāmad* + adjective ms emphatic	adjective ms emphatic	peal active participle ms
to guide	blind	blind	being able

Translation: Are the blind able to guide the blind...

Luke 6:39

Note that ܡܫܟܚ forms the peal active participle of ܫܟܚ ("to be able"). The most common usage is here as a participle.

Pael Participles

Pael participles can be either active or passive, as expected. The difference between the two is the use of an *e*-vowel over the second consonant of the root for the active (mCaCCeC); the passive takes an *a*-vowel (mCaCCaC). Also, note the absence of a vowel after the *mīm* prefix. This is an important identifying feature of the pael participle, and a characteristic that it shares with the pael infinitive and imperfect. When a text does not have vowel pointing, it is important to let context guide the translation as to which should be chosen.

Active	Passive
ܡܟܬܒ	ܡܟܬܒ
mkatteb	*mkattab*
writing	being written

The pael participle takes the same endings that have already been introduced. Remember to look for the tell-tale sign that the participle is pael: the absence of a vowel over the initial *mīm*.

Active Participles

Masculine		Feminine	
Singular	Plural	Singular	Plural
ܡܟܰܬܶܒ	ܡܟܰܬܒܺܝܢ	ܡܟܰܬܒܳܐ	ܡܟܰܬܒܳܢ
mkatteb	*mkattbin*	*mkattbān*	*mkattbān*

Passive Participles

Masculine		Feminine	
Singular	Plural	Singular	Plural
ܡܟܰܬܰܒ	ܡܟܰܬܒܺܝܢ	ܡܟܰܬܒܳܐ	ܡܟܰܬܒܳܢ
mkattab	*mkattbin*	*mkattbā*	*mkattbān*

Additionally, note how many of the passive and active forms are identical to one another. In these cases, context will determine which to use. While the pael stem will change the translation of a passage, the actual use of the pael participle is identical to that of the peal participle: it is typically used to show an action that is currently happening, whether the subject is active or passive.

ܐܰܢ݁ܬ݁	ܕܰܡܨܰܠܶܐ	ܘܡܳܐ
-att	*damṣalle*	*w-mā*
pronoun 2ms	*dālat* + peal active participle ms	*waw* + interrogative pronoun
you are	praying	and when

Translation: And when you are praying…

Matthew 6:5

Use of the Pael

In the fifth edition of *Robinson's Paradigms and Exercises in Syriac Grammar*, J. F. Coakley identifies six different uses and meanings for the pael.[2] This highlights the complexity of finding a precise lexical equivalent for a particular word. The five categories are:

1. Intensive: This is the use that most think about when translating the pael conjugation.

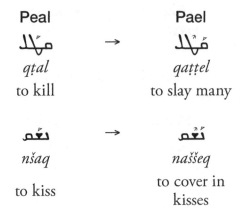

Peal		Pael
ܩܛܰܠ	→	ܩܰܛܶܠ
qṭal		*qaṭṭel*
to kill		to slay many
ܢܫܰܩ	→	ܢܰܫܶܩ
nšaq		*naššeq*
to kiss		to cover in kisses

2. No distinction: Sometimes, the pael will exhibit no change in meaning. Note the following words:

Peal		Pael
ܥܕܰܪ	→	ܥܰܕܰܪ
ʿdar		*ʿaddar*
to help		to help
ܦܩܰܕ	→	ܦܰܩܶܕ
pqad		*paqqed*
to command		to command
ܙܡܰܪ	→	ܙܰܡܰܪ
zmar		*zammar*
to sing		to sing

2. J. F. Coakley, *Robinson's Paradigms and Exercises in Syriac Grammar*, 5th ed. (Oxford: Oxford University Press, 2002), 75–76.

3. Transitively: As a review, a transitive verb is one that must have a direct object. For example:

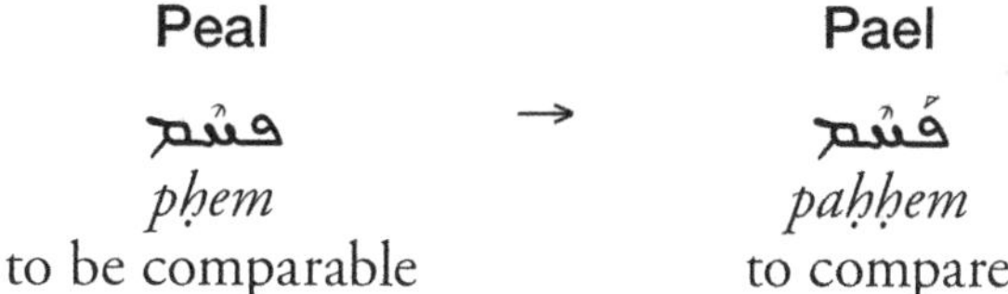

4. Change in meaning: Some verbs will change the meaning of the entire word when they go from the peal to the pael. For example:

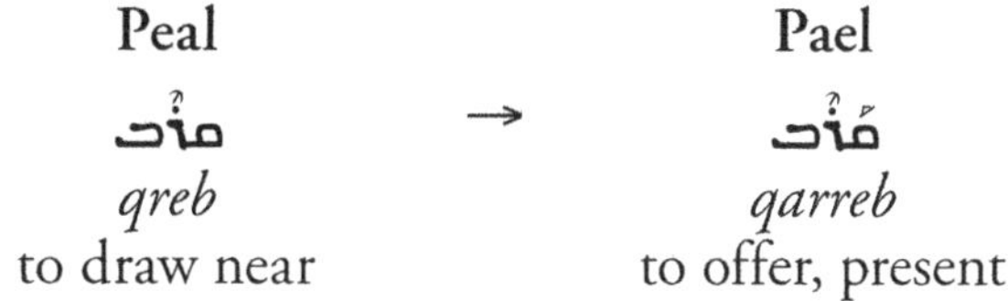

5. Verbs occurring only in the pael: Some verbs do not occur in the peal form of the verb; they only occur in the pael. For example:

ܫܕܪ	ܩܒܠ
šaddar	*qabbel*
to send	to receive

6. Denominative: A denominative verb is a verb that is derived from a noun or adjective. For example, the noun ܚܝܠܐ (*ḥaylā*, "strength") is made into a verb by applying the pael vowels to the root, ܚܝܠ (*ḥayyel*, to "strengthen"):

Noun		Pael Verb
ܚܝܠܐ	→	ܚܝܠ
ḥaylā		*ḥayyel*
strength		to strengthen

Vocabulary

Nouns

ܙܪܥܐ *zarʿā* seed
ܝܕܥܬܐ *idaʿtā* knowledge
ܡܗܝܡܢܐ *mhaymnā* believer
ܡܘܗܒܬܐ *mawhabtā* gift
ܡܬܠܐ *matlā* parable
ܣܒܪܬܐ *sbartā* message, good news
ܣܛܢܐ *sāṭānā* satan, adversary
ܨܠܘܬܐ *ṣlutā* prayer
ܫܐܕܐ *šidā* demon, evil spirit
ܬܫܡܫܬܐ *tešmeštā* administration, service

Verbs

ܐܣܪ *esar* to bind, fasten
ܒܪܟ *brek* to kneel, bless
ܕܟܐ *dkā* to cleanse
ܕܡܐ *dmā* to resemble, compare
ܕܡܪ *dmar* to marvel, be amazed
ܙܒܢ *zban* to buy, sell
ܙܕܩ *zdaq* to be right, fitting
ܚܫܒ *ḥšab* to think, deliberate
ܛܝܒ *ṭayyeb* to make ready
ܛܥܐ *ṭʿā* to go astray, err
ܡܛܐ *mṭā* to arrive
ܣܓܕ *sged* to worship, pay homage
ܥܡܪ *ʿmar* to live, dwell
ܦܠܚ *plaḥ* to work, labor, serve
ܦܢܐ *pnā* to return
ܪܕܐ *rdā* to journey, proceed, instruct

Other

ܗܽܘܝܽܘ	*huyu*	that is to say / he is
ܚܰܟܺܝܡܳܐ	*ḥakimā*	wise, prudent
ܡܶܣܟܺܝܢܳܐ	*meskinā*	poor
ܫܰܪܺܝܪܳܐܝܺܬ	*šarirāit*	truly

Exercises

Matthew 13:34 (1)

ܗܳܠܶܝܢ ܟܽܠܗܶܝܢ ܡܰܠܶܠ ܝܶܫܽܘܥ ܒܦܶܠܐܬܳܐ[3] ܠܟܶܢܫܶܐ ܘܕܠܳܐ ܦܶܠܐܬܳܐ ܠܳܐ

ܡܡܰܠܶܠ ܗܘܳܐ ܥܰܡܗܽܘܢ܀

Matthew 14:29 (2)

ܝܶܫܽܘܥ ܕܶܝܢ ܐܶܡܰܪ ܠܶܗ ܬܳܐ[4] ܘܢܶܚܶܬ ܟܺܐܦܳܐ ܡܶܢ ܐܶܠܦܳܐ[5] ܘܗܰܠܶܟ ܥܰܠ

ܡܰܝܳܐ ܕܢܺܐܬܶܐ[6] ܠܘܳܬ ܝܶܫܽܘܥ

Matthew 22:41–43 (3)

ܟܰܕ ܟܢܺܝܫܺܝܢ ܕܶܝܢ ܦܪ̈ܺܝܫܶܐ ܫܰܐܶܠ ܐܶܢܽܘܢ ܝܶܫܽܘܥ ܘܶܐܡܰܪ ܡܳܢܳܐ ܐܳܡܪܺܝܢ

ܐܢ̄ܬܽܘܢ ܥܰܠ ܡܫܺܝܚܳܐ ܒܰܪ ܡܰܢܽܘ ܐܳܡܪܺܝܢ ܠܶܗ ܒܰܪ ܕܰܘܺܝܕ ܐܶܡܰܪ ܠܗܽܘܢ܀

ܘܐܰܝܟܰܢܳܐ ܕܰܘܺܝܕ ܒܪܽܘܚ ܩܳܪܶܐ ܠܶܗ ܡܳܪܝܳܐ

---

3. ܦܶܠܐܬܳܐ = parables (x2).
4. ܬܳܐ = come (imperative).
5. ܐܶܠܦܳܐ = boat.
6. This is a I-*alap* root. Note the addition of the vowel above the *alap*.

John 5:8–9 (4)

ܐܡܪ ܠܗ ܝܫܘܥ ܩܘܡ[7] ܫܩܘܠ ܥܪܣܟ[8] ܘܗܠܟ ܘܒܪ ܫܥܬܗ ܐܬܐܣܝ

ܓܒܪܐ ܗܘ ܘܩܡ[9] ܫܩܠ ܥܪܣܗ ܘܗܠܟ ܘܗܘܐ ܗܘ ܝܘܡܐ ܫܒܬܐ ܗܘܬ

John 6:63 (5)

ܡܠܐ ܕܐܢܐ ܡܠܠܬ ܥܡܟܘܢ ܪܘܚܐ ܐܢܝܢ ܘܚܝܐ ܐܢܝܢ

Matthew 16:20 (6)

ܗܝܕܝܢ ܦܩܕ ܠܬܠܡܝܕܘܗܝ ܕܠܐܢܫ ܠܐ ܢܐܡܪܘܢ ܕܗܘܝܘ[10] ܡܫܝܚܐ

Matthew 18:5 (7)

ܘܡܢ ܕܢܩܒܠ ܐܝܟ ܛܠܝܐ ܗܢܐ ܒܫܡܝ ܠܝ ܡܩܒܠ

Luke 4:10 (8)

ܟܬܝܒ ܓܝܪ ܕܠܡܠܐܟܘܗܝ ܢܦܩܕ ܥܠܝܟ ܕܢܛܪܘܢܟ[11]

John 9:19 (9)

ܘܫܐܠܘ ܐܢܘܢ ܐܢ ܗܢܘ ܒܪܟܘܢ ܗܘ ܕܐܡܪܝܢ ܐܢܬܘܢ ܕܟܕ

ܣܡܝܐ[12] ܐܬܝܠܕ ܐܝܟܢܐ ܗܫܐ ܚܙܐ

7. ܩܘܡ = get up! (imperative, but the root is a hollow verb).
8. ܥܪܣܐ = pallet (x2).
9. ܘܩܡ = and he got up.
10. ܕܗܘܝܘ = that he is.
11. This is a verb with a pronominal suffix: pael imperfect 3mp + 2ms.
12. This is a peal passive participle ms.

Luke 13:34 (10)

ܐܘܪܫܠܡ ܐܘܪܫܠܡ ܩܛܠܬ[13] ܢܒܝܐ ܘܪܓܡܬ[14] ܠܐܝܠܝܢ ܕܫܠܝܚܝܢ ܠܘܬܗ
ܟܡܐ ܙܒܢܝܢ ܨܒܝܬ[15] ܠܡܟܢܫܘ ܒܢܝܟܝ

John 7:1 (11)

ܒܬܪ ܗܠܝܢ ܡܗܠܟ ܗܘܐ ܝܫܘܥ ܒܓܠܝܠܐ ܠܐ ܓܝܪ ܨܒܐ ܗܘܐ
ܠܡܗܠܟܘ ܒܝܗܘܕ ܡܛܠ ܕܝܗܘܕܝܐ ܒܥܝܢ[16] ܗܘܘ ܠܡܩܛܠܗ[17]

John 12:49 (12)

ܕܐܢܐ ܡܢ ܢܦܫܝ ܠܐ ܡܠܠܬ ܐܠܐ ܐܒܐ ܕܫܕܪܢܝ[18] ܗܘ ܝܗܒ ܠܝ
ܦܘܩܕܢܐ ܡܢܐ ܐܡܪ[19] ܘܡܢܐ ܐܡܠܠ

John 18:21 (13)

ܡܢܐ ܡܫܐܠ ܐܢܬ ܠܝ ܫܐܠ ܠܗܢܘܢ ܕܫܡܥܘ ܡܢܐ ܡܠܠܬ ܥܡܗܘܢ
ܗܐ ܗܢܘܢ ܝܕܥܝܢ ܟܠ ܡܕܡ ܕܐܡܪܬ

John 20:22–23 (14)

ܘܟܕ ܐܡܪ ܗܠܝܢ ܢܦܚ[20] ܒܗܘܢ ܘܐܡܪ ܠܗܘܢ ܩܒܠܘ ܪܘܚܐ ܕܩܘܕܫܐ
ܐܢ ܬܫܒܩܘܢ ܚܛܗܐ ܠܐܢܫ ܢܫܬܒܩܘܢ ܠܗ

13. This is a participle with a 2 ms ending.
14. ܪܓܡܬ = stoning.
15. ܨܒܝܬ = I desire.
16. ܒܥܝܢ = seeking.
17. This is a verb with a pronominal suffix: peal infinitive + 3ms.
18. This is a verb with a pronominal suffix: pael perfect 3ms + 1cs.
19. This is a peal imperfect 1 cs.
20. ܢܦܚ = he breathed.

Matthew 10:14 (15)

ܡܢ ܕܠܐ ܢܩܒܠ ܠܟܘܢ ܘܠܐ ܢܫܡܥ ܡܠܝܟܘܢ ܟܕ ܢܦܩܝܢ ܐܢܬܘܢ

ܡܢ ܒܝܬܐ ܐܘ ܡܢ ܩܪܝܬܐ ܗܝ، ܦܨܘ[21] ܚܠܐ[22] ܡܢ ܪܓܠܝܟܘܢ

Matthew 10:41 (16)

ܡܢ ܕܡܩܒܠ ܢܒܝܐ ܒܫܡ ܢܒܝܐ ܐܓܪܐ[23] ܕܢܒܝܐ ܢܣܒ ܘܡܢ ܕܡܩܒܠ

ܙܕܝܩܐ ܒܫܡ ܙܕܝܩܐ ܐܓܪܐ ܕܙܕܝܩܐ ܢܣܒ

Mark 6:48 (17)

ܐܬܐ ܠܘܬܗܘܢ ܝܫܘܥ ܟܕ ܡܗܠܟ ܥܠ ܡܝܐ ܘܨܒܐ ܗܘܐ ܕܢܥܒܪ

ܐܢܘܢ

Luke 1:64 (18)

ܘܡܚܕܐ ܐܬܦܬܚ ܦܘܡܗ ܘܠܫܢܗ[24] ܘܡܠܠ ܘܫܒܚ[25] ܠܐܠܗܐ

Luke 1:70 (19)

ܐܝܟ ܕܡܠܠ ܒܦܘܡܐ ܕܢܒܝܘܗܝ، ܩܕܝܫܐ ܕܡܢ ܥܠܡ

Matthew 26:1 (20)

ܘܗܘܐ ܕܟܕ ܫܠܡ ܝܫܘܥ ܟܠܗܘܢ ܡܠܐ ܗܠܝܢ ܐܡܪ ܠܬܠܡܝܕܘܗܝ،

---

21. ܦܨܘ = shake off (imperative).
22. ܚܠܐ = dust.
23. ܐܓܪܐ = reward (x2).
24. ܘܠܫܢܗ = and his tongue.
25. ܘܫܒܚ = he praised (pael).

Additional Exercises

Exodus 20:19–22

ܘܐܡܪܘ ܠܡܘܫܐ ܡܠܠ ܐܢܬ ܥܡܢ ܘܢܫܡܥ ܘܠܐ ܢܡܠܠ ܥܡܢ ܐܠܗܐ v.19
ܕܠܐ ܢܡܘܬ[26]

ܘܐܡܪ ܡܘܫܐ ܠܥܡܐ ܠܐ ܬܕܚܠܘܢ ܡܛܠ ܕܠܡܢܣܝܘܬܟܘܢ[27] ܐܬܐ v.20
ܐܠܗܐ ܘܡܛܠ ܕܬܗܘܐ ܕܚܠܬܗ ܥܠ ܐܦ̈ܝܟܘܢ ܘܕܠܐ ܬܚܛܘܢ

ܘܩܡܘ[28] ܥܡܐ ܡܢ ܪܘܚܩܐ[29] ܘܡܘܫܐ ܩܪܒ ܠܘܬ ܥܪܦܠܐ[30] ܕܬܡܢ v.21
ܐܠܗܐ

ܘܐܡܪ ܡܪܝܐ ܠܡܘܫܐ ܗܟܢܐ ܬܐܡܪ ܠܒܢ̈ܝ ܐܝܣܪܝܠ ܐܢܬܘܢ v.22
ܚܙܝܬܘܢ[31] ܕܡܢ ܫܡܝܐ ܡܠܠܬ ܥܡܟܘܢ

---

26. ܢܡܘܬ = we will die.
27. ܕܠܡܢܣܝܘܬܟܘܢ = that he will test you.
28. ܘܩܡܘ = and they stood
29. ܪܘܚܩܐ = far place.
30. ܥܪܦܠܐ = dark cloud.
31. ܚܙܝܬܘܢ = you have seen.

14

Ethpaal (Dp)

	Perfect	Participle	Imperfect	Imperative	Infinitive
Ethpeel	ܐܶܬܟܰܬܰܒ	ܡܶܬܟܰܬܰܒ	ܢܶܬܟܰܬܰܒ	ܐܶܬܟܰܬܰܒ	ܡܶܬܟܰܬܳܒܽܘ
	etkattab	*metkattab*	*netkattab*	*etkattab*	*metkattābu*

Introduction

In the same way that adding an *et-* to the beginning of a peal makes it passive (the ethpeel stem), the ethpaal is the passive form of the pael stem. It is formed the same way, by adding the prefix *et-* to the front of the verb. The basic understanding of the ethpaal is the same as the pael: typically an intensified action. However, the same rules that apply to the pael apply to the ethpaal, so be careful that you do not oversimplify your translation (see ch. 13 for further uses of the pael). In examining the chart above, what sets the ethpaal apart from the ethpeel is the presence of two *a*-vowels found above the first and second consonants of the root.

Ethpaal Perfect

The ethpaal perfect is similar to the pael perfect, with the exception that the *e*-stem vowel is typically transformed into an *a*-vowel (etCaCCaC). As a reminder, the pael perfect of ܟܬܒ ("to read") is *katteb*—note the *e*-stem vowel. The *e*-stem vowel is changed to an *a*- and the prefix is added to the word. If you need a reminder, look at the name of the stem: ethpaal. Note the two *a*-vowels. Also, compare this with the ethpeel perfect and note the differences: etCaCCaC vs. etCCeC.

	Singular		Plural	
3m	ܐܶܬ݂ܟ݁ܰܬ݁ܰܒ݂	*etkattab* he/it was written	ܐܶܬ݂ܟ݁ܰܬ݁ܰܒ݂ܘ ܐܶܬ݂ܟ݁ܰܬ݁ܰܒ݂ܘܽܢ	*etkattab* *etkattabun* they were written
3f	ܐܶܬ݂ܟ݁ܰܬ݁ܒ݂ܰܬ݂	*etkattbat* she/it was written	ܐܶܬ݂ܟ݁ܰܬ݁ܰܒ݂ ܐܶܬ݂ܟ݁ܰܬ݁ܰܒ݂ܝ̈ ܐܶܬ݂ܟ݁ܰܬ݁ܰܒ݂̈ܶܢ	*etkattab* *etkattab* *etkattabēn* they were written
2m	ܐܶܬ݂ܟ݁ܰܬ݁ܰܒ݂ܬ݁	*etkattabt* you were written	ܐܶܬ݂ܟ݁ܰܬ݁ܰܒ݂ܬ݁ܘܿܢ ܐܶܬ݂ܟ݁ܰܬ݁ܰܒ݂ܬ݁ܘܽܢ	*etkattabton* *etkattabtun* you were written
2f	ܐܶܬ݂ܟ݁ܰܬ݁ܰܒ݂ܬ݁ܝ	*etkattabt* you were written	ܐܶܬ݂ܟ݁ܰܬ݁ܰܒ݂ܬ݁̈ܶܝܢ	*etkattabtēn* you were written
1c	ܐܶܬ݂ܟ݁ܰܬ݁ܒ݂ܶܬ݂	*etkattbet* I was written	ܐܶܬ݂ܟ݁ܰܬ݁ܰܒ݂ܢ ܐܶܬ݂ܟ݁ܰܬ݁ܰܒ݂ܢܰܢ	*etkattabn* *etkattabnan* we were written

Below is a common use of the ethpaal perfect, where the root ܪܚܡ ("to love") translates "to have compassion" in the ethpaal.

ܥܠܰܝܗܘܽܢ	ܘܶܐܬ݂ܪܰܚܰܡ
ʿlayhun	*w-etraḥḥam*
preposition + 3mp	*waw* + ethpaal perfect 3ms
concerning them	and he had compassion

Translation: And he had compassion concerning them.

Matthew 14:14

Metathesis

Just as in the ethpeel conjugations, the addition of the *et-* at the beginning of a word will cause the *taw* to switch with the first consonant of the root if it begins with a *šīn* or *semkat* (examples 1 and 2 below). With *zayn* and *ṣādē*, the same switch takes place, but there is also an alteration of the *taw*: with *zayn* it becomes a *dālat* (3), while with *ṣādē* the *taw* becomes a *ṭēt* (4).

(1)	ܫ	→	ܫܠܡ *šlek* to die	→	ܐܫܬܠܡ *eštallam* to be completed
(2)	ܣ	→	ܣܡܟ *smak* to lean	→	ܐܣܬܡܟ *estammak* to recline
(3)	ܙ	→	ܙܒܢ *zban* to buy	→	ܐܙܕܒܢ *ezdabban* to be sold
(4)	ܨ	→	ܨܠܒ *ṣlab* to crucify	→	ܐܨܛܠܒ *eṣṭallab* to be crucified

To illustrate this further, notice the metathesis in the following example. Note the stem vowels as well, as this is the best way to distinguish it from the ethpeel conjugation.

ܢܫܬܠܛ	ܠܐ	ܐܢܫ	ܥܠܝ
neštalaṭ	*lā*	*nāš*	*ʿal*
ethpaal imperfect 3ms	negative particle	noun ms absolute	preposition + 1cs
he will be given authority	not	man	concerning me

Translation: Concerning me, man will not have authority.

1 Corinthians 6:12

Ethpaal Imperfect

Like the ethpaal perfect, the ethpaal imperfect is recognized by the *a*-stem vowel that is present in the ethpaal (netCaCCaC). This is the primary feature available to distinguish this stem from the ethpeel imperfect (netCCeC), so it is important to pay attention to what stem vowel is being used. When there is no vowel pointing, context must be used to guide the translation.

	Singular		Plural	
3m	ܢܬܟܬܒ	*netkattab* he/it will be written	ܢܬܟܬܒܘܢ	*netkattbun* they will be written
3f	ܬܬܟܬܒ ܬܬܟܬܒ	*tetkattab* *tetkattab* she/it will be written	ܢܬܟܬܒܢ	*netkattbān* they will be written
2m	ܬܬܟܬܒ	*tetkattab* you will be written	ܬܬܟܬܒܘܢ	*tetkattbun* you will be written
2f	ܬܬܟܬܒܝܢ	*tetkattbin* you will be written	ܬܬܟܬܒܢ	*tetkattbān* you will be written
1c	ܐܬܟܬܒ	*etkattab* I will be written	ܢܬܟܬܒ	*netkattab* we will be written

Note how the following ethpaal imperfect is translated in 2 Peter.

ܒܟܘܢ	ܢܬܬܓܪܘܢ	ܕܒܕܝܐ	ܘܒܡܠܐ
b-kun	*nettaggrun*	*d-bedyā*	*wa-b-melte*
bēth + 2mp	ethpaal imperfect 3mp	*dālat* + noun ms emphatic	*waw* + *bēth* + noun fp emphatic
with you	they will make gain	of folly	and with words

Translation: And with words of folly they will make gain (exploit) you.

2 Peter 2:3

The translation here is typical—the imperfect shows a predicated action (taking place in the future). Also note that the root of this verb begins with a *taw*, ܬܓܪ ("to make gain, trade"). This is important because the presence of a double *taw* typically signifies a verb in the ettaphal stem (see ch. 16). However, in this case the second *taw* is from the root of the verb.

Ethpaal Imperative

Predictably, the *a*-stem vowel distinguishes the ethpaal imperative from the ethpeel imperative (etCaCCaC vs. etCCaC). Keep in mind that the stem vowel is the vowel over the middle consonant of the root. This can be somewhat confusing because the ethpeel conjugation also has the same *a*-vowel but, it appears over the initial consonant of the root. To help remember this, think back to the name of the verb stem: ethpaal has two *a*'s. The basic endings also remain the same as with other imperatival forms.

	Singular	Plural I	Plural II
Masculine	ܐܶܬ݂ܟܰܬܰܒ *etkattab* Be written!	ܐܶܬ݂ܟܰܬܰܒܘ *etkattab* Be written!	ܐܶܬ݂ܟܰܬܰܒܽܘܢ *etkattabun* Be written!
Feminine	ܐܶܬ݂ܟܰܬܰܒܝ *etkattab* Be written!	ܐܶܬ݂ܟܰܬܰܒ̈ܝ *etkattab* Be written!	ܐܶܬ݂ܟܰܬܰܒܶܝܢ *etkattabēn* Be written!

Like the ethpeel, the ethpaal also attests the *linea occultans* under the second consonant. What makes this difficult is that the forms become identical to one another (ethpeel vs. ethpaal). While this characteristic is more prevalent in the ethpeel, make sure to look for context to help determine which is being used.

	Singular	Plural I	Plural II
Masculine	ܐܶܬ݂ܟܰܬ݂ܒ *etkab* Be written!	ܐܶܬ݂ܟܰܬ݂ܒܘ *etkab* Be written!	ܐܶܬ݂ܟܰܬ݂ܒܽܘܢ *etkabun* Be written!
Feminine	ܐܶܬ݂ܟܰܬ݂ܒܝ *etkab* Be written!	ܐܶܬ݂ܟܰܬ݂ܒ̈ܝ *etkab* Be written!	ܐܶܬ݂ܟܰܬ݂ܒܶܝܢ *ehkabēn* Be written!

For example, the verb below is an ethpaal even though it is similar in form to an ethpeel:

ܕܰܐܠܳܗܳܐ	ܪܰܒܬ݂ܳܐ	ܠܰܚܫܳܡܺܝܬ݂ܳܐ	ܐܶܬ݂ܟܰܢܫܘ
d-alāhā	*rabtā*	*la-ḥšāmitā*	*etkaš*
dālat + noun ms emphatic	adjective fs emphatic	*lāmad* + noun fs emphatic	ethpaal imperative mp
of God	great	for the feast	assemble

Translation: Assemble for the great feast of God.

Revelation 19:17

The following example demonstrates a typical use of the ethpaal imperative: a command in the second person. In this specific instance, the *dālat* at the beginning is signifying that this is a quote (see ch. 4) Here, the author is quoting from Isaiah 54:1:

ܥܩܰܪܬܳܐ	ܕܶܐܬܒܰܣܰܡܝ
ʿqartā	*d-etbassam*
adjective fs emphatic	*dālat* + ethpaal imperative fs
barren (one)	rejoice

Translation: Rejoice, barren (one)!
Galatians 4:27

Ethpaal Infinitive

It can be very difficult to distinguish the ethpaal from ethpeel when it comes to the infinitive (metCaCCāCu vs. metCCāCu). Really, the only distinction here is the *a*-vowel that is above the initial consonant of the root. Beyond this, the two are identical.

ܡܶܬܟܰܬܳܒܘ
metkattābu

The following example displays a *lāmad*-prefix attached to the ethpaal infinitive. The use is common in the New Testament. Note how the medio-passive aspect of the ethpaal is exhibited in this translation.

ܟܬܳܒ̈ܶܐ	ܠܡܶܣܬܰܟܳܠܘ	ܪ̈ܶܥܝܳܢܗܘܢ	ܦܬܰܚ
ktābe	*l-mestakkālu*	*reʿyānhun*	*ptaḥ*
noun ms emphatic	*lāmad* + ethpaal infinitive	noun + 3mp	peal perfect 3ms
the Scriptures	to understand	their mind	he opened

Translation: He opened their mind to understand the Scriptures.
Luke 24:45

Note also that the ethpaal infinitive exhibits metathesis; the *semkat* and the *taw* have switched places.

Ethpaal Participle

The ethpaal participle has an *a*-stem vowel with an *a* above the first consonant of the root (metCaCCaC) whereas the ethpeel has an *e*-stem vowel (metCaCCaC vs. metCCeC). Since they both take the typical *mīm* prefix common to non-peal stems of participles, the vowel is the only way to distinguish the two forms apart. Remember, the ethpaal stem is passive in nature, just as the ethpeel.

Masculine		Feminine	
Singular	Plural	Singular	Plural
ܡܶܬܟܰܬܰܒ	ܡܶܬܟܰܬܒܺܝܢ	ܡܶܬܟܰܬܒܳܐ	ܡܶܬܟܰܬܒܳܢ
metkattab	*metkattbin*	*metkattbā*	*metkattbān*

Below is an example where the participle is used with the *hwā* verb. These two words are pronounced as a single word: *metdammarwā*.

ܗ݇ܘܳܐ	ܡܶܬܕܰܡܰܪ	ܟܽܠܢܳܫ
-wā	*metdammar*	*kulnāš*
peal perfect 3ms	ethpaal participle ms	noun cs absolute
he was	marveling	every man

Translation: Every man was marveling.

Luke 9:43

Vocabulary

Nouns

ܐܶܕܢܳܐ	*ednā*	ear
ܐܶܠܦܳܐ	*elpā*	ship, boat
ܒܰܥܠܳܐ	*baʿlā*	husband, lord
ܒܰܪܬܳܐ	*bartā*	daughter
ܕܰܗܒܳܐ	*dahbā*	gold
ܚܰܪܬܳܐ	*ḥartā*	end
ܛܽܘܒܳܐ	*ṭubā*	blessedness
ܝܰܘܡܳܢܳܐ	*yawmānā*	today
ܡܰܠܦܳܢܳܐ	*malpānā*	teacher
ܡܫܰܡܫܳܢܳܐ	*mšammšānā*	servant

Verbs

ܒܛܶܠ *bṭel* to be idle
ܒܢܳܐ *bnā* to build
ܙܩܰܦ *zqap* to crucify, lift up
ܙܪܰܥ *zraʿ* to sow
ܚܳܪ *ḥār* to look, behold
ܠܒܶܫ *lbeš* to wear, put on (clothes)
ܣܡܰܟ *smak* to recline, rest
ܣܥܰܪ *sʿar* to do
ܦܠܰܓ *plag* to distribute, divide
ܦܪܰܩ *praq* to depart, save
ܦܪܰܫ *praš* to separate, appoint
ܩܕܰܡ *qdam* to go before
ܪܗܶܛ *rheṭ* to run
ܪܳܡ *rām* to be high, exalted
ܫܠܶܡ *šlem* to be finished, follow
ܫܡܰܫ *šmaš* to serve, minister

Other

ܫܰܒܥܳܐ *šabʿā* seven
ܬܠܳܬܳܐ *tlātā* three
ܬܪܶܝܢ *trēn* two
ܬܪܶܥܣܰܪ *treʿsar* twelve

Exercises

Matthew 20:34 (1)

ܘܐܬܪܚܡ ܥܠܝܗܘܢ ܝܫܘܥ ܘܩܪܒ ܠܥܝܢܝܗܘܢ ܘܒܪ ܫܥܬܗ[1] ܐܬܦܬܚ

ܥܝܢܝܗܘܢ ܘܐܙܠܘ ܒܬܪܗ

Matthew 17:7 (2)

ܘܐܬܩܪܒ ܠܘܬܗܘܢ ܝܫܘܥ ܘܩܪܒ ܠܗܘܢ ܘܐܡܪ ܩܘܡܘ[2] ܠܐ ܬܕܚܠܘܢ

Mark 11:31–33 (3)

ܘܐܬܚܫܒܘ ܒܢܦܫܗܘܢ ܘܐܡܪܘ ܕܐܢ ܢܐܡܪ ܠܗ ܕܡܢ ܫܡܝܐ ܐܡܪ ܠܢ

ܘܠܡܢܐ ܠܐ ܗܝܡܢܬܘܢܝܗܝ[3] ܘܐܢ ܢܐܡܪ ܕܡܢ ܒܢܝܢܫܐ ܕܚܠܝܢ ܗܘܘ ܡܢ

ܥܡܐ ܟܠܗܘܢ ܓܝܪ ܐܚܝܕܝܢ ܗܘܘ ܠܗ ܠܝܘܚܢܢ ܕܫܪܝܪܐܝܬ ܢܒܝܐ ܗܘ

ܘܥܢܘ[4] ܘܐܡܪܝܢ ܠܗ ܠܝܫܘܥ ܠܐ ܝܕܥܝܢܢ[5] ܐܡܪ ܠܗܘܢ ܐܦ ܠܐ ܐܢܐ

ܐܡܪ ܐܢܐ ܠܟܘܢ ܒܐܝܢܐ ܫܘܠܛܢܐ ܗܠܝܢ ܥܒܕ ܐܢܐ

Matthew 26:3 (4)

ܗܝܕܝܢ ܐܬܟܢܫܘ ܪܒܝ ܟܗܢܐ ܘܣܦܪܐ ܘܩܫܝܫܐ ܕܥܡܐ ܠܕܪܬܗ[6] ܕܪܒ

ܟܗܢܐ ܕܡܬܩܪܐ ܩܝܦܐ

---

1. ܒܪ ܫܥܬܗ = lit: the son of the hour, i.e., "immediately."
2. ܩܘܡܘ = get up (imperative). Notice the pattern used for hollow verbs. These will be covered later.
3. This is the verbal form of "faith" + 3ms ending. "You are believing him."
4. ܥܢܘ = they answered.
5. This is a participle with a pronominal suffix: peal active mp + 1cp.
6. ܠܕܪܬܗ = the court of.

Hebrews 12:22 (5)

ܐܰܢ̱ܬܽܘܢ ܕܶܝܢ ܐܶܬܩܰܪܰܒܬܽܘܢ ܠܛܽܘܪܳܐ ܕܨܶܗܝܽܘܢ ܘܰܠܡܕܺܝܢܬܳܐ ܕܰܐܠܳܗܳܐ

ܚܰܝܳܐ ܠܽܐܘܪܺܫܠܶܡ ܕܒܰܫܡܰܝܳܐ ܘܰܠܟܶܢܫܳܐ ܕܪ̈ܶܒܘܳܬܳܐ[7] ܕܡܰܠܰܐܟ̈ܶܐ

Matthew 26:13 (6)

ܘܰܐܡܺܝܢ ܐܳܡܰܪ ܐ̱ܢܳܐ ܠܟܽܘܢ ܕܰܐܝܟܳܐ ܕܬܶܬܟܪܶܙ[8] ܣܒܰܪܬܝ ܗܳܕܶܐ ܒܟܽܠܶܗ

ܥܳܠܡܳܐ ܢܶܬܡܰܠܰܠ ܐܳܦ ܡܶܕܶܡ ܕܥܶܒܕܰܬ ܗܳܕܶܐ ܠܕܽܘܟܪܳܢܳܗ̇[9]

Matthew 6:9 (7)

ܐܰܒܽܘܢ ܕܒܰܫܡܰܝܳܐ ܢܶܬܩܰܕܰܫ ܫܡܳܟ

John 3:7–8 (8)

ܠܳܐ ܬܶܬܕܰܡܰܪ ܕܶܐܡܪܶܬ ܠܳܟ ܕܘܳܠܶܐ ܠܟܽܘܢ ܠܡܶܬܺܝܠܳܕܽܘ ܡܶܢ ܕܪܺܝܫ ܪܽܘܚܳܐ ܐܰܝܟܳܐ

ܕܨܳܒܝܳܐ[10] ܢܳܫܒܳܐ[11] ܘܩܳܠܳܗ̇ ܫܳܡܰܥ ܐܰܢ̱ܬ

John 20:17 (9)

ܐܳܡܰܪ ܠܳܗ̇ ܝܶܫܽܘܥ ܠܳܐ ܬܶܬܩܰܪܒܺܝܢ ܠܝ ܠܳܐ ܓܶܝܪ ܥܕܰܟܺܝܠ[12] ܣܠܶܩܶܬ ܠܘܳܬ

ܐܳܒܝ ܙܶܠܝ[13] ܕܶܝܢ ܠܘܳܬ ܐܰܚ̈ܰܝ ܘܶܐܡܰܪܝ[14] ܠܗܽܘܢ ܣܳܠܶܩ ܐ̱ܢܳܐ ܠܘܳܬ ܐܳܒܝ

ܘܰܐܒܽܘܟܽܘܢ ܘܰܐܠܳܗܝ ܘܰܐܠܳܗܟܽܘܢ

---

7. ܪ̈ܶܒܘܳܬܳܐ = one thousand.
8. ܬܶܬܟܪܶܙ = it is preached.
9. ܠܕܽܘܟܪܳܢܳܗ̇ = to her memory.
10. ܨܳܒܝܳܐ = desiring (participle).
11. ܢܳܫܒܳܐ = blowing.
12. ܥܕܰܟܺܝܠ = yet.
13. ܙܶܠܝ = go!
14. ܐܶܡܰܪܝ = say!

Matthew 25:32 (10)

ܘܢܬܟܢܫܘܢ ܩܕܡܘܗܝ ܟܠܗܘܢ ܥܡܡܐ ܘܢܦܪܫ[15] ܐܢܘܢ ܚܕ ܡܢ ܚܕ

Luke 6:19 (11)

ܘܟܠܗ ܟܢܫܐ ܒܥܝܢ[16] ܗܘܘ ܠܡܬܩܪܒܘ ܠܗ ܚܝܠܐ ܓܝܪ ܢܦܩ ܗܘܐ
ܡܢܗ ܘܠܟܠܗܘܢ ܡܐܣܐ[17] ܗܘܐ

John 9:30 (12)

ܥܢܐ ܗܘ ܓܒܪܐ ܘܐܡܪ ܠܗܘܢ ܒܗܕܐ ܗܘ ܡܩܒܠ ܠܡܬܕܡܪܘ
ܕܐܢܬܘܢ ܠܐ ܝܕܥܝܢ ܐܢܬܘܢ ܡܢ ܐܝܡܟܐ[18] ܗܘ ܘܥܝܢܝ ܕܝܠܝ ܦܬܚ[19]

Mark 10:47 (13)

ܘܠܡܐܡܪ[20] ܒܪܗ ܕܕܘܝܕ ܐܬܪܚܡ ܥܠܝ

Mark 8:16 (14)

ܘܡܬܚܫܒܝܢ ܗܘܘ ܚܕ ܥܡ ܚܕ ܘܐܡܪܝܢ ܕܠܚܡܐ ܠܝܬ ܠܢ

Matthew 12:23 (15)

ܘܡܬܕܡܪܝܢ ܗܘܘ ܟܠܗܘܢ ܟܢܫܐ ܘܐܡܪܝܢ ܕܠܡܐ ܗܢܘ ܒܪܗ ܕܕܘܝܕ

---

15. ܘܢܦܪܫ = he will separate.
16. ܒܥܝܢ = seeking.
17. ܡܐܣܐ = healing.
18. ܐܝܡܟܐ = whence.
19. This is a pael perfect. Note the variable vowel because of the guttural.
20 This is a peal infinitive. Since it is a I-*ālap* verb, note the vowel that accompanies the *ālap*.

Matthew 16:8 (16)

ܝܶܫܽܘܥ ܕܶܝܢ ܝܺܕܰܥ ܘܶܐܡܰܪ ܠܗܽܘܢ ܡܳܢܳܐ ܡܶܬ݂ܚܰܫܒܺܝܢ ܐܢ݈ܬܽܘܢ ܒܢܰܦܫܟ݂ܽܘܢ
ܙܥܽܘܪܰܝ ܗܰܝܡܳܢܽܘܬ݂ܳܐ ܕܠܰܚܡܳܐ ܠܳܐ ܢܣܰܒܬܽܘܢ

Mark 8:2 (17)

ܡܶܬ݂ܪܰܚܰܡ ܐ̱ܢܳܐ ܥܰܠ ܟܶܢܫܳܐ ܗܳܢܳܐ ܕܗܳܐ ܬܠܳܬ݂ܳܐ ܝܰܘܡܺܝܢ ܩܰܘܝܽܘ[21] ܠܘܳܬ݂ܝ
ܘܠܰܝܬ݂ ܠܗܽܘܢ ܡܳܢܳܐ ܢܶܐܟ݂ܠܽܘܢ[22]

John 11:54 (18)

ܘܬܰܡܳܢ ܡܶܬ݂ܗܰܦܶܟ ܗܘܳܐ ܥܰܡ ܬܰܠܡܺܝܕ݂ܰܘܗ݈ܝ

Luke 9:43 (19)

ܘܶܐܬ݂ܕܰܡܰܪܘ ܟܽܠܗܽܘܢ ܒܪܰܒܽܘܬ݂ܶܗ ܕܰܐܠܳܗܳܐ ܘܟ݂ܰܕ ܟܽܠܢܳܫ ܡܶܬ݂ܕܰܡܰܪ ܗܘܳܐ ܥܰܠ
ܟܽܠ ܕܥܳܒܶܕ ܝܶܫܽܘܥ ܐܶܡܰܪ ܠܬܰܠܡܺܝܕ݂ܰܘܗ݈ܝ

Mark 1:41 (20)

ܗܽܘ ܕܶܝܢ ܝܶܫܽܘܥ ܐܶܬ݂ܪܰܚܰܡ ܥܠܰܘܗ݈ܝ ܘܰܦܫܰܛ[23] ܐܺܝܕܶܗ ܩܪܶܒ ܠܶܗ ܘܶܐܡܰܪ
ܨܳܒܶܐ ܐ̱ܢܳܐ ܐܶܬ݂ܕܰܟܳܐ[24]

---

21. ܩܰܘܝܽܘ = they remain.
22. This is a I-*ālap* imperfect.
23. ܘܰܦܫܰܛ = he stretched out.
24. This is an ethpaal imperative. The form is a little different because it is a III-*ālap* verb.

Additional Exercises

Isaiah 48:8 (21)

ܠܐ ܫܡܥܬ ܐܦ ܠܐ ܝܕܥ ܐܢܬ ܠܗܝܢ ܘܡܢ ܩܕܝܡ ܠܐ ܐܬܦܬܚ
ܐܕܢܝܟ[25]

Genesis 11:6 (22)

ܘܐܡܪ ܡܪܝܐ. ܗܐ ܥܡܐ ܚܕ ܘܠܫܢܐ ܚܕ ܠܟܠܗܘܢ. ܘܗܢܐ ܐܬܚܫܒܘ
ܠܡܥܒܕ. ܡܟܝܠ ܠܐ ܢܬܟܣܪ ܡܢܗܘܢ ܟܠܡܕܡ ܕܐܬܚܫܒܘ ܠܡܥܒܕ.

Genesis 49:2 (23)

ܐܬܟܢܫܘ ܘܫܡܥܘ ܒܢܘܗܝ ܕܝܥܩܘܒ. ܫܡܥܘ ܠܐܝܣܪܐܝܠ ܐܒܘܟܘܢ

2 Samuel 11:20 (24)

ܐܢܗܘ[26] ܕܣܠܩܬ ܚܡܬܗ[27] ܕܡܠܟܐ ܘܐܡܪ ܠܟ ܠܡܢܐ ܐܬܩܪܒܬܘܢ ܠܘܬ
ܩܪܝܬܐ ܠܡܬܟܬܫܘ[28]

Sirach 11:21 (25)

ܠܐ ܬܬܕܡܪ ܒܥܒܕܐ ܕܥܘܠܐ ܐܠܐ ܣܟܐ[29] ܠܡܪܝܐ

Micah 4:11 (26)

ܡܟܝܠ ܢܬܟܢܫܘܢ ܥܠܝܟܝ ܥܡܡܐ ܣܓܝܐܐ

---

24. ܐܕܢܝܟ = your ears.
25. ܐܢܗܘ = if.
26. ܚܡܬܗ = his wrath.
27. ܠܡܬܟܬܫܘ = to fight.
28. ܣܟܐ = trust.

15

Aphel (A)

	Perfect	Participle	Imperfect	Imperative	Infinitive
Aphel	ܐܟܬܒ	ܡܟܬܒ	ܢܟܬܒ	ܐܟܬܒ	ܡܟܬܒܘ
	akteb	*makteb*	*nakteb*	*akteb*	*maktābu*

Introduction

As the name implies, the aphel stem is identified by the *alāp* prefix attached to the front of the verb. The aphel stem indicates an active causative action of the verb, meaning, the subject is causing the action to be performed. It is also used in a factitive function—where the verb implies a particular result to the action. For example, in the sentence "The boss promoted me to manager," "promoted" would be factitive because it implies the result of me being manager.

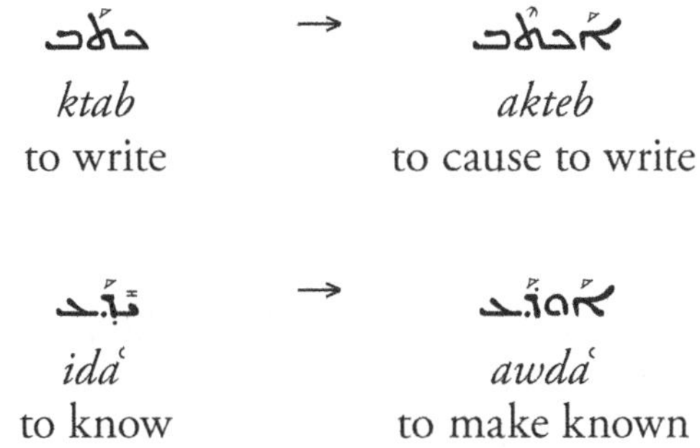

In the second example above, the verb has changed form because the initial consonant is a *yūd*, a weak consonant (see earlier discussion in ch. 7); these are known as weak verbs and will be examined later in the grammar.

Aphel Perfect

The best way to identity the aphel conjugation is by the *alāp* preformative that is added to the front of the word. The stem vowel, as the name aphel suggests, is an *e* (aCCeC), but this is not always a hard and fast rule. Note that the 3fs form does not have this as a characteristic.

	Singular		Plural	
3m	ܐܰܟ݂ܬܶܒ݂	*akteb* he/it was caused to write	ܐܰܟ݂ܬܶܒ݂ܘ ܐܰܟ݂ܬܶܒ݂ܘܿܢ	*akteb* *aktebun* they were caused to write
3f	ܐܰܟ݂ܬܒ݂ܰܬ݂	*aktbat* she/it was caused to write	ܐܰܟ݂ܬܶܒ݂ ܐܰܟ݂ܬܶܒ݂ܝ̈ ܐܰܟ݂ܬܶܒ݂ܶܝܢ	*akteb* *akteb* *aktebēn* they were caused to write
2m	ܐܰܟ݂ܬܶܒ݂ܬ݁	*aktebt* you were caused to write	ܐܰܟ݂ܬܶܒ݂ܬܘܿܢ ܐܰܟ݂ܬܶܒ݂ܬܘܿܢ	*aktebton* *aktebtun* you were caused to write
2f	ܐܰܟ݂ܬܶܒ݂ܬ݁ܝ	*aktebt* you were caused to write	ܐܰܟ݂ܬܶܒ݂ܬܶܝܢ	*aktebtēn* you were caused to write
1c	ܐܰܟ݂ܬܒ݂ܶܬ݂	*aktbet* I was caused to write	ܐܰܟ݂ܬܶܒ݂ܢ ܐܰܟ݂ܬܶܒ݂ܢܰܢ	*atktebn* *aktebnan* we were caused to write

Note how the causative action is drawn out from the verb below. For an initial attempt at translation, it is fine to add a suggestive "caused to" to the translation, as in "he caused to pour," and then smooth out the English. The context of the passage will often suggest the causative nuance, but it is a good reminder as one translates to keep in mind the causative facets of the conjugation.

ܡܳܐܢ̈ܶܐ	ܥܰܠ	ܪ̈ܰܚܡܰܘܗ̄ܝ	ܘܰܐܫܦܰܥ
māne	*ʿal*	*raḥmaw*	*wašpaʿ*
noun mp emphatic	preposition	noun mp emphatic + 3 ms	waw + aphel perfect 3ms
the vessels	on	his mercy	and he caused to pour

Translation: And he poured his mercy on the vessels.

Romans 9:23

Note: The form above, ܗܰܐܫܡܰܥ, is another example of a root with a variable vowel. Always keep in mind as you continue to translate Syriac that if the final consonant in a verb is a guttural (*ālap*, *hē*, *ḥēt*, *ʿē*) or a *rīš*, then the final vowel will always be *a*.

Aphel Imperfect

There are two preformatives added to the front of the verb in the aphel imperfect (the *alāp* prefix of the aphel stem + the imperfect preformative). In the imperfect conjugation, the *alāp* prefix is absorbed into the imperfect prefix and the distinguishing *ālap* of the aphel stem disappears. Therefore, the primary way to identify the aphel imperfect is by the vowel on the prefix (naCCeC).

ܢ	+	ܐܰ	→	ܢܰܟܬܶܒ
Imperfect Prefix *n*		Aphel Prefix *a-*		Aphel Imperfect *nakteb*

The full paradigm is below. While the *alāp* prefix is typically a giveaway for the aphel stem, keep in mind that the *e*-vowel is also often present as a stem vowel of the second root consonant.

	Singular		Plural	
3m	ܢܰܟܬܶܒ	*nakteb* he/it will be caused to write	ܢܰܟܬܒܽܘܢ	*naktbun* they will be caused to write
3f	ܬܰܟܬܶܒ ܬܰܟܬܶܒ	*takteb* *takteb* she/it will be caused to write	ܢܰܟܬܒܳܢ	*naktbān* they will be caused to write
2m	ܬܰܟܬܶܒ	*takteb* you will be caused to write	ܬܰܟܬܒܽܘܢ	*taktbun* you will be caused to write
2f	ܬܰܟܬܒܺܝܢ	*taktbin* you will be caused to write	ܬܰܟܬܒܳܢ	*taktbān* you will be caused to write
1c	ܐܰܟܬܶܒ	*akteb* I will be caused to write	ܢܰܟܬܶܒ	*nakteb* we will be caused to write

Note: Note that the 1cs form of the imperfect could easily be mistaken for the 3ms of the perfect because it has no *nūn* or *taw* preformative. In these cases, context will have to guide the translation, as the forms are identical.

The example below demonstrates a typical use of the aphel imperfect. Note how the causative is somewhat assumed in the translation, as if it said "do not let your youth cause men to despise you." This is an important grammatical characteristic to keep in mind when translating. Additionally, since the sentence has the negative particle *lā*, the form can be understood as an imperative.

ܛܠܝܘܬܟ	ܥܠ	ܢܒܣܐ	ܢܫ	ܘܠܐ
ṭalyutāk	*ʿal*	*nabse*	*nāš*	*w-lā*
noun fs emphatic + 2ms	preposition	aphel imperfect 3ms	noun ms absolute	waw + particle
your youth	concerning	cause to despise	man	and not

Translation: And (do) not let man despise you concerning your youth.

1 Timothy 4:12

Aphel Imperative

As with other conjugations, the aphel imperative is formed in the same manner as the aphel imperfect, with the imperfect prefix taken away (aCCeC). Removing the prefix causes the *ālap* to reappear; the *e*-stem vowel remains. This creates an unusual situation where the imperative has the same form as the 1cs imperfect and the 3ms perfect (*akteb*). The good news is that the imperative is usually easy to identify.

	Singular	Plural I	Plural II
Masculine	ܐܟܬܒ *akteb* (Cause to) Write!	ܐܟܬܒܘ *akteb* (Cause to) Write!	ܐܟܬܒܘܢ *aktebun* (Cause to)Write!
Feminine	ܐܟܬܒܝ *akteb* (Cause to) Write!	ܐܟܬ̈ܒܝ *akteb* (Cause to) Write!	ܐܟܬ̈ܒܝܢ *aktebēn* (Cause to) Write!

The passage below can be somewhat difficult to translate, even though the context (Paul's admonition to Timothy) makes the imperative clear. Rendering the verb itself is where the difficulty lies.

ܕܠܥܠܡ	ܚܝ̈ܐ	ܘܐܕܪܟ
dalʿālam	*ḥaye*	*wadrek*
dālat + noun ms absolute	noun mp emphatic	*waw* + aphel imperative ms
of eternity	life	overtake/comprehend

Translation: Take hold (of) eternal life!

1 Timothy 6:12

Note that ܪܕܶܟ (*rdek*) is typically translated as "to overtake" or "to comprehend." However, if this were simply plugged into the verse, it would sound very awkward: "cause to overtake eternal life." In cases like these, a slight departure within the semantic domain of the word will help the English reader comprehend the meaning. This also emphasizes the need for a good lexicon when doing translations.

Aphel Infinitive

As with the imperfect tense, when the *ālap* prefix meets the *mīm* prefix of the infinitive, the *ālap* is swallowed up by the *mīm*. However, an *a*-vowel remains above the *mīm* in order to identify that the infinitive is an aphel (maCCāCu). This vowel is the distinguishing feature of the aphel infinitive.

ܡ	+	ܐܰ	→	ܡܰܟܬܳܒܘ
Infinitive Prefix		Aphel Prefix		Aphel Infinitive
m		*a-*		*maktābu*

The following is an example of an infinitive absolute in the aphel stem. Once again, the causative action of the verb is implied, but in order to be more specific it could be added to the translation if desired.

ܐܰܣܟܠܶܬ	ܡܰܣܟܳܠܘ	ܕܰܠܡܳܐ	ܐܰܘ
asklet	*maskālu*	*dalmā*	*aw*
verb: aphel perfect 1 CS	verb: aphel infitive	particle	particle
I have offended	to offend	lest	or

Translation: Or lest I have offended . . . / Or lest I have caused to offend . . .

2 Corinthians 11:7

Aphel Participle

The aphel stem is the last stem that will be covered which attests both an active and a passive participle form. The distinguishing feature, as with the infinitive, is the *a*-vowel above the *mīm* (maCCeC). As we might expect, the *alāp* prefix of the aphel stem assmilate into the *mīm* and disappear, leaving only the *a*-vowel.

It is easy to distinguish the aphel participle from the infinitive because of the different endings (the infinitive carries a *waw*). Distinguishing between the passive and the active is more difficult, as only the ms form has a distinction in the stem vowels: *a* in the passive and *e* in the active. The active and passive forms for the other forms in the aphel conjugation are identical. This can make the translation somewhat ambiguous, but once again context will guide your translation.

Active	Passive
ܡܲܟܬܸܒ	ܡܲܟܬܲܒ
makteb	*maktab*
causing to write	being caused to write

Active Participles

Masculine		Feminine	
Singular	Plural	Singular	Plural
ܡܲܟܬܸܒ	ܡܲܟܬܒܝܼܢ	ܡܲܟܬܒܵܐ	ܡܲܟܬܒܵܢ
makteb	*maktbin*	*maktbā*	*maktbān*

Passive Participles

Masculine		Feminine	
Singular	Plural	Singular	Plural
ܡܲܟܬܲܒ	ܡܲܟܬܒܝܼܢ	ܡܲܟܬܒܵܐ	ܡܲܟܬܒܵܢ
maktab	*maktbin*	*maktbā*	*maktbān*

Below is an example of a typical use of the aphel active participle. Note how it is recognizable as the active because of the stem vowel that is used. In the active the stem vowel is an *e*; in the passive it is an *a*.

ܠܝܼ	ܡܲܫܠܸܡ	ܡܸܢܟ݂ܘܿܢ	ܚܲܕ
li	*mašlem*	*menkun*	*ḥad*
lāmad + 1cs	aphel active participle ms	preposition + 2mp	number
to me	delivering up	from you	one

Translation: One from you (will) deliver me.
Matthew 26:21

Lastly, in some words (such as with the *mīm* preformative) there is no distinction between the pael and aphel conjugations when there is no vowel pointing. A dot is again sometimes applied to the word in order to make the distinction. However, this time it is applied above the letter that has the vowel:

ܡܟܬܒ	ܡܟܬܒ
mkateb	*makteb*
Pael	Aphel

Vocabulary

Nouns

ܐܝܩܪܐ	*iqārā*	honor, glory, majesty
ܐܡܪܐ	*emrā*	lamb
ܗܕܡܐ	*haddāmā*	limb, member
ܙܕܝܩܘܬܐ	*zadiqutā*	justice, righteousness
ܟܣܦܐ	*kespā*	money, silver
ܡܘܠܟܢܐ	*mulkānā*	promise
ܣܦܝܢܬܐ	*spittā*	boat, ship
ܥܘܠܐ	*ʿawlā*	unrighteousness
ܪܚܡܐ	*raḥme*	mercy, bowels
ܫܪܟܐ	*šarkā*	remainder, rest

Verbs

ܐܠܨ	*elaṣ*	to compel, constrain
ܐܣܐ	*asse*	to heal
ܓܒܐ	*gbā*	to choose, gather
ܙܥ	*zāʿ*	to be shaken, confused, trouble (aphel), stir (aphel)
ܚܒ	*ḥāb*	to owe, be condemned
ܝܕܐ	*yade*	to confess, give thanks
ܟܦܪ	*kpar*	to deny, renounce
ܟܪܙ	*kraz*	to be preached, proclaimed
ܡܚܐ	*mḥā*	to strike, smite
ܡܠܟ	*mlak*	to council, reign
ܣܟܠ	*skal*	to understand, perceive
ܥܪܩ	*ʿraq*	to flee
ܦܝܣ	*payes*	to convince, persuade
ܩܘܐ	*qwā*	to abide, remain
ܪܥܐ	*rʿā*	to think, feed, tend
ܫܒܚ	*šbaḥ*	to commend, praise

Other

ܐܝܢ	*in*	truly, so, yes
ܐܦܢ	*āpen*	even if
ܠܘ	*law*	no, is not (*lā* + *hu*)
ܥܬܝܪܐ	*ʿaytirā*	rich, wealthy

Exercises

Mark 15:15 (1)

ܦܝܠܛܘܣ ܕܝܢ ܨܒܐ ܕܢܥܒܕ ܨܒܝܢܐ ܠܟܢܫܐ ܘܫܪܐ ܠܗܘܢ ܠܒܪܐܒܐ

ܘܐܫܠܡ ܠܗܘܢ ܠܝܫܘܥ

John 3:16 (2)

ܗܟܢܐ ܓܝܪ ܐܚܒ[1] ܐܠܗܐ ܠܥܠܡܐ

John 13:1 (3)

ܩܕܡ ܕܝܢ ܥܐܕܐ ܕܦܨܚܐ[2] ܝܕܥ ܗܘܐ ܝܫܘܥ ܕܡܛܬ[3] ܫܥܬܐ ܕܢܫܢܐ[4]

ܡܢ ܗܢܐ ܥܠܡܐ ܠܘܬ ܐܒܘܗܝ ܘܐܚܒ[5] ܠܕܝܠܗ ܕܒܗܢܐ ܥܠܡܐ

ܘܥܕܡܐ ܠܚܪܬܐ ܐܚܒ ܐܢܘܢ

---

1. This is a hollow verb (a *waw* is the middle consonant of the root). Note how the aphel stem appears in these situations. Aphel perfect 3ms of ܚܒ, "to love."
2. ܥܐܕܐ ܕܦܨܚܐ = Feast of Passover.
3. ܡܛܬ = had arrived.
4. ܕܢܫܢܐ = that he would depart.
5. This is an aphel from the hollow root ܚܒ, "to love." This verb appears twice in this verse.

Acts 19:4 (4)

ܐܡܪ ܠܗܘܢ ܦܘܠܘܣ ܝܘܚܢܢ ܐܥܡܕ ܡܥܡܘܕܝܬܐ ܕܬܝܒܘܬܐ[6] ܠܥܡܐ
ܟܕ ܐܡܪ ܗܘܐ ܕܢܗܝܡܢܘܢ[7] ܒܡܢ ܕܐܬܐ ܒܬܪܗ ܕܐܝܬܘܗܝ ܝܫܘܥ
ܡܫܝܚܐ

1 Cor. 11:23 (5)

ܐܢܐ ܓܝܪ ܩܒܠܬ ܡܢ ܡܪܢ ܗܘ ܡܕܡ ܕܐܫܠܡܬ ܠܟܘܢ ܕܡܪܢ ܝܫܘܥ
ܒܗܘ ܠܠܝܐ ܕܡܫܬܠܡ ܗܘܐ ܢܣܒ ܗܘܐ ܠܚܡܐ

Mark 7:13 (6)

ܘܡܣܠܝܢ[8] ܐܢܬܘܢ ܡܠܬܗ ܕܐܠܗܐ ܡܛܠ ܡܫܠܡܢܘܬܐ[9] ܕܐܫܠܡܬܘܢ
ܘܕܪܡܝܢ[10] ܠܗܠܝܢ ܣܓܝܐܬܐ ܥܒܕܝܢ ܐܢܬܘܢ

Matthew 3:9 (7)

ܘܠܐ ܬܣܒܪܘܢ ܘܬܐܡܪܘܢ ܒܢܦܫܟܘܢ ܕܐܒܐ ܐܝܬ ܠܢ ܐܒܪܗܡ ܐܡܪ
ܐܢܐ ܠܟܘܢ ܓܝܪ ܕܡܫܟܚ[11] ܐܠܗܐ ܡܢ ܗܠܝܢ ܟܐܦܐ ܠܡܩܡܘ[12]
ܒܢܝܐ ܠܐܒܪܗܡ

---

6. ܡܥܡܘܕܝܬܐ ܕܬܝܒܘܬܐ = baptism of repentance.
7. This is another example of the paiel stem, conjugated the same as a pael with the addition of a *yūd*. Let the prefix and the ending guide your parsing of the word.
8. ܡܣܠܝܢ = despising (participle).
9. ܡܫܠܡܢܘܬܐ = tradition.
10. ܘܕܪܡܝܢ = and resembling (participle).
11. ܡܫܟܚ = peal participle of ܫܟܚ.
12. ܠܡܩܡܘ = to raise up.

Matthew 10:19–20 (8)

ܐܡܬܝ ܕܝܢ ܕܢܫܠܡܘܢܟܘܢ[13] ܠܐ ܬܐܨܦܘܢ[14] ܐܝܟܢܐ ܐܘ ܡܢܐ

ܬܡܠܠܘܢ ܡܬܝܗܒ[15] ܠܟܘܢ ܓܝܪ ܒܗܝ ܫܥܬܐ ܡܢܐ ܕܬܡܠܠܘܢ

ܠܐ ܗܘܐ ܓܝܪ ܐܢܬܘܢ ܡܡܠܠܝܢ ܐܠܐ ܪܘܚܐ ܕܐܒܘܟܘܢ ܡܡܠܠܐ

ܒܟܘܢ

Mark 13:12 (9)

ܢܫܠܡ ܕܝܢ ܐܚܐ ܠܐܚܘܗܝ ܠܡܘܬܐ ܘܐܒܐ ܠܒܪܗ ܘܢܩܘܡܘܢ[16] ܒܢܝܐ

ܥܠ ܐܒܗܝܗܘܢ

Matthew 5:43–44 (10)

ܫܡܥܬܘܢ ܕܐܬܐܡܪ ܕܬܪܚܡ ܠܩܪܝܒܟ ܘܬܣܢܐ[17] ܠܒܥܠܕܒܒܟ ܐܢܐ ܕܝܢ

ܐܡܪ ܐܢܐ ܠܟܘܢ ܐܚܒܘ[18] ܠܒܥܠܕܒܒܝܟܘܢ

Matthew 26:52 (11)

ܗܝܕܝܢ ܐܡܪ ܠܗ ܝܫܘܥ ܐܗܦܟ ܣܦܣܪܐ[19] ܠܕܘܟܬܗ ܟܠܗܘܢ ܓܝܪ

ܗܢܘܢ ܕܢܣܒܘ ܣܦܣܝܪܐ ܒܣܦܣܝܪܐ ܢܡܘܬܘܢ[20]

---

13. This is a verb with a pronominal suffix: aphel imperfect 3mp + 2mp.
14. ܬܐܨܦܘܢ = be anxious (imperfect).
15 This is a I-*yūd* verb. Note the addition of the vowel over the *yūd*.
16. ܘܢܩܘܡܘܢ = and he will rise.
17. ܘܣܢܐ = hate.
18. This is an aphel from the hollow root ܚܒ, "to love." Here it is an imperative
19. ܣܦܣܪܐ = sword (x3). Note the slight change in spelling here (singular) versus the plural (the other two).
20. ܢܡܘܬܘܢ = they will die.

Matthew 7:5 (12)

ܢܣܒ ܒܐܦܐ[21] ܐܦܩ[22] ܠܘܩܕܡ ܩܪܝܬܐ[23] ܡܢ ܥܝܢܟ ܘܗܝܕܝܢ ܬܬܚܙܐ

ܠܟ ܠܡܦܩܘ[24] ܓܠܐ[25] ܡܢ ܥܝܢܗ ܕܐܚܘܟ

Matthew 3:11 (13)

ܐܢܐ ܡܥܡܕ ܐܢܐ ܠܟܘܢ ܒܡܝܐ ܠܬܝܒܘܬܐ[26] ܗܘ ܕܝܢ ܕܒܬܪܝ ܐܬܐ

ܚܝܠܬܢ[27] ܗܘ ܡܢܝ ܗܘ ܕܠܐ ܫܘܐ ܐܢܐ ܡܣܢܘܗܝ[28] ܠܡܫܩܠ ܗܘ

ܢܥܡܕ ܠܟܘܢ ܒܪܘܚܐ ܕܩܘܕܫܐ ܘܒܢܘܪܐ

Matthew 6:30 (14)

ܐܢ ܕܝܢ ܠܥܣܒܐ ܕܚܩܠܐ[29] ܕܝܘܡܢܐ ܐܝܬܘܗܝ ܘܡܚܪ ܢܦܠ ܒܬܢܘܪܐ[30]

ܐܠܗܐ ܗܟܢܐ ܡܠܒܫ ܠܗ ܣܓܝ ܝܬܝܪ ܠܟܘܢ ܙܥܘܪܝ ܗܝܡܢܘܬܐ

Matthew 12:28 (15)

ܘܐܢ ܒܪܘܚܐ ܕܐܠܗܐ ܐܢܐ ܡܦܩ[31] ܐܢܐ ܫܐܕܐ[32] ܩܪܒܬ ܠܗ

ܥܠܝܟܘܢ ܡܠܟܘܬܐ ܕܐܠܗܐ

---

21. ܢܣܒ ܒܐܦܐ = lit: "being with face," i.e., hypocrite.
22. ܐܦܩ = The *nūn* disappears from *npaq* ("to go out") in the aphel stem. The reason for this will be discussed later in the book.
23. ܩܪܝܬܐ = plank.
24. ܠܡܦܩܘ = *npaq*. The vowels reveal that it is an aphel infinitive and as before, the initial *nūn* is assimilated.
25. ܓܠܐ = straw.
26. ܬܝܒܘܬܐ = repentance.
27. ܚܝܠܬܢ = greater.
28. ܡܣܢܘܗܝ = his sandal.
29. ܥܣܒܐ ܕܚܩܠܐ = grass of the field.
30. ܒܬܢܘܪܐ = in the furnace.
31. The *nūn* disappears from *npaq* ("to go out") in the aphel stem.
32. ܫܐܕܐ = demons.

Matthew 26:21 (16)

ܘܟܕ ܠܥܣܝܢ[33] ܐܡܪ ܐܡܝܢ ܐܡܪ ܐܢܐ ܠܟܘܢ ܕܚܕ ܡܢܟܘܢ ܡܫܠܡ ܠܝ

Luke 22:48 (17)

ܐܡܪ ܠܗ ܝܫܘܥ ܝܗܘܕܐ ܒܢܘܫܩܬܐ[34] ܡܫܠܡ ܐܢܬ ܠܗ ܠܒܪܗ
ܕܐܢܫܐ

John 5:39 (18)

ܒܨܘ[35] ܟܬܒܐ ܕܒܗܘܢ ܡܣܒܪܝܢ ܐܢܬܘܢ ܕܚܝܐ ܕܠܥܠܡ ܐܝܬ ܠܟܘܢ
ܘܗܢܘܢ ܣܗܕܝܢ[36] ܥܠܝ

Luke 8:54 (19)

ܗܘ ܕܝܢ ܐܦܩ[37] ܠܟܠܢܫ ܠܒܪ ܘܐܚܕܗ[38] ܒܐܝܕܗ ܘܩܪܝܗ[39] ܘܐܡܪ ܛܠܝܬܐ
ܩܘܡܝ[40]

---

33. ܠܥܣܝܢ = eating.
34. ܒܢܘܫܩܬܐ = with a kiss.
35. ܒܨܘ = you search.
36. ܣܗܕܝܢ = are testifying.
37. ܐܦܩ = The *nūn* disappears from *npaq* ("to go out") in the aphel stem.
38. This is a verb with a pronominal suffix: peal perfect 3ms + 3fs.
39. ܩܪܝܗ = called to her.
40. ܩܘܡܝ = arise!

John 18:16 (20)

ܘܢܦܩ ܗܘ ܬܠܡܝܕܐ ܐܚܪܢܐ ܕܝܕܝܥ ܗܘܐ ܠܗ ܠܪܒ ܟܗܢܐ ܘܐܡܪ

ܠܢܛܪܬ[41] ܬܪܥܐ ܘܐܥܠܗ[42] ܠܫܡܥܘܢ

Additional Exercises

Numbers 21:34 (21)

ܘܐܡܪ ܡܪܝܐ ܠܡܘܫܐ. ܠܐ ܬܕܚܠ ܡܢܗ. ܡܛܠ ܕܒܐܝܕܝܟ ܡܫܠܡ

ܐܢܐ ܠܗ ܘܠܟܠܗ ܥܡܗ. ܘܠܟܠܗ ܐܪܥܗ. ܘܬܥܒܕ ܠܗ ܐܝܟ ܕܥܒܕܬ

ܠܣܝܚܘܢ[43] ܡܠܟܐ

1 Chronicles 21:27 (22)

ܘܐܡܪ ܡܪܝܐ ܠܡܠܐܟܐ ܟܕ ܚܙܐ ܐܗܦܟ ܣܝܦܗ[44] ܠܬܠܝܬܗ[45]

Malachi 2:6 (23)

ܢܡܘܣܐ ܕܩܘܫܬܐ[46] ܗܘܐ ܒܦܘܡܗ ܘܥܘܠܐ[47] ܠܐ ܐܫܬܟܚ ܒܣܦܘܬܗ[48]

ܒܫܠܡܐ ܘܒܬܪܝܨܘܬܐ[49] ܗܠܟ ܥܡܝ ܘܣܓܝܐܐ ܐܗܦܟ ܡܢ ܥܘܠܐ

---

41. ܠܢܛܪܬ = guarding.
42. ܥܠ = to enter. This is an aphel stem plus a 3ms ending.
43. This is a name.
44. ܣܝܦܗ = his sword.
45. ܠܬܠܝܬܗ = to his sheath.
46. ܕܩܘܫܬܐ = of truth.
47. ܥܘܠܐ= unrighteousness (x2).
48. ܒܣܦܘܬܗ = on his lip.
49. ܒܬܪܝܨܘܬܐ = uprightness.

Judges 20:28 (24)

ܘܐܡܪ ܡܪܝܐ ܣܩܘ[50] ܡܛܠ ܕܡܚܪ[51] ܡܫܠܡ ܐܢܐ ܠܗ ܒܐܝ̈ܕܝܟܘܢ

Genesis 33:14 (25)

ܢܥܒܪ ܡܪܝ ܩܕܡ ܥܒܕܗ. ܘܐܢܐ ܐܗܠܟ

Exodus 6:13 (26)

ܠܡܦܩܘ[52] ܠܒܢ̈ܝ ܐܝܣܪܝܠ ܡܢ ܐܪܥܐ ܕܡܨܪܝܢ[53]

50. ܣܩܘ = go up.
51. ܡܚܪ= tomorrow.
52. This is the root ܢܦܩ, *npaq*, the *nūn* assimilates into the *mīm*.
53. ܡܨܪܝܢ= Egypt.

16

Ettaphal (Ap)

	Perfect	Participle	Imperfect	Imperative	Infinitive
Ettaphal	ܐܶܬܬܰܟܬܰܒ	ܡܶܬܬܰܟܬܰܒ	ܢܶܬܬܰܟܬܰܒ	ܐܶܬܬܰܟܬܰܒ	ܡܶܬܬܰܟܬܳܒܽܘ
	ettaktab	*mettaktab*	*nettaktab*	*ettaktab*	*mettaktābu*

Introduction

One of the nice things about Semitic languages, and especially Syriac, is that they are very predictable in their structure. Consequently, some of this grammar might seem repetitive at various points, but that is good in that it reveals a predictability about the language. With that said, as you have come to expect from the other verb stems, the addition of the *et-* prefix to the aphel stem indicates that the verb acts like an aphel, but in the passive. Therefore, an ettaphal verb is one that typically functions as causative and passive. This stem is rare enough that it is worth examining a lexicon for an accurate translation.

One of the distinct characteristics of the ettaphal stem is that it usually attests a double *taw* in the prefix of the verb. This recognizable trait is present for all of the forms of the conjugations–perfect, imperfect, imperative, and participle.

Ettaphal Perfect

The ettaphal perfect paradigm, as one would expect from the name of the stem, has an *alāp-taw-taw* prefix and the stem vowel is usually an *a* (ettaCCaC). The endings are familiar and predictable from the other stems you have learned.

	Singular		Plural	
3m	ܐܬܬܟܬܒ	*ettaktab* he/it was caused to be written	ܐܬܬܟܬܒܘ ܐܬܬܟܬܒܘܢ	*ettaktab* *ettaktabun* they were caused to be written
3f	ܐܬܬܟܬܒܬ	*ettaktbat* she/it was caused to be written	ܐܬܬܟܬܒ ܐܬܬܟܬܒ̈ ܐܬܬܟܬܒ̈ܝܢ	*ettaktab* *ettaktab* *ettaktabēn* they were caused to be written
2m	ܐܬܬܟܬܒܬ	*ettaktabt* you were caused to be written	ܐܬܬܟܬܒܬܘܢ ܐܬܬܟܬܒܬܘܢ	*ettaktabton* *ettaktabtun* you were caused to be written
2f	ܐܬܬܟܬܒܬܝ	*ettaktabt* you were caused to be written	ܐܬܬܟܬܒ̈ܬܝܢ	*ettaktabtēn* you were caused to be written
1c	ܐܬܬܟܬܒܬ	*ettaktbet* I was caused to be written	ܐܬܬܟܬܒܢ ܐܬܬܟܬܒܢܢ	*ettatktabn* *ettaktabnan* we were caused to be written

Note that in the following example the root of the verb is altered slightly (the *yūd* is changed to a *waw* from the root ܝܣܦ, "to add, increase"). Verbs undergo predictable transformations depending on the presence of various consonants placed throughout the root. This will be covered in the next section on weak verbs; for now it is enough simply to notice the change. Also, keep in mind that the causative dimension of the verb is still present even in the passive form of the verb. One might wish to translate this as "he was caused to be added."

ܐܒܗ̈ܘܗܝ	ܥܠ	ܘܐܬܬܘܣܦ
abāhaw	*ʿal*	*w-ettawsap*
noun mp emphatic + 3ms	preposition	*waw* + ettaphal perfect 3ms
his fathers	concerning	and he was added

Translation: And he was added with his fathers.

Acts 13:36

Ettaphal Imperfect

As with the other imperfect stems that have the *et-* prefix, the ettaphal imperfect must interact with two prefixes. However, the very noticeable double-*taw* should enable you to identify these particular verbs. With the double prefix, the *nūn* takes on the *e*-vowel, and the typical *a*-vowel is added to the end of the prefix (nettaCCaC). This is paired with the *a*-stem vowel in most cases to form the full conjugation. Beyond these issues with the prefix, the various forms of the verb are formed regularly.

ܢ	+	ܐܬܬ	→	ܢܬܬܟܬܒ
Imperfect Prefix *n*		Aphel Prefix *etta-*		Ettaphal Imperfect *nettaktab*

There is one interesting feature to note regarding the ettaphal imperfect: the prefix in the second and third feminine forms should technically have three *taws* lined up together.

ܬ	+	ܐܬܬ	→	ܬܬܬܟܬܒ	→	ܬܬܟܬܒ
Imperfect Prefix *t*		Aphel Prefix *etta-*		Ettaphal Imperfect *tettaktab*		Ettaphal Imperfect *tetaktab*

The language does not tolerate this and the prefix is reduced to only two *taws*, with the second one doubling. The full paradigm is below.

	Singular		Plural	
3m	ܢܬܬܟܬܒ	*nettaktab* he/it will be caused to be written	ܢܬܬܟܬܒܘܢ	*nettaktbun* they will be caused to be written
3f	ܬܬܟܬܒ ܬܬܟܬܒ	*tetaktab* *tetaktab* she/it will be caused to be written	ܢܬܬܟܬܒܢ	*nettaktbān* they will be caused to be written
2m	ܬܬܟܬܒ	*tetaktab* you will be caused to be written	ܬܬܟܬܒܘܢ	*tetaktbun* you will be caused to be written
2f	ܬܬܟܬܒܝܢ	*tetaktbin* you will be caused to be written	ܬܬܟܬܒܢ	*tetaktbān* you will be caused to be written
1c	ܐܬܬܟܬܒ	*ettaktab* I will be caused to be written	ܢܬܬܟܬܒ	*nettaktab* we will be caused to be written

The following example illustrates a fairly typical use of the ettaphal imperfect. Once again, note the transformation of the root (the *yūd* is changed to a *waw* in ܘܣܦ). In this example, the imperfect is functioning as an imperative; remember, Syriac doesn't allow the negative particle *lā* to appear with the imperative. Instead, the imperfect plus *lā* is used for negative commands.

ܥܡܗܘܢ	ܢܬܡܠܠ	ܢܬܬܘܣܦ	ܕܠܐ
ʿamhun	*netmalal*	*nettawsap*	*d-lā*
preposition + 3mp	ethpaal imperfect 3ms	ettaphal imperfect 3ms	*dālat* + negative particle
with them	it was spoken	it will be added	not

Translation: Do not add (what) was spoken with them.
Hebrews 12:19

Ettaphal Imperative

The ettaphal imperative requires a little more finagling with the prefixes. The imperative is normally formed by dropping the prefix from the imperfect. Following this convention, the ettaphal drops the prefix, which allows the *alāp* consonant to reappear, as we might expect (ettaCCaC). In doing this, the ettaphal ms imperative is identical to the 3ms of the ettaphal perfect. Once again, context must be relied upon in determining which translation is appropriate.

	Singular	Plural I	Plural II
Masculine	ܐܬܬܟܬܒ *ettaktab* Be written!	ܐܬܬܟܬܒܘ *ettaktab* Be written!	ܐܬܬܟܬܒܘܢ *ettaktabun* Be written!
Feminine	ܐܬܬܟܬܒܝ *ettaktab* Be written!	ܐܬܬܟ̈ܬܒܝ *ettaktab* Be written!	ܐܬܬܟ̈ܬܒܝܢ *ettaktabēn* Be written!

The root of the ettaphal verb in the following example is ܢܘܚ ("to rest"). Note the behavior of the root (known as a hollow verb) when it is conjugated. This pattern is typical of hollow verbs and will be covered in chapter 22.

ܫܥܬܐ	ܡܛܬ	ܗܐ	ܘܐܬܬܢܝܚܘ
šaʿtā	*mṭāt*	*hā*	*w-ettniḥ*
noun fs emphatic	peal perfect 3fs	particle	*waw* + ettaphal imperative mp
hour	it has arrived	behold	and resting

Translation: And are you (sleeping) resting?! Behold. The hour has arrived.
Matthew 26:45

Notice that the use of ܘܐܬܬܢܝܚܘ is somewhat irregular, as the imperative is being used as a direct address, while at the same time a question is being asked. This illustrates the flexibility that the imperative has in the various ways that it is used. Additionally, the peal perfect form is a III-weak verb, ܡܛܐ ("to arrive"), which alters the typical peal perfect form by dropping the *ālap* from the end of the word and adding a long *a*-vowel.

Ettaphal Infinitive

With the ettaphal infinitive, the *alāp* predictably is overpowered by the *mīm* and only the *e*-vowel remains above the *mīm* (mettaCCāCu). This is typical of how the infinitive is formed with the other *et-* conjugations. Additionally, the infinitive will still have the *waw* ending that is typical of the other derived stems. Remember that the double-*taw* that is present in the prefix is your clue that this is the ettaphal stem.

ܡ	+	ܐܬܬ	→	ܡܬܬܟܬܒܘ
Infinitive Prefix		Aphel Prefix		Ettaphal Infinitive
m		*etta-*		*mettaktābu*

A fairly representative use of the ettaphal infinitive is given in the following example. Note the *lāmad* prefix that is present, a common characteristic (but not required) in biblical usage of the infinitive. This is also another example of a hollow verb; the root of the ettaphal is ܪܘܡ and the middle *waw* will drop.

ܕܐܢܫܐ	ܒܪܗ	ܠܡܬܬܪܡܘ	ܥܬܝܕ
d-nāšā	*breh*	*l-mettrāmu*	*ʿtid*
dālat + noun ms emphatic	noun ms emphatic + 3ms	*lāmad* + ettaphal infinitive	peal passive participle ms
of man	son of him	to be exalted	being prepared

Translation: The son of man is being prepared to be exalted.
John 3:14

Ettaphal Participle

The ettaphal participle takes the *mīm* prefix just as the other non-peal stems (mettaCCaC). The various endings of this paradigm are predictable and follow the basic patterns of the other participle conjugations.

Masculine		Feminine	
Singular	Plural	Singular	Plural
ܡܬܬܟܬܒ	ܡܬܬܟܬܒܝܢ	ܡܬܬܟܬܒܐ	ܡܬܬܟܬܒܢ
mettaktab	*mettaktbin*	*mettaktbā*	*mettaktabān*

In the example below, it would be very hard to bring out the nuance of the ettaphal participle in translation. Remember that this verb will have a passive element as well as a causative element attached to its translation. However, this would often stretch the bounds of the English language, thus rendering an odd translation. In most scenarios, the translator can only do his or her best to bring out the depth of these nuances in meaning.

ܠܟܘܢ	ܡܬܬܘܣܦܢ	ܗܠܝܢ	ܘܟܠܗܝܢ
l-kun	*mettawspan*	*halēn*	*w-kullhēn*
lāmad + 2mp	ettaphal participle fp	demonstrative pronoun fp	*waw* + particle + 3fp
to you	being added	these	and all of them

Translation: And all of these (things) will be added to you.
Matthew 6:33

Again, note that this is a I-*yūd* verb ܝܣܦ (*ysp*, "to add/increase"), so the *waw* takes the place of the *yūd* in the conjugation.

Vocabulary

Nouns

ܓܙܘܪܬܐ	*gzurtā*	circumcision
ܚܡܪܐ	*ḥamrā*	wine
ܟܣܐ	*kāsā*	cup
ܥܠܬܐ	*ʿeltā*	reason, cause
ܦܪܨܘܦܐ	*parṣupā*	person, face, aspect (Gk. πρόσωπον)
ܨܒܘܬܐ	*ṣbutā*	thing, affair
ܩܒܘܪܐ	*qburā*	tomb
ܩܝܡܬܐ	*qyāmtā*	resurrection
ܪܘܓܙܐ	*rugzā*	anger, wrath
ܫܡܫܐ	*šemšā*	sun

Verbs

ܒܗܬ	*bhet*	to be ashamed
ܒܟܐ	*bkā*	to weep
ܓܡܪ	*gmar*	to accomplish, fulfill, perfect
ܙܗܪ	*zher*	to warn, beware
ܚܒܠ	*ḥbal*	to corrupt, destroy
ܚܛܐ	*ḥṭā*	to sin
ܝܩܪ	*iqqar*	to be heavy, honor
ܟܪܟ	*krak*	to lead, wrap
ܢܚ	*nāḥ*	to rest
ܢܣܐ	*nse*	to try, test, prove
ܢܩܦ	*nqep*	to adhere, follow
ܣܢܐ	*snā*	to hate
ܥܪ	*ʿer*	to wake up, watch
ܦܪܥ	*praʿ*	to repay
ܫܕܐ	*šdā*	to throw, cast down
ܬܒ	*tāb*	to repent, return

Other

ܒܪܰܡ	*bram*	but, yet, nonetheless
ܓܰܘ	*gaw*	in, within
ܛܰܢܦܳܐ	*ṭanpā*	impure, defiled
ܥܓܰܠ	*ʿgal*	quickly

Exercises

Note: The scarcity of ettaphal forms in the New Testament will require brief explanation in order to parse out most of the words. This is mainly because they are roots with weak consonants, which alter their shape in certain scenarios when conjugated. The rules for these alterations are covered in the chapters that follow this one; for now simply take note of how certain roots are altered. Unfortunately, there are few strong verbs, so be aware that the *a*-stem vowel may be altered. Hint: Let the ending be the ultimate guide in determining the parsing of the verb.

John 3:14–15 (1)

ܗܳܟܰܢܳܐ ܥܬܺܝܕ ܠܡܶܬܬܪܳܡܽܘ[1] ܒܪܶܗ ܕܐ݈ܢܳܫܳܐ ܕܟܽܠ ܐ݈ܢܳܫ ܕܡܗܰܝܡܶܢ[2] ܒܶܗ ܠܳܐ
ܢܐܒܰܕ ܐܶܠܳܐ ܢܶܗܘܶܐ ܠܶܗ ܚܰܝܶܐ ܕܰܠܥܳܠܰܡ

Matthew 2:3–4 (2)

ܫܡܰܥ ܕܶܝܢ ܗܶܪܳܘܕܶܤ ܡܰܠܟܳܐ ܘܶܐܬܬܙܺܝܥ[3] ܘܟܽܠܳܗ ܐܽܘܪܺܫܠܶܡ ܥܰܡܶܗ ܘܟܰܢܶܫ
ܟܽܠܗܽܘܢ ܪ̈ܰܒܰܝ ܟܳܗ̈ܢܶܐ ܘܣܳܦܪ̈ܶܐ ܕܥܰܡܳܐ ܘܡܶܫܬܰܐܶܠ ܗܘܳܐ ܠܗܽܘܢ ܕܰܐܝܟܳܐ
ܡܶܬܺܝܠܶܕ[4] ܡܫܺܝܚܳܐ

---

1. This is an ettaphal from the hollow root ܪܳܡ (*rām*, "be lifted up"). Notice how the vowels are altered slightly to accommodate the hollow verb.
2. ܡܗܰܝܡܶܢ = believe.
3. Ettaphal from the root word ܙܳܥ, "to be shaken or troubled." Note the addition of the *yūd* in the middle of the root; this is because it is a hollow verb (a *waw* is the second consonant in the root).
4. ܡܶܬܺܝܠܶܕ = was being born.

Matthew 11:23 (3)

ܘܐܢܬܝ ܟܦܪܢܚܘܡ ܗܝ ܕܥܕܡܐ ܠܫܡܝܐ ܐܬܬܪܝܡܬܝ[5] ܥܕܡܐ ܠܫܝܘܠ
ܬܬܚܬܝܢ[6] ܕܐܠܘ ܒܣܕܘܡ[7] ܗܘܘ ܚܝܠܐ ܐܝܠܝܢ ܕܗܘܘ ܒܟܝ ܡܩܘܝܐ[8]
ܗܘܬ ܥܕܡܐ ܠܝܘܡܢܐ

Matthew 25:13 (4)

ܐܬܬܥܝܪܘ[9] ܗܟܝܠ ܕܠܐ ܝܕܥܝܢ ܐܢܬܘܢ ܠܝܘܡܐ ܗܘ ܘܠܐ ܠܫܥܬܐ

Matthew 25:29 (5)

ܠܡܢ ܓܝܪ ܕܐܝܬ ܠܗ ܢܬܝܗܒ ܠܗ ܘܢܬܬܘܣܦ[10] ܠܗ ܘܗܘ ܕܝܢ ܕܠܝܬ
ܠܗ ܘܐܦ ܗܘ ܕܐܝܬ ܠܗ ܢܫܬܩܠ ܡܢܗ

Matthew 26:45 (6)

ܗܝܕܝܢ ܐܬܐ ܠܘܬ ܬܠܡܝܕܘܗܝ ܘܐܡܪ ܠܗܘܢ ܕܡܟܘ ܡܟܝܠ
ܘܐܬܬܢܝܚܘ[11] ܗܐ ܡܛܬ[12] ܫܥܬܐ ܘܒܪܗ ܕܐܢܫܐ ܡܫܬܠܡ
ܒܐܝܕܝܗܘܢ ܕܚܛܝܐ

5. ܐܬܬܪܝܡܬܝ = ettaphal from the root meaning "to exalt."
6. ܠܫܝܘܠ ܬܬܚܬܝܢ = you will be brought to Sheol.
7. ܒܣܕܘܡ = in Sodom.
8. ܡܩܘܝܐ = remained.
9. Ettaphal from the root ܥܝܪܐ, "to be awakened." Look at the ending (which is shared among a few different forms) and the context to guide your translation.
10. Ettaphal from the root ܝܣܦ, "to add." Note the *yūd* changes to a *waw* when in the ettaphal.
11. Ettaphal from the root ܢܚ, "to rest." This is a hollow verb (a *waw* is the second consonant in the root), so look at the ending of the verb in order to determine the parsing.
12. ܡܛܬ = it has arrived.

John 12:34 (7)

ܐܡܪܝܢ ܠܗ ܟ̈ܢܫܐ ܚܢܢ ܫܡܥܢ ܡܢ ܢܡܘܣܐ ܕܡܫܝܚܐ ܠܥܠܡ ܡܩܘܐ[13]
ܐܝܟܢܐ ܐܡܪ ܐܢܬ ܕܥܬܝܕ[14] ܗܘ ܕܢܬܬܪܝܡ[15] ܒܪܗ ܕܐܢܫܐ ܡܢܘ ܗܢܐ
ܒܪܗ ܕܐܢܫܐ

Luke 10:6 (8)

ܘܐܢ ܐܝܬ ܬܡܢ ܒܪ ܫܠܡܐ ܢܬܬܢܝܚ[16] ܥܠܘܗܝ ܫܠܡܟܘܢ ܐܢ ܕܝܢ
ܠܐ ܥܠܝܟܘܢ ܢܗܦܘܟ

Philemon 20 (9)

ܐܝܢ ܐܚܝ ܐܢܐ ܐܬܬܢܝܚ[17] ܒܟ ܒܡܪܢ ܐܢܝܚ[18] ܪ̈ܚܡܝ ܒܡܫܝܚܐ

Mark 14:36–37 (10)

ܘܐܡܪ ܐܒܐ ܐܒܝ ܟܠ ܡܕܡ ܡܫܟܚ[19] ܐܢܬ ܐܥܒܪ ܡܢܝ ܟܣܐ
ܗܢܐ ܐܠܐ ܠܐ ܨ̈ܒܝܢܝ ܕܝܠܝ ܐܠܐ ܕܝܠܟ ܘܐܬܐ ܐܫܟܚ[20] ܐܢܘܢ ܟܕ

13. ܡܩܘܐ = will remain.
14. ܥܬܝܕ = preparing.
15. Ettaphal from the root ܪܡ, "to be lifted up." This is another hollow verb (a *waw* is the second consonant of the root); note the addition of the *yūd* into the middle of the verb. Look at the ending of the verb in order to determine the parsing.
16. Ettaphal from the root ܢܚ, "to rest." This is another hollow verb; note the addition of the *yūd* in the middle of the verb. Look at the ending of the verb in order to determine the parsing.
17. Ettaphal from the root ܢܚ, "to rest." This is another hollow verb; note the addition of the *yūd* in the middle of the verb. Look at the ending of the verb in order to determine the parsing.
18. ܐܢܝܚ = refresh.
19. ܡܫܟܚ = peal participle of ܫܟܚ.
20. Be careful. The *ālap* on the front of this word can be deceiving. Hint: it is not an aphel.

ܕܡܟܝܢ[21] ܘܐܡܪ ܠܟܐܦܐ ܫܡܥܘܢ ܕܡܟܬ[22] ܠܟ ܠܐ ܐܫܟܚܬ ܚܕܐ

ܫܥܐ ܠܡܬܬܥܪܘ[23]

Matthew 24:42 (11)

ܐܬܬܥܝܪܘ[24] ܗܟܝܠ ܕܠܐ ܝܕܥܝܢ ܐܢܬܘܢ ܒܐܝܕܐ ܫܥܬܐ ܐܬܐ

ܡܪܟܘܢ

1 Peter 4:7 (12)

ܡܛܝܬ[25] ܠܗ ܕܝܢ ܚܪܬܐ ܕܟܠ ܡܛܠ ܗܢܐ ܐܬܢܟܦܘ[26] ܘܐܬܬܥܝܪܘ[27]

ܠܨܠܘܬܐ

Matthew 6:33 (13)

ܒܥܘ[28] ܕܝܢ ܠܘܩܕܡ ܡܠܟܘܬܗ ܕܐܠܗܐ ܘܙܕܝܩܘܬܗ ܘܟܠܗܝܢ ܗܠܝܢ

ܡܬܬܘܣܦܢ[29] ܠܟܘܢ

---

21. ܕܡܟܝܢ = sleeping.
22. ܕܡܟܬ = sleeping.
23. Ettaphal from the root ܥܝܪ, "to be awake." Note how the *yūd* disappears when the verb is conjugated.
24. Ettaphal from the root ܥܝܪ, "to be awake." In this case, the *yūd* reappears in the conjugation. Note the ending and context to guide your translation.
25. ܡܛܝܬ = it arrives, draws near.
26. ܐܬܢܟܦܘ = be modest.
27. Ettaphal from the root ܥܝܪ, "to be awake." In this case, the *yūd* reappears in the conjugation. Note the ending and context to guide your translation.
28. ܒܥܘ = seek, search for.
29. Ettaphal from the root ܝܣܦ, "to add." Note that in this form the *yūd* becomes a *waw*, but the ending will remain the same.

Luke 16:25 (14)

ܐܡܪ ܠܗ ܐܒܪܗܡ ܒܪܝ ܐܬܕܟܪ ܕܩܒܠܬ[30] ܛܒܬܟ ܒܚܝܝܟ ܘܠܥܙܪ[31]

ܒܝܫܬܗ ܘܗܫܐ ܗܐ ܡܬܬܝܚ[32] ܗܪܟܐ ܘܐܢܬ ܡܫܬܢܩ[33]

Acts 5:14 (15)

ܘܝܬܝܪ ܡܬܬܘܣܦܝܢ[34] ܗܘܘ ܐܝܠܝܢ ܕܡܗܝܡܢܝܢ[35] ܗܘܘ ܒܡܪܢ ܟܢܫܐ

ܕܓܒܪܐ ܘܕܢܫܐ

Romans 2:17 (16)

ܐܢ ܐܢܬ ܕܝܢ ܝܗܘܕܝܐ ܡܬܩܪܐ ܐܢܬ ܘܡܬܬܝܚ[36] ܐܢܬ ܥܠ

ܢܡܘܣܐ ܘܡܫܬܒܗܪ[37] ܐܢܬ ܒܐܠܗܐ

Hebrews 12:28 (17)

ܡܛܠ ܗܟܝܠ ܕܩܒܠܢ ܡܠܟܘܬܐ ܕܠܐ ܡܬܙܝܥܐ[38]

---

30. ܐܬܕܟܪ ܕܩܒܠܬ = remember you received.
31. ܠܥܙܪ = Lazarus.
32. Ettaphal from the root ܢܚ, "to rest." This is a hollow verb; note the addition of the *yūd* in the middle of the verb.
33. ܡܫܬܢܩ = tormented.
34. Ettahpal from the root ܝܣܦ, "to add." Note that this form switches the *yūd* to a *waw*, but the ending will remain the same.
35. ܕܡܗܝܡܢܝܢ = those believing.
36. Ettaphal from the root ܢܚ, "to rest." This is a hollow verb; note the addition of the *yūd* in the middle of the verb. Look at the ending of the verb in order to determine the parsing.
37. ܡܫܬܒܗܪ = glorified.
38. Ettaphal from the root word ܙܥ, "to be shaken or troubled." This is a hollow verb; note the addition of the *yūd* in the middle of the verb. Also, this is an interesting case where the first letter of the root (*zayn*) absorbs the second *taw* of the prefix. Look at the ending of the verb in order to determine the parsing.

John 12:32 (18)

ܘܐܢܐ ܡܐ ܕܐܬܬܪܝܡܬ[39] ܡܢ ܐܪܥܐ ܐܓܕ[40] ܟܠܢܫ ܠܘܬܝ.

1 Peter 5:5 (19)

ܡܛܠ ܕܐܠܗܐ ܣܩܘܒܠܐ[41] ܗܘ ܕܐܠܝܢ ܕܡܬܬܪܝܡܝܢ[42] ܘܠܡܟܝܟܐ[43]
ܝܗܒ ܛܝܒܘܬܐ[44]

Hebrews 4:4 (20)

ܐܝܟ ܕܐܡܪ ܥܠ ܫܒܬܐ ܕܐܬܬܢܝܚ[45] ܐܠܗܐ ܒܝܘܡܐ ܫܒܝܥܝܐ[46] ܡܢ
ܥܒܕܘܗܝ ܟܠܗܘܢ

Additional Exercises

Jonah 1:1-4

ܘܗܘܐ ܦܬܓܡܗ[47] ܕܡܪܝܐ ܥܠ ܝܘܢܢ ܒܪ ܡܬܝ ܠܡܐܡܪ v.1

ܩܘܡ[48] ܙܠ[49] ܠܢܝܢܘܐ ܡܕܝܢܬܐ ܪܒܬܐ ܘܐܟܪܙ ܥܠܝܗ ܡܛܠ ܕܣܠܩܬ v.2
ܒܝܫܬܗܘܢ ܩܕܡܝ

ܘܩܡ ܝܘܢܢ ܠܡܥܪܩ ܠܬܪܫܝܫ ܡܢ ܩܕܡ ܡܪܝܐ ܘܢܚܬ ܠܝܘܦܐ ܘܐܫܟܚ v.3

---

39. Ettaphal from the root ܪܡ, "to be lifted up" This is a hollow verb; note the addition of the *yūd* in the middle of the verb. Look at the ending of the verb in order to determine the parsing.
40. ܐܓܕ = I will lead.
41. ܣܩܘܒܠܐ = opposes.
42. Ettaphal from the root ܪܡ, "to be exalted, proud." This is a hollow verb; note the addition of the *yūd* in the middle of the verb. Look at the ending of the verb in order to determine the parsing.
43. ܠܡܟܝܟܐ = humble, lowly.
44. ܛܝܒܘܬܐ = grace.
45. Ettaphel from the hollow verb ܢܚ, "to rest." Note the lack of a double *taw*. This reduction is characteristic of some hollow verbs.
46. ܫܒܝܥܝܐ = seventh.
47. ܦܬܓܡܗ = his word.
48. ܩܘܡ = get up.
49. ܙܠ = go.

ܐܠܦܐ ܕܡܗܠܟܐ[50] ܠܬܪܫܝܫ ܘܝܗܒ ܐܓܪܐ[51] ܘܢܚܬ ܠܗ ܠܡܥܠ[52]

ܥܡܗܘܢ ܠܬܪܫܝܫ ܠܡܥܪܩ ܡܢ ܩܕܡ ܡܪܝܐ

v.4 ܘܡܪܝܐ ܐܪܝܡ[53] ܪܘܚܐ ܪܒܬܐ ܒܝܡܐ ܘܗܘܐ ܡܥܠܘܠܐ[54] ܪܒܐ

[55]ܒܝܡܐ ܘܐܠܦܐ ܡܬܗܦܟܐ[56] ܗܘܬ ܠܡܬܬܒܪܘ

50. ܕܡܗܠܟܐ = that was traveling.
51. ܐܓܪܐ = payment.
52. ܠܡܥܠ = to enter.
53. This is an aphel perfect of ܪܡܐ.
54. ܡܥܠܘܠܐ = storm.
55. ܡܬܗܦܟܐ = it was overturning.
56. ܠܡܬܬܒܪܘ = to break.

17

I-*ālap* Verbs

	Perfect	Participle	Imperfect	Imperative	Infinitive
I-*ālap*	ܐܶܟ݂ܰܠ	ܐܳܟ݂ܶܠ	ܢܶܐܟ݂ܽܘܠ	ܐܶܟ݂ܽܘܠ	ܡܶܐܟ݂ܰܠ
	ekal	*ākel*	*nekul*	*akul*	*mekal*

Introduction to Weak Verbs

The final chapters serve as a brief introduction to the numerous ways that verbs morph according to certain patterns in verbal roots. The student should note, however, that these few chapters by no means cover all of these forms. Every language has numerous irregular verbs which must be learned.[1] Therefore, the following chapters will only cover some basic rules of morphology in irregular verbs.

As one ventures further into the language, and especially when dealing with irregular verbs, two items are important to keep in mind.

1. Remember that many of the rules will follow phonetic patterns because of pronunciation. Ancient languages were birthed in a period of oral/aural culture that tended to follow vocal patterns above concern for word structure. Therefore, one of the most helpful things is to be familiar with the vocalization of the language. Most of the rules that are learned in the following chapters are logical contractions and phonetical emendations when the various verbs are spoken in conjugated form. A proficiency at reading the language is important in order to fully understand why some of the words morph the way that they do.

2. Second, be flexible when dealing with the finer nuances of Syriac. Remember to focus mainly on the consonantal structures and syntax of a word in order to determine its translation. Some students become overly involved with why or why not a certain vowel appears on a verb, regardless of its correct conjugation. These sorts of battles, while useful in truly understanding the language, can be an unnecessary distraction for the student new to the language. Therefore, find a good balance between being inquisitive and flexible.

---

1. An irregular verb is one that doesn't necessarily follow the strict conjugation rules.

Introduction

Verbs that begin with an *ālap* are unique in that the quiescent aspect of the *ālap* requires that it take a vowel. Some of the more frequent I-*ālap* verbs include:

ܐܶܙܰܠ	ܐܶܚܰܕ	ܐܶܟ݂ܰܠ	ܐܶܡܰܪ	ܐܶܬ݂ܳܐ
ezal	*eḥad*	*ekal*	*emar*	*etā*
to go	to take	to eat	to say	*to come*

Often, but not always, I-*ālap* verbs will be regularly formed, just with variations on the vowel that accompanies the *ālap* at the front of the root.

I-*ālap* Peal Perfect

As the above forms indicate, the typical vowel that accompanies the *ālap* in the peal perfect is an *e*-vowel. The verbs are otherwise regularly formed.

	Singular		Plural	
3m	ܐܶܟ݂ܰܠ	*ekal* he ate	ܐܶܟ݂ܰܠܘ ܐܶܟ݂ܰܠܘܢ	*ekal* *ekalun* they ate
3f	ܐܶܟ݂ܠܰܬ݂	*eklat* she ate	ܐܶܟ݂ܰܠ ܐܶܟ݂ܰܠ̈ ܐܶܟ݂ܰܠܶܝܢ	*ekal* *ekal* *ekalēn* they ate
2m	ܐܶܟ݂ܰܠܬ݁	*ekalt* you ate	ܐܶܟ݂ܰܠܬ݁ܘܢ ܐܶܟ݂ܰܠܬ݁ܘܢ	*ekalton* *ekaltun* you ate
2f	ܐܶܟ݂ܰܠܬ݁ܝ	*ekalt* you ate	ܐܶܟ݂ܰܠ̈ܬ݁ܶܝܢ	*ekaltēn* you ate
1c	ܐܶܟ݂ܠܶܬ݂	*eklet* I ate	ܐܶܟ݂ܰܠܢ ܐܶܟ݂ܰܠܢܰܢ	*ekaln* *ekalnān* we ate

I-*ālap* Peal Imperfect

The vowel that appears with the *ālap* in the peal imperfect is dependent on which stem vowel the root takes when it is conjugated. If the imperfect form takes an *o*/*u*-vowel, which adds a *waw* to the word, then the *ālap* takes an *e*-vowel. Consider the paradigm of ܐܶܟ݂ܰܠ (*ekal*, "to eat").

	Singular		Plural	
3m	ܢܐܟܘܠ ܢܐܟܘܠ	*nekol* *nekul* he will eat	ܢܐܟܠܘܢ	*neklun* they will eat
3f	ܬܐܟܘܠ ܬܐܟܘܠ	*tekol* *tekul* she will eat	ܢܐܟܠܢ	*neklān* they will eat
2m	ܬܐܟܘܠ ܬܐܟܘܠ	*tekol* *tekul* you will eat	ܬܐܟܠܘܢ	*teklun* you will eat
2f	ܬܐܟܠܝܢ	*teklin* you will eat	ܬܐܟܠܢ	*teklān* you will eat
1c	ܐܟܘܠ ܐܟܘܠ	*ekol* *ekul* I will eat	ܢܐܟܘܠ ܢܐܟܘܠ	*nekol* *nekul* we will eat

Likewise, if the imperfect is formed with an *a*-vowel then the paradigm does not include a *waw* and the vowel that is paired with the *ālap* is an *i*. Notice the conjugations of ܐܡܪ (*emar*, “to say/speak”) below.

	Singular		Plural	
3m	ܢܐܡܪ	*nimar* he will say	ܢܐܡܪܘܢ	*nimrun* they will say
3f	ܬܐܡܪ	*timar* she will say	ܢܐܡܪܢ	*nimrān* they will say
2m	ܬܐܡܪ	*timar* you will say	ܬܐܡܪܘܢ	*timrun* you will say
2f	ܬܐܡܪܝܢ	*timrin* you will say	ܬܐܡܪܢ	*timrān* you will say
1c	ܐܡܪ	*imar* I will say	ܢܐܡܪ	*nimar* we will say

Notice that in each paradigm the 1cs form does not double the *ālap* as we might anticipate in a strong verb. Rather, the two *ālap*’s are assimilated.

I-*ālap* Peal Imperative

Since the imperative form removes the suffix of the imperfect, there are two different forms that the imperative can take: either an *e*-vowel with the *o/u* forms or an *i*-vowel with the *a* forms.

o/u-class

	Singular	Plural I	Plural II
Masculine	ܐܶܟܘܿܠ ܐܶܟܘܼܠ *akol* *akul* Eat!	ܐܶܟܘܿܠܘ ܐܶܟܘܼܠܘ *akol* *akul* Eat!	ܐܶܟܘܿܠܘܢ ܐܶܟܘܼܠܘܢ *akolun* *akulun* Eat!
Feminine	ܐܶܟܘܿܠܝ ܐܶܟܘܼܠܝ *akol* *akul* Eat!	ܐܶܟ̈ܘܿܠܝ ܐܶܟ̈ܘܼܠܝ *akol* *akul* Eat!	ܐܶܟ̈ܘܿܠܶܝܢ ܐܶܟ̈ܘܼܠܶܝܢ *akolēn* *akulēn* Eat!

a-class

	Singular	Plural I	Plural II
Masculine	ܐܶܡܰܪ ܐ̱ܡܰܪ *emar* *mar* Speak!	ܐܶܡܰܪܘ ܐ̱ܡܰܪܘ *emar* *mar* Speak!	ܐܶܡܰܪܘܢ ܐ̱ܡܰܪܘܢ *emarun* *marun* Speak!
Feminine	ܐܶܡܰܪܝ ܐ̱ܡܰܪܝ *emar* *mar* Speak!	ܐܶܡ̈ܰܪܝ ܐ̱ܡ̈ܰܪܝ emar *mar* Speak!	ܐܶܡ̈ܰܪܶܝܢ ܐ̱ܡ̈ܰܪܶܝܢ *emarēn* *marēn* Speak!

Note in the *a*-vowel form of the imperative that sometimes the *ālap* will be written with a *linea occultans* and no vowel. This provides distinction from the peal perfect form.

I-*ālap* Peal Infinitive

As with the imperfect and imperative, the vowel that is associated with the *ālap* will vary depending on the verb that is being used. Note that each of the forms below receive an *a*-stem vowel and therefore the *o*/*u*-class doesn't take the additional *waw*. The only difference between the two is that the *o*/*u* verbs take an *e*-vowel, and the *a* verbs take an *i* above the *mīm*.

o/*u*-vowel	*a*-vowel
ܡܶܐܟܰܠ	ܡܺܐܡܰܪ
mekal	*mimar*
to eat	to speak

I-*ālap* Peal Participle

Active

The participles are formed in a fairly regular manner, with a few exceptions. The distinction between the *o*/*u* verbs and the *a*-vowel verbs can be seen with a change in the stem vowel of the ms participle: an *e*-vowel for the *o*/*u* verbs and an *a*-vowel for the *a* verbs.

o/*u*-class

Masculine		Feminine	
Singular	Plural	Singular	Plural
ܐܳܟܶܠ	ܐܳܟܠܺܝܢ	ܐܳܟܠܳܐ	ܐܳܟܠ̈ܳܢ
ākel	*āklin*	*āklā*	*āklān*

a-class

Masculine		Feminine	
Singular	Plural	Singular	Plural
ܐܳܡܰܪ	ܐܳܡܪ̈ܺܝܢ	ܐܳܡܪܳܐ	ܐܳܡܪ̈ܳܢ
āmar	*āmrin*	*āmrā*	*āmrān*

Passive

All passive participles take an *a*-vowel over the initial *ālap*. For the passive forms, there is no distinction between the *o/u*-class verbs and the *a*-class verbs. Besides the addition of the vowel over the *ālap*, these are regularly formed.

Masculine		Feminine	
Singular	Plural	Singular	Plural
ܐܟܝܠ	ܐܟܝܠܝܢ	ܐܟܝܠܐ	ܐܟܝܠܢ
akil	*akilin*	*akilā*	*akilān*

Introduction to Derived Stems

For the derived stems, the only real significant change is apparent in the aphel and ettaphal stems. Here, the *ālap* is replaced with a *waw*. The one exception to this is the verb ܐܬܐ ("to come"). This verb takes a *yûd* instead of a *waw* in the aphel and ettaphal stems. For example, note: ܐܝܬܝ (aphel perfect 3ms) in Acts 14:13.

I- *ālap* Aphel (A)

ܐܘܟܠ	ܢܘܟܠ	ܐܘܟܠ	ܡܘܟܠܘ	ܡܘܟܠ	ܡܘܟܠ
awkel	*nawkel*	*awkel*	*mawkel*	*mawkālu*	*mawkal*
Perfect	Imperfect	Imperative	Infinitive	Active Participle	Passive Participle

I- *ālap* Ettaphal (Ap)

ܐܬܬܘܟܠ	ܢܬܬܘܟܠ	ܐܬܬܘܟܠ	ܡܬܬܘܟܠܘ	ܡܬܬܘܟܠ
ettawkal	*nettawkal*	*ettawkal*	*mettawkālu*	*mettawkal*
Perfect	Imperfect	Imperative	Infinitive	Participle

Vocabulary and Exercises

Since this chapter marks the transition into the weak verbs, we will deviate from the usual vocabulary and homework exercises to give a chance to review the previous material and vocabulary.

18

III-Weak

	Perfect	Participle	Imperfect	Imperative	Infinitive
III-Weak	ܒܢܵܐ	ܒܵܢܹܐ	ܢܸܒܢܹܐ	ܒܢܝ	ܡܸܒܢܵܐ
	bnā	*bāne*	*nebne*	*bni*	*mebnā*

Introduction

III-weak verbs are those whose third consonant is weak. Some of the more popular III-weak verbs include:

ܐܸܬܵܐ	ܒܢܵܐ	ܒܥܵܐ	ܚܕܝ	ܚܙܵܐ	ܩܪܵܐ	ܨܒܵܐ
eta	*bnā*	*b'ā*	*ḥdi*	*ḥzā*	*qrā*	*sbā*
to come	to build	to seek	to rejoice	to see	to call	to want

Note that even if the final verb is an *ālap*, the root of the verb is actually a *yūd*, as the *ālap* takes the place of the *yūd* in parsing. Therefore, the above list should technically have all *yūd*s as the final consonant. However, most lexicons show the root with the *ālap* (with the exception of ܚܕܝ, however this can also sometimes appear as ܚܕܐ). It is for this reason that many of the paradigms below will often alternate between *ālap* and *yūd*.

III-Weak Peal Perfect

First Paradigm

III-weak verbs have two forms in the peal perfect and are fairly typical in how they are formed. The first paradigm is the most typical of the III-weak verbs and is represented by the root *bnā*, "to build." The major differences in the III-weak peal perfect conjugation are in how the III-weak consonant presents itself. Notice how the *ālap* is present only in the 3ms form, as well as occasionally in the 3mp form. Other than this, the *ālap* will disappear (as is the case with the 3fs) or will turn into a *yūd*, as is the case with the majority of the other forms. Also, note the shortening of the *a*-vowel after the 3ms and 3fs forms.

	Singular		Plural	
3m	ܒܢܐ	*bnā* he/it built	ܒܢܘ ܒܢܐܘܢ	*bnaw* *bnaun* they built
3f	ܒܢܬ	*bnāt* she/it built	ܒܢܝ ܒܢܝ̈ܢ	*bnay* *bnayēn* they built
2m	ܒܢܝܬ	*bnayt* you built	ܒܢܝܬܘܢ ܒܢܝܬܘܢ	*bnayton* *bnaytun* you built
2f	ܒܢܝܬܝ	*bnayt* you built	ܒܢܝܬܝܢ	*bnaytēn* you built
1c	ܒܢܝܬ	*bnit* I built	ܒܢܝܢ ܒܢܝܢܢ	*bnayn* *bnaynan* we built

Second Paradigm

The second paradigm is similar, but in this case the *yūd* is present throughout the entire paradigm in place of the *ālap*. Along with this change, the stem vowel is altered to an *i*. The root in the following paradigm is ܚܕܝ (*ḥdi*), "to rejoice."

As far as the verb endings, each of them is regularly formed according to typical peal perfect conjugations. One important element to point out is the subtle difference between the 2ms and 1cs forms (just the softening of the final consonant). These two can otherwise be very hard to distinguish from one another.

	Singular		Plural	
3m	ܚܕܝ	*ḥdi* he/it rejoiced	ܚܕܝܘ ܚܕܝܘܢ	*ḥdi* *ḥdiun* they rejoiced
3f	ܚܕܝܬ	*ḥedyat* she/it rejoiced	ܚܕܝ̈ ܚܕܝܢ	*ḥdi* *ḥdiēn* they rejoiced
2m	ܚܕܝܬ	*ḥdit* you rejoiced	ܚܕܝܬܘܢ ܚܕܝܬܘܢ	*ḥditon* *ḥditun* you rejoiced
2f	ܚܕܝܬܝ	*ḥdit* you rejoiced	ܚܕܝܬܝܢ	*ḥditēn* you rejoiced
1c	ܚܕܝܬ	*ḥdit* I rejoiced	ܚܕܝܢ ܚܕܝܢܢ	*ḥdin* *ḥdinan* we rejoiced

III-Weak Peal Imperfect

The peal imperfect of the III-weak verbs all follow a single paradigm (as opposed to two in the perfect). Note how the feminine singular and plural are very similar.

	Singular		Plural	
3m	ܢܶܒܢܶܐ	*nebne* he/it will build	ܢܶܒܢܘܿܢ ܢܶܒܢܽܘܢ	*nebnon* *nebnun* they will build
3f	ܬܶܒܢܶܐ	*tebne* she/it will build	ܢܶܒܢܝܳܢ	*nebnyān* they will build
2m	ܬܶܒܢܶܐ	*tebne* you will build	ܬܶܒܢܘܿܢ ܬܶܒܢܽܘܢ	*tebnon* *tebnun* you will build
2f	ܬܶܒܢܶܝܢ	*tebnēn* you will build	ܬܶܒܢܝܳܢ	*tebnyān* you will build
1c	ܐܶܒܢܶܐ	*ebne* I will build	ܢܶܒܢܶܐ	*nebne* we will build

III-Weak Peal Imperative

There are two things to note in regards to the III-weak peal imperative paradigm: (1) the masculine singular, feminine singular, and feminine plural forms lose the weak *ālap* in favor of a *yūd* with various vowels. (2) The masculine plural form also loses the *ālap*, but it is not replaced with anything. Instead, it just has the common ending. Additionally, if there is no vowel pointing provided, then the feminine singular and the feminine plural are identical. In these cases, a *seyame* will be used to make the distinction.

	Singular	Plural I	Plural II
Masculine	ܒܢܺܝ *bni* Build!	ܒܢܰܘ *bnaw* Build!	ܒܢܰܝܽܘܢ *bnayun* Build!
Feminine	ܒܢܳܝ *bnāy* Build!	ܒܢܳܝ̈ bnāy Build!	ܒܢܳܝ̈ܶܢ *bnāyēn* Build!

III-Weak Peal Infinitive

The III-weak peal infinitive is formed as we might expect, with the *mīm* prefix and the *ālap* present at the end of the form. In these cases, the root is obvious to ascertain.

ܡܶܒܢܳܐ
mebnā
to build

III-Weak Peal Participles

The tricky part about identifying participles in the III-weak category is that the active and the passive are so similar. When translating, be sure to look for the initial vowel on the first consonant as a hint that points towards the active or passive nature of the participle. If it is a long *a*-class vowel, then it is an active participle; if not, then it is passive.

The masculine singular form is fairly easy to identify because the *ālap* remains. Outside of this form, the *ālap* is replaced with a *yūd*. Since this is one of the ways that is commonly used to distinguish a passive participle from an active participle, this distinction can be somewhat difficult without vowel pointing.

Active

Masculine		Feminine	
Singular	Plural	Singular	Plural
ܒܳܢܶܐ	ܒܳܢܶܝܢ	ܒܳܢܝܳܐ	ܒܳܢܝܳܢ
bāne	*bānēn*	*bānyā*	*bānyān*
building	building	building	building

Passive

Masculine		Feminine	
Singular	Plural	Singular	Plural
ܒܢܶܐ	ܒܢܶܝܢ	ܒܰܢܝܳܐ	ܒܰܢܝܳܢ
bne	*bnēn*	*banyā*	*banyān*
being built	being built	being built	being built

III-Weak Verbs and Pronominal Suffixes

Like with the nominal endings, when an object suffix is attached to the ending of a III-weak verb, the *ālap* will disappear and the connecting vowel will be transferred to the middle consonant. Note how the *ālap* disappears in the following examples:

ܩܪܐ (*qrā*, "to call")

ܩܪܳܝܗ̱ܝ

qrāy

peal perfect 3ms + 3ms suffix

he called him

Translation: He called him.

Matthew 18:32

ܡܚܐ (*mḥā*, "to hit, strike")

ܡܚܳܟ	ܡܰܢܘ
mḥāk	*manu*
peal perfect 3ms + 2ms suffix	pronoun + 3ms contraction
he hit you	who is it

Translation: Who hit you?

Luke 22:63

However, if the conjugation has a *waw* at the end (as in the peal perfect 3mp), the *ālap* does disappear. Note Psalm 77:17:

ܘܕܚܶܠܘ	ܡܰܝ̈ܳܐ	ܚܙܰܐܘܟ	ܐܰܠܳܗܳܐ	ܡܰܝ̈ܳܐ	ܚܙܰܐܘܟ
wa-dḥel	*mayyā*	*ḥzauk*	*alāhā*	*mayyā*	*ḥzauk*
waw + peal perfect 3mp	noun mp emphatic	peal perfect 3mp + 2ms suffix	noun: ms emphatic	noun:mp emphatic	peal perfect 3mp + 2ms suffix
and they were afraid	the waters	they saw you	God	the waters	they saw you

Translation:
The waters saw you, God.
The waters saw you and were afraid.

Introduction to Derived Stems

For the purpose of this general introduction, the stems outside of the peal stem will only be briefly reviewed. These sections are treated as additional information and resources for translation. Therefore, they are broad strokes of the different paradigms, and the student should observe major thematic tendencies over nuances. This same pattern will be followed in the ensuing chapters on weak verbs. This is not to downplay the importance of knowing how each weak verb operates outside of the peal stem but rather is an effort to not overwhelm students with paradigm after paradigm (some might think it is too late for that!). The following charts, along with the exercises in the homework, provide a good introduction to how the verbs are altered in each of the derived stems.

In the following paradigms, note the presence or absence of the *ālap*. For example, in the perfect the final consonant is a *yūd*, and in the imperfect it is an *ālap*. Keep in mind that sometimes the III-weak verbs, if their ending is an *ālap*, will have the tendency to switch between an *ālap* and a *yūd*. This is again in relation to the fact that the root of most III-weak verbs have *yūd* endings, and the *ālap* takes the place of the *yūd*. For example, the imperative conjugation will go from an *ālap* in the masculine singular to a *yūd* in the other forms (mp, fs, and fp). Keep in mind the typical rules of the conjugations in order to correctly parse certain verbs.

The general pattern with III-weak verbs is that the form will have a *yūd* in the perfect, infinitive, and passive participle, and switch to an *ālap* in the imperfect, imperative, and active participle. Note the patterns in the following paradigms.

III-Weak Pael (D)

ܒܰܢܺܝ	ܢܒܰܢܶܐ	ܒܰܢܳܐ	ܡܒܰܢܳܝܽܘ	ܡܒܰܢܶܐ	ܡܒܰܢܰܝ
banni	*nbanne*	*bannā*	*mbannāyu*	*mbanne*	*mbannay*
Perfect	Imperfect	Imperative	Infinitive	Active Participle	Passive Participle

III-Weak Aphel (A)

ܐܰܒܢܺܝ	ܢܰܒܢܶܐ	ܐܰܒܢܳܐ	ܡܰܒܢܳܝܽܘ	ܡܰܒܢܶܐ	ܡܰܒܢܰܝ
abni	*nabne*	*abnā*	*mabnāyu*	*mabne*	*mabnay*
Perfect	Imperfect	Imperative	Infinitive	Active Participle	Passive Participle

III-Weak Ethpeel (Gp)

ܐܬܒܢܝ	ܢܬܒܢܐ	ܐܬܒܢܝ	ܡܬܒܢܝܘ	ܡܬܒܢܐ
etbni	*netbne*	*etbnay*	*metbnāyu*	*metbne*
Perfect	Imperfect	Imperative	Infinitive	Participle

III-Weak Ethpaal (Dp)

ܐܬܒܢܝ	ܢܬܒܢܐ	ܐܬܒܢܐ	ܡܬܒܢܝܘ	ܡܬܒܢܐ
etbanni	*netbanne*	*etbannā*	*metbannāyu*	*metbanne*
Perfect	Imperfect	Imperative	Infinitive	Participle

III-Weak Ettaphal (Ap)

ܐܬܬܒܢܝ	ܢܬܬܒܢܐ	ܐܬܬܒܢܐ	ܡܬܬܒܢܝܘ	ܡܬܬܒܢܐ
ettabni	*nettabne*	*ettabnā*	*mettabnāyu*	*mettabne*
Perfect	Imperfect	Imperative	Infinitive	Participle

Vocabulary
Nouns

ܐܓܪܐ	*agrā*	payment, reward
ܐܘܢܓܠܝܘܢ	*ewangeliyān*	Gospel (Gk. εὐαγγέλιον)
ܐܝܡܡܐ	*imāmā*	daytime
ܕܝܘܐ	*daywā*	demon, devil
ܕܝܬܩܐ	*diatāqā*	covenant (Gk. διαθήκη)
ܚܘܪܒܐ	*ḥurbā*	wilderness, desolation
ܡܣܝܒܪܢܘܬܐ	*msaybrānutā*	endurance, patience
ܡܥܡܘܕܝܬܐ	*maʿmuditā*	baptism, washing, pool
ܩܘܪܒܢܐ	*qurbānā*	gift, offering
ܩܘܫܬܐ	*quštā*	truth

Verbs

ܓܕܰܦ	*gdap*	to blaspheme, revile
ܕܟܰܪ	*dkar*	to remember
ܕܡܶܟ	*dmek*	to sleep
ܙܟܳܐ	*zkā*	to conquer, overcome
ܚܰܫ	*ḥaš*	to suffer, feel
ܝܡܳܐ	*imā*	to swear (oath)
ܝܨܶܦ	*iṣep*	to be anxious, careful
ܝܩܶܕ	*iqed*	to burn
ܟܣܳܐ	*ksā*	to hide, conceal, clothe, cover
ܥܶܗܰܕ	*ʿehad*	to remember
ܦܣܰܩ	*psaq*	to cut off, break
ܪܒܳܐ	*rbā*	to grow, increase
ܪܕܰܦ	*rdap*	to follow, persecute
ܫܢܳܐ	*šnā*	to depart, be mad
ܫܦܰܪ	*špar*	to seem good, please
ܫܰܪ	*šar*	to be strong

Other

ܐܰܝܡܶܟܳܐ	*aymekā*	hence, therefore
ܥܰܕ	*ʿad*	until, up to, while
ܥܶܕܰܟܺܝܠ	*ʿedakil*	still, yet
ܫܬܳܐ	*štā*	six

Exercises

Matthew 2:15 (1)

ܘܰܗܘܳܐ ܬܰܡܳܢ ܥܕܰܡܳܐ ܠܡܰܘܬܶܗ ܕܗܶܪܳܘܕܶܣ ܕܢܶܬܡܰܠܶܐ ܡܶܕܶܡ ܕܶܐܬܶܐܡܰܪ ܡܶܢ

ܡܳܪܝܳܐ ܒܝܰܕ ܢܒܺܝܳܐ ܕܰܐܡܰܪ ܡܶܢ ܡܨܪܶܝܢ[1] ܩܪܺܝܬ ܠܒܶܪܝ.

1. ܡܨܪܶܝܢ = Egypt.

Matthew 23:37–39 (2)

ܐܘܪܫܠܡ ܐܘܪܫܠܡ ܩܛܠܬ[2] ܢܒܝܐ ܘܪܓܡܬ[3] ܠܐܝܠܝܢ ܕܫܠܝܚܝܢ ܠܘܬܗ
ܟܡܐ ܙܒܢܝܢ ܨܒܝܬ ܕܐܟܢܫ ܒܢܝܟܝ ܐܝܟ ܕܟܢܫܐ ܬܪܢܓܘܠܬܐ[4]
ܦܪܘܓܝܗ[5] ܬܚܝܬ ܓܦܝܗ[6] ܘܠܐ ܨܒܝܬܘܢ ܗܐ ܡܫܬܒܩ ܠܟܘܢ
ܒܝܬܟܘܢ ܚܪܒܐ ܐܡܪܢܐ[7] ܠܟܘܢ ܓܝܪ ܕܠܐ ܬܚܙܘܢܢܝ[8] ܡܢ ܗܫܐ
ܥܕܡܐ ܕܬܐܡܪܘܢ ܒܪܝܟ ܗܘ ܕܐܬܐ ܒܫܡܗ ܕܡܪܝܐ

Matthew 24:33–37 (3)

ܗܟܢܐ ܐܦ ܐܢܬܘܢ ܡܐ ܕܚܙܝܬܘܢ ܗܠܝܢ ܟܠܗܝܢ ܕܥܘ[9] ܕܡܛܬ[10] ܠܗ
ܠܬܪܥܐ ܐܡܝܢ ܐܡܪ ܐܢܐ ܠܟܘܢ ܕܠܐ ܬܥܒܪ ܫܪܒܬܐ ܗܕܐ ܥܕܡܐ
ܕܗܠܝܢ ܟܠܗܝܢ ܢܗܘܝܢ ܫܡܝܐ ܘܐܪܥܐ ܢܥܒܪܘܢ ܘܡܠܝ[11] ܠܐ ܢܥܒܪܢ ܥܠ
ܝܘܡܐ ܕܝܢ ܗܘ ܘܥܠ ܫܥܬܐ ܗܝ ܐܢܫ ܠܐ ܝܕܥ ܐܦܠܐ[12] ܡܠܐܟܐ
ܕܫܡܝܐ ܐܠܐ ܐܒܐ ܒܠܚܘܕ ܐܝܟܢܐ ܕܝܢ ܕܒܝܘܡܝ ܢܘܚ[13] ܗܟܢܐ ܬܗܘܐ
ܡܐܬܝܬܗ ܕܒܪܗ ܕܐܢܫܐ

---

2. This is a contraction: "killing."
3. ܪܓܡܬ = stoned.
4. ܬܪܢܓܘܠܬܐ = hen.
5. ܦܪܘܓܝܗ = her chicks.
6. ܓܦܝܗ = her wings.
7. This is a participle with a pronominal suffix: peal active ms + 1cp.
8. This is a verb with a pronominal suffix: peal imperfect 2mp + 1cs.
9. The is the imperative of the verb ܝܕܥ.
10. ܕܡܛܬ = that he arrived.
11. The *taw* drops out here from ܡܠܬܐ.
12. ܐܦܠܐ = not even
13. ܢܘܚ = Noah.

Matthew 8:11 (4)

ܐܡܪ ܐܢܐ ܠܟܘܢ ܕܣܓܝܐܐ ܢܐܬܘܢ[14] ܡܢ ܡܕܢܚܐ[15] ܘܡܢ
ܡܥܪܒܐ[16] ܘܢܣܬܡܟܘܢ ܥܡ ܐܒܪܗܡ ܘܐܝܣܚܩ ܘܝܥܩܘܒ ܒܡܠܟܘܬܐ
ܕܫܡܝܐ

John 1:38–39 (5)

ܘܐܬܦܢܝ ܝܫܘܥ ܘܚܙܐ ܐܢܘܢ ܕܐܬܝܢ ܒܬܪܗ ܘܐܡܪ ܠܗܘܢ ܡܢܐ ܒܥܝܢ
ܐܢܬܘܢ ܐܡܪܝܢ ܠܗ ܪܒܢ ܐܝܟܐ ܗܘ ܐܝܬܝܟ ܐܡܪ ܠܗܘܢ ܬܘ[17] ܘܬܚܙܘܢ
ܗܢܘܢ ܕܝܢ ܐܬܘ ܘܚܙܘ ܐܝܟܐ ܕܗܘܐ ܘܠܘܬܗ ܗܘܘ ܝܘܡܐ ܗܘ

Matthew 16:21–23 (6)

ܡܢ ܗܝܕܝܢ ܫܪܝ ܝܫܘܥ ܠܡܚܘܝܘ ܠܬܠܡܝܕܘܗܝ ܕܥܬܝܕ ܗܘ ܕܢܐܙܠ[18]
ܠܐܘܪܫܠܡ ܘܣܓܝ ܢܚܫ[19] ܡܢ ܩܫܝܫܐ ܘܡܢ ܪܒܝ ܟܗܢܐ ܘܣܦܪܐ
ܘܢܬܩܛܠ ܘܠܝܘܡܐ ܕܬܠܬܐ ܢܩܘܡ[20] ܘܕܒܪܗ[21] ܟܐܦܐ ܘܫܪܝ ܠܡܟܐܐ[22]
ܒܗ ܘܐܡܪ ܚܣ[23] ܠܟ ܡܪܝ ܕܬܗܘܐ ܠܟ ܗܕܐ ܗܘ ܕܝܢ ܐܬܦܢܝ
ܘܐܡܪ ܠܟܐܦܐ ܙܠ[24] ܠܟ ܠܒܣܬܪܝ[25] ܣܛܢܐ ܬܘܩܠܬܐ[26] ܐܢܬ ܠܝ ܕܠܐ
ܡܬܪܥܐ ܐܢܬ ܕܐܠܗܐ ܐܠܐ ܕܒܢܝ ܐܢܫܐ

---

14. Note the vowel that appears over the *ālap* in this I-*ālap* verb.
15. ܡܕܢܚܐ = east.
16. ܡܥܪܒܐ = west (setting of the sun).
17. ܬܘ = come!
18. Since this is also a I-*ālap* verb, note the vowel that appears over the *ālap*.
19. ܢܚܫ = suffer.
20. ܢܩܘܡ = he would rise.
21. This is a verb with a pronominal suffix: peal perfect 3ms + 3ms.
22. ܠܡܟܐܐ = to rebuke.
23. ܚܣ = God forbid!
24. ܙܠ = go!
25. ܠܒܣܬܪܝ = behind me.
26. ܬܘܩܠܬܐ = stumbling block, offense.

Matthew 5:43–48 (7)

ܫܡܥܬܘܢ ܕܐܬܐܡܪ ܕܬܪܚܡ ܠܩܪܝܒܟ ܘܬܣܢ ܠܒܥܠܕܒܒܟ ܐܢܐ ܕܝܢ
ܐܡܪ ܐܢܐ ܠܟܘܢ ܐܚܒܘ[27] ܠܒܥܠܕܒܒܝܟܘܢ ܘܒܪܟܘ ܠܡܢ ܕܠܐܛ[28]
ܠܟܘܢ ܘܥܒܕܘ ܕܫܦܝܪ ܠܡܢ ܕܣܢܐ[29] ܠܟܘܢ ܘܨܠܘ ܥܠ ܐܝܠܝܢ ܕܕܒܪܝܢ
ܠܟܘܢ ܒܩܛܝܪܐ[30] ܘܪܕܦܝܢ ܠܟܘܢ ܐܝܟ ܕܬܗܘܘܢ ܒܢܘܗܝ ܕܐܒܘܟܘܢ
ܕܒܫܡܝܐ ܗܘ ܕܡܕܢܚ[31] ܫܡܫܗ ܥܠ ܛܒܐ ܘܥܠ ܒܝܫܐ ܘܡܚܬ ܡܛܪܗ[32]
ܥܠ ܟܐܢܐ ܘܥܠ ܥܘܠܐ ܐܢ ܓܝܪ ܪܚܡܝܢ[33] ܐܢܬܘܢ ܠܐܝܠܝܢ ܕܪܚܡܝܢ
ܠܟܘܢ ܡܢܘ ܐܓܪܐ ܐܝܬ ܠܟܘܢ ܠܐ ܗܐ ܐܦ ܡܟܣܐ[34] ܗܝ ܗܕܐ
ܥܒܕܝܢ ܘܐܢ ܫܐܠܝܢ ܐܢܬܘܢ ܒܫܠܡܐ ܕܐܚܝܟܘܢ ܒܠܚܘܕ ܡܢܐ ܝܬܝܪ
ܥܒܕܝܢ ܐܢܬܘܢ ܠܐ ܗܐ ܐܦ ܡܟܣܐ ܗܝ ܗܕܐ ܥܒܕܝܢ ܗܘܘ ܗܟܝܠ
ܐܢܬܘܢ ܓܡܝܪܐ[35] ܐܝܟܢܐ ܕܐܒܘܟܘܢ ܕܒܫܡܝܐ ܓܡܝܪ[36] ܗܘ

Mark 15:31–34 (8)

ܘܗܟܢܐ ܐܦ ܪܒܝ ܟܗܢܐ ܓܚܟܝܢ[37] ܗܘܘ ܚܕ ܥܡ ܚܕ ܘܣܦܪܐ
ܘܐܡܪܝܢ ܠܐܚܪܢܐ ܐܚܝ ܢܦܫܗ ܠܐ ܡܫܟܚ[38] ܠܡܚܝܘ ܡܫܝܚܐ ܡܠܟܗ

27. ܐܚܒܘ = love. This is an aphel imperative of a geminate verb (the final two consonants are identical).
28. ܕܠܐܛ = that is cursing.
29. ܣܢܐ = enemy.
30. ܩܛܝܪܐ = violence.
31. ܡܕܢܚ = causes to rise.
32. ܡܚܬ ܡܛܪܗ = causes his rain to descend.
33. ܪܚܡܝܢ = loving (x2).
34. ܡܟܣܐ = tax collectors (x2).
35. ܓܡܝܪܐ = perfect.
36. ܓܡܝܪ = is being (perfect).
37. ܓܚܟܝܢ = laughing.
38. This is a peal participle.

ܕܐܝܣܪܝܠ ܢܚܘܬ ܗܫܐ ܡܢ ܙܩܝܦܐ[39] ܕܢܚܙܐ ܘܢܗܝܡܢ[40] ܒܗ ܘܐܦ

ܗܢܘܢ ܕܐܙܕܩܦܘ ܗܘܘ ܥܡܗ ܡܚܣܕܝܢ[41] ܗܘܘ ܠܗ ܘܡܢ ܗܝ

ܫܬ[42] ܫܥܝܢ ܗܘܐ ܚܫܘܟܐ[43] ܥܠ ܟܠܗ ܐܪܥܐ ܥܕܡܐ ܠܫܥܐ ܬܫܥ[44]

ܘܒܬܫܥ ܫܥܝܢ ܩܥܐ ܝܫܘܥ ܒܩܠܐ ܪܡܐ ܘܐܡܪ ܐܝܠ ܐܝܠ ܠܡܢܐ

ܫܒܩܬܢܝ[45] ܕܐܝܬܘܗܝ ܐܠܗܝ ܐܠܗܝ ܠܡܢܐ ܫܒܩܬܢܝ

Matthew 12:38–40 (9)

ܗܝܕܝܢ ܥܢܘ ܐܢܫܐ ܡܢ ܣܦܪܐ ܘܡܢ ܦܪܝܫܐ ܘܐܡܪܝܢ ܠܗ ܡܠܦܢܐ

ܨܒܝܢ ܚܢܢ ܕܢܚܙܐ ܡܢܟ ܐܬܐ ܗܘ ܕܝܢ ܥܢܐ ܘܐܡܪ ܠܗܘܢ ܫܪܒܬܐ

ܒܝܫܬܐ ܘܓܝܘܪܬܐ[46] ܐܬܐ ܒܥܝܐ ܘܐܬܐ ܠܐ ܬܬܝܗܒ[47] ܠܗ ܐܠܐ

ܐܬܗ ܕܝܘܢܢ ܢܒܝܐ ܐܝܟܢܐ ܓܝܪ ܕܗܘܐ ܝܘܢܢ ܒܟܪܣܗ ܕܢܘܢܐ[48]

ܬܠܬܐ ܝܘܡܝܢ ܘܬܠܬܐ ܠܠܘܢ ܗܟܢܐ ܢܗܘܐ ܒܪܗ ܕܐܢܫܐ ܒܠܒܗ

ܕܐܪܥܐ ܬܠܬܐ ܐܝܡܡܝܢ[49] ܘܬܠܬܐ ܠܠܘܢ[50]

---

39. ܙܩܝܦܐ = the cross.
40. ܘܢܗܝܡܢ = and we will believe.
41. ܡܚܣܕܝܢ = mocking.
42. ܫܬ = sixth.
43. ܚܫܘܟܐ = dark.
44. ܬܫܥ = ninth (x2).
45. This is a verb with a pronominal suffix (x2): peal perfect 2ms + 1cs.
46. ܓܝܘܪܬܐ = adulterous.
47 Note the addition of the *i*-vowel in this I-*yūd* verb.
48. ܒܟܪܣܗ ܕܢܘܢܐ = in the belly of the fish.
49. ܐܝܡܡܝܢ = daytimes.
50. ܠܠܘܢ = nighttimes.

ܐܦ ܐܢܐ ܐܡܪ ܐܢܐ ܠܟ ܕܐܢܬ ܗܘ ܟܐܦܐ ܘܥܠ ܗܕܐ ܟܐܦܐ
ܐܒܢܝܗ̇[51] ܠܥܕܬܝ ܘܬܪܥܐ ܕܫܝܘܠ[52] ܠܐ ܢܚܣܢܘܢܗ̇[53] ܠܟ ܐܬܠ[54] ܩܠܝܕܐ[55]
ܕܡܠܟܘܬܐ ܕܫܡܝܐ ܘܟܠ ܡܕܡ ܕܬܐܣܘܪ ܒܐܪܥܐ ܢܗܘܐ ܐܣܝܪ
ܒܫܡܝܐ ܘܡܕܡ ܕܬܫܪܐ ܒܐܪܥܐ ܢܗܘܐ ܫܪܐ ܒܫܡܝܐ ܗܝܕܝܢ ܦܩܕ
ܠܬܠܡܝܕܘܗܝ ܕܠܐܢܫ ܠܐ ܢܐܡܪܘܢ ܕܗܘܝܘ[56] ܡܫܝܚܐ

Additional Exercises

Genesis 11:5-8

v.5 ܘܢܚܬ ܡܪܝܐ ܠܡܚܙܐ ܩܪܝܬܐ ܘܡܓܕܠܐ ܕܒܢܝܢ ܒܢܝܢܫܐ

v.6 ܘܐܡܪ ܡܪܝܐ ܗܐ ܥܡܐ ܚܕ ܘܠܫܢܐ ܚܕ ܠܟܠܗܘܢ ܘܗܢܐ ܐܬܚܫܒܘ
ܠܡܥܒܕ ܡܟܝܠ ܠܐ ܢܬܒܨܪ[57] ܡܢܗܘܢ ܟܠܡܕܡ ܕܐܬܚܫܒܘ ܠܡܥܒܕ

v.7 ܬܘ[58] ܢܚܘܬ ܘܢܦܠܓ ܬܡܢ ܠܫܢܐ ܕܠܐ ܢܫܡܥܘܢ ܚܕ ܠܫܢ ܚܒܪܗ[59]

v.8 ܘܒܕܪ[60] ܐܢܘܢ ܡܪܝܐ ܡܢ ܬܡܢ ܥܠ ܐܦܝ ܟܠܗ̇ ܐܪܥܐ ܘܦܫܘ[61] ܡܢ
ܕܠܡܒܢܐ ܩܪܝܬܐ

51. This is a verb with a pronominal suffix: peal imperfect 1cs + 3fs.
52. ܫܝܘܠ = Sheol.
53. ܢܚܣܢܘܢܗ̇ = prevail [against] it.
54. ܐܬܠ = I give.
55. ܩܠܝܕܐ = keys.
56. ܕܗܘܝܘ = that he is.
57. ܢܬܒܨܪ = it will be decreased / withheld (impossible).
58. ܬܘ = come.
59. ܚܒܪܗ = his neighbor.
60. ܘܒܕܪ = and he scattered.
61. ܘܦܫܘ = and they stopped.

19

I-*yūd*

	Perfect	Participle	Imperfect	Imperative	Infinitive
I-*yūd*	ܝܺܠܶܕ *iled*	ܝܳܠܶܕ *yāled*	ܢܺܐܠܰܕ *nilad*	ܝܺܠܰܕ *ilad*	ܡܺܐܠܰܕ *milad*

Introduction

I-*yūd* verbs are those that have a *yūd* as the first consonant of the word. The alteration of I-*yūd* verbs is typically minor, dealing with either a change in vowel or the addition of an *ālap*. Some of the more popular I-*yūd* verbs include:

ܝܺܬܶܒ	ܝܺܕܰܥ	ܝܰܗ̱ܒ	ܝܺܠܶܦ	ܝܺܠܶܕ
iteb	*ida'*	*yab*	*ilep*	*iled*
to sit	to know	to give	to learn	to beget

I-*yūd* Peal Perfect

Verbs in the peal that begin with *yūd* without a given vowel over the *yūd* will automatically take an *i*-vowel attached to them—with the exception of the 3fs and 1cs. These two forms will take an *e*-vowel above the initial *yūd*. In the case of the I-*yūd* peal perfect conjugation, that means that the majority of the verbs begin with this *yūd* and *i*-vowel combination. The endings are predictably formed, with no alteration from the basic pattern of the perfect conjugation.

	Singular		Plural	
3m	ܝܠܕ	*iled* he/it beget	ܝܠܕܘ ܝܠܕܘܢ	*iled* *iledun* they beget
3f	ܝܠܕܬ	*yeldat* she/it beget	ܝܠܕ ܝܠܕܝ ܝܠܕܝܢ	*iled* *iled* *iledēn* they beget
2m	ܝܠܕܬ	*iledt* you beget	ܝܠܕܬܘܢ ܝܠܕܬܘܢ	*iledton* *iledtun* you beget
2f	ܝܠܕܬܝ	*iledt* you beget	ܝܠܕܬܝܢ	*iledtēn* you beget
1c	ܝܠܕܬ	*yeldet* I beget	ܝܠܕܢ ܝܠܕܢܢ	*iledn* *iled̄nan* we beget

I-*yūd* Peal Imperfect

In the peal imperfect, I-*yūd* verbs are formed in the exact same way as I-*ālap* verbs: the *yūd* will become an *ālap* in the conjugation with an *i*-vowel over the prefix. They are formed regularly after the addition of the *ālap*. Because of this similarity, it is easy to get the I-*yūd* and I-*ālap* verbs confused when looking for the root of the verb.

	Singular		Plural	
3m	ܢܐܠܕ	*nilad* he/it will beget	ܢܐܠܕܘܢ	*nildun* they will beget
3f	ܬܐܠܕ	*tilad* she/it will beget	ܢܐܠܕܢ	*nildān* they will beget
2m	ܬܐܠܕ	*tilad* you will beget	ܬܐܠܕܘܢ	*tildun* you will beget
2f	ܬܐܠܕܝܢ	*tildin* you will beget	ܬܐܠܕܢ	*tildān* you will beget
1c	ܐܐܠܕ	*ilad* I will beget	ܢܐܠܕ	*nilad* we will beget

There are some classes of I-*yūd* verbs where the *ālap* does not appear in place of the *yūd*. With these particular verbs, the initial consonant disappears altogether and the *yūd* is simply assimilated into the prefix. Most notable in this case are the verbs ܝܺܕܰܥ ("to know") and ܝܺܬܶܒ ("to sit"). Also note the difference in the stem vowels between the two (*a* in the first paradigm vs. *e* in the paradigm below). These verbs are parsed similar to I-*n* forms of the verb (these will be covered later in the grammar). Finally, this particular form of verb doubles the *taw* when it is pronounced. Note the differences below with the paradigm above.

	Singular		Plural	
3m	ܢܶܬܶܒ	*netteb* he/it will sit	ܢܶܬܒܽܘܢ	*nettbun* they will sit
3f	ܬܶܬܶܒ	*tetteb* she/it will sit	ܢܶܬܒܳܢ	*nettbān* they will sit
2m	ܬܶܬܶܒ	*tetteb* you will sit	ܬܶܬܒܽܘܢ	*tettbun* you will sit
2f	ܬܶܬܒܺܝܢ	*tettbin* you will sit	ܬܶܬܒܳܢ	*tettbān* you will sit
1c	ܐܶܬܶܒ	*etteb* I will sit	ܢܶܬܶܒ	*netteb* we will sit

The Conjugation of *yab*

There is one last element to note regarding the imperfect tense of I-*yūd* verbs and that is in regards to the verb ܝܗܰܒ ("to give"). This verb is irregular and changes its appearance in the imperfect, infinitive, imperative, and participle forms.

ܝܗܰܒ	→	ܢܶܬܶܠ
perfect 3ms		imperfect 3ms

Note the usage in Matthew 4:9.

ܐܶܬܶܠ	ܠܳܟ	ܟܽܠܗܶܝܢ	ܗܳܠܶܝܢ
ettel	*l-āk*	*kullhēn*	*hālēn*
peal imperfect 1cs	*lāmad* + 2ms	particle + 3fs	pronoun 1cp
I will give	to you	all of them	these

Translation: All of these I will give to you.

This verb is fairly prevalent in Syriac, and so it is worth looking at the full paradigm in order to note the alterations in the verb. This verb, ܢܬܠ, acts like a I-*nūn* verb and so will follow the typical I-*nūn* conjugation patterns discussed in the next chapter.

	Singular		Plural	
3m	ܢܶܬܶܠ	*nettel* he/it will give	ܢܶܬܠܽܘܢ	*nettlun* they will give
3f	ܬܶܬܶܠ	*tettel* she/it will give	ܢܶܬܠܳܢ	*nettlān* they will give
2m	ܬܶܬܶܠ	*tettel* you will give	ܬܶܬܠܽܘܢ	*tettlun* you will give
2f	ܬܶܬܠܺܝܢ	*tettlin* you will give	ܬܶܬܠܳܢ	*tettlān* you will give
1c	ܐܶܬܶܠ	*ettel* I will give	ܢܶܬܶܠ	*nettel* we will give

Finally, note that the verb goes back to being regularly formed in the Ethpeel conjugation. For example, note Matthew 7:7:

ܠܟܽܘܢ	ܘܢܶܬܝܗܶܒ	ܫܰܐܠܘ
l-kun	*w-netiheb*	*šal*
lāmad + particle	waw + ethpeel imperfect 3ms	peal imperative
to you	and it will be given	ask

Translation: Ask and it will be given to you.

I-*yūd* Peal Imperative

The I-*yūd* peal imperative is formed by dropping the imperfect prefix. This allows the *yūd* to reappear. The endings are typical of the imperative.

	Singular	Plural I	Plural II
Masculine	ܝܺܠܰܕ *ilad* Beget!	ܝܺܠܰܕܘ *ilad* Beget!	ܝܺܠܰܕܘܢ *iladun* Beget!
Feminine	ܝܺܠܰܕܝ *ilad* Beget!	ܝܺܠܰܕ̈ܝ *ilad* Beget!	ܝܺܠܰܕ̈ܶܝܢ *iladēn* Beget!

I-*yūd* Peal Infinitive

The peal infinitive is formed by replacing the initial *yūd* consonant with an *ālap* and then adding an *i*-vowel above the *mīm*. This can be somewhat confusing when looking for the roots of verbs because the initial thought might be to look for a verbal root that begins with an *ālap*. One of the key indicators that this is a I-*yūd* peal verb is the *i*-vowel that is present above the *mīm*.

ܡܺܐܠܰܕ
milad
to beget

I-*yūd* Peal Participle

The I-*yūd* peal participle is regularly formed. Since the I-*yūd* verbs alter the initial consonant, there is no interaction or alteration with the endings of the participles. The masculine singular forms for each will be enough to get an idea of how the verbs are formed, and the other arrangements are predictably formed. In general, look for the long *a*-vowel (*ā*) above the *yūd* for the active, and the *i*-vowel for the passive.

Active

Masculine Singular	Masculine Plural	Feminine Singular	Feminine Plural
ܝܳܠܶܕ	ܝܳܠܕܺܝܢ	ܝܳܠܕܳܐ	ܝܳܠܕܳܢ
yāled	*yāldin*	*yāldā*	*yāldān*
begetting	begetting	begetting	begetting

Passive

Masculine Singular	Masculine Plural	Feminine Singular	Feminine Plural
ܝܺܠܺܝܕ	ܝܺܠܺܝܕܺܝܢ	ܝܺܠܺܝܕܳܐ	ܝܺܠܺܝܕܳܢ
ilid	*ilidin*	*ilidā*	*ilidān*
being begotten	being begotten	being begotten	being begotten

Note: For the pronunciation of the passives forms, the *yūd* assumes the *i*-vowel and drops out of the transliteration.

Introduction to Derived Stems

As with the previous chapter, the I-*yūd* verbs in the various conjugations other than the pael will be briefly overviewed below. The best thing to do with these generalities is to look for the overall patterns in the words, particularly how the word is altered in the initial consonant.

The largest departure from normal conjugations appears in the aphel and ettaphal conjugations. Here, many of the I-*yūd* verbs have the tendency to alter the *yūd* to a *waw*. Outside of this, many will keep the initial *yūd* in the verb.

I-*yūd* Pael (D)

ܝܰܠܶܕ	ܢܝܰܠܶܕ	ܝܰܠܶܕ	ܡܝܰܠܳܕܽܘ	ܡܝܰܠܶܕ	ܡܝܰܠܰܕ
yalled	*nyalled*	*yalled*	*myallādu*	*myalled*	*myallad*
Perfect	Imperfect	Imperative	Infinitive	Active Participle	Passive Participle

I-*yūd* Aphel (A)

ܐܰܘܠܶܕ	ܢܰܘܠܶܕ	ܐܰܘܠܶܕ	ܡܰܘܠܳܕܽܘ	ܡܰܘܠܶܕ	ܡܰܘܠܰܕ
awled	*nawled*	*awled*	*mawlādu*	*mawled*	*mawlad*
Perfect	Imperfect	Imperative	Infinitive	Active Participle	Passive Participle

I-*yūd* Ethpeel (Gp)

ܐܶܬܺܝܠܶܕ	ܢܶܬܺܝܠܶܕ	ܐܶܬܝܰܠܕ	ܡܶܬܺܝܠܳܕܽܘ	ܡܶܬܺܝܠܶܕ
etiled	*netiled*	*etyald*	*metilādu*	*metiled*
Perfect	Imperfect	Imperative	Infinitive	Participle

I-*yūd* Ethpaal (Dp)

ܐܶܬܝܰܠܰܕ	ܢܶܬܝܰܠܰܕ	ܐܶܬܝܰܠܰܕ	ܡܶܬܝܰܠܳܕܽܘ	ܡܶܬܝܰܠܰܕ
etyallad	*netyallad*	*etyallad*	*metyallādu*	*metyallad*
Perfect	Imperfect	Imperative	Infinitive	Participle

I-*yūd* Ettaphal (Ap)

ܐܶܬܬܰܘܠܰܕ	ܢܶܬܬܰܘܠܰܕ	ܐܶܬܬܰܘܠܰܕ	ܡܶܬܬܰܘܠܳܕܽܘ	ܡܶܬܬܰܘܠܰܕ
ettawlad	*nettawlad*	*ettawlad*	*mettawladu*	*mettawlad*
Perfect	Imperfect	Imperative	Infinitive	Participle

Vocabulary

Nouns

ܐܓܪܬܐ	*eggartā*	letter, epistle
ܪܙܐ	*rāzā*	mystery
ܚܒܪܐ	*ḥabrā*	companion, friend
ܚܙܘܐ	*ḥezwā*	appearance
ܟܘܟܒܐ	*kawkbā*	star, planet
ܟܘܡܪܐ	*kumrā*	priest
ܟܪܝܗܐ	*krihā*	sick, weak in faith
ܡܐܟܘܠܬܐ	*mekultā*	food (also *meklā*)
ܡܨܥܬܐ	*mṣaʿtā*	middle
ܢܘܢܐ	*nunā*	fish
ܣܗܕܐ	*sāhdā*	witness, martyr
ܥܢܢܐ	*ʿnānā*	cloud
ܥܪܣܐ	*ʿarsā*	bed, pallet
ܪܚܡܐ	*rāḥmā*	friend

Verbs

ܒܝܐ	*byā*	to comfort, encourage
ܟܐܐ	*kā*	to rebuke
ܟܪܐ	*krā*	to have sorrow, be sad
ܟܪܗ	*krah*	to be sick, weak
ܟܫܠ	*kšel*	to offend, stumble
ܠܥܣ	*lʿes*	to eat
ܢܒܐ	*nbā*	to prophesy
ܢܓܕ	*ngad*	to beat, lead, drag
ܢܗܪ	*nhar*	to shine
ܣܓܐ	*sgā*	to increase, be great
ܣܟܐ	*skā*	to expect, wait for
ܫܥܐ	*šʿa*	to narrate, play

Other

ܥܣܪܐ	*ʿesrā*	ten
ܦܨܚܐ	*peṣḥā*	Passover
ܪܫܝܬܐ	*rišitā*	beginning
ܬܡܢ	*tammān*	there

Exercises

Matthew 5:19–20 (1)

ܟܠ ܡܢ ܗܟܝܠ ܕܢܫܪܐ ܚܕ ܡܢ ܦܘܩܕܢܐ ܗܠܝܢ ܙܥܘܪܐ ܘܢܠܦ ܗܟܢܐ
ܠܒܢܝܢܫܐ[1] ܒܨܝܪܐ[2] ܢܬܩܪܐ ܒܡܠܟܘܬܐ ܕܫܡܝܐ ܟܠ ܕܝܢ ܕܢܥܒܕ ܘܢܠܦ
ܗܢܐ ܪܒܐ ܢܬܩܪܐ ܒܡܠܟܘܬܐ ܕܫܡܝܐ ܐܡܪ ܐܢܐ ܠܟܘܢ ܓܝܪ
ܕܐܠܐ ܬܬܝܬܪ ܟܐܢܘܬܟܘܢ ܝܬܝܪ ܡܢ ܕܣܦܪܐ ܘܦܪܝܫܐ ܠܐ ܬܥܠܘܢ[3]
ܠܡܠܟܘܬܐ ܕܫܡܝܐ

Matthew 16:24–28 (2)

ܗܝܕܝܢ ܐܡܪ ܝܫܘܥ ܠܬܠܡܝܕܘܗܝ ܡܢ ܕܨܒܐ ܕܢܐܬܐ ܒܬܪܝ ܢܟܦܘܪ
ܒܢܦܫܗ ܘܢܫܩܘܠ ܙܩܝܦܗ[4] ܘܢܐܬܐ ܒܬܪܝ ܡܢ ܕܨܒܐ ܓܝܪ ܕܢܚܐ[5]
ܢܦܫܗ ܢܘܒܕܝܗ[6] ܘܡܢ ܕܢܘܒܕ[7] ܢܦܫܗ ܡܛܠܬܝ[8] ܢܫܟܚܝܗ[9] ܗܢܐ ܓܝܪ

---

1. This is the compound of two familiar words.
2. ܒܨܝܪܐ = least, inferior.
3. ܬܥܠܘܢ = you will enter.
4. ܙܩܝܦܗ = his cross.
5. ܢܚܐ = he will save.
6. ܢܘܒܕܝܗ = he will perish [it].
7. ܢܘܒܕ = he will perish.
8. This is a particle with a pronominal suffix attached to the end.
9. This is a verb plus a pronominal suffix: peal imperfect 3ms + 3fs.

ܡܬܗܢܐ[10] ܒܪܢܫܐ ܐܢ ܟܠܗ ܥܠܡܐ ܢܩܢܐ[11] ܘܢܦܫܗ ܢܚܣܪ[12] ܐܘ
ܡܢܐ ܢܬܠ ܒܪܢܫܐ ܚܠܘܦܐ[13] ܕܢܦܫܗ ܥܬܝܕ ܗܘ ܓܝܪ ܒܪܗ ܕܐܢܫܐ
ܕܢܐܬܐ ܒܫܘܒܚܐ ܕܐܒܘܗܝ ܥܡ ܡܠܐܟܘܗܝ ܩܕܝܫܐ ܘܗܝܕܝܢ
ܢܦܪܘܥ ܠܟܠ ܐܢܫ ܐܝܟ ܥܒܕܘܗܝ ܐܡܝܢ ܐܡܪ ܐܢܐ ܠܟܘܢ ܕܐܝܬ
ܐܢܫܐ ܕܩܝܡܝܢ[14] ܗܪܟܐ[15] ܕܠܐ ܢܛܥܡܘܢ[16] ܡܘܬܐ ܥܕܡܐ ܕܢܚܙܘܢ
ܠܒܪܗ ܕܐܢܫܐ ܕܐܬܐ ܒܡܠܟܘܬܗ

Mark 3:31–35 (3)

ܘܐܬܘ ܐܡܗ ܘܐܚܘܗܝ ܩܝܡܝܢ[17] ܠܒܪ ܘܫܕܪܘ ܕܢܩܪܘܢܗ[18] ܠܘܬܗܘܢ ܝܬܒ
ܗܘܐ ܕܝܢ ܚܕܪܘܗܝ[19] ܟܢܫܐ ܘܐܡܪܝܢ ܠܗ ܗܐ ܐܡܟ ܘܐܚܝܟ ܠܒܪ
ܒܥܝܢ ܠܟ ܘܥܢܐ ܘܐܡܪ ܠܗܘܢ ܡܢ ܗܝ ܐܡܝ ܘܡܢ ܐܢܘܢ ܐܚܝ ܘܚܪ[20]
ܒܐܝܠܝܢ[21] ܕܝܬܒܝܢ ܠܘܬܗ ܘܐܡܪ ܗܐ ܐܡܝ ܘܗܐ ܐܚܝ ܡܢ ܕܥܒܕ
ܓܝܪ ܨܒܝܢܗ ܕܐܠܗܐ ܗܢܘ[22] ܐܚܝ ܘܚܬܝ ܘܐܡܝ

10. ܡܬܗܢܐ = profit.
11. ܢܩܢܐ = he gains.
12. ܢܚܣܪ = he loses.
13. ܚܠܘܦܐ = in exchange.
14. ܩܝܡܝܢ = standing.
15. ܗܪܟܐ = here.
16. ܢܛܥܡܘܢ = partake of.
17. ܩܝܡܝܢ = standing.
18. This is a verb plus a pronominal suffix: peal imperfect 3mp + 3ms.
19. ܚܕܪܘܗܝ = surrounding him.
20. ܘܚܪ = and he looked.
21. ܒܐܝܠܝܢ = at who.
22. ܗܢܘ = he is.

Matthew 13:10–13 (4)

ܘܩܪܒܘ ܬܠܡܝܕܘܗܝ ܘܐܡܪܝܢ ܠܗ ܠܡܢܐ ܒܦܠܐܬܐ[23] ܡܡܠܠ ܐܢܬ
ܥܡܗܘܢ ܗܘ ܕܝܢ ܥܢܐ ܘܐܡܪ ܠܗܘܢ ܠܟܘܢ ܗܘ ܝܗܝܒ ܠܡܕܥ
ܐܪܙܐ[24] ܕܡܠܟܘܬܐ ܕܫܡܝܐ ܠܗܢܘܢ ܕܝܢ ܠܐ ܝܗܝܒ ܠܡܢ ܓܝܪ ܕܐܝܬ
ܠܗ ܢܬܝܗܒ ܠܗ ܘܢܬܝܬܪ ܠܗ ܘܠܡܢ ܕܠܝܬ ܠܗ ܘܗܘ ܕܐܝܬ ܠܗ
ܢܫܬܩܠ[25] ܡܢܗ ܡܛܠ ܗܢܐ ܒܦܠܐܬܐ[26] ܡܡܠܠ ܐܢܐ ܥܡܗܘܢ ܡܛܠ
ܕܚܙܝܢ ܘܠܐ ܚܙܝܢ ܘܫܡܥܝܢ ܘܠܐ ܫܡܥܝܢ ܘܠܐ ܡܣܬܟܠܝܢ[27]

John 5:23–24 (5)

ܕܟܠܢܫ ܢܝܩܪ ܠܒܪܐ ܐܝܟ ܕܡܝܩܪ ܠܐܒܐ ܗܘ ܕܠܐ ܡܝܩܪ ܠܒܪܐ ܠܐ
ܡܝܩܪ ܠܐܒܐ ܕܫܕܪܗ[28] ܐܡܝܢ ܐܡܝܢ ܐܡܪ ܐܢܐ ܠܟܘܢ ܕܡܢ ܕܫܡܥ
ܡܠܬܝ ܘܡܗܝܡܢ[29] ܠܡܢ ܕܫܕܪܢܝ[30] ܐܝܬ ܠܗ ܚܝܐ ܕܠܥܠܡ ܘܠܕܝܢܐ ܠܐ
ܐܬܐ ܐܠܐ ܫܢܐ[31] ܠܗ ܡܢ ܡܘܬܐ ܠܚܝܐ

Matthew 28:18–20 (6)

ܘܩܪܒ ܝܫܘܥ ܡܠܠ ܥܡܗܘܢ ܘܐܡܪ ܠܗܘܢ ܐܬܝܗܒ ܠܝ ܟܠ ܫܘܠܛܢ
ܒܫܡܝܐ ܘܒܐܪܥܐ ܐܝܟܢܐ ܕܫܕܪܢܝ[32] ܐܒܝ ܡܫܕܪ ܐܢܐ ܠܟܘܢ

23. ܦܠܐܬܐ = parables.
24. ܐܪܙܐ = mysteries.
25. ܢܫܬܩܠ = it will be taken.
26. ܦܠܐܬܐ = parables.
27. ܡܣܬܟܠܝܢ = understanding.
28. This is a verb with a pronominal suffix: pael perfect 3ms + 3ms.
29. ܘܡܗܝܡܢ = and believing.
30. This is a verb with a pronominal suffix: pael perfect 3ms + 1cs.
31. ܫܢܐ = he departs.
32. This is a verb with a pronominal suffix: pael perfect 3ms + 1cs.

ܙܠܘ[33] ܗܟܝܠ ܬܠܡܕܘ[34] ܟܠܗܘܢ ܥܡܡܐ ܘܐܥܡܕܘ ܐܢܘܢ ܒܫܡ
ܐܒܐ ܘܒܪܐ ܘܪܘܚܐ ܕܩܘܕܫܐ ܘܐܠܦܘ ܐܢܘܢ ܕܢܛܪܘܢ[35] ܟܠ ܡܐ
ܕܦܩܕܬܟܘܢ[36] ܘܗܐ ܐܢܐ ܥܡܟܘܢ ܐܢܐ ܟܠܗܘܢ ܝܘܡܬܐ ܥܕܡܐ
ܠܫܘܠܡܗ[37] ܕܥܠܡܐ ܐܡܝܢ

Matthew 6:23–24 (7)

ܐܢ ܕܝܢ ܥܝܢܟ ܬܗܘܐ ܒܝܫܐ ܟܠܗ ܦܓܪܟ ܚܫܘܟܐ ܢܗܘܐ ܐܢ
ܗܟܝܠ ܢܘܗܪܐ ܕܒܟ ܚܫܘܟܐ ܗܘ ܚܫܘܟܟ ܟܡܐ ܢܗܘܐ ܠܐ ܐܢܫ
ܡܫܟܚ[38] ܠܬܪܝܢ ܡܪܘܢ ܠܡܦܠܚ ܐܘ ܓܝܪ ܠܚܕ ܢܣܢܐ ܘܠܐܚܪܢܐ ܢܪܚܡ
ܐܘ ܠܚܕ ܢܝܩܪ ܘܠܐܚܪܢܐ ܢܫܘܛ[39] ܠܐ ܡܫܟܚܝܢ ܐܢܬܘܢ ܠܐܠܗܐ
ܠܡܦܠܚ ܘܠܡܡܘܢܐ[40]

Matthew 4:14–17 (8)

ܕܢܬܡܠܐ ܡܕܡ ܕܐܬܐܡܪ ܒܝܕ ܐܫܥܝܐ ܢܒܝܐ ܕܐܡܪ ܐܪܥܐ ܕܙܒܘܠܘܢ[41]
ܐܪܥܐ ܕܢܦܬܠܝ[42] ܐܘܪܚܐ ܕܝܡܐ ܥܒܪܘܗܝ ܕܝܘܪܕܢܢ[43] ܓܠܝܠܐ ܕܥܡܡܐ
ܥܡܐ ܕܝܬܒ ܒܚܫܘܟܐ ܢܘܗܪܐ ܪܒܐ ܚܙܐ ܘܐܝܠܝܢ ܕܝܬܒܝܢ ܒܐܬܪܐ

---

33. ܙܠܘ = go.
34. ܬܠܡܕܘ = teach.
35. ܕܢܛܪܘܢ = that they should keep.
36. This is a verb and a pronominal suffix: pael perfect 1cs + 2mp.
37. ܠܫܘܠܡܗ = to the end of it.
38. This is a peal active participle.
39. ܢܫܘܛ = he will despise.
40. ܡܡܘܢܐ = mammon.
41. ܙܒܘܠܘܢ = Zebulun.
42. ܢܦܬܠܝ = Naphtali.
43. ܥܒܪܘܗܝ ܕܝܘܪܕܢܢ = the crossing of the Jordan.

ܘܒܛܠܠܐ[44] ܕܡܘܬܐ ܢܘܗܪܐ ܕܢܚ[45] ܠܗܘܢ ܡܢ ܗܝܕܝܢ ܫܪܝ ܝܫܘܥ
ܠܡܟܪܙܘ[46] ܘܠܡܐܡܪ ܬܘܒܘ[47] ܩܪܒܬ ܠܗ ܓܝܪ ܡܠܟܘܬܐ ܕܫܡܝܐ

Matthew 10:5–8 (9)

ܠܗܠܝܢ ܬܪܥܣܪ[48] ܫܕܪ ܝܫܘܥ ܘܦܩܕ ܐܢܘܢ ܘܐܡܪ ܒܐܘܪܚܐ ܕܥܡܡܐ[49] ܠܐ
ܬܐܙܠܘܢ ܘܠܡܕܝܢܬܐ ܕܫܡܪܝܐ ܠܐ ܬܥܠܘܢ ܙܠܘ[50] ܠܟܘܢ ܕܝܢ ܝܬܝܪܐܝܬ
ܠܘܬ ܥܢܐ ܕܐܒܕܘ ܡܢ ܒܝܬ ܝܣܪܝܠ ܘܟܕ ܐܙܠܝܢ ܐܢܬܘܢ ܐܟܪܙܘ[51]
ܘܐܡܪܘ ܕܩܪܒܬ ܡܠܟܘܬܐ ܕܫܡܝܐ... ܡܓܢ[52] ܢܣܒܬܘܢ ܡܓܢ ܗܒܘ

Mark 6:2–4 (10)

ܘܟܕ ܗܘܬ ܫܒܬܐ ܫܪܝ ܠܡܠܦܘ ܒܟܢܘܫܬܐ ܘܣܓܝܐܐ ܕܫܡܥܘ
ܐܬܕܡܪܘ ܘܐܡܪܝܢ ܗܘܘ ܐܝܡܟܐ[53] ܠܗ ܗܠܝܢ ܠܗܢܐ ܘܐܝܕܐ ܗܝ
ܚܟܡܬܐ ܕܐܬܝܗܒܬ ܠܗ ܕܚܝܠܐ ܐܝܟ ܗܠܝܢ ܒܐܝܕܘܗܝ ܢܗܘܘܢ
ܠܐ ܗܘܐ ܗܢܐ ܢܓܪܐ[54] ܒܪܗ ܕܡܪܝܡ ܘܐܚܘܗܝ ܕܝܥܩܘܒ ܘܕܝܘܣܐ
ܘܕܝܗܘܕܐ ܘܕܫܡܥܘܢ[55] ܘܠܐ ܗܐ ܐܚܘܬܗ ܬܢܢ[56] ܠܘܬܢ ܘܡܬܟܫܠܝܢ[57]

---

44. ܛܠܠܐ = shadow.
45. ܕܢܚ = that is shining.
46. ܠܡܟܪܙܘ = to preach.
47. ܬܘܒܘ = repent!
48. ܬܪܥܣܪ = twelve.
49. ܕܥܡܡܐ = gentiles.
50. ܙܠܘ = go.
51. ܐܟܪܙܘ = preach.
52. ܡܓܢ = freely (x2).
53. . ܐܝܡܟܐ = whence.
54. ܢܓܪܐ = carpenter.
55. ܕܝܥܩܘܒ ܘܕܝܘܣܐ ܘܕܝܗܘܕܐ ܘܕܫܡܥܘܢ = of James and of Josis and Judas and Simon.
56. ܬܢܢ = here.
57. ܘܡܬܟܫܠܝܢ = offended.

ܗܘܰܘ ܒܶܗ ܘܐܳܡܰܪ ܠܗܽܘܢ ܝܶܫܽܘܥ ܕܠܰܝܬ ܢܒܺܝܳܐ ܕܫܺܝܛ[58] ܐܶܠܳܐ ܐܶܢ

ܒܡܕܺܝܢ݈ܬܶܗ ܘܒܰܝܬ ܐܰܚ̈ܝܳܢܰܘܗ̱ܝ[59] ܘܰܒܒܰܝܬܶܗ

Additional Exercises

Numbers 16:28–30

v.28 ܘܐܡܪ ܡܘܫܐ ܒܗܕܐ ܬܕܥܘܢ ܕܡܪܝܐ ܫܕܪܢܝ[60] ܠܡܥܒܕ ܗܠܝܢ ܟܠܗܘܢ

ܥܒ̈ܕܐ ܘܠܐ ܗܘܐ ܡܢ ܪܥܝܢܝ

v.29 ܐܢ ܐܝܟ ܡܘܬܐ ܕܟܠ ܒܢܝܢܫ ܢܡܘܬܘܢ[61] ܗܠܝܢ ܘܦܘܩܕܢܐ ܐܝܟ ܕܟܠ

ܒܢܝܢܫ ܢܬܦܩܕ ܥܠܝܗܘܢ ܠܐ ܗܘܐ ܡܪܝܐ ܫܕܪܢܝ

v.30 ܘܐܢ ܒܪܝܬܐ[62] ܢܒܪܐ[63] ܡܪܝܐ ܘܬܦܬܚ ܐܪܥܐ ܦܘܡܗ̇ ܘܬܒܠܥ[64] ܐܢܘܢ

ܠܗܘܢ ܘܠܟܠ ܡܕܡ ܕܐܝܬ ܠܗܘܢ ܘܢܚܬܘܢ ܗ̇ܢܘܢ ܘܟܠ ܡܕܡ ܕܐܝܬ

ܠܗܘܢ ܚܝܝܢ[65] ܠܫܝܘܠ[66] ܬܕܥܘܢ ܕܐܪܓܙܘ[67] ܓܒܪ̈ܐ ܗܠܝܢ ܠܡܪܝܐ

---

58. ܕܫܺܝܛ = that is despised.
59. ܐܰܚ̈ܝܳܢܰܘܗ̱ܝ = his kinsman.
60. ܫܕܪܢܝ = he sent me (x2).
61. ܢܡܘܬܘܢ = they will die.
62. ܒܪܝܬܐ = creation.
63. ܢܒܪܐ = he creates.
64. ܬܒܠܥ= swallows up.
65. ܚܝܝܢ = living.
66. ܠܫܝܘܠ = to Sheol.
67. ܬܕܥܘܢ = they made angry.

20

I-*nūn*

	Perfect	Participle	Imperfect	Imperative	Infinitive
I-*nūn*	ܢܦܰܩ *npaq*	ܢܳܦܶܩ *nāpeq*	ܢܶܦܽܘܩ *neppuq*	ܦܽܘܩ *puq*	ܡܶܦܰܩ *mepaq*

Introduction

Verbs with a *nūn* in the first position are called I-*nūn* verbs. Some of the more frequent verbs include:

ܢܣܰܒ	ܢܛܰܪ	ܢܦܰܠ	ܢܚܶܬ	ܢܶܬܶܠ	ܢܦܰܩ
nsab	*nṭar*	*npal*	*nḥet*	*nettel*	*npaq*
to take	to keep	to fall	to go down	to give	to go out
				This is the imperfect form of ܝܗܒ (*yab*)	

I-*nūn* verbs have the tendency to assimilate the *nūn* into whatever consonant comes after it. This mainly comes into play whenever there is a prefix added to a word, such as with the imperfect, imperative, and infinitive forms of the verb. In these cases, the initial *nūn* assimilates into the following consonant, which is then doubled in its pronunciation.

The verbs in the conjugations that do not have a prefix, such as the perfect, are not affected, as the *nūn* typically functions as a strong consonant. Therefore, these forms behave as a strong form when conjugated and will not be reviewed in this chapter (one less paradigm to memorize!).

I-*nūn* Peal Imperfect

For the I-*nūn* peal imperfect conjugation, the *nūn* seems to disappear from the verb. This can be difficult to handle if one is looking for the root of a verb that has a I-*nūn*. One of the effects of the assimilation of the *nūn* with the consonant that comes after it is that the following letter is doubled. For example, note the following noun:

ܡܕ݂ܺܝܢ݇ܬܳܐ
mdittā
city

Here the *nūn* is assimilated, and the result is that *taw* is doubled in pronunciation. This assimilation of the *nūn* with the next consonant happens when there is a *nūn* and a consonant that are not separated by a vowel. When pronounced, notice how the consonants tend to run together into a single sound. For example, if ܢܦܩ ("to go out") was conjugated according to the typical imperfect, it would be:

ܢ	+	ܢܦܰܩ	=	ܢܶܢܦܽܘܩ	=	ܢܶܢ݇ܦܽܘܩ	=	ܢܶܦܽܘܩ
n		*npaq*		*nenpoq*		*neppoq*		*neppoq*

The parsing, then, becomes:

	Singular		Plural	
3m	ܢܶܦܽܘܩ ܢܶܦܘܼܩ	*neppoq* *neppuq* he/it will go out	ܢܶܦܩܽܘܢ	*neppqun* they will go out
3f	ܬܶܦܽܘܩ ܬܶܦܽܘܩܝ ܬܶܦܘܼܩ ܬܶܦܘܼܩܝ	*teppoq* *teppoq* *teppuq* *teppuq* she/it will go out	ܢܶܦܩܳܢ	*neppqān* they will go out
2m	ܬܶܦܽܘܩ ܬܶܦܘܼܩ	*teppoq* *teppuq* you will go out	ܬܶܦܩܽܘܢ	*teppqon* you will go out
2f	ܬܶܦܩܺܝܢ	*teppqin* you will go out	ܬܶܦܩܳܢ	*teppqān* you will go out
1c	ܐܶܦܽܘܩ ܐܶܦܘܼܩ	*eppoq* *eppuq* I will go out	ܢܶܦܽܘܩ ܢܶܦܘܼܩ	*neppoq* *neppuq* we will go out

Keep in mind that, as with any other verb in the peal imperfect or imperative, some of the stem vowels will change from a *u*- to an *a*- or an *e*-class verb. In these cases, there will be no *waw* that appears in the middle of the imperfect and imperative forms. The *waw* is necessary for the *u*-sound that is present in the different conjugations. For example:

ܢܣܰܒ	→	ܢܶܣܰܒ	not	ܢܶܣܽܘܒ
ܢܦܰܠ	→	ܢܶܦܶܠ	not	ܢܶܦܽܘܠ

I-*nūn* Peal Imperative

As we might expect, the imperative is formed from the imperfect with the absence of the prefix. In these cases, the *nūn* remains assimilated to the second consonant of the root and does not reappear for this conjugation. Additionally, the doubling that takes place due to the assimilated *nūn* is not carried with it in the imperative, and is dropped. Keep in mind also that the *waw* may or may not be present, depending on the stem vowel for the imperfect.

	Singular	Plural I	Plural II
Masculine	ܦܽܘܩ ܦܘܼܩ *poq* *puq* Go out!	ܦܽܘܩܘ ܦܘܼܩܘ *poq* *puq* Go out!	ܦܽܘܩܽܘܢ ܦܘܼܩܘܼܢ *poqun* *puqun* Go out!
Feminine	ܦܽܘܩܝ ܦܘܼܩܝ *puq* Go out!	ܦܽܘܩ̈ܝ ܦܘܼܩ̈ܝ *puq* Go out!	ܦܽܘܩ̈ܶܝܢ ܦܘܼܩ̈ܶܝܢ *puqeyn* Go out!

I-*nūn* Peal Infinitive

Because the infinitive takes a *mīm* prefix, the *nūn* assimilates into the following consonant. This can make it difficult to identify the root. With experience, you will learn the more common I-*nūn* verbs and it will become second nature to recognize them.

ܡܶܦܰܩ

meppaq

to go out

Introduction to Derived Stems

Other verb forms that show significant change in the I-*nūn* configuration are the aphel and the ettaphal stems. In each of these stems, the *nūn* is assimilated to the following consonant. Keep in mind that this means that the following consonant will be doubled whenever assimilation takes place with the *nūn*. In the other stems, the I-*nun* verbs are formed regularly. These will not be reviewed in this brief introduction and overview.

I-*nūn* Aphel (A)

ܐܰܦܶܩ	ܢܰܦܶܩ	ܐܰܦܶܩ	ܡܰܦܳܩܽܘ	ܡܰܦܶܩ	ܡܰܦܰܩ
appeq	*nappeq*	*appeq*	*mappāqu*	*mappeq*	*mappaq*
Perfect	Imperfect	Imperative	Infinitive	Active Participle	Passive Participle

I-*nūn* Ettaphal (Ap)

ܐܶܬܬܰܦܰܩ	ܢܶܬܬܰܦܰܩ	ܐܶܬܬܰܦܰܩ	ܡܶܬܬܰܦܳܩܽܘ	ܡܶܬܬܰܦܰܩ
ettappaq	*nettappaq*	*ettappaq*	*mettappāqu*	*mettappaq*
Perfect	Imperfect	Imperative	Infinitive	Participle

Vocabulary

Nouns

ܐܝܠܢܐ	*ilānā*	tree
ܐܪܡܠܬܐ	*armaltā*	widow
ܓܠܝܢܐ	*gelyānā*	revelation, assurance
ܕܒܚܐ	*debḥā*	sacrifice, victim
ܕܝܢܐ	*dayānā*	judge
ܙܢܝܘܬܐ	*zānyutā*	adultery
ܙܩܝܦܐ	*zqipā*	cross
ܟܪܡܐ	*karmā*	vineyard
ܟܪܣܐ	*karsā*	womb, belly
ܡܟܣܐ	*māksā*	tax collector
ܢܚܬܐ	*naḥtā*	garment
ܣܝܡܬܐ	*simtā*	treasure
ܥܒܪܐ	*ʿebrā*	crossing
ܦܬܓܡܐ	*petgāmā*	word
ܦܬܟܪܐ	*ptakrā*	idol, image
ܩܒܪܐ	*qabrā*	grave
ܩܢܛܪܘܢܐ	*qenṭrunā*	centurion (Gk. κένταρχος)
ܪܓܝܓܬܐ	*rgigtā*	lust
ܫܘܩܐ	*šuqā*	marketplace
ܬܐܪܬܐ	*tirtā*	conscience

Verbs

ܠܐܐ	*lā*	to labor, toil
ܥܕܪ	*ʿdar*	to help, give advantage
ܦܣ	*pas*	to allow, permit
ܩܕܫ	*qdāš*	to sanctify, make holy
ܫܘܬܦ	*šawtep*	to partake, share
ܬܡܗ	*tmah*	to be astonished

Other

ܐܟܚܕܐ	*akḥdā*	together
ܐܪܒܥܝܢ	*arbʿin*	forty
ܕܟܝܐ	*dakyā*	clean, pure
ܦܩܚܐ	*paqāḥā*	better, profitable

Exercises

Matthew 26:26–29 (1)

ܟܕ ܕܝܢ ܠܥܣܝܢ ܗܘܘ ܢܣܒ ܝܫܘܥ ܠܚܡܐ ܘܒܪܟ ܘܩܨܐ[1] ܘܝܗܒ
ܠܬܠܡܝܕܘܗܝ܂ ܘܐܡܪ ܣܒܘ ܐܟܘܠܘ ܗܢܘ ܦܓܪܝ܂ ܘܢܣܒ ܟܣܐ ܘܐܘܕܝ܂
ܘܝܗܒ ܠܗܘܢ ܘܐܡܪ ܣܒܘ ܐܫܬܘ ܡܢܗ ܟܠܟܘܢ܂ ܗܢܘ ܕܡܝ ܕܕܝܬܩܐ
ܚܕܬܐ ܕܚܠܦ ܣܓܝܐܐ ܡܬܐܫܕ[2] ܠܫܘܒܩܢܐ[3] ܕܚܛܗܐ܂ ܐܡܪ ܐܢܐ
ܠܟܘܢ ܕܝܢ ܕܠܐ ܐܫܬܐ[4] ܡܢ ܗܫܐ ܡܢ ܗܢܐ ܝܠܕܐ ܕܓܦܬܐ[5] ܥܕܡܐ
ܠܝܘܡܐ ܕܒܗ ܐܫܬܝܘܗܝ[6] ܥܡܟܘܢ ܚܕܬܐ ܒܡܠܟܘܬܗ ܕܐܒܝ

Matthew 12:25–28 (2)

ܝܫܘܥ ܕܝܢ ܝܕܥ ܡܚܫܒܬܗܘܢ[7] ܘܐܡܪ ܠܗܘܢ ܟܠ ܡܠܟܘ[8] ܕܬܬܦܠܓ
ܥܠ ܢܦܫܗ ܬܚܪܒ[9] ܘܟܠ ܒܝܬ[10] ܘܡܕܝܢܐ[11] ܕܬܬܦܠܓ ܥܠ ܢܦܫܗ ܠܐ

---

1. ܘܩܨܐ = and broke it.
2. ܡܬܐܫܕ = being poured out.
3. ܠܫܘܒܩܢܐ = for forgiveness.
4. This is a peal imperfect 1cs.
5. ܝܠܕܐ ܕܓܦܬܐ = fruit of the vine.
6. This is a verb with a pronominal suffix: peal imperfect 1cs + 3ms.
7. ܡܚܫܒܬܗܘܢ = their thoughts.
8. This is the absolute form of ܡܠܟܘܬܐ.
9. ܬܚܪܒ = will be desolate.
10. This is the absolute form of ܒܝܬܐ.
11. This is the absolute form of ܡܕܝܢܬܐ.

ܢܩܘܡ[12] ܘܐܢ ܣܛܢܐ ܠܣܛܢܐ ܡܦܩ ܥܠ ܢܦܫܗ ܐܬܦܠܓ ܐܝܟܢܐ
ܗܟܝܠ ܩܝܡܐ[13] ܡܠܟܘܬܗ ܘܐܢ ܐܢܐ ܒܒܥܠܙܒܘܒ ܡܦܩ ܐܢܐ ܫܐܕܐ
ܒܢܝܟܘܢ ܒܡܢܐ ܡܦܩܝܢ ܠܗܘܢ ܡܛܠ ܗܢܐ ܗܢܘܢ ܢܗܘܘܢ ܠܟܘܢ
ܕܝܢܐ[14] ܘܐܢ ܒܪܘܚܐ ܕܐܠܗܐ ܐܢܐ ܡܦܩ ܐܢܐ ܫܐܕܐ ܩܪܒܬ ܠܗ
ܥܠܝܟܘܢ ܡܠܟܘܬܐ ܕܐܠܗܐ

John 8:55–58 (3)

ܘܠܐ ܝܕܥܬܘܢܝܗܝ[15] ܐܢܐ ܕܝܢ ܝܕܥ ܐܢܐ ܠܗ ܘܐܢ ܐܡܪ ܐܢܐ ܕܠܐ
ܝܕܥ ܐܢܐ ܠܗ ܗܘܐ ܐܢܐ ܠܝ ܟܕܒܐ[16] ܐܟܘܬܟܘܢ[17] ܐܠܐ ܝܕܥ
ܐܢܐ ܠܗ ܘܡܠܬܗ ܢܛܪ ܐܢܐ ܐܒܪܗܡ ܐܒܘܟܘܢ ܡܣܘܚ[18] ܗܘܐ
ܕܢܚܙܐ ܝܘܡܝ ܘܚܙܐ ܘܚܕܝ ܐܡܪܝܢ ܠܗ ܝܗܘܕܝܐ ܥܕܟܝܠ ܒܪ ܚܡܫܝܢ[19]
ܫܢܝܢ[20] ܠܐ ܡܛܝܬ ܘܠܐܒܪܗܡ ܚܙܝܬ ܐܡܪ ܠܗܘܢ ܝܫܘܥ ܐܡܝܢ ܐܡܝܢ
ܐܡܪ ܐܢܐ ܠܟܘܢ ܕܥܕܠܐ ܢܗܘܐ ܐܒܪܗܡ ܐܢܐ ܐܝܬܝ

12. ܢܩܘܡ = it will stand.
13. ܩܝܡܐ = stand.
14. ܕܝܢܐ = judges.
15. This is a verb plus a pronominal suffix: peal perfect 2mp + 3ms.
16. ܟܕܒܐ = liar.
17. ܐܟܘܬܟܘܢ = like you.
18. ܡܣܘܚ = desired.
19. ܚܡܫܝܢ = fifty.
20 This is the plural absolute of ܫܢܬܐ (year).

John 14:11 – 15 (4)

ܗܝܡܢܘ[21] ܕܐܢܐ ܒܐܒܝ ܘܐܒܝ ܒܝ ܘܐܠܐ ܐܦ[22] ܡܛܠ ܥܒܕ̈ܐ

ܗܝܡܢܘ ܐܡܝܢ ܐܡܝܢ ܐܡܪ ܐܢܐ ܠܟܘܢ ܕܡܢ ܕܡܗܝܡܢ[23] ܒܝ ܥܒܕ̈ܐ

ܐܝܠܝܢ ܕܐܢܐ ܥܒܕ ܐܢܐ ܐܦ ܗܘ ܢܥܒܕ ܘܕܝܬܝܪ̈ܢ ܡܢ ܗܠܝܢ ܢܥܒܕ

ܕܐܢܐ ܠܘܬ ܐܒܝ ܐܙܠ ܐܢܐ ܘܡܕܡ ܕܬܫܐܠܘܢ ܒܫܡܝ ܐܥܒܕ ܠܟܘܢ

ܕܢܫܬܒܚ ܐܒܐ ܒܒܪܗ ܘܐܢ ܬܫܐܠܘܢܢܝ[24] ܒܫܡܝ ܐܢܐ ܥܒܕܢܐ[25] ܐܢ

ܪܚܡܝܢ ܐܢܬܘܢ ܠܝ ܦܘܩܕܢܝ ܛܪܘ

Matthew 18:9 – 11 (5)

ܘܐܢ ܗܘ ܕܥܝܢܟ ܡܟܫܠܐ ܠܟ ܚܨܝܗ̇[26] ܘܫܕܝܗ̇[27] ܡܢܟ ܛܒ ܗܘ

ܠܟ ܕܒܚܕܐ ܥܝܢܐ ܬܥܘܠ[28] ܠܚܝܐ ܘܠܐ ܟܕ ܐܝܬ ܠܟ ܬܪ̈ܬܝܢ

ܥܝ̈ܢܝܢ ܬܦܠ ܒܓܗܢܐ[29] ܕܢܘܪܐ ܚܙܘ ܠܐ ܬܒܣܘܢ[30] ܚܕ ܡܢ ܗܠܝܢ

ܙܥܘܪ̈ܐ ܐܡܪ ܐܢܐ ܠܟܘܢ ܓܝܪ ܕܡܠܐܟܝܗܘܢ ܒܫܡܝܐ ܒܟܠܙܒܢ

ܚܙܝܢ ܦܪܨܘܦܗ ܕܐܒܝ ܕܒܫܡܝܐ ܐܬܐ ܓܝܪ ܒܪܗ ܕܐܢܫܐ ܕܢܚܐ ܡܕܡ

ܕܐܒܝܕ ܗܘܐ

---

21. ܗܝܡܢܘ = believe.
22. ܐܦ = even if.
23. ܡܗܝܡܢ = believing.
24. This is a verb with a pronominal suffix: peal imperfect 2mp + 1cs.
25. This is a participle with a pronominal suffix: peal active ms + 1cs.
26. ܚܨܝܗ̇ = pluck it out.
27. This is an imperative with a 3fs pronominal suffix.
28. ܬܥܘܠ = you will enter.
29. ܓܗܢܐ = Gihannā (hell).
30. ܬܒܣܘܢ = you will despise.

John 17:14–16 (6)

ܐܢܐ ܝܗܒܬ ܠܗܘܢ ܡܠܬܟ ܘܥܠܡܐ ܣܢܐ ܐܢܘܢ ܕܠܐ ܗܘܘ ܡܢ
ܥܠܡܐ ܐܝܟܢܐ ܕܐܢܐ ܠܐ ܗܘܝܬ ܡܢ ܥܠܡܐ ܠܐ ܗܘܐ ܕܬܫܩܘܠ
ܐܢܘܢ ܡܢ ܥܠܡܐ ܒܥܐ ܐܢܐ ܐܠܐ ܕܬܛܪ ܐܢܘܢ ܡܢ ܒܝܫܐ ܠܐ
ܗܘܘ ܓܝܪ ܡܢ ܥܠܡܐ ܐܝܟܢܐ ܕܐܢܐ ܠܐ ܗܘܝܬ ܡܢ ܥܠܡܐ

Matthew 19:4–6 (7)

ܗܘ ܕܝܢ ܥܢܐ ܘܐܡܪ ܠܗܘܢ ܠܐ ܩܪܝܬܘܢ ܕܗܘ ܕܥܒܕ ܡܢ ܒܪܫܝܬ
ܕܟܪܐ ܘܢܩܒܬܐ[31] ܥܒܕ ܐܢܘܢ ܘܐܡܪ ܡܛܠ ܗܢܐ ܢܫܒܘܩ ܓܒܪܐ
ܠܐܒܘܗܝ ܘܠܐܡܗ ܘܢܩܦ ܠܐܢܬܬܗ ܘܢܗܘܘܢ ܬܪܝܗܘܢ ܚܕ ܒܣܪ[32] ܡܟܝܠ
ܠܐ ܗܘܘ ܬܪܝܢ ܐܠܐ ܚܕ ܦܓܪ ܡܕܡ ܗܟܝܠ ܕܐܠܗܐ ܙܘܓ[33] ܒܪܢܫܐ
ܠܐ ܢܦܪܫ

Luke 6:42–44a (8)

ܐܘ ܐܝܟܢܐ ܡܫܟܚ ܐܢܬ ܠܡܐܡܪ ܠܐܚܘܟ ܐܚܝ ܫܒܘܩ ܐܦܩ
ܓܠܐ[34] ܡܢ ܥܝܢܟ ܘܗܐ ܩܪܝܬܐ ܕܒܥܝܢܟ ܠܐ ܡܬܚܙܝܐ ܠܟ
ܢܣܒ ܒܐܦܐ[35] ܐܦܩ ܠܘܩܕܡ ܩܪܝܬܐ[36] ܡܢ ܥܝܢܟ ܘܗܝܕܝܢ ܢܬܚܙܐ
ܠܟ ܠܡܦܩܘ ܓܠܐ ܡܢ ܥܝܢܗ ܕܐܚܘܟ ܠܐ ܐܝܬ ܐܝܠܢܐ ܛܒܐ

---

31. ܕܟܪܐ ܘܢܩܒܬܐ = male and female.
32. ܒܣܪ = flesh.
33. ܙܘܓ = joined together.
34. ܓܠܐ = straw (x2).
35. ܢܣܒ ܒܐܦܐ = hypocrite.
36. ܩܪܝܬܐ = beam (x2).

ܕܥܒܕ ܦܐܪ̈ܐ ܒܝܫ̈ܐ ܐܦ ܠܐ ܐܝܠܢܐ ܒܝܫܐ ܕܥܒܕ ܦܐܪ̈ܐ ܛܒ̈ܐ ܟܠ

ܐܝܠܢܐ ܓܝܪ ܡܢ ܦܐܪ̈ܘܗܝ ܗܘ ܡܬܝܕܥ

Matthew 7:21 – 23a (9)

ܠܐ ܗܘܐ ܟܠ ܕܐܡܪ ܠܝ ܡܪܝ ܡܪܝ ܥܐܠ[37] ܠܡܠܟܘܬܐ ܕܫܡܝܐ ܐܠܐ

ܡܢ ܕܥܒܕ ܨܒܝܢܗ ܕܐܒܝ ܕܒܫܡܝܐ ܣܓܝܐܐ ܢܐܡܪܘܢ ܠܝ ܒܗܘ ܝܘܡܐ

ܡܪܝ ܡܪܝ ܠܐ ܒܫܡܟ ܐܬܢܒܝܢ ܘܒܫܡܟ ܫܐܕܐ ܐܦܩܢ ܘܒܫܡܟ

ܚܝܠܐ ܣܓܝܐܐ ܥܒܕܢ ܘܗܝܕܝܢ ܐܘܕܐ[38] ܠܗܘܢ ܕܡܢ ܡܬܘܡ[39] ܠܐ

ܝܕܥܬܟܘܢ[40]

John 10:17 – 18 (10)

ܡܛܠ ܗܢܐ ܐܒܝ ܪܚܡ ܠܝ ܕܐܢܐ ܣܐܡ[41] ܐܢܐ ܢܦܫܝ ܕܬܘܒ

ܐܣܒܝܗ̇[42] ܠܐ ܗܘܐ ܐܢܫ ܫܩܠ ܠܗ̇ ܡܢܝ ܐܠܐ ܐܢܐ ܣܐܡ[43] ܐܢܐ

ܠܗ̇ ܡܢ ܨܒܝܢܝ ܫܠܝܛ ܐܢܐ ܓܝܪ ܕܐܣܝܡܝܗ̇[44] ܘܫܠܝܛ ܐܢܐ ܕܬܘܒ

ܐܣܒܝܗ̇[45] ܕܗܢܐ ܦܘܩܕܢܐ ܩܒܠܬ ܡܢ ܐܒܝ

37. ܥܐܠ = entering.
38. ܐܘܕܐ = I will declare.
39. ܡܬܘܡ = ever.
40. This is a verb with a pronominal suffix: peal perfect 1cs + 2mp.
41. ܣܐܡ = laying down (x2).
42. This is a verb with a pronominal suffix: peal imperfect 1cs + 3fs.
43. ܣܐܡ = placing.
44. ܕܐܣܝܡܝܗ̇ = that I could lay it down.
45. This is a verb with a pronominal suffix: peal imperfect 1cs + 3fs.

Additional Exercises

Psalm 136:1–9

v.1 ܐܘܕܘ[46] ܠܡܪܝܐ ܕܛܒ ܗܘ ܘܠܥܠܡ ܪ̈ܚܡܘܗܝ

v.2 ܐܘܕܘ ܠܐܠܗ ܐ̈ܠܗܝܢ ܕܠܥܠܡ ܪ̈ܚܡܘܗܝ

v.3 ܐܘܕܘ ܠܡܪܝܐ ܡܪ̈ܘܬܐ[47] ܕܠܥܠܡ ܪ̈ܚܡܘܗܝ

v.4 ܠܥܒܕ ܬܕܡܪ̈ܬܐ[48] ܪ̈ܘܪܒܬܐ ܒܠܚܘܕܘܗܝ ܕܠܥܠܡ ܪ̈ܚܡܘܗܝ

v.5 ܠܥܒܕ ܫܡܝܐ ܒܣܘܟܠܬܗ ܕܠܥܠܡ ܪ̈ܚܡܘܗܝ

v.6 ܠܕܪܩܥ ܐܪܥܐ ܥܠ ܡ̈ܝܐ ܕܠܥܠܡ ܪ̈ܚܡܘܗܝ

v.7 ܠܥܒܕ ܢܗܝܪ̈ܐ ܪ̈ܘܪܒܐ ܕܠܥܠܡ ܪ̈ܚܡܘܗܝ

v.8 ܫܡܫܐ ܠܫܘܠܛܢܐ ܕܐܝܡܡܐ ܕܠܥܠܡ ܪ̈ܚܡܘܗܝ

v.9 ܣܗܪܐ[49] ܘܟܘ̈ܟܒܐ ܠܫܘܠܛܢܐ ܕܠܠܝܐ ܕܠܥܠܡ ܪ̈ܚܡܘܗܝ

---

46. ܐܘܕܘ = give thanks.
47. ܡܪ̈ܘܬܐ = dominions.
48. ܡܪ̈ܘܬܐ = wonders.
49. ܣܗܪܐ = moon.

21

Geminate

	Perfect	Participle	Imperfect	Imperative	Infinitive
Geminate	ܥܰܠ	ܥܳܐܶܠ	ܢܶܥܽܘܠ	ܥܽܘܠ	ܡܶܥܰܠ
	ʿal	*ʿāel*	*neʿʿol*	*ʿul*	*meʿʿal*

Introduction

Geminate (meaning doubled) verbs are verbs in which the second and the third consonants are the same letter. One of the more common geminate verb is ܥܰܠ (*ʿal*), meaning "to enter." This will be used for the majority of the paradigms. Below is a short list of other geminate verbs:

ܥܰܠ	ܫܰܒ	ܒܰܙ	ܚܰܫ	ܓܰܫ	ܡܰܠ
ʿal	*šab*	*baz*	*ḥaš*	*gaš*	*mal*
to enter	to put down	to plunder	to suffer	to touch	to speak

Note that only two consonants from the root of the verb appear.

Geminate Peal Perfect

The peal perfect conjugation of geminate verbs follows a pattern similar to that of the strong peal perfect verb. The strong verb forms that typically have different vowels above the initial consonant (such as the 3fs and 1cs) exhibit similar characteristics in the geminate, with a shift of the vowel from *a* to *e*. Likewise, the endings are similar and predictable from the peal paradigm. Therefore, in the peal perfect the only real change in the geminate verb is the absence of one of the consonants. The basic overall pattern remains intact.

	Singular		Plural	
3m	ܥܰܠ	*ʿal* he/it entered	ܥܰܠܘ ܥܰܠܘܢ	*ʿal* *ʿallun* they entered
3f	ܥܶܠܰܬ	*ʿellat* she/it entered	ܥܰܠ ܥܰܠ̈ ܥܰܠ̈ܶܝܢ	*ʿal* *ʿal* *ʿallēn* they entered
2m	ܥܰܠܬ	*ʿalt* you entered	ܥܰܠܬܘܿܢ ܥܰܠܬܽܘܢ	*ʿalton* *ʿaltun* you entered
2f	ܥܰܠܬܝ	*ʿalt* you entered	ܥܰܠܬܶܝܢ	*ʿaltēn* you entered
1c	ܥܶܠܶܬ	*ʿellet* I entered	ܥܰܠܢ ܥܰܠܢܰܢ	*ʿaln* *ʿalnan* we entered

Geminate Peal Imperfect

As expected with imperfect verbs, the geminate peal imperfect can take either a *u*- or an *a*-vowel, depending on the stem vowel that is present. The *o/u*-vowel is added with the occurrence of the *waw* in the 3ms, 3fs, 2ms, 1cs, and 1cp forms. The *a*-class vowels will not have the accompanying *waw* and will place the vowel above the initial consonant. Keep in mind that both forms of the geminate peal imperfect (*a*- and *o/u*-class) will double the first consonant in pronunciation.

	Singular		Plural	
3m	ܢܶܥܘܿܠ ܢܶܥܽܘܠ	*neʿʿol* *neʿʿul* he/it will enter	ܢܶܥܠܽܘܢ	*neʿʿlun* they will enter
3f	ܬܶܥܘܿܠ ܬܶܥܽܘܠ	*teʿʿol* *teʿʿul* she/it will enter	ܢܶܥܠ̈ܳܢ	*neʿʿlān* they will enter
2m	ܬܶܥܘܿܠ ܬܶܥܽܘܠ	*teʿʿol* *teʿʿul* you will enter	ܬܶܥܠܽܘܢ	*teʿʿlun* you will enter
2f	ܬܶܥܠܺܝܢ	*teʿʿlin* you will enter	ܬܶܥܠ̈ܳܢ	*teʿʿlān* you will enter
1c	ܐܶܥܘܿܠ ܐܶܥܽܘܠ	*eʿʿol* *eʿʿul* I will enter	ܢܶܥܘܿܠ ܢܶܥܽܘܠ	*neʿʿol* *neʿʿul* we will enter

Geminate Peal Imperative

Since dropping the preformative forms the imperative, the *waw* is present in the geminate imperative if it is an *o/u*-class verb. If it is an *a*-class verb, then there will be no *waw*.

Outside of this predictable change, the verb forms are regular. As a reminder, look for the *seyame* to distinguish the feminine singular and plural if there are no vowel markings present.

	Singular	Plural I	Plural II
Masculine	ܥܘܿܠ ܥܘܼܠ *ʿol* *ʿul* Enter!	ܥܘܿܠܘ ܥܘܼܠܘ *ʿol* *ʿul* Enter!	ܥܘܿܠܘܢ ܥܘܼܠܘܢ *ʿolun* *ʿulun* Enter!
Feminine	ܥܘܿܠܝ ܥܘܼܠܝ *ʿol* *ʿul* Enter!	ܥܘ̈ܿܠܝ ܥܘܼ̈ܠܝ *ʿol* *ʿul* Enter!	ܥܘ̈ܿܠܝܢ ܥܘܼ̈ܠܝܢ *ʿolēn* *ʿulēn* Enter!

Geminate Peal Infinitive

The geminate infinitive is formed regularly considering just the two consonants for the root. The vowel patterns remain consistent with the *a*-stem vowel.

ܡܶܥܰܠ

meʿʿal

to enter

Geminate Peal Participle

With most geminate peal participles an *ālap* will appear in the middle of the word. In some cases this is only present in the masculine singular form, and in the other forms (mp, fs, fp) the *ālap* will drop out, leaving just the two-consonant root. However, with ܥܰܠ (*ʿal*) the *ālap* is present throughout. The presence of the *ālap* does not alter the pronunciation, just the appearance of the word.

Active

Masculine		Feminine	
Singular	Plural	Singular	Plural
ܥܳܐܶܠ	ܥܳܐܠܺܝܢ	ܥܳܐܠܳܐ	ܥܳܐܠܳܢ
ʿāel	*ʿāllin*	*ʿāllā*	*ʿāllān*
entering	entering	entering	entering

An example of a participle that does not carry the *ālap* throughout the conjugation can be seen below. The root here is ܒܙ, *baz*, "to plunder."

Masculine		Feminine	
Singular	Plural	Singular	Plural
ܒܳܐܙ	ܒܳܙܺܝܢ	ܒܳܙܳܐ	ܒܳܙܳܢ
bāz	*bāzin*	*bāzā*	*bāzān*
plundering	plundering	plundering	plundering

In the passive participle, the second letter of the root makes an appearance after the characteristic *yūd* of the passive participle.

Passive

Masculine		Feminine	
Singular	Plural	Singular	Plural
ܥܰܠܺܝܠ	ܥܰܠܺܝܠܺܝܢ	ܥܰܠܺܝܠܳܐ	ܥܰܠܺܝܠܳܢ
ʿalil	*ʿalilin*	*ʿalilā*	*ʿalilān*
causing to enter	causing to enter	causing to enter	causing to enter

Introduction to Derived Stems

The verb used in the following examples is ܡܰܠܶܠ (*mll*), "to speak." The illustrations demonstrate the typical behavior of a geminate verb in the derived stems. Look for the larger patterns that are present in each of the various categories.

Many of the geminate verbs are regularly formed in the various stems. Pay attention to the final consonant, which will sometimes be doubled in geminate verbs. This can make it confusing when looking for verbal roots in a lexicon. With that said, notice how the aphel and ettaphal stems revert to a single final consonant.

Geminate Pael (D)

ܡܰܠܶܠ	ܢܡܰܠܶܠ	ܡܰܠܶܠ	ܡܰܠܳܠܽܘ	ܡܡܰܠܶܠ	ܡܡܰܠܰܠ
mallel	*nmallel*	*mallel*	*mallālu*	*mmallel*	*mmallal*
Perfect	Imperfect	Imperative	Infinitive	Active Participle	Passive Participle

Geminate Aphel (A)

ܐܰܡܶܠ	ܢܰܡܶܠ	ܐܰܡܶܠ	ܡܰܡܳܠܽܘ	ܡܰܡܶܠ	ܡܰܡܰܠ
amel	*namel*	*amel*	*mamālu*	*mamel*	*mamal*
Perfect	Imperfect	Imperative	Infinitive	Active Participle	Passive Participle

Geminate Ethpeel (Gp)

ܐܶܬܡܠܶܠ	ܢܶܬܡܠܶܠ	ܐܶܬܡܰܠ	ܡܶܬܡܠܳܠܽܘ	ܡܶܬܡܰܠܶܠ
etmlel	*netmlel*	*etmall*	*metmelālu*	*metmellel*
Perfect	Imperfect	Imperative	Infinitive	Participle

Geminate Ethpaal (Dp)

ܐܶܬܡܰܠܰܠ	ܢܶܬܡܰܠܰܠ	ܐܶܬܡܰܠܰܠ	ܡܶܬܡܰܠܳܠܽܘ	ܡܶܬܡܰܠܰܠ
etmallal	*netmallal*	*etmallal*	*metmallālu*	*metmallal*
Perfect	Imperfect	Imperative	Infinitive	Participle

Geminate Ettaphal (Ap)

ܐܶܬܬܰܡܰܠ	ܢܶܬܬܰܡܰܠ	ܐܶܬܬܰܡܰܠ	ܡܶܬܬܰܡܳܠܽܘ	ܡܶܬܬܰܡܰܠ
ettamal	*nettamal*	*ettamal*	*mettamalu*	*mettamal*
Perfect	Imperfect	Imperative	Infinitive	Participle

Vocabulary

Nouns

ܒܘܝܐܐ	*buyāā*	comfort, encouragement
ܒܪܝܬܐ	*britā*	creation
ܓܒܐ	*gabā*	side, sect
ܚܕܪܐ	*ḥdārā*	neighbor, surroundings
ܚܪܝܢܐ	*ḥeryānā*	altercation, strife
ܚܬܐ	*ḥātā*	sister
ܟܘܪܗܢܐ	*kurhānā*	ailment, disease
ܡܐܬܝܬܐ	*metitā*	advent, coming
ܡܕܒܚܐ	*madbḥā*	altar
ܡܚܘܬܐ	*mḥutā*	wound, plague
ܡܚܫܒܬܐ	*maḥšabtā*	counsel, thought, reasoning
ܥܕܒܐ	*ʿedbā*	sheep
ܥܕܢܐ	*ʿedānā*	moment, time, season
ܥܐܕܥܝܕܐ	*ʿadʿidā*	feast, festival
ܦܘܪܩܢܐ	*purqānā*	salvation, redemption
ܦܠܚܐ	*pālḥā*	servant, soldier
ܨܦܪܐ	*ṣaprā*	morning
ܩܪܢܐ	*qarnā*	horn, corner
ܫܘܒܗܪܐ	*šubhārā*	glorying
ܬܝܒܘܬܐ	*tyābutā*	repentance

Verbs

ܐܫܕ	*ešad*	to pour out, shed
ܝܒܠ	*ybel*	to conduct, lead away
ܝܣܦ	*ysap*	to add, increase
ܟܠܐ	*klā*	to forbid, restrain
ܨܡ	*ṣām*	to fast
ܪܓ	*rag*	to covet, desire
ܫܓ	*šāg*	to wash (pael)

Other

ܓܒܝܐ	*gabyā*	chosen, elect
ܝܩܝܪܐ	*yaqirā*	heavy, precious, honor
ܡܐܐ	*mā*	one hundred

Exercises

John 3:4–6 (1)

ܐܡܪ ܠܗ ܢܝܩܕܡܘܣ ܐܝܟܢܐ ܡܫܟܚ[1] ܕܢܬܝܠܕ ܓܒܪܐ ܣܒܐ[2] ܕܠܡܐ
ܡܫܟܚ ܬܘܒ ܠܟܪܣܐ ܕܐܡܗ ܕܬܪܬܝܢ ܙܒܢܝܢ ܠܡܥܠ ܘܢܬܝܠܕ ܥܢܐ
ܝܫܘܥ ܘܐܡܪ ܠܗ ܐܡܝܢ ܐܡܝܢ ܐܡܪ ܐܢܐ ܠܟ ܕܐܢ ܐܢܫ ܠܐ
ܡܬܝܠܕ ܡܢ ܡܝܐ ܘܪܘܚܐ ܠܐ ܡܫܟܚ ܕܢܥܘܠ ܠܡܠܟܘܬܐ ܕܐܠܗܐ
ܡܕܡ ܕܝܠܝܕ ܡܢ ܒܣܪܐ ܒܣܪܐ ܗܘ ܘܡܕܡ ܕܝܠܝܕ ܡܢ ܪܘܚܐ ܪܘܚܐ ܗܘ

Matthew 15:10–12 (2)

ܘܩܪܐ ܠܟܢܫܐ ܘܐܡܪ ܠܗܘܢ ܫܡܥܘ ܘܐܣܬܟܠܘ ܠܐ ܗܘܐ ܡܕܡ
ܕܥܐܠ ܠܦܘܡܐ ܡܛܢܦ[3] ܠܒܪܢܫܐ ܐܠܐ ܡܕܡ ܕܢܦܩ ܡܢ ܦܘܡܐ ܗܘ
ܗܘ ܡܛܢܦ ܠܒܪܢܫܐ ܗܝܕܝܢ ܩܪܒܘ ܬܠܡܝܕܘܗܝ ܘܐܡܪܝܢ ܠܗ ܝܕܥ ܐܢܬ
ܕܦܪܝܫܐ ܕܫܡܥܘ ܡܠܬܐ ܗܕܐ ܐܬܟܫܠܘ

---

1. This is the peal active participle of ܫܟܚ ("to find, be able to") (x3).
2. ܣܒܐ = old.
3. ܡܛܢܦ = defiling (x2).

Matthew 19:16–26 (3)

ܘܐܬܐ ܚܕ ܩܪܒ ܘܐܡܪ ܠܗ ܡܠܦܢܐ ܛܒܐ ܡܢܐ ܕܛܒ ܐܥܒܕ
ܕܢܗܘܘܢ ܠܝ ܚܝܐ ܕܠܥܠܡ ܗܘ ܕܝܢ ܐܡܪ ܠܗ ܡܢܐ ܩܪܐ ܐܢܬ ܠܝ
ܛܒܐ ܠܝܬ ܛܒܐ ܐܠܐ ܐܢ ܚܕ ܐܠܗܐ ܐܢ ܕܝܢ ܨܒܐ ܐܢܬ
ܕܬܥܘܠ ܠܚܝܐ ܛܪ ܦܘܩܕܢܐ ܐܡܪ ܠܗ ܐܝܠܝܢ ܗܘ ܕܝܢ ܝܫܘܥ ܐܡܪ
ܠܗ ܕܠܐ ܬܩܛܘܠ ܘܠܐ ܬܓܘܪ[4] ܘܠܐ ܬܓܢܘܒ[5] ܘܠܐ ܬܣܗܕ ܣܗܕܘܬ
ܫܘܩܪܐ[6] ܘܝܩܪ ܠܐܒܘܟ ܘܠܐܡܟ ܘܬܐܚܒ[7] ܠܩܪܝܒܟ ܐܝܟ ܢܦܫܟ
ܐܡܪ ܠܗ ܗܘ ܥܠܝܡܐ[8] ܗܠܝܢ ܟܠܗܝܢ ܢܛܪܬ ܐܢܝܢ ܡܢ ܛܠܝܘܬܝ
ܡܢܐ ܚܣܝܪ[9] ܐܢܐ ܐܡܪ ܠܗ ܝܫܘܥ ܐܢ ܨܒܐ ܐܢܬ ܓܡܝܪܐ[10]
ܠܡܗܘܐ ܙܠ[11] ܙܒܢ ܩܢܝܢܝܟ[12] ܘܗܒ ܠܡܣܟܢܐ ܘܬܗܘܐ ܠܟ ܣܝܡܬܐ
ܒܫܡܝܐ ܘܬܐ ܒܬܪܝ، ܫܡܥ ܕܝܢ ܗܘ ܥܠܝܡܐ ܡܠܬܐ ܗܕܐ ܘܐܙܠ
ܟܕ ܟܪܝܐ[13] ܠܗ ܐܝܬ ܗܘܐ ܠܗ ܓܝܪ ܩܢܝܢܐ[14] ܣܓܝܐܐ ܝܫܘܥ ܕܝܢ
ܐܡܪ ܠܬܠܡܝܕܘܗܝ، ܐܡܝܢ ܐܡܪ ܐܢܐ ܠܟܘܢ ܕܥܛܠܐ[15] ܗܝ، ܠܥܬܝܪܐ[16]
ܕܢܥܘܠ ܠܡܠܟܘܬ ܫܡܝܐ ܬܘܒ ܕܝܢ ܐܡܪܢܐ[17] ܠܟܘܢ ܕܦܫܝܩ[18] ܗܘ

4. ܬܓܘܪ = commit adultery.
5. ܬܓܢܘܒ = steal.
6. ܫܘܩܪܐ = false.
7. ܬܐܚܒ = love.
8. ܥܠܝܡܐ = young man.
9. ܚܣܝܪ = lacking.
10. ܓܡܝܪܐ = perfect.
11. ܙܠ = go.
12. ܩܢܝܢܝܟ = your possessions.
13. ܟܪܝܐ = sad.
14. ܩܢܝܢܐ = possessions.
15. ܥܛܠܐ = difficult.
16. ܥܬܝܪܐ = wealthy (x2).
17. This is a participle with a pronominal suffix: peal active ms + 1cs.
18. ܦܫܝܩ = it is easier.

ܠܓܡܠܐ[19] ܠܡܥܠ ܒܚܪܘܪܐ ܕܡܚܛܐ[20] ܐܘ ܥܬܝܪܐ ܕܢܥܘܠ ܠܡܠܟܘܬܐ
ܕܐܠܗܐ ܬܠܡܝܕܐ ܕܝܢ ܟܕ ܫܡܥܘ ܬܡܝܗܝܢ[21] ܗܘܘ ܛܒ ܘܐܡܪܝܢ ܡܢܘ
ܟܝ[22] ܡܫܟܚ[23] ܕܢܚܐ[24] ܚܪ ܒܗܘܢ ܝܫܘܥ ܘܐܡܪ ܠܗܘܢ ܠܘܬ ܒܢܝܢܫܐ
ܗܕܐ ܠܐ ܡܫܟܚܐ ܠܘܬ ܐܠܗܐ ܕܝܢ ܟܠܡܕܡ ܡܫܟܚܐ

Luke 9:59–62 (4)

ܘܐܡܪ ܠܐܚܪܢܐ ܬܐ[25] ܒܬܪܝ ܗܘ ܕܝܢ ܐܡܪ ܠܗ ܡܪܝ ܐܦܣ ܠܝ ܠܘܩܕܡ
ܐܙܠ[26] ܐܩܒܘܪ[27] ܐܒܝ ܐܡܪ ܠܗ ܝܫܘܥ ܫܒܘܩ ܡܝܬܐ ܩܒܪܝܢ[28]
ܠܡܝܬܝܗܘܢ ܘܐܢܬ ܙܠ[29] ܣܒܪ ܡܠܟܘܬܗ ܕܐܠܗܐ ܐܡܪ ܠܗ ܐܚܪܢܐ
ܐܬܐ[30] ܒܬܪܟ ܡܪܝ ܠܘܩܕܡ ܕܝܢ ܐܦܣ ܠܝ ܐܙܠ ܐܫܠܡ[31] ܠܒܢܝ ܒܝܬܝ
ܘܐܬܐ ܐܡܪ ܠܗ ܝܫܘܥ ܠܐ ܐܢܫ ܪܡܐ ܐܝܕܗ ܥܠ ܣܟܬܐ ܕܦܕܢܐ[32]
ܘܚܐܪ[33] ܠܒܣܬܪܗ[34] ܘܡܬܚܫܚ[35] ܠܡܠܟܘܬܗ ܕܐܠܗܐ

---

19. ܓܡܠܐ = camel.
20. ܚܪܘܪܐ ܕܡܚܛܐ = eye of a needle.
21. ܬܡܝܗܝܢ = peal passive participle of "to be amazed."
22. ܟܝ = indeed.
23. This is the peal active participle of ܫܟܚ ("to find, happen, be able") (x2).
24. ܕܢܚܐ = that he will be saved.
25. ܬܐ = come.
26. ܐܙܠ = I will go.
27. ܐܩܒܘܪ = I will bury.
28. ܩܒܪܝܢ = burying.
29. ܙܠ = go.
30. ܐܬܐ = I will come (x2).
31. ܐܫܠܡ = I will say bye (deliver, complete).
32. ܣܟܬܐ ܕܦܕܢܐ = plough handle.
33. ܘܚܐܪ = and he looks.
34. ܠܒܣܬܪܗ = behind him.
35. ܡܬܚܫܚ = he is useful.

John 13:34–35 (5)

ܦܘܩܕܢܐ ܚܕܬܐ ܝܗܒ ܐܢܐ ܠܟܘܢ ܕܬܚܒܘܢ ܚܕ ܠܚܕ ܐܝܟܢܐ

ܕܐܢܐ ܐܚܒܬܟܘܢ[36] ܐܦ ܐܢܬܘܢ ܬܚܒܘܢ ܚܕ ܠܚܕ ܒܗܕܐ ܢܕܥ ܟܠ

ܐܢܫ ܕܬܠܡܝܕܝ ܐܢܬܘܢ ܐܢ ܚܘܒܐ ܢܗܘܐ ܒܟܘܢ ܚܕ ܠܘܬ ܚܕ

John 15:12–14 (6)

ܗܢܘ ܦܘܩܕܢܝ ܕܬܚܒܘܢ ܚܕ ܠܚܕ ܐܝܟܢܐ ܕܐܢܐ ܐܚܒܬܟܘܢ[37] ܚܘܒܐ

ܕܪܒ ܡܢ ܗܢܐ ܠܝܬ ܕܐܢܫ ܢܦܫܗ ܢܣܝܡ[38] ܚܠܦ ܪܚܡܘܗܝ ܐܢܬܘܢ

ܪܚܡܝ ܐܢܬܘܢ ܐܢ ܬܥܒܕܘܢ ܟܠ ܕܡܦܩܕ ܐܢܐ ܠܟܘܢ

Matthew 8:8–10 (7)

ܥܢܐ ܩܢܛܪܘܢܐ ܗܘ ܘܐܡܪ ܡܪܝ ܠܐ ܫܘܐ ܐܢܐ ܕܬܥܘܠ ܬܚܝܬ

ܡܛܠܠܝ[39] ܐܠܐ ܒܠܚܘܕ ܐܡܪ ܒܡܠܬܐ ܘܢܬܐܣܐ ܛܠܝܝ[40] ܐܦ

ܐܢܐ ܓܝܪ ܓܒܪܐ ܐܢܐ ܕܬܚܝܬ ܫܘܠܛܢܐ ܘܐܝܬ ܬܚܝܬ ܐܝܕܝ

ܐܣܛܪܛܝܘܛܐ[41] ܘܐܡܪ ܐܢܐ ܠܗܢܐ ܕܙܠ[42] ܘܐܙܠ ܘܠܐܚܪܢܐ

ܕܬܐ[43] ܘܐܬܐ ܘܠܥܒܕܝ ܕܥܒܕ ܗܕܐ ܘܥܒܕ ܟܕ ܫܡܥ ܕܝܢ ܝܫܘܥ

---

36. This is a verb with a pronominal suffix: aphel perfect 1cs + 2mp.
37. Ibid.
38. ܢܣܝܡ = he will put.
39. ܡܛܠܠܝ = my shelter.
40 ܛܠܝܝ = my servant.
41. ܐܣܛܪܛܝܘܛܐ = soldiers.
42. ܙܠ = go.
43. ܬܐ = come.

ܐܬܕܡܪ ܘܐܡܪ ܠܕܐܬܝܢ ܒܬܪܗ ܐܡܝܢ ܐܡܪ ܐܢܐ ܠܟܘܢ ܕܐܦ ܠܐ
ܒܐܝܣܪܝܠ ܐܫܟܚܬ ܐܝܟ ܗܕܐ ܗܝܡܢܘܬܐ

Luke 16:16 – 17 (8)

ܢܡܘܣܐ ܘܢܒܝܐ ܥܕܡܐ ܠܝܘܚܢܢ ܡܢ ܗܝܕܝܢ ܡܠܟܘܬܐ ܕܐܠܗܐ
ܡܣܬܒܪܐ ܘܟܠ ܠܗ ܚܒܝܨ[44] ܕܢܥܘܠ ܦܫܝܩ[45] ܗܘ ܕܝܢ ܕܫܡܝܐ ܘܐܪܥܐ
ܢܥܒܪܘܢ ܐܘ ܐܬܘܬܐ[46] ܚܕܐ ܡܢ ܢܡܘܣܐ ܬܥܒܪ

John 10:1 – 2 (9)

ܐܡܝܢ ܐܡܝܢ ܐܡܪ ܐܢܐ ܠܟܘܢ ܕܡܢ ܕܠܐ ܥܐܠ ܡܢ ܬܪܥܐ ܠܛܝܪܐ
ܕܥܢܐ[47] ܐܠܐ ܣܠܩ ܡܢ ܕܘܟܐ ܐܚܪܢܐ ܗܘ ܓܢܒܐ[48] ܗܘ ܘܓܝܣܐ[49]
ܗܘ ܕܝܢ ܕܥܐܠ ܡܢ ܬܪܥܐ ܪܥܝܐ[50] ܗܘ ܕܥܢܐ[51]

1 John 4:7 – 12 (10)

ܚܒܝܒܝ ܢܚܒ ܚܕ ܠܚܕ ܡܛܠ ܕܚܘܒܐ ܡܢ ܐܠܗܐ ܗܘ ܘܟܠ ܡܢ
ܕܡܚܒ ܡܢ ܐܠܗܐ ܝܠܝܕ ܘܝܕܥ ܠܐܠܗܐ ܡܛܠ ܕܐܠܗܐ ܚܘܒܐ ܗܘ
ܘܟܠ ܕܠܐ ܡܚܒ ܠܐ ܝܕܥ ܠܐܠܗܐ ܒܗܕܐ ܐܬܝܕܥ ܚܘܒܗ ܕܐܠܗܐ
ܠܘܬܢ ܕܠܒܪܗ ܝܚܝܕܝܐ[52] ܫܕܪ ܐܠܗܐ ܠܥܠܡܐ ܕܢܚܐ ܒܐܝܕܗ ܒܗܕܐ

---

44. ܚܒܝܨ = crowding.
45. ܦܫܝܩ = easier.
46. ܐܬܘܬܐ = letter.
47. ܛܝܪܐ ܕܥܢܐ = flock of sheep.
48. ܓܢܒܐ = thief.
49. ܓܝܣܐ = robber.
50. ܪܥܝܐ = shepherd.
51. ܥܢܐ = flock.
52. ܝܚܝܕܝܐ = only.

ܐܺܝܬܰܘܗ̱ܝ ܚܽܘܒܳܐ ܠܳܐ ܗ̱ܘܳܐ ܕܰܚܢܰܢ ܐܰܚܶܒܢ ܠܰܐܠܳܗܳܐ ܐܶܠܳܐ ܗܽܘ ܐܰܚܒܰܢ[53]

ܘܫܰܕܰܪ ܠܒܶܪܶܗ ܚܽܘܣܳܝܳܐ[54] ܥܰܠ ܐܰܦܰܝ ܚܛܳܗܰܝܢ ܚܰܒܺܝܒܰܝ ܐܶܢ ܗܳܟܰܢܳܐ ܐܰܚܒܰܢ[55]

ܐܰܠܳܗܳܐ ܐܳܦ ܚܢܰܢ ܚܰܝܳܒܺܝܢܰܢ ܚܰܕ ܠܚܰܕ ܠܡܰܚܒܽܘ ܠܰܐܠܳܗܳܐ ܡܶܡܬܽܘܡ[56] ܐ݇ܢܳܫ

ܠܳܐ ܚܙܳܝܗ̱ܝ[57] ܐܶܢ ܢܰܚܶܒ ܚܰܕ ܠܚܰܕ ܐܰܠܳܗܳܐ ܒܰܢ ܡܩܰܘܶܐ[58] ܘܚܽܘܒܶܗ

ܡܫܰܡܠܝܳܐ[59] ܒܰܢ

Additional Exercises

Starting in this chapter, the additional exercises will be taken from Ephrem's Commentary on the Diatessaron (an early harmony of the four gospels that was used extensively in the early Syriac church).[60] Additionally, the text will be given without any footnotes for help. This may require the aid of a lexicon, if available. To help with difficult or rare words, an English translation has been provided. Make your own translation and use the provided translation only when necessary.

Commentary on the Diatessaron 12.10[61]

ܡܢܐ ܠܟ ܐܬܐ ܒܒܪܬ ܕܫܝܢܐ ܘܢܘܫܩ ܒܝ. ܘܗܘܐ ܦܘܠܓܐ

ܕܬܠܡ̈ܝܕܘܗܝ ܘܪܚܡܘܗܝ ܕܢܟܝܢ ܗܘܘ. ܘܡܛܠ ܕܠܫܝܢܐ ܗܘܪܒܢ ܗܘܘ.

ܫܒܩ ܐܢܫ ܠܟܠܗܘܢ ܕܒܒܪ. ܐܝܟ ܗܘ ܕܐܠܦܐ ܠܦܘܡܗ ܢܫܩ

ܒܐܪ̈ܚܝܗܘܢ. ܘܐܝܟܢܐ ܗ̇ ܗܝ ܕܒܗ ܢܟܝܢ ܗܘܘ. ܐܠܐ ܗܝ ܕܐܡܘܪܗ

53. This is a verb with a pronominal suffix: aphel perfect 3ms + 1cp.
54. ܚܽܘܣܳܝܳܐ = propitiation.
55. This is a verb with a pronominal suffix: aphel perfect 3ms + 1cp.
56. ܡܶܡܬܽܘܡ = ever.
57. This is a verb with a pronominal suffix: peal perfect 3ms + 3ms.
58. ܡܩܰܘܶܐ = abides.
59. ܡܫܰܡܠܝܳܐ = is complete.
60. The authorship of this text is in dispute but for convenience and familiarity, the commentary will be attributed to Ephrem.
61. Text (here and subsequent chapters) from Ephrem's *Commentary on the Diatessaron*. Found in: Louis LeLoir, *Saint Ephrem: Commentaire de l'Evangile Concordant Texte Syriaque (Manuscrit Chester Beatty 709)*, Chester Beatty Monographs 8a (Dublin: Hodges Figgis, 1963) and Louis LeLoir, *Saint Ephrem: Commentaire de l'Evangile Concordant Texte Syriaque (Manuscrit Chester Beatty 709) Folios Additionnels*, Chester Beatty Monographs 8b (Leuven: Peeters, 1990).

ܠܗ ܓܠܝܐܝܬ. ܕܐܒ̈ܗܝܢ ܠܡ ܡܢܢܐ ܐܟܠܘ. ܐܝܟ ܕܟܬܝܒ ܕܠܚܡܐ

ܡܢ ܫܡܝܐ ܝܗܒ ܠܗܘܢ.

English Translation: "*What sign will you do, that we may see and believe in you*? For lo, a multitude of miracles had been arrayed before them. But, because they wanted only one [thing], they despised all [the others] he had performed, as if his fame had not reached their ears. What then was it that they wanted, if not that about which they had spoken openly to him, *Our fathers ate manna in the desert, as it is written, He gave them bread from heaven*."[62]

---

58. English translation (here and subsequent chapters): Carmel McCarthy, *Saint Ephrem's Commentary on Tatian's Diatessaron: An English Translation of Chester Beatty Syriac MS 709 with Introduction and Notes*, Journal of Semitic Studies Supplement 2 (New York: Oxford University Press, 1993).

22

Hollow

Hollow	Perfect	Participle	Imperfect	Imperative	Infinitive
	ܩܳܡ	ܩܳܐܶܡ	ܢܩܽܘܡ	ܩܽܘܡ	ܡܩܳܡ
	qām	*qāem*	*nqum*	*qum*	*mqām*

Introduction

Verbs that have a *waw* or *yūd* as the middle letter in the root are known as hollow verbs. Some of these include:

ܩܘܡ	ܣܘܡ	ܡܝܬ	ܪܘܡ	ܬܘܒ
qām	*sām*	*mit*	*rām*	*tāb*
to rise	to put	to die	to be lifted up (aphel)	to repent

It is important to note that just because a word attests a *waw* in the 3ms form does not necessarily mean that it is a hollow verb. In fact, it is indicative of a strong verb since the *waw* is functioning as a strong consonant and is parsed accordingly. The key to determining if a verb is hollow, therefore, is to look at how the verb behaves in the peal perfect paradigm. If there are only two letters, then it is a hollow verb, and if the *waw* is attested in the form it is a strong verb. For instance, the example used in the paradigm below is from the root ܩܘܡ, *qām,* "to get up or arise." While technically the root attests a *waw* as the second consonant, it disappears in the conjugations.

Hollow Peal Perfect

Since only the middle consonant is affected in hollow verbs, the peal perfect paradigm is formed as we might expect. The endings remain the same as other peal perfect conjugations. Additionally, the 2ms, 3fs, and 1cs look nearly identical, with the only difference being the stem vowel (or lack thereof). This can make translating unpointed texts somewhat difficult, and context must be consulted in order to find the right option.

The vowel that often appears above the initial consonant of the root is a long *a*-vowel. This is not always the case (see immediately below), but the presence of only two consonants and a long *a* can be very good clues to a translator that this is a hollow peal verb.

	Singular		Plural	
3m	ܩܳܡ	*qām* he/it arose	ܩܳܡܘ ܩܳܡܘܢ	*qām* *qāmun* they arose
3f	ܩܳܡܰܬ	*qāmat* she/it arose	ܩܳܡ ܩܳܡܝ̈ ܩܳܡܶܝ̈ܢ	*qām* *qām* *qāmēn* they arose
2m	ܩܳܡܬ	*qāmt* you arose	ܩܳܡܬܘܢ ܩܳܡܬܘܢ	*qāmton* *qāmtun* you arose
2f	ܩܳܡܬܝ	*qāmt* you arose	ܩܳܡܬܶܝ̈ܢ	*qāmtēn* you arose
1c	ܩܳܡܶܬ	*qāmet* I arose	ܩܳܡܢ ܩܳܡܢܰܢ	*qāmn* *qamnan* we arose

In the perfect, the *yūd* occurs only with the verb ܡܘܬ, "to die." The verb occurs relatively frequently in Syriac and so the paradigm is worth examining.

	Singular		Plural	
3m	ܡܺܝܬ	*mit* he/it died	ܡܺܝܬܘ ܡܺܝܬܘܢ	*mit* *mitun* they died
3f	ܡܺܝܬܰܬ	*mitat* she/it died	ܡܺܝܬ ܡܺܝܬܝ̈ ܡܺܝܬܶܝ̈ܢ	*mit* *mit* *mitēn* they died
2m	ܡܺܝܬܬ	*mitt* you died	ܡܺܝܬܬܘܢ ܡܺܝܬܬܘܢ	*mitton* *mittun* you died
2f	ܡܺܝܬܬܝ	*mitt* you died	ܡܺܝܬܬܶܝ̈ܢ	*mittēn* you died
1c	ܡܺܝܬܶܬ	*mitet* I died	ܡܺܝܬܢ ܡܺܝܬܢܰܢ	*mitn* *mitnan* we died

However, note that this irregularity (of having the *yūd*) is only present in the perfect. If the verb is rendered in the imperfect, for example, it becomes regular. Note the following example from Matthew 15:3, which doesn't have the *yūd* and is regularly formed:

ܢܡܽܘܬ	ܡܡܳܬ
nmut	*mmāt*
peal imperfect 3ms	peal infinitive
he will die	to die

Translation: He will die (infinitive absolute).

Hollow Peal Imperfect

One interesting characteristic of the peal imperfect conjugation of hollow verbs is that the middle *waw* reemerges in the middle of the word. This is actually not a characteristic of the hollow verb, per se, but a characteristic of imperfect verbs. Remember that imperfect verbs will often add a *waw* to the middle of a word to accommodate the *u*-sound in the stem vowel. It is just a coincidence that with hollow verbs it resembles the root.

Another interesting aspect of hollow peal imperfect verbs is that there is no vowel on the preformative (except in the 1cs). This is a distinguishable trait that can point to the fact that the root is a hollow verb (as well as being a phonetic challenge, in some cases). Keep in mind that this is a trait that is shared with the pael imperfect. Finally, note that the vowel that is paired with the *waw* is a *u* (and not *o/u*).

	Singular		Plural	
3m	ܢܩܽܘܡ	*nqum* he/it will arise	ܢܩܽܘܡܽܘܢ	*nqumun* they will arise
3f	ܬܩܽܘܡ	*tqum* she/it will arise	ܢܩܽܘܡ̈ܳܢ	*nqumān* they will arise
2m	ܬܩܽܘܡ	*tqum* you will arise	ܬܩܽܘܡܽܘܢ	*tqumun* you will arise
2f	ܬܩܽܘܡܺܝܢ	*tqumin* you will arise	ܬܩܽܘܡ̈ܳܢ	*tqumān* you will arise
1c	ܐܶܩܽܘܡ	*equm* I will arise	ܢܩܽܘܡ	*nqum* we will arise

In the imperfect (and imperative), the verb ܣܳܡ (*sam*, "to put/place") shows the pattern of a hollow verb with the *yūd* as the middle consonant. This is similar to ܡܘܬ, "to die" above, where the change only is present in these forms. There is no vowel over the preformative and the stem vowel is an *i*. With this in mind, the verbs form in the same manner as above, just with a *yūd* instead of a *waw* in the middle.

	Singular		Plural	
3m	ܢܣܺܝܡ	*nsim* he/it will put	ܢܣܺܝܡܽܘܢ	*nsimun* they will put
3f	ܬܣܺܝܡ	*tsim* she/it will put	ܢܣܺܝܡܳܢ	*nsimān* they will put
2m	ܬܣܺܝܡ	*tsim* you will put	ܬܣܺܝܡܽܘܢ	*tsimun* you will put
2f	ܬܣܺܝܡܺܝܢ	*tsimin* you will put	ܬܣܺܝܡܳܢ	*tsimān* you will put
1c	ܐܣܺܝܡ	*esim* I will put	ܢܣܺܝܡ	*nsim* we will put

Hollow Peal Imperative

In typical fashion, the peal imperative is formed the same as the imperfect, just without the preformative. Hence, the paradigms look similar to the two forms above. The actual patterns themselves are predictably formed as imperatives, just with two consonants as the root. This first is an example with a *u*-stem vowel—keep in mind that the *waw* is added not because it is a hollow verb but because this is the typical behavior of imperative conjugations.

	Singular	Plural I	Plural II
Masculine	ܩܽܘܡ *qum* Get up!	ܩܽܘܡܘ *qum* Get up!	ܩܽܘܡܽܘܢ *qumun* Get up!
Feminine	ܩܽܘܡܝ *qum* Get up!	ܩܽܘ̈ܡܝ *qum* Get up!	ܩܽܘܡܶܝܢ *qumēn* Get up!

The following is another example from ܣܡ (*sam*, "to put/place") with an *i*-stem vowel in the imperfect tense and a *yūd* instead of a *waw* in the middle of the root.

	Singular	Plural I	Plural II
Masculine	ܣܺܝܡ *sim* Put!	ܣܺܝܡܘ *sim* Put!	ܣܺܝܡܶܘܢ *simēn* Put!
Feminine	ܣܺܝܡܝ *sim* Put!	ܣܺܝ̈ܡܝ *sim* Put!	ܣܺܝ̈ܡܶܝܢ *simēn* Put!

Hollow Peal Infinitive

The hollow peal infinitive will appear in one of two forms. However, even with the various endings, the basic form of the two verbs is similar, with a *mīm* prefix and long *a*-stem vowel. Note the differences in the two below.

1. The *-u* ending absent:

ܡܩܳܡ
mqām
to arise

2. The *-u* ending present:

ܡܣܳܡܽܘ
msāmu
to put / place

Hollow Peal Participles

The hollow peal participles behave in a manner similar to geminate verbs; the active masculine singular form takes an *ālap* as the middle consonant, and all others take a *yūd* in the middle of the verb. This can make the identification of the root somewhat difficult because the masculine singular resembles the paradigm of the II-*ālap* and geminate verbs even down to having similar vowel pointing. In these instances, when the root is hard to distinguish keep in mind the options that are available and let context rule out the various possibilities.

One nice thing about the participles is that there is only one paradigm to examine. In the previous conjugations, there was typically a *u*-class verb and an *i*-class verb. In the case of hollow peal participles there is only one pattern to follow as both types will take a similar form.

Finally, note that the two forms of the active and the passive participles are very similar to one another. The main difference between them is the initial vowel of the passive participle: an *i* instead of an *a*.

Active

Masculine		Feminine	
Singular	**Plural**	**Singular**	**Plural**
ܩܳܐܶܡ	ܩܳܝܡܺܝܢ	ܩܳܝܡܳܐ	ܩܳܝܡܳܢ
qāem	*qāymin*	*qāymā*	*qāymān*
arising	arising	arising	arising

Passive

Masculine		Feminine	
Singular	**Plural**	**Singular**	**Plural**
ܩܺܝܡ	ܩܺܝܡܺܝܢ	ܩܺܝܡܳܐ	ܩܺܝܡܳܢ
qim	*qimin*	*qimā*	*qimān*
being raised	being raised	being raised	being raised

Introduction to Derived Stems

Outside of the peal perfect paradigms, the other stems of hollow verbs will typically have the middle consonant appear as a *yūd*. This occurs regardless of whether the middle consonant is an original *yūd* or *waw*; hollow verbs are otherwise conjugated as we might expect. Note, however, that there is no hollow ethpeel conjugation in Syriac. It is replaced by the hollow ettaphal conjugation.

Hollow Pael (D)

ܩܰܝܶܡ	ܢܩܰܝܶܡ	ܩܰܝܶܡ	ܡܩܰܝܳܡܽܘ	ܡܩܰܝܶܡ	ܡܩܰܝܰܡ
qayyem	*nqayyem*	*qayyem*	*mqayyāmu*	*mqayyem*	*mqayyam*
Perfect	Imperfect	Imperative	Infinitive	Active Participle	Passive Participle

Hollow Aphel (A)

ܐܰܩܺܝܡ	ܢܩܺܝܡ	ܐܰܩܺܝܡ	ܡܩܳܡܽܘ	ܡܩܺܝܡ	ܡܩܳܡ
aqim	*nqim*	*aqim*	*mqāmu*	*mqim*	*mqām*
Perfect	Imperfect	Imperative	Infinitive	Active Participle	Passive Participle

Hollow Ethpaal (Dp)

ܐܶܬܩܰܝܰܡ	ܢܶܬܩܰܝܰܡ	ܐܶܬܩܰܝܰܡ	ܡܶܬܩܰܝܳܡܽܘ	ܡܶܬܩܰܝܰܡ
etqayyam	*netqayyam*	*etqayyam*	*metqayyāmu*	*metqayyam*
Perfect	Imperfect	Imperative	Infinitive	Participle

Hollow Ettaphal (Ap)

ܐܶܬܬܩܺܝܡ	ܢܶܬܬܩܺܝܡ	ܐܶܬܬܩܺܝܡ	ܡܶܬܬܩܳܡܽܘ	ܡܶܬܬܩܺܝܡ
ettqim	*nettqim*	*ettqim*	*mettqāmu*	*mettqim*
Perfect	Imperfect	Imperative	Infinitive	Participle

Vocabulary
Nouns

ܐܰܒܕܳܢܳܐ	*abdānā*	loss, waste
ܐܶܣܛܪܰܛܺܝܳܛܳܐ	*esṭraṭiāṭā*	soldier (Gk. στρατιώτης)
ܒܶܣܡܳܐ	*besmā*	ointment, incense, aroma
ܝܰܪܚܳܐ	*yarḥā*	month
ܟܽܠܝܽܘܡ	*kullyum*	everyday
ܠܒܽܘܫܳܐ	*lbušā*	clothing
ܢܶܣܝܽܘܢܳܐ	*nesyunā*	trial, temptation
ܣܽܘܓܳܐܐ	*sugā*	abundance, many
ܣܰܟܠܘܳܬܳܐ	*saklwātā*	error, wrongdoing
ܥܽܘܬܪܳܐ	*ʿutrā*	riches
ܫܶܬܶܐܣܬܳܐ	*šetestā*	foundation
ܬܺܝܬܳܐ	*titā*	fig tree

Verbs

ܒܩܐ	*bqā*	to examine, prove
ܛܥܡ	*ṭʿem*	to taste, partake
ܛܫܐ	*ṭšā*	to hide
ܟܦܢ	*kpen*	to hunger
ܣܝܒ	*syeb*	to defile
ܣܢܩ	*sneq*	to need
ܣܦܩ	*spaq*	to be sufficient, able
ܦܨܐ	*pṣā*	to deliver
ܦܫܩ	*pašeq*	to interpret
ܫܬܩ	*šteq*	to be silent
ܬܟܠ	*tkel*	to be confident, trust
ܬܩܢ	*tqen*	to be restored, make right

Other

ܒܝܢܝ	*bayna*	between, among
ܚܘܪܐ	*ḥewwārā*	white
ܗܟܘܬ	*hākwāt*	likewise, so
ܚܣܝܪܐ	*ḥasirā*	deficient, shame, reproach
ܟܐܢܐ	*kinā*	just, righteous
ܡܟܝܟܐ	*makkikā*	gentle, humble
ܢܘܟܪܝܐ	*nukrāyā*	foreign, strange
ܢܨܪܝܐ	*naṣrāyā*	Nazarene
ܪܚܝܩܐ	*raḥiqā*	far, distant

Exercises

Matthew 28:6–9 (1)

ܠܐ ܗܘܐ ܬܢܢ[1] ܩܡ ܠܗ ܓܝܪ ܐܝܟܢܐ ܕܐܡܪ ܬܘ ܚܙܝܘ ܕܘܟܬܐ
ܕܣܝܡ ܗܘܐ ܒܗ ܡܪܢ ܘܙܠܝܢ ܒܥܓܠ[2] ܐܡܪܝܢ ܠܬܠܡܝܕܘܗܝ، ܕܩܡ ܡܢ
ܒܝܬ ܡܝܬܐ ܘܗܐ ܩܕܡ ܠܟܘܢ ܠܓܠܝܠܐ ܬܡܢ ܬܚܙܘܢܝܗܝ[3] ܗܐ
ܐܡܪܬ ܠܟܝܢ ܘܐܙܠ ܥܓܠ[4] ܡܢ ܩܒܪܐ ܒܕܚܠܬܐ ܘܒܚܕܘܬܐ ܪܒܬܐ
ܘܪܗܛ ܠܡܐܡܪ ܠܬܠܡܝܕܘܗܝ، ܘܗܐ ܝܫܘܥ ܦܓܥ[5] ܒܗܝܢ ܘܐܡܪ ܠܗܝܢ
ܫܠܡ ܠܟܝܢ ܗܢܝܢ ܕܝܢ ܩܪܒ ܐܚܕ ܪܓܠܘܗܝ، ܘܣܓܕܝܢ ܠܗ

Matthew 9:5–8 (2)

ܐܝܢܐ ܓܝܪ ܦܫܝܩ[6] ܠܡܐܡܪ ܕܫܒܝܩܝܢ ܠܟ ܚܛܗܝܟ ܐܘ ܠܡܐܡܪ
ܩܘܡ ܗܠܟ ܕܬܕܥܘܢ ܕܝܢ ܕܫܠܝܛ ܒܪܗ ܕܐܢܫܐ ܒܐܪܥܐ
ܠܡܫܒܩ ܚܛܗܐ ܐܡܪ ܠܗܘ ܡܫܪܝܐ[7] ܩܘܡ ܫܩܘܠ ܥܪܣܟ ܘܙܠ
ܠܒܝܬܟ ܘܩܡ ܐܙܠ ܠܒܝܬܗ ܟܕ ܚܙܘ ܕܝܢ ܟܢܫܐ ܕܚܠܘ ܘܫܒܚܘ
ܠܐܠܗܐ ܕܝܗܒ ܫܘܠܛܢܐ ܐܝܟ ܗܢܐ ܠܒܢܝܢܫܐ

1. ܬܢܢ = here.
2. ܒܥܓܠ = quickly.
3. This is a verb with a pronominal suffix: peal imperfect 2mp + 3ms.
4. ܥܓܠ = quickly.
5. ܦܓܥ = he met.
6. ܦܫܝܩ = easier (this verb actually could have a number of different interpretations. For now, consider "easier" as an appropriate translation).
7. ܡܫܪܝܐ = paralytic.

Matthew 6:19–21 (3)

ܠܐ ܬܣܝܡܘܢ ܠܟܘܢ ܣܝܡܬܐ[8] ܒܐܪܥܐ ܐܬܪ ܕܣܣܐ ܘܐܟܠܐ
ܡܚܒܠܝܢ[9] ܘܐܝܟܐ ܕܓܢܒܐ ܦܠܫܝܢ ܘܓܢܒܝܢ[10] ܐܠܐ ܣܝܡܘ ܠܟܘܢ
ܣܝܡܬܐ ܒܫܡܝܐ ܐܝܟܐ ܕܠܐ ܣܣܐ ܘܠܐ ܐܟܠܐ ܡܚܒܠܝܢ ܘܐܝܟܐ
ܕܓܢܒܐ ܠܐ ܦܠܫܝܢ ܘܠܐ ܓܢܒܝܢ ܐܝܟܐ ܓܝܪ ܕܐܝܬܘܗܝ ܣܝܡܬܟܘܢ
ܬܡܢ ܗܘ ܐܦ ܠܒܟܘܢ

John 13:34–38 (4)

ܦܘܩܕܢܐ ܚܕܬܐ ܝܗܒ ܐܢܐ ܠܟܘܢ ܕܬܗܘܘܢ ܡܚܒܝܢ ܚܕ ܠܚܕ
ܐܝܟܢܐ ܕܐܢܐ ܐܚܒܬܟܘܢ[11] ܐܦ ܐܢܬܘܢ ܬܚܒܘܢ ܚܕ ܠܚܕ ܒܗܕܐ
ܢܕܥ ܟܠ ܐܢܫ ܕܬܠܡܝܕܝ ܐܢܬܘܢ ܐܢ ܚܘܒܐ ܢܗܘܐ ܒܟܘܢ ܚܕ ܠܘܬ
ܚܕ ܐܡܪ ܠܗ ܫܡܥܘܢ ܟܐܦܐ ܡܪܢ ܠܐܝܟܐ ܐܙܠ ܐܢܬ ܥܢܐ ܝܫܘܥ
ܘܐܡܪ ܠܗ ܠܐܝܟܐ ܕܐܙܠ ܐܢܐ ܠܐ ܡܫܟܚ[12] ܐܢܬ ܗܫܐ ܕܬܐܬܐ
ܒܬܪܝ ܠܚܪܬܐ[13] ܕܝܢ ܬܐܬܐ ܐܡܪ ܠܗ ܫܡܥܘܢ ܟܐܦܐ ܡܪܝ ܠܡܢܐ
ܠܐ ܡܫܟܚ ܐܢܐ ܕܐܬܐ ܒܬܪܟ ܗܫܐ ܢܦܫܝ ܚܠܦܝܟ ܣܐܡ ܐܢܐ
ܐܡܪ ܠܗ ܝܫܘܥ ܢܦܫܟ ܚܠܦܝ ܣܐܡ ܐܢܬ ܐܡܝܢ ܐܡܝܢ ܐܡܪ ܐܢܐ
ܠܟ ܕܠܐ ܢܩܪܐ ܬܪܢܓܠܐ[14] ܥܕܡܐ ܕܬܟܦܘܪ[15] ܒܝ ܬܠܬ ܙܒܢܝܢ

8. ܣܝܡܬܐ = treasures (x2).
9. ܕܣܣܐ ܘܐܟܠܐ ܡܚܒܠܝܢ = that moth and bugs corrupt. These words appear twice in the verse.
10. ܕܓܢܒܐ ܦܠܫܝܢ ܘܓܢܒܝܢ = that thieves break in and steal. These words appear twice in the verse.
11. This is a verb with a pronominal suffix: aphel perfect 1cs + 2mp.
12. Remember, this is the peal perfect of this particular verb (x2).
13. ܠܚܪܬܐ = (at) the end.
14. ܬܪܢܓܠܐ = rooster.
15. ܕܬܟܦܘܪ = you deny.

Luke 2:16–20 (5)

ܘܐܬܘ ܡܣܘܪܗܒܐܝܬ[16] ܘܐܫܟܚܘܗ̇ ܠܡܪܝܡ ܘܠܝܘܣܦ ܘܠܥܘܠܐ[17] ܕܣܝܡ
ܒܐܘܪܝܐ[18] ܘܟܕ ܚܙܘ ܐܘܕܥܘ ܠܡܠܬܐ ܕܐܬܡܠܠܬ ܥܡܗܘܢ ܥܠܘܗܝ
ܥܠ ܛܠܝܐ ܘܟܠܗܘܢ ܕܫܡܥܘ ܐܬܕܡܪܘ ܥܠ ܐܝܠܝܢ ܕܐܬܡܠܠ ܠܗܘܢ
ܡܢ ܪ̈ܥܘܬܐ[19] ܡܪܝܡ ܕܝܢ ܢܛܪܐ ܗܘܬ ܟܠܗܝܢ ܡ̈ܠܐ ܗܠܝܢ ܘܡܦܚܡܐ[20]
ܒܠܒܗ̇ ܘܗܦܟܘ ܪ̈ܥܘܬܐ ܗܢܘܢ ܟܕ ܡܫܒܚܝܢ ܘܡܗܠܠܝܢ[21] ܠܐܠܗܐ ܥܠ
ܟܠ ܕܫܡܥܘ ܘܚܙܘ ܐܝܟܢܐ ܕܐܬܡܠܠ ܥܡܗܘܢ

John 10:14–18 (6)

ܐܢܐ ܐܢܐ ܪܥܝܐ[22] ܛܒܐ ܘܝܕܥ ܐܢܐ ܠܕܝܠܝ ܘܡܬܝܕܥ ܐܢܐ ܡܢ
ܕܝܠܝ ܐܝܟܢܐ ܕܝܕܥ ܠܝ ܐܒܝ ܘܐܢܐ ܝܕܥ ܐܢܐ ܠܐܒܝ ܘܢܦܫܝ ܣܐܡ
ܐܢܐ ܚܠܦ ܥܢܐ[23] ܐܝܬ ܠܝ ܕܝܢ ܐܦ ܥ̈ܪܒܐ ܐ̈ܚܪܢܐ ܐܝܠܝܢ ܕܠܐ
ܗܘܘ ܡܢ ܛܝܪܐ[24] ܗܢܐ ܘܐܦ ܠܗܘܢ ܘܠܐ ܠܝ ܠܡܝܬܝܘ[25] ܐܢܘܢ
ܘܢܫܡܥܘܢ ܩܠܝ ܘܬܗܘܐ ܥܢܐ ܟܠܗ̇ ܚܕܐ ܘܪܥܝܐ ܚܕ. ܡܛܠ ܗܢܐ
ܐܒܝ ܪܚܡ ܠܝ ܕܐܢܐ ܣܐܡ ܐܢܐ ܢܦܫܝ ܕܬܘܒ ܐܣܒܝܗ̇[26] ܠܐ ܗܘܐ
ܐܢܫ ܫܩܠ ܠܗ̇ ܡܢܝ ܐܠܐ ܐܢܐ ܣܐܡ ܐܢܐ ܠܗ̇ ܡܢ ܨܒܝܢܝ ܫܠܝܛ[27]

16. ܡܣܘܪܗܒܐܝܬ = quickly.
17. ܘܠܥܘܠܐ = and the child.
18. ܒܐܘܪܝܐ = in the manger.
19. ܪ̈ܥܘܬܐ = the shepherds.
20. ܘܡܦܚܡܐ = and she pondered.
21. ܘܡܗܠܠܝܢ = and praising.
22. ܪܥܝܐ = shepherd (x2).
23. ܥܢܐ = the flock (x2).
24. ܛܝܪܐ = flock.
25. This is the peal infinitive of ܐܬܐ.
26. This is a verb with a pronominal suffix: peal imperfect 1cs + 3fs.
27. ܫܠܝܛ = permitted.

ܐܝܬ ܠܝ ܕܐܣܝܡܝܗ̇[28] ܘܫܘܠܛܢܐ ܐܝܬ ܠܝ ܕܬܘܒ ܐܣܒܝܗ̇[29] ܗܕܐ

ܦܘܩܕܢܐ ܩܒܠܬ ܡܢ ܐܒܝ

John 11:21–29 (7)

ܘܐܡܪܬ ܡܪܬܐ ܠܝܫܘܥ ܡܪܝ ܐܠܘ ܬܢܢ[30] ܗܘܝܬ ܠܐ ܡܐܬ ܗܘܐ

ܐܚܝ ܐܠܐ ܐܦ ܗܫܐ ܝܕܥܐ ܐܢܐ ܕܟܡܐ ܕܬܫܐܠ ܠܐܠܗܐ ܝܗܒ

ܠܟܝ ܐܡܪ ܠܗ̇ ܝܫܘܥ ܩܐܡ ܐܚܘܟܝ ܐܡܪܐ ܠܗ ܡܪܬܐ ܝܕܥܐܢܐ[31]

ܕܩܐܡ ܒܩܝܡܬܐ[32] ܒܝܘܡܐ ܐܚܪܝܐ ܐܡܪ ܠܗ̇ ܝܫܘܥ ܐܢܐ ܐܢܐ

ܩܝܡܬܐ[33] ܘܚܝܐ ܡܢ ܕܡܗܝܡܢ[34] ܒܝ ܐܦܢ ܢܡܘܬ ܢܚܐ ܘܟܠ ܕܚܝ

ܘܡܗܝܡܢ ܒܝ ܠܥܠܡ ܠܐ ܢܡܘܬ ܡܗܝܡܢܐܢܬܝ[35] ܗܕܐ ܐܡܪܐ ܠܗ ܐܝܢ

ܡܪܝ ܐܢܐ ܡܗܝܡܢܐ ܐܢܐ ܕܐܢܬ ܗܘ ܡܫܝܚܐ ܒܪܗ ܕܐܠܗܐ ܕܐܬܐ

ܠܥܠܡܐ ܘܟܕ ܐܡܪܬ ܗܠܝܢ ܐܙܠܬ ܩܪܬ ܠܡܪܝܡ ܚܬܗ ܒܛܘܫܝܐܝܬ[36]

ܘܐܡܪܐ ܠܗ̇ ܪܒܢ ܐܬܐ ܘܩܪܐ ܠܟܝ ܘܡܪܝܡ ܟܕ ܫܡܥܬ ܩܡܬ ܥܓܠ[37]

ܘܐܬܝܐ ܗܘܬ ܠܘܬܗ

---

28. This is a verb with a pronominal suffix: peal imperfect 1cs + 3fs.
29. Ibid.
30. ܬܢܢ = here.
31. This is a participle with a pronominal suffix: peal active fs + 1cs.
32. ܒܩܝܡܬܐ = in the resurrection.
33. ܩܝܡܬܐ = the resurrection.
34. ܡܗܝܡܢ = believing (participle). This verb appears a few times in this verse. Look for the endings as clues to the parsing.
35. ܡܗܝܡܢܐܢܬܝ = you are believing.
36. ܒܛܘܫܝܐܝܬ = secretly.
37. ܥܓܠ = quickly.

John 12:47–50 (8)

ܘܡܢ ܕܫܡܥ ܡܠܝ ܘܠܐ ܢܛܪ ܠܗܝܢ ܐܢܐ ܠܐ ܕܐܢ ܐܢܐ ܠܗ ܠܐ
ܓܝܪ ܐܬܝܬ ܕܐܕܘܢ ܠܥܠܡܐ ܐܠܐ ܕܐܚܐ ܠܥܠܡܐ ܡܢ ܕܛܠܡ[38] ܠܝ
ܘܠܐ ܡܩܒܠ ܡܠܝ ܐܝܬ ܠܗ ܡܢ ܕܕܐܢ ܠܗ ܡܠܬܐ ܕܡܠܠܬ ܗܝ ܕܐܢܐ ܠܗ
ܒܝܘܡܐ ܐܚܪܝܐ ܕܐܢܐ ܡܢ ܢܦܫܝ ܠܐ ܡܠܠܬ ܐܠܐ ܐܒܐ ܕܫܕܪܢܝ[39] ܗܘ
ܝܗܒ ܠܝ ܦܘܩܕܢܐ ܡܢܐ ܐܡܪ ܘܡܢܐ ܐܡܠܠ ܘܝܕܥ ܐܢܐ ܕܦܘܩܕܢܗ
ܚܝܐ ܐܢܘܢ ܕܠܥܠܡ ܐܠܝܢ ܗܟܝܠ ܕܡܡܠܠ ܐܢܐ ܐܝܟܢܐ ܕܐܡܪ ܠܝ
ܐܒܝ ܗܟܢܐ ܡܡܠܠ ܐܢܐ

Luke 16:27–31 (9)

ܐܡܪ ܠܗ ܡܕܝܢ ܒܥܐ ܐܢܐ ܡܢܟ ܐܒܝ ܕܬܫܕܪܝܘܗܝ[40] ܠܒܝܬ ܐܒܝ
ܚܡܫܐ[41] ܓܝܪ ܐܚܝܢ ܐܝܬ ܠܝ ܢܐܙܠ ܢܣܗܕ ܐܢܘܢ ܕܠܐ ܐܦ
ܗܢܘܢ ܢܐܬܘܢ ܠܐܬܪܐ ܗܢܐ ܕܬܫܢܝܩܐ[42] ܐܡܪ ܠܗ ܐܒܪܗܡ ܐܝܬ
ܠܗܘܢ ܡܘܫܐ ܘܢܒܝܐ ܢܫܡܥܘܢ ܐܢܘܢ ܗܘ ܕܝܢ ܐܡܪ ܠܗ ܠܐ ܐܒܝ
ܐܒܪܗܡ ܐܠܐ ܐܢ ܐܢܫ ܡܢ ܡܝܬܐ ܢܐܙܠ ܠܘܬܗܘܢ ܬܝܒܝܢ ܐܡܪ
ܠܗ ܐܒܪܗܡ ܐܢ ܠܡܘܫܐ ܘܠܢܒܝܐ ܠܐ ܫܡܥܝܢ ܐܦ ܠܐ ܐܢ ܐܢܫ
ܡܢ ܡܝܬܐ ܢܩܘܡ ܡܗܝܡܢܝܢ[43] ܠܗ

38. ܕܛܠܡ = rejects.
39. This is a verb with a pronominal suffix: pael perfect 3ms + 1cs.
40. This is a verb with a pronominal suffix: pael imperfect 2ms + 3ms.
41. ܚܡܫܐ = five.
42. ܕܬܫܢܝܩܐ = of torment.
43. ܡܗܝܡܢܝܢ = believing (participle).

Matthew 4:5–10 (10)

ܗܝܕܝܢ ܕܒܪܗ[44] ܐܟܠܩܪܨܐ[45] ܠܡܕܝܢܬܐ ܩܕܝܫܬܐ ܘܐܩܝܡܗ[46] ܥܠ ܟܢܦܐ[47]
ܕܗܝܟܠܐ ܘܐܡܪ ܠܗ ܐܢ ܒܪܗ ܐܢܬ ܕܐܠܗܐ ܫܕܝ ܢܦܫܟ ܠܬܚܬ[48]
ܟܬܝܒ ܗܘ ܓܝܪ ܕܠܡܠܐܟܘܗܝ ܢܦܩܕ ܥܠܝܟ ܘܥܠ ܐܝܕܝܗܘܢ ܢܛܠܘܢܟ
ܕܠܐ ܬܬܩܠ[49] ܪܓܠܟ ܒܟܐܦܐ ܐܡܪ ܠܗ ܝܫܘܥ ܬܘܒ ܟܬܝܒ ܕܠܐ
ܬܢܣܐ ܠܡܪܝܐ ܐܠܗܟ ܬܘܒ ܕܒܪܗ[50] ܐܟܠܩܪܨܐ ܠܛܘܪܐ ܕܪܡ
ܛܒ ܘܚܘܝܗ[51] ܟܠܗܝܢ ܡܠܟܘܬܐ ܕܥܠܡܐ ܘܫܘܒܚܗܝܢ ܘܐܡܪ ܠܗ
ܗܠܝܢ ܟܠܗܝܢ ܠܟ ܐܬܠ[52] ܐܢ ܬܦܠ ܬܣܓܘܕ ܠܝ ܗܝܕܝܢ ܐܡܪ ܠܗ
ܝܫܘܥ ܙܠ ܠܟ ܣܛܢܐ ܟܬܝܒ ܗܘ ܓܝܪ ܕܠܡܪܝܐ ܐܠܗܟ ܬܣܓܘܕ ܘܠܗ
ܠܚܘܕܘܗܝ ܬܦܠܘܚ

44. Be careful on this one. It looks like another common word but is actually a verb with a pronominal suffix: peal perfect 3ms + 3ms.
45. ܐܟܠܩܪܨܐ = the accuser (x2).
46. This is a verb with a pronominal suffix: aphel perfect 3ms + 3ms.
47. ܟܢܦܐ = side.
48. ܠܬܚܬ = under.
49. ܬܬܩܠ = you will stumble.
50. This is a verb with a pronominal suffix: peal perfect 3ms + 3ms.
51. This is a verb with a pronominal suffix: pael perfect 3ms + 3ms.
52. ܐܬܠ = I will give.

Commentary on the Diatessaron 16.25

ܘܕܩܐܡ ܗܘܐ ܡܪܢ ܘܩܥܐ. ܕܟܠ ܕܨܗܐ[53] ܢܐܬܐ ܠܘܬܝ ܘܢܫܬܐ.

ܗ̇ܝ ܗܝ ܕܢܒܝܐ. ܕܐܘ ܟܠ ܕܨܗܐ ܐܙܠܘ ܠܡ̈ܝܐ. ܢܒܝܐ ܫܕܪ ܠܡܒܘܥܐ.[54]

ܘܡܫܠܡܢܐ[55] ܕܢܒ̈ܝܐ ܩܪܐ ܠܡܫܬܝܐ. ܗܝ ܕܐܡܪܬ ܚܟܡܬܐ ܕܬܘ

ܐܟܘܠܘ ܡܢ ܠܚܡܝ. ܘܐܫܬܘ ܡܢ ܚܡܪܐ ܕܡܙܓܬ.[56] ܘܐܫܝܘ ܡܢܟܘܢ

ܫܛܝܘܬܐ[57] ܕܬܚܝܘܢ ܘܚܝܘ.

English Translation (McCarthy): "The [text], *Our Lord stood up and proclaimed, Let all who are thirsty come to me and drink,* is like that of the prophet, *Let all who thirst come to the waters.* The prophet sent [them] to the spring, but the One who fulfills the prophets' [words] invited [them] to drink. [That is] what Wisdom said, *Come and eat my bread and drink the wine I have mixed, leave folly behind and you will live!*"

53. ܨܗܐ = thirsty (x2).
54. ܠܡܒܘܥܐ = to the fountain.
55. ܡܫܠܡܢܐ = fulfilling
56. ܕܡܙܓܬ = that I have mixed.
57. ܫܛܝܘܬܐ = defect

23

II-*ālap*

	Perfect	Participle	Imperfect	Imperative	Infinitive
II-*ālap*	ܫܶܐܠ	ܫܳܐܶܠ	ܢܶܫܰܐܠ	ܫܰܐܠ	ܡܶܫܰܐܠ
	šel	*šāel*	*nešal*	*šal*	*mešal*

Introduction

Verbs that have an *ālap* as the second consonant of the root show minor variation compared to strong verbs. Verbs in this form include:

ܫܶܐܠ	ܒܶܐܫ	ܛܶܐܒ
šel	*beš*	*ṭeb*
to ask	to be evil	to be good

Since the *ālap* is a very weak consonant, it takes its accompanying vowel and has no pronunciation (called a quiescent *ālap*, meaning that it has no pronunciation). Additionally, the vowel that appears as the stem vowel on a II-*ālap* verb will move forward onto the first consonant of the root.

II-*ālap* Peal Perfect

In the II-*ālap* peal perfect paradigm, notice how the stem vowel is an *e* appearing above the first (not second) consonant. Outside of this unique change, the paradigm is predictably formed according to the strong conjugation. Keep in mind the typical vowel change from the 2ms, 3fs, and 1cs forms.

	Singular		Plural	
3m	ܫܶܐܠ	*šel* he/it asked	ܫܶܐܠܘ ܫܶܐܠܘܢ	*šel* *šelun* they asked
3f	ܫܶܐܠܰܬ	*šelat* she/it asked	ܫܶܐܠ ܫܶܐܠ̈ ܫܶܐܠ̈ܶܝܢ	*šel* *šel* *šelēn* they asked
2m	ܫܶܐܠܬ	*šelt* you asked	ܫܶܐܠܬܽܘܢ ܫܶܐܠܬܘܢ	*šelton* *šeltun* you asked
2f	ܫܶܐܠܬܝ	*šelt* you asked	ܫܶܐܠ̈ܬܶܝܢ	*šeltēn* you asked
1c	ܫܶܐܠܶܬ	*šelet* I asked	ܫܶܐܠܢ ܫܶܐܠܢܰܢ	*šeln* *šelnan* we asked

II-*ālap* Peal Imperfect

The II-*ālap* peal imperfect is formed in a manner similar to the perfect, with the stem vowel appearing over the initial consonant. The rest of the paradigm is regularly formed according to the typical peal imperfect paradigm.

	Singular		Plural	
3m	ܢܶܫܰܐܠ	*nešal* he/it will ask	ܢܶܫܶܐܠܘܢ	*nešelun* they will ask
3f	ܬܶܫܰܐܠ	*tešal* she/it will ask	ܢܶܫܶܐܠ̈ܳܢ	*nešelān* they will ask
2m	ܬܶܫܰܐܠ	*tešal* you will ask	ܬܶܫܶܐܠܘܢ	*tešelun* you will ask
2f	ܬܶܫܶܐܠܺܝܢ	*tešelin* you will ask	ܬܶܫܶܐܠ̈ܳܢ	*tešelān* you will ask
1c	ܐܶܫܰܐܠ	*ešal* I will ask	ܢܶܫܰܐܠ	*nešal* we will ask

II-*ālap* Peal Imperative

As we might expect, the stem vowel appears above the initial consonant in the II-*ālap* peal imperative. As with other verb types, the II-*ālap* imperative is a duplication of the 3ms imperfect form, just without the preformative.

	Singular	Plural I	Plural II
Masculine	ܫܰܐܠ *šal* Ask!	ܫܰܐܠܘ *šal* Ask!	ܫܰܐܠܘܢ *šalun* Ask!
Feminine	ܫܰܐܠܝ *šal* Ask!	ܫܰܐ̈ܠܝ *šal* Ask!	ܫܰܐ̈ܠܝܢ *šalēn* Ask!

II-*ālap* Peal Infinitive

The peal infinitive for II-*ālap* verbs takes the usual *mīm* prefix with an *e*-vowel, ܡܶ (*me-*), attached to the front as well as the stem vowel over the first letter.

ܡܶܫܰܐܠ
mešal
to ask

II-*ālap* Participles

Peal participles are one type of conjugation that breaks the expected pattern for the II-*ālap* verbs. Here the *ālap* does take a vowel in the masculine singular active, the most common form of the participle.

One other interesting fact is that the *ālap* remains in the root with the passive. Further, the stem vowel still appears above the initial consonant of the root, but it is paired with the *yūd* that appears after the *ālap*. In other words, the *ālap* does not assimilate into the *yūd–i* combination, but remains where it is placed in the root of the word and quiesces.

Active

Masculine		Feminine	
Singular	**Plural**	**Singular**	**Plural**
ܫܳܐܶܠ	ܫܳܐܠܺܝܢ	ܫܳܐܠܳܐ	ܫܳܐܠܳܢ
šāel	*šālin*	*šālā*	*šālān*
asking	asking	asking	asking

Passive

Masculine		Feminine	
Singular	**Plural**	**Singular**	**Plural**
ܫܺܐܝܠ	ܫܺܐܝܠܺܝܢ	ܫܺܐܝܠܳܐ	ܫܺܐܝܠܳܢ
šil	*šilin*	*šilā*	*šilān*
being asked	being asked	being asked	being asked

Introduction to Derived Stems

When surveying the derived stems of the II-*ālap* verbs, note that in the pael and ethpaal stems of the verbs there are vowels above the *ālap* consonant. This is due to the fact that there is a glottal stop[1] where the *ālap* is "pronounced" in order to account for the doubling of the middle consonant. This causes the *ālap* to take a vowel. In the following tables, this doubling will be labeled with double apostrophes but remember that these are not pronounced.

Finally, notice the metathesis of the *š* and the *t* in the *et-* conjugations.

1. Think of a glottal stop as a short break in pronunciation where the glottis (vocal tract) is briefly obstructed.

II-*ālap* Pael (D)

ܫܐܠ	ܢܫܐܠ	ܫܐܠ	ܡܫܐܠܘ	ܡܫܐܠ	ܡܫܐܠ
ša''el	*nša''el*	*ša''el*	*mša''ālu*	*mša''el*	*mša''al*
Perfect	Imperfect	Imperative	Infinitive	Active Participle	Passive Participle

II-*ālap* Aphel (A)

ܐܫܐܠ	ܢܫܐܠ	ܐܫܐܠ	ܡܫܐܠܘ	ܡܫܐܠ	-
ašel	*našel*	*ašel*	*mašālu*	*mašel*	-
Perfect	Imperfect	Imperative	Infinitive	Active Participle	Passive Participle

II-*ālap* Ethpeel (Gp)

ܐܫܬܐܠ	ܢܫܬܐܠ	ܐܫܬܐܠ	ܡܫܬܐܠܘ	ܡܫܬܐܠ
eštel	*neštel*	*eštal*	*meštālu*	*meštel*
Perfect	Imperfect	Imperative	Infinitive	Participle

II-*ālap* Ethpaal (Dp)

ܐܫܬܐܠ	ܢܫܬܐܠ	ܐܫܬܐܠ	ܡܫܬܐܠܘ	ܡܫܬܐܠ
ešta''al	*nešta''al*	*ešta''al*	*meštā'' lu*	*mša''al*
Perfect	Imperfect	Imperative	Infinitive	Participle

Vocabulary

This chapter will be used to take a break from the usual rigorous vocabulary memorization in order to learn how to count in Syriac. There is a more in-depth chapter in the appendix that covers the numbers and dates, but for now focus on being able to count from one to twenty. All of these will be in the masculine form, but note that there is a feminine form as well.

ܚܰܕ	*ḥad*	one
ܬܪܶܝܢ	*trēn*	two
ܬܠܳܬܳܐ	*tlātā*	three
ܐܰܪܒܥܳܐ	*arbʿā*	four
ܚܰܡܫܳܐ	*ḥamšā*	five
ܐܶܫܬܳܐ	*eštā*	six
ܫܰܒܥܳܐ	*šabʿā*	seven
ܬܡܳܢܝܳܐ	*tmānyā*	eight
ܬܶܫܥܳܐ	*tešʿā*	nine
ܥܶܣܪܳܐ	*ʿesrā*	ten
ܚܕܰܥܣܰܪ	*ḥdaʿsar*	eleven
ܬܪܶܥܣܰܪ	*treʿsar*	twelve
ܬܠܳܬܬܰܥܣܰܪ	*tlāttaʿsar*	thirteen
ܐܰܪܒܰܥܬܰܥܣܰܪ	*arbaʿtaʿsar*	fourteen
ܚܰܡܶܫܬܰܥܣܰܪ	*ḥammeštaʿsar*	fifteen
ܫܬܰܥܣܰܪ	*šttaʿsar*	sixteen
ܫܒܰܥܬܰܥܣܰܪ	*šbaʿtaʿsar*	seventeen
ܬܡܳܢܬܰܥܣܰܪ	*tmāntaʿsar*	eighteen
ܬܫܰܥܬܰܥܣܰܪ	*tšaʿtaʿsar*	nineteen
ܥܶܣܪܺܝܢ	*ʿesrin*	twenty

Exercises

Part 1

The purpose of this homework assignment is to begin translating larger sections of Scripture. To start, begin with the first chapter of 1 John. Because the Syriac is a little difficult in certain sections make sure that your English translation reflects what the author is saying, as a word-for-word translation may not be possible in several lines.

This portion of John is somewhat more challenging to translate than what has been seen previously. Remember to take time with each verse and make sure that each clause is properly understood and parsed. Also, if the student is familiar with the Greek, feel free to utilize the Greek New Testament to make comparison with the Syriac text. Note the similarities, differences, and translation techniques.

1 John 1:1–10

v.1 ܡܣܒܪܝܢܢ[2] ܠܟܘܢ ܠܗܘ ܕܐܝܬܘܗܝ ܗܘܐ ܡܢ ܒܪܫܝܬ[3] ܗܘ ܕܫܡܥܢ

ܘܚܙܝܢܝܗܝ[4] ܒܥܝܢܝܢ ܚܪܝܢ ܘܓܫܢ[5] ܒܐܝܕܝܢ ܗܘ ܕܐܝܬܘܗܝ ܡܠܬܐ ܕܚܝܐ

v.2 ܘܚܝܐ ܐܬܓܠܝܘ ܘܚܙܝܢ ܘܣܗܕܝܢܢ[6] ܘܡܟܪܙܝܢܢ[7] ܠܟܘܢ ܚܝܐ ܕܠܥܠܡ

ܗܘ ܕܐܝܬܘܗܝ ܗܘܐ ܠܘܬ ܐܒܐ ܘܐܬܓܠܝ ܠܢ

---

2. This is a participle with a pronominal suffix: peal active mp + 1cp.
3. ܒܪܫܝܬ = in the beginning.
4. This is a verb with a pronominal suffix: peal perfect 1cp + 3ms.
5. ܘܓܫܢ = and we touched.
6. This is a participle with a pronominal suffix: peal active mp + 1cp.
7. This is a participle with a pronominal suffix: aphel active mp + 1cp.

v.3 ܘܡܕܡ ܕܚܙܝܢ ܘܫܡܥܢ ܡܚܘܝܢܢ[8] ܐܦ ܠܟܘܢ ܕܬܗܘܐ ܠܟܘܢ
ܫܘܬܦܘܬܐ[9] ܥܡܢ ܘܫܘܬܦܘܬܢ ܕܝܢ ܕܝܠܢ ܐܝܬܝܗ ܥܡ ܐܒܐ ܘܥܡ
ܒܪܗ ܝܫܘܥ ܡܫܝܚܐ

v.4 ܘܗܠܝܢ ܟܬܒܝܢܢ[10] ܠܟܘܢ ܕܚܕܘܬܢ ܕܒܟܘܢ ܬܗܘܐ ܡܫܡܠܝܐ[11]

v.5 ܘܗܕܐ ܗܝ ܣܒܪܬܐ ܕܫܡܥܢ ܡܢܗ ܘܡܣܒܪܝܢܢ[12] ܠܟܘܢ ܕܐܠܗܐ
ܢܘܗܪܐ ܗܘ ܘܚܫܘܟܐ ܟܠ ܟܠܗ ܠܝܬ ܒܗ

v.6 ܘܐܢ ܐܡܪܝܢܢ[13] ܕܫܘܬܦܘܬܐ[14] ܐܝܬ ܠܢ ܥܡܗ ܘܡܗܠܟܝܢܢ[15] ܒܚܫܘܟܐ
ܕܓܠܝܢ ܚܢܢ ܘܠܐ[16] ܒܫܪܪܐ ܪܕܝܢܢ[17]

8. This is a participle with a pronominal suffix: aphel active mp + 1cp.
9. ܫܘܬܦܘܬܐ = fellowship (x2).
10. This is a participle with a pronominal suffix: peal active mp + 1cp.
11. ܡܫܡܠܝܐ = being complete.
12. This is a participle with a pronominal suffix: pael active mp + 1cp.
13. This is a participle with a pronominal suffix: peal active mp + 1cp.
14. ܫܘܬܦܘܬܐ = fellowship.
15. This is a participle with a pronominal suffix: pael active mp + 1cp.
16. ܘܠܐ = and not.
17. This is a participle with a pronominal suffix: peal active mp + 1cp.

v.7 ܐܢ ܕܝܢ ܒܢܘܗܪܐ ܡܗܠܟܝܢܢ[18] ܐܝܟ ܕܗܘ ܐܝܬܘܗܝ ܒܢܘܗܪܐ ܐܝܬ
ܠܢ ܫܘܬܦܘܬܐ[19] ܥܡ ܚܕܕܐ[20] ܘܕܡܐ ܕܝܫܘܥ ܒܪܗ ܡܕܟܐ[21] ܠܢ ܡܢ
ܟܠܗܘܢ ܚܛܗܝܢ

v.8 ܘܐܢ ܢܐܡܪ ܕܠܝܬ ܠܢ ܚܛܝܬܐ ܢܦܫܢ ܡܛܥܝܢܢ[22] ܘܫܪܪܐ ܠܝܬ ܒܢ

v.9 ܐܢ ܕܝܢ ܡܘܕܝܢܢ[23] ܒܚܛܗܝܢ ܡܗܝܡܢ ܗܘ ܘܟܐܢ ܕܢܫܒܘܩ ܠܢ ܚܛܗܝܢ
ܘܢܕܟܝܢ[24] ܡܢ ܟܠܗ ܥܘܠܢ

v.10 ܘܐܢ ܐܡܪܝܢܢ[25] ܕܠܐ ܚܛܝܢ ܥܒܕܝܢܢ[26] ܠܗ ܕܓܠܐ ܘܡܠܬܗ ܠܝܬ ܠܘܬܢ

18. This is a participle with a pronominal suffix: pael active mp + 1cp.
19. ܫܘܬܦܘܬܐ = fellowship.
20. ܚܕܕܐ = one another.
21. ܡܕܟܐ = cleanses.
22. This is a participle with a pronominal suffix: aphel active mp + 1cp.
23. This is a participle with a pronominal suffix: aphel active mp + 1cp.
24. ܘܢܕܟܝܢ = and cleanse us.
25. This is a participle with a pronominal suffix: peal active mp + 1cp.
26. This is a participle with a pronominal suffix: peal active mp + 1cp.

Part 2

This is an excerpt from Matthew 6:5–13. Note that this is also a somewhat challenging passage to translate in various areas. It is also the first passage that you were asked to transliterate in the opening chapter, so note the progress that has been made in translation ability.

v.5 ܘܡܐ ܕܡܨܠܐ ܐܢܬ ܠܐ ܬܗܘܐ ܐܝܟ ܢܣܒܝ ܒܐܦܐ[27] ܕܪܚܡܝܢ ܠܡܩܡ
ܒܟܢܘܫܬܐ ܘܒܙܘܝܬܐ ܕܫܘܩܐ ܠܡܨܠܝܘ ܕܢܬܚܙܘܢ ܠܒܢܝ ܐܢܫܐ ܘܐܡܝܢ ܐܡܪ
ܐܢܐ ܠܟܘܢ ܕܩܒܠܘ ܐܓܪܗܘܢ

v.6 ܐܢܬ ܕܝܢ ܐܡܬܝ ܕܡܨܠܐ ܐܢܬ ܥܘܠ ܠܬܘܢܟ[28] ܘܐܚܘܕ ܬܪܥܟ ܘܨܠܐ
ܠܐܒܘܟ ܕܒܟܣܝܐ ܘܐܒܘܟ ܕܚܙܐ ܒܟܣܝܐ[29] ܢܦܪܥܟ[30] ܒܓܠܝܐ[31]

v.7 ܘܡܐ ܕܡܨܠܝܢ ܐܢܬܘܢ ܠܐ ܗܘܝܬܘܢ ܡܦܩܩܝܢ[32] ܐܝܟ ܚܢܦܐ ܣܒܪܝܢ ܓܝܪ
ܕܒܡܡܠܠܐ[33] ܣܓܝܐܐ ܡܫܬܡܥܝܢ

v.8 ܠܐ ܗܟܝܠ ܬܬܕܡܘܢ ܠܗܘܢ ܐܒܘܟܘܢ ܓܝܪ ܝܕܥ ܡܢܐ ܡܬܒܥܐ ܠܟܘܢ
ܥܕܠܐ[34] ܬܫܐܠܘܢܝܗܝ[35]

---

27. ܒܐܦܐ ܢܣܒܝ = hypocrites.
28. ܬܘܢܐ = small room.
29. ܒܟܣܝܐ = in secret (x2).
30. This is a verb with a pronominal suffix: peal imperfect 3ms + 2ms.
31. ܒܓܠܝܐ = in the open.
32. ܡܦܩܩܝܢ = stammer.
33. ܕܒܡܡܠܠܐ = that with discourse.
34. ܥܕܠܐ = before.
35. This is a verb with a pronominal suffix: peal imperfect 2mp + 3ms.

v.9 ܗܟܢܐ ܗܟܝܠ ܨܠܘ ܐܢܬܘܢ ܐܒܘܢ ܕܒܫܡܝܐ ܢܬܩܕܫ ܫܡܟ

v.10 ܬܐܬܐ ܡܠܟܘܬܟ ܢܗܘܐ ܨܒܝܢܟ ܐܝܟܢܐ ܕܒܫܡܝܐ ܐܦ ܒܐܪܥܐ

v.11 ܗܒ ܠܢ ܠܚܡܐ[36] ܕܣܘܢܩܢܢ[37] ܝܘܡܢܐ

v.12 ܘܫܒܘܩ ܠܢ ܚܘܒܝܢ[38] ܐܝܟܢܐ ܕܐܦ ܚܢܢ ܫܒܩܢ ܠܚܝܒܝܢ[39]

v.13 ܘܠܐ ܬܥܠܢ[40] ܠܢܣܝܘܢܐ ܐܠܐ ܦܨܢ[41] ܡܢ ܒܝܫܐ ܡܛܠ ܕܕܝܠܟ ܗܝ ܡܠܟܘܬܐ
ܘܚܝܠܐ ܘܬܫܒܘܚܬܐ[42] ܠܥܠܡ ܥܠܡܝܢ

36. ܠܚܡܐ = bread.
37. ܕܣܘܢܩܢܢ = of our need.
38. ܚܘܒܝܢ = our wrongs/debts.
39. ܠܚܝܒܝܢ = our debtors.
40. This is a verb with a pronominal suffix: aphel imperfect 2mp + 1cp.
41. This is a verb with a pronominal suffix: pael imperative + 1cp.
42. ܘܬܫܒܘܚܬܐ = glory.

Additional Exercise

Commentary on the Diatessaron 5.18

ܠܠܝܐ ܠܡ ܟܠܗ ܠܐܝܢ. ܐܪܙ[43] ܢܒ̈ܝܐ. ܡܠܦܢܘܬܗ ܕܝܢ ܢܚܬ ܡܢ ܪܘܡܐ

ܠܥܠܡܐ ܕܡܬܠ ܒܝܡܐ. ܣܦ̈ܝܢܐ ܬܪܬܝܢ.[44] ܓܙܘܪܬܐ ܘܥܘܪܠܘܬܐ[45]

ܘܪܡܙܘ[46] ܠܚܒ̈ܪܝܗܘܢ. ܐܪܙ ܫܒܥܝܢ ܘܬܪܝܢ.[47] ܕܒܨܝܪܝܢ ܗܘܘ ܒܡܢܝܢ ܗܢܘܢ

ܠܨܝܕܐ ܘܠܚܨܕܐ.[48]

English Translation (McCarthy): "*We have been toiling all night.* [This refers] symbolically to the prophets. His teaching came down from on high on the world, which stands by way of parable for the sea. *The two boats* [represent] circumcision and uncircumcision. *They made a sign to their companions.* [This refers] symbolically to the seventy-two, for these [disciples] were too few in number for the catch and the harvest."

Additional Practice

Note that the following is not considered original to Ephrem in the Commentary on the Diatessaron. It appears at the very end of Chester Beatty manuscript 709. This is being left in the text as a challenging exercise. It will require the use of an additional lexicon to complete the translation but is a good project for the student who is looking for a challenge.

Appendix to the Commentary of the Diatessaron.

ܐܘܢܓܠ̈ܝܣܛܐ.

ܕܠܐ ܕܝܢ ܫܠܡ ܬܠ̈ܡܝܕܘܗܝ ܕܫܠܝ̈ܚܐ ܡܛܠ ܕܠܘ ܐܚܪܢܐ ܐܟܬܒܘܗܝ

ܠܐܘܢܓܠܝܘܢ. ܠܐ ܓܝܪ ܐܬܦܩܕܘ ܐܝܟ ܡܫܚܐ. ܕܟ̈ܠܗܝܢܐ. ܐܠܐ

ܐܝܟ ܕܐܡܪ ܢܒܝܐ. ܕܐܬܠ ܘܚܠ ܠܗܘܢ ܕܢܬܠܐ ܠܐ ܐܝܟ ܗܿܝ ܐܠܐ

ܕܢܟܬܒܘܢ ܟܬ̈ܒܝܗܘܢ: ܘܟܠ ܠܒܢ̈ܝܗܘܢ ܐܟܬܒܘܗܝ. ܘܬܠܬܬܐ ܗܘ

43. ܐܪܙ = symbolically (x2).
44. ܣܦ̈ܝܢܐ ܬܪܬܝܢ = two boats.
45. ܥܘܪܠܘܬܐ = uncircumcision.
46. ܪܡܙܘ = they made a sign.
47. ܫܒܥܝܢ ܘܬܪܝܢ = seventy-two.
48. ܠܨܝܕܐ ܘܠܚܨܕܐ = catch (of fish) and harvest.

ܓܪܝ ܐܢܘܢ ܘܟܬܒܘ. ܡܬܝ ܒܥܒܪܐܝܬ ܐܟܬܒܗ. ܘܡܢ ܢܦܩ ܠܝܘܢܝܐ.

ܡܪܩܘܣ ܕܝܢ ܕܢܩܦ ܗܘܐ ܠܫܡܥܘܢ ܟܐܦܐ. ܟܕ ܐܙܠ ܠܪܗܘܡܝ.

ܕܗܘܘ ܥܗܕܝܢ ܡܫܠܡܢܘܬܐ. ܕܕܡ ܒܢܘܓܪܐ ܬܬܛܥܐ ܠܗ. ܐܦܝܣܘܗܝ،

ܘܟܬܒ ܡܕܡ ܕܐܕܪܟ. ܠܘܩܐ ܕܝܢ ܫܪܝ ܡܢ ܡܥܡܘܕܝܘܬܗ ܕܝܘܚܢܢ. ܟܕ

ܕܝܢ ܚܕ ܥܠ ܦܓܪܢܘܬܗ ܐܡܪ ܘܥܠ ܡܠܟܘܬܗ ܕܡܢ ܕܘܝܕ. ܘܐܚܪܢܐ

ܕܡܢ ܐܒܪܗܡ. ܐܬܐ ܝܘܚܢܢ ܐܫܟܚ ܕܡܟܪܙܝܢ ܡ̈ܠܝܗܘܢ

ܣܓܝ̈ܢ ܕܐܟܬܒܘ ܫܪ̈ܒܬܗ ܕܒܪ ܐܢܫܐ ܗܘ. ܐܟܬܒ ܗܘ ܕܠܘ ܒܪܢܫܐ

ܗܘܐ ܐܠܐ ܕܒܪܫܝܬ ܐܝܬܘܗܝ، ܗܘܐ ܡܠܬܐ.

English Translation (McCarthy): "The Evangelists. The words of the apostles are not in agreement because they did not write the Gospel at the same time. They did not receive the command like Moses, on tablets, but, as the prophet has said, *I will give them a covenant, not like this one, but my Law in their spirit, and I will write it on their heart.* [Various] reasons summoned them, and they wrote. Matthew wrote it in Hebrew, and it was then translated into Greek. Mark followed Simon Peter. When he went to Rome [the faithful] persuaded him [to write] so that they would remember the tradition, lest it be forgotten after a long time. He wrote what he had grasped. Luke began with the baptism of John. Since one had spoken of his incarnation and of his kingdom springing from David, and the other [had begun] with Abraham, John came and found their words were proclaiming many things, for they had composed genealogies concerning his human origins. Consequently he wrote that he had been not just a man, but, *In the beginning was the Word.*"

Appendix 1

Next Steps

Next Steps

After finishing an introductory grammar, a very common question to ask is, "What's next?" The nice thing about learning Syriac is that learning the basics of the language opens up a lot of doors in terms of research, and so it really depends on your own interests.

It it probably a good idea to invest in a few resources that will be helpful as you continue your studies in Syriac. The first is Theodor Nöldeke's *Compendious Syriac Grammar*.[1] This is the standard research grammar available today.

A second useful tool is a good lexicon. Two immediately come to mind. First is Michael Sokoloff's *A Syriac Lexicon*.[2] This is a translation from a Latin Syriac lexicon written by C. Brockelmann and is a good research lexicon for the field. Note that it uses the Eastern vowel points. This can be used in conjunction with J. Payne Smith's *A Compendious Syriac Lexicon*, which is another standard research lexicon.[3]

As far as developing your new-found skills in Syriac, there are a couple of areas that you will want to develop. First, it is important to continue to read Syriac in all three of the main families of the language—Estrangela, Eastern, and Western. The last two were only briefly introduced in the first and last chapters of this grammar, yet it is important to become proficient at reading and writing in both scripts.

The good news is that, as far as the grammar is concerned, you should be able to make your way through both an Estrangela (with no vowel pointing) text and a Western text, because of the vowel pointing, with minimal practice. The Eastern text might take a little while longer due to the fact that the vowel pointing is a bit different.

If you are looking for a grammar that predominately uses a particular type of text, here are a few recommendations.

Estrangela (no vowel pointing):

1. Theodor Nöldeke, *Compendious Syriac Grammar*, 2nd ed., tr. James A. Crichton (Winona Lake, IN: Eisenbrauns, 2001).
2. Michael Sokoloff, *A Syriac Lexicon: A Translation from the Latin, Correction, Expansion, and Update of C. Brockelmann's Lexicon Syriacum* (Winona Lake, IN: Eisenbrauns; Piscataway, NJ: Gorgias Press, 2009).
3. J. Payne Smith, *A Compendious Syriac Dictionary* (Oxford: Oxford University Press, 1903; repr. Winona Lake, IN: Eisenbrauns, 1998).

Thackston, Wheeler M., Jr. *Introduction to Syriac: An Elementary Grammar with Readings from Syriac Literature*. Bethesda, MD: IBEX, 1999.

Western:

Coakley, J. F. *Robinson's Paradigms and Exercises in Syriac Grammar*. 5th ed. New York: Oxford University Press, 2002.

Eastern:

Arayathinal, Thomas. *Aramaic Grammar*. 2 vols. Kerala State, India: St. Joseph's Press, 1957–1959.

Regarding the latter book, it is difficult to find a grammar that is written from a purely Eastern phonological model. This grammar is written in this manner, but it is older and can be confusing to navigate.

Finally, it is also a good idea to continue to build your Syriac vocabulary. For this, I would recommend a handy little reference from George Kiraz entitled *Lexical Tools to the Syriac New Testament*, which includes vocabulary lists as well as several other useful tools and references for sharpening Syriac skills.[4] This grammar that you are using has covered a good majority of these words, but it is always a good idea to continue to build the discipline of expanding vocabulary.

From here you could either dive into the New Testament, Old Testament, or church fathers. My primary encouragement is that you do not take a break from a disciplined translating regimen. Languages are much like going to the gym—a little bit of time off can result in starting back at ground zero. Remember to translate at least a verse or a couple of sentences a day in order to stay sharp.

4. George Kiraz, *Lexical Tools to the Syriac New Testament* (Piscataway, NJ: Gorgias Press, 2002).

Appendix 2

Reading Eastern and Western Texts

Reading in Eastern and Western Scripts

As mentioned in chapter 1, there are three distinct types of Syriac script used in Classical Syriac: Estrangela, Eastern, and Western. In this grammar, the Estrangela was chosen because of its antiquity, as well as ease of recognition among similar-looking letters. The other two will be further discussed here. If more study is desired in Syriac, it is highly recommended that the student become familiar with all three of the scripts, as each have a beauty and importance all of their own.

Name	Transliteration	Estrangela	Eastern	Western
ālap	ʾ	ܐ	ܐ	ܐ
bēth	*b*	ܒ	ܒ	ܒ
gāmal	*g*	ܓ	ܓ	ܓ
dālat	*d*	ܕ	ܕ	ܕ
hē	*h*	ܗ	ܗ	ܗ
waw	*w*	ܘ	ܘ	ܘ
zayn	*z*	ܙ	ܙ	ܙ
ḥēt	*ḥ*	ܚ	ܚ	ܚ
ṭēt	*ṭ*	ܛ	ܛ	ܛ
yūd	*y*	ܝ	ܝ	ܝ

Name	Transliteration	Estrangela	Eastern	Western
*kāp** (Beginning/ Middle)	*k*	ܟـ	ܟـ	ܟـ
kāp (Final)	*k*	ܟ	ܟ	ܟ
lāmad	*l*	ܠ	ܠ	ܠ
*mīm** (Beginning/ Middle)	*m*	ܡـ	ܡـ	ܡـ
mīm (Ending)	*m*	ܡ	ܡ	ܡ
*nūn** (Beginning/ Middle)	*n*	ܢـ	ܢـ	ܢـ
nūn (Final, no connecting prefix)	*n*	ܢ	ܢ	ܢ
semkat	*s*	ܣ	ܣ	ܣ
ʿē	ʿ	ܥ	ܥ	ܥ
pē	*p*	ܦ	ܦ	ܦ
ṣādē	*ṣ*	ܨ	ܨ	ܨ
qop	*q*	ܩ	ܩ	ܩ
rīš	*r*	ܪ	ܪ	ܪ
šīn	*š*	ܫ	ܫ	ܫ
taw	*t*	ܬ	ܬ	ܬ

The differences among various words can be somewhat drastic. Note the distinctions in the following passage.

Estrangelo

ܐܝܟܢܐ ܕܒܪܗ ܕܐܢܫܐ ܠܐ ܐܬܐ ܕܢܫܬܡܫ.
ܐܠܐ ܕܢܫܡܫ. ܘܢܬܠ ܢܦܫܗ ܦܘܪܩܢܐ ܚܠܦ ܣܓܝܐܐ

Eastern

ܐܝܟܢܐ ܕܒܪܗ ܕܐܢܫܐ ܠܐ ܐܬܐ ܕܢܫܬܡܫ
ܐܠܐ ܕܢܫܡܫ ܘܢܬܠ ܢܦܫܗ ܦܘܪܩܢܐ ܚܠܦ ܣܓܝܐܐ

Western

ܐܝܟܢܐ ܕܒܪܗ ܕܐܢܫܐ ܠܐ ܐܬܐ ܕܢܫܬܡܫ
ܐܠܐ ܕܢܫܡܫ ܘܢܬܠ ܢܦܫܗ ܦܘܪܩܢܐ ܚܠܦ ܣܓܝܐܐ

Translation: As the son of man did not come that he would be served,
but that he would serve, and give his life for deliverance (of) many (people).
Matthew 20:28

There are also a few combinations of letters that change when they are placed next to one another. In the Western text, the most common is the *lāmad-ālap* combination, which places the two characters straight up and down: ܠܐ (see the text above for several examples).

The good news is that the general patterns are the same between the different scripts, even if the scripts themselves look different. However, the two other scripts do take some time to get used to when becoming proficient with the language.

Appendix 3

Numbers and Dates

Numbers

There are two ways that numbers can be written in Classical Syriac: (1) an abbreviated form that is based off of the Syriac alphabet and (2) the adjectival form, based off the vocabulary words that represent the numbers. This is common in Semitic languages. Only the very basic numbers will be covered in this chapter.

1. A number can be represented with letters from the Syriac alphabet. Typically, when a number is represented with a letter, the scribe will place a line over the number in order to draw attention to the fact that it is a number. The basic rules of this are as follows.

   ālap to *yūd* represent the first ten numbers, just as they appear in order in the alphabet:

ܐ	1
ܒ	2
ܓ	3
ܕ	4
ܗ	5
ܘ	6
ܙ	7
ܚ	8
ܛ	9
ܝ	10

kāp to *ṣādē* represent the numbers from 20 to 90, counting by 10:

ܟ	20
ܠ	30
ܡ	40
ܢ	50
ܣ	60
ܥ	70
ܦ	80
ܨ	90

As an example, if one wished to represent the number 34, they could write:

ܠ̄ܕ̄

dālat = 4 + *lāmad* = 30

Again, note the line above the letters, an indicator that the consonants form a number.

2. The written names for the numbers are treated mostly as adjectives, and therefore they have a masculine or feminine ending. However, the names for the numbers follow a somewhat unusual pattern that is similar to other Semitic languages such as Hebrew. The numbers one and two are irregular, but numbers three through nine all accompany nouns that are of the opposite grammatical gender. For example, if one was to write the words "four men" the grammatical gender would be "four (feminine) men (masculine)."

The following chart is arranged according to which style of noun the number is accompanying.

Number + Masculine Noun		Number + Feminine Noun
ܚܕ *ḥad*	one	ܚܕܐ *ḥdā*
ܬܪܝܢ *treyn*	two	ܬܪܬܝܢ *tarten*
ܬܠܬܐ *tlātā*	three	ܬܠܬ *tlāt*
ܐܪܒܥܐ *arbʿā*	four	ܐܪܒܥ *arbaʿ*
ܚܡܫܐ *ḥamšā*	five	ܚܡܫ *ḥameš*
ܐܫܬܐ / ܫܬܐ *eštā, štā*	six	ܫܬ *šet*
ܫܒܥܐ *šbʿā*	seven	ܫܒܥ *šbāʿ*
ܬܡܢܝܐ *tmānyā*	eight	ܬܡܢܐ *tmāne*
ܬܫܥܐ *tešʿā*	nine	ܬܫܥ *tšaʿ*
ܥܣܪܐ *ʿesrā*	ten	ܥܣܪ *ʿsar*
ܚܕܥܣܪ *ḥdaʿsar*	eleven	ܚܕܥܣܪܐ *ḥdaʿesre*
ܬܪܥܣܪ *treʿsar*	twelve	ܬܪܥܣܪܐ *treʿesre*
ܬܠܬܬܥܣܪ *tlāttaʿsar*	thirteen	ܬܠܬܬܥܣܪܐ *tlāttaʿesre*
ܐܪܒܥܬܥܣܪ *arbaʿtaʿsar*	fourteen	ܐܪܒܥܬܥܣܪܐ *arbaʿtaʿesre*
ܚܡܫܬܥܣܪ *ḥameštaʿsar*	fifteen	ܚܡܫܬܥܣܪܐ *ḥameštaʿesre*
ܫܬܥܣܪ *štaʿsar*	sixteen	ܫܬܥܣܪܐ *štaʿesre*
ܫܒܥܬܥܣܪ *šbaʿtaʿsar*	seventeen	ܫܒܥܬܥܣܪܐ *šbaʿtaʿesre*
ܬܡܢܬܥܣܪ *tmāntaʿsar*	eighteen	ܬܡܢܬܥܣܪܐ *tmāntaʿesre*
ܬܫܥܣܪ *tšaʿsar*	nineteen	ܬܫܥܣܪܐ *tšaʿesre*

Note the use of gender in the following example:

ܠܠܝܘܢ	ܘܬܠܬܐ	ܝܘܡܝܢ	ܬܠܬܐ
laylawān	*wa-tāltā*	*yawmin*	*tlātā*
noun mp absolute	*waw* + adjective feminine	noun mp absolute	adjective feminine
nights	and three	days	three

Translation: Three days and three nights.
Matthew 12:40

Additionally, there are the numbers above 20, but these only have one form.

ܥܣܪܝܢ	*ʿesrin*	twenty
ܬܠܬܝܢ	*tlātin*	thirty
ܐܪܒܥܝܢ	*arbʿin*	forty
ܚܡܫܝܢ	*ḥamšin*	fifty
ܐܫܬܝܢ ܫܬܝܢ	*eštin* *štin*	sixty
ܫܒܥܝܢ	*šabʿin*	seventy
ܬܡܢܝܢ	*tmānin*	eighty
ܬܫܥܝܢ	*tešʿin*	ninety
ܡܐܐ	*mā*	one hundred
ܡܐܬܝܢ	*maten*	two hundred
ܐܠܦ	*ālep*	one thousand

After the number two-hundred, the numbers are regularly formed by taking the last *ālap* away and adding the proper ending. For example, four hundred would be:

ܬܠܬܐ	+	ܡܐܐ	→	ܬܠܬܡܐܐ
tlātā		*mā*		*tlātmā*
three		hundred		three hundred

Finally, when putting the numbers together, the larger numbers come first, and the subsequent smaller numbers are connected with a *waw* prefix. For example:

ܥܣܪܝܢ ܘܚܡܫܐ

ʿesrin wa-ḥmšā

lit: "twenty and five"

25

Dates

In order to round out the use of numbers, it is good to know the names of the months, as well:

Month	Syriac	Transliteration
January	ܟܢܘܢ ܐܚܪܝ	*kānun ḥrāy*
February	ܫܒܛ	*šbāṭ*
March	ܐܕܪ	*ādar*
April	ܢܝܣܢ	*nisān*
May	ܐܝܪ	*iyār*
June	ܚܙܝܪܢ	*ḥzirān*
July	ܬܡܘܙ	*tāmmuz*
August	ܐܒ	*āb*
September	ܐܠܘܠ	*elul*
October	ܬܫܪܝ ܩܕܝܡ	*tešri qdim*
November	ܬܫܪܝ ܐܚܪܝ	*tešri ḥrāy*
December	ܟܢܘܢ ܩܕܝܡ	*kānun qdim*

Finally, the days of the week are all centered around the Sabbath, which is Saturday. From there, the numbers count up from the Sabbath until Friday.

English	Syriac	Transliteration
Saturday	ܫܰܒܬܳܐ	*šabtā*
Sunday	ܚܰܕܒܫܰܒܳܐ	*ḥadbšabbā*
Monday	ܬܪܶܝܢܒܫܰܒܳܐ	*trēnbšabbā*
Tuesday	ܬܠܳܬܒܫܰܒܳܐ	*tlātbšabbā*
Wednesday	ܐܰܪܒܥܳܒܫܰܒܳܐ	*arbʿābšabbā*
Thursday	ܚܰܡܶܫܒܫܰܒܳܐ	*ḥammešbšabbā*
Friday	ܥܪܽܘܒܬܳܐ	*ʿrubtā*

Appendix 4

Comparative Chart of Syriac and Hebrew

Syriac Script	Hebrew Script	Hebrew Name	Syriac Name	Transliteration
ܐ	א	*aleph*	*ālap*	ʾ
ܒ	ב	*bet*	*bēth*	*b*
ܓ	ג	*gimel*	*gāmal*	*g*
ܕ	ד	*dalet*	*dālat*	*d*
ܗ	ה	*he*	*hē*	*h*
ܘ	ו	*waw*	*waw*	*w*
ܙ	ז	*zayin*	*zayn*	*z*
ܚ	ח	*ḥet*	*ḥēt*	*ḥ*
ܛ	ט	*ṭet*	*ṭēt*	*ṭ*
ܝ	י	*yod*	*yūd*	*y*

Syriac Script	Hebrew Script	Hebrew Name	Syriac Name	Transliteration
ܟ	כ	*kaph*	*kāp** (Initial/Medial)	*k*
ܟ	ך	*kaph*	*kāp* (Final)	*k*
ܠ	ל	*lamed*	*lāmad*	*l*
ܡ	מ	*mem*	*mīm** (Initial/Medial)	*m*
ܡ	ם	*mem*	*mīm* (Final)	*m*
ܢ	נ	*nun*	*nūn** (Initial/Medial)	*n*
ܢ	ן	*nun*	*nūn* (Final, no connecting prefix)	*n*
ܣ	ס	*samek*	*semkat*	*s*
ܥ	ע	*ayin*	*ʿē*	ʿ
ܦ	פ	*pe*	*pē*	*p*
ܨ	צ	*ṣade*	*ṣādē*	*ṣ*
ܩ	ק	*qoph*	*qop*	*q*
ܪ	ר	*resh*	*rīš*	*r*
ܫ	ש	*sin/šin*	*šīn*	*š*
ܬ	ת	*tav*	*taw*	*t*

Appendix 5

Similar Syriac and Hebrew Roots

In *Basics of Biblical Aramaic*, Miles Van Pelt draws attention to the fact that there are many shared roots between Biblical Hebrew and Aramaic. The Aramaic of the Bible is Imperial Aramaic, which is earlier than Classical Syriac. However, the language of Aramaic (of which Syriac belongs) has shown amazing resilience and so much of the vocabulary and roots for Imperial Aramaic are the same for Syriac. Note the following chart, which is taken from *Basics of Biblical Aramaic* and modified here.[1]

The roots below are displayed according to their lexical entries. However, since the root of a word also forms nouns and adjectives, knowing the root will lead to more than just verbal similarities. For example, the verbal form of the root ܡܠܟ is ܡܠܰܟ (*mlak*, to rule), yielding the nominal forms:

מֶלֶךְ	=	ܡܰܠܟܳܐ
melek		*malkā*
king		king

Only the exact matches for roots in Biblical Hebrew and Syriac (with one exception) are listed here. Yet, consider that there are many other roots that are similar in both languages (with some predictability) but are not identical.[2] For example: יָשַׁב (*yāšab*, to sit) → ܝܺܬܶܒ (*iteb*, to sit); שׁוּב (*šûb*, to return) → ܬܳܒ (*tāb*, to return).

1. Miles V. Van Pelt, *Basics of Biblical Aramaic: Complete Grammar, Lexicon, and Annotated Text* (Grand Rapids: Zondervan, 2011), 80–81.
2. See Van Pelt's discussion on consonantal variation on pages 3–4, *Basics of Biblical Aramaic.*

Syriac	Biblical Hebrew	Translation
ܐܶܒܰܕ *ebad*	אָבַד *ʾābad*	to perish
ܐܶܟܰܠ *ekal*	אָכַל *ʾākal*	to eat
ܐܶܡܰܪ *emar*	אָמַר *ʾāmar*	to say / speak
ܒܢܳܐ *bnā*	בָּנָה *bānāh*	to build
ܒܪܶܟ *brek*	בָּרַךְ *bārak*	to bless
ܓܠܳܐ *glā*	גָּלָה *gālāh*	to reveal
ܗܘܳܐ *hwā*	הָיָה *hāyāh*	to be (This root is similar but not identical)
ܗܰܠܶܟ *hallek*	הָלַךְ *hālak*	to walk
ܚܙܳܐ *ḥzā*	חָזָה *ḥāzāh*	to see
ܚܝܳܐ *ḥyā*	חָיָה *ḥāyāh*	to live
ܝܺܕܰܥ *idaʿ*	יָדַע *yādaʿ*	to know
ܟܬܰܒ *ktab*	כָּתַב *kātab*	to write

ܡܠܟ *mlak*	מָלַךְ *mālak*	to rule
ܢܦܠ *npal*	נָפַל *nāpal*	to fall
ܥܢܐ *ʿnā*	עָנָה *ʿānāh*	to answer
ܩܡ *qām*	קוּם *qûm*	to rise
ܩܪܐ *qrā*	קָרָא *qārāʾ*	to call (out)
ܩܪܒ *qreb*	קָרַב *qārab*	to draw near
ܪܒܐ *rbā*	רָבָה *rābāh*	to grow, become great
ܪܡ *rām*	רוּם *rûm*	to be high
ܣܡ *sām*	שׂוּם *sûm*	to put, place
ܫܐܠ *šel*	שָׁאַל *šāʾal*	to ask
ܫܠܚ *šlaḥ*	שָׁלַח *šālaḥ*	to send
ܫܡܥ *šmaʿ*	שָׁמַע *šāmaʿ*	to hear

Appendix 6

Verbs with Pronominal Endings

Peal Perfect — Singular Verbs

Note: There are no formal 3mp and 3fp pronominal endings that are added to verbs. In these cases the typical 3mp or 3fp independent pronouns will often be added to the end of a word but they are not enclitic. The Western Syriac convention is used here.

Singular	Verb	Verb + him	Verb + them	Verb + them	Verb + her	Verb + you	Verb + you	Verb + you(pl)	Verb+you(pl)	Verb + me	Verb + us
Suffix	None	3ms	3mp	3fp	3fs	2ms	2fs	2mp	2fp	1cs	1cp
3m	ܟܬܰܒ	ܟܬܰܒܶܗ	ܟܬܰܒ ܐܶܢܽܘܢ	ܟܬܰܒ ܐܶܢܶܝܢ	ܟܬܰܒܳܗ	ܟܬܰܒܳܟ	ܟܬܰܒܶܟܝ	ܟܬܰܒܟܽܘܢ	ܟܬܰܒܟܶܝܢ	ܟܬܰܒܰܢܝ	ܟܬܰܒܰܢ
3f	ܟܶܬܒܰܬ	ܟܬܰܒܬܶܗ	ܟܶܬܒܰܬ ܐܶܢܽܘܢ	ܟܶܬܒܰܬ ܐܶܢܶܝܢ	ܟܬܰܒܬܳܗ	ܟܬܰܒܬܳܟ	ܟܬܰܒܬܶܟܝ	ܟܶܬܒܰܬܟܽܘܢ	ܟܶܬܒܰܬܟܶܝܢ	ܟܬܰܒܰܬܢܝ	ܟܬܰܒܬܰܢ
2m	ܟܬܰܒܬ	ܟܬܰܒܬܳܝܗܝ	ܟܬܰܒܬ ܐܶܢܽܘܢ	ܟܬܰܒܬ ܐܶܢܶܝܢ	ܟܬܰܒܬܳܗ	–	–	–	–	ܟܬܰܒܬܳܢܝ	ܟܬܰܒܬܳܢ
2f	ܟܬܰܒܬܝ	ܟܬܰܒܬܝܳܘܗܝ	ܟܬܰܒܬܝ ܐܶܢܽܘܢ	ܟܬܰܒܬܝ ܐܶܢܶܝܢ	ܟܬܰܒܬܝܗ	–	–	–	–	ܟܬܰܒܬܺܝܢܝ	ܟܬܰܒܬܺܝܢ
1c	ܟܶܬܒܶܬ	ܟܬܰܒܬܶܗ	ܟܶܬܒܶܬ ܐܶܢܽܘܢ	ܟܶܬܒܶܬ ܐܶܢܶܝܢ	ܟܬܰܒܬܳܗ	ܟܬܰܒܬܳܟ	ܟܬܰܒܬܶܟܝ	ܟܬܰܒܬܟܽܘܢ	ܟܬܰܒܬܟܶܝܢ	–	–
Suffix	–	ܗ	ܐܶܢܽܘܢ	ܐܶܢܶܝܢ	ܗ̇	ܟ	ܟܝ	ܟܽܘܢ	ܟܶܝܢ	ܢܝ	ܢ

Peal Perfect — Plural Verbs

Plural	Suffix	3m	3f	2m	2f	1c	Suffix
Verb	None	ܟܬܒܘ	ܟܬܒ	ܟܬܒܬܘܢ	ܟܬܒܬܝܢ	ܟܬܒܢ	–
Verb + him	3ms	ܟܬܒܘܗܝ	ܟܬܒܝܗܝ	ܟܬܒܬܘܢܝܗܝ	ܟܬܒܬܝܢܝܗܝ	ܟܬܒܢܝܗܝ	ܝܗܝ
Verb + them	3mp	ܟܬܒܘ ܐܢܘܢ	ܟܬܒ ܐܢܘܢ	ܟܬܒܬܘܢ ܐܢܘܢ	ܟܬܒܬܝܢ ܐܢܘܢ	ܟܬܒܢ ܐܢܘܢ	ܐܢܘܢ
Verb + them	3fp	ܟܬܒܘ ܐܢܝܢ	ܟܬܒ ܐܢܝܢ	ܟܬܒܬܘܢ ܐܢܝܢ	ܟܬܒܬܝܢ ܐܢܝܢ	ܟܬܒܢ ܐܢܝܢ	ܐܢܝܢ
Verb + her	3fs	ܟܬܒܘܗ	ܟܬܒܗ	ܟܬܒܬܘܢܗ	ܟܬܒܬܝܢܗ	ܟܬܒܢܗ	ܗ
Verb + you	2ms	ܟܬܒܘܟ	ܟܬܒܟ	–	–	ܟܬܒܢܟ	ܟ
Verb + you	2fs	ܟܬܒܘܟܝ	ܟܬܒܟܝ	–	–	ܟܬܒܢܟܝ	ܟܝ
Verb + you(pl)	2mp	ܟܬܒܘܟܘܢ	ܟܬܒܟܘܢ	–	–	ܟܬܒܢܟܘܢ	ܟܘܢ
Verb+you(pl)	2fp	ܟܬܒܘܟܝܢ	ܟܬܒܟܝܢ	–	–	ܟܬܒܢܟܝܢ	ܟܝܢ
Verb + me	1cs	ܟܬܒܘܢܝ	ܟܬܒܢܝ	ܟܬܒܬܘܢܢܝ	ܟܬܒܬܝܢܢܝ	–	ܢܝ
Verb + us	1cp	ܟܬܒܘܢ	ܟܬܒܢ	ܟܬܒܬܘܢܢ	ܟܬܒܬܝܢܢ	–	ܢ

Peal Imperfect — Singular Verbs

Singular	Suffix	3m	3f	2m	2f	1c	Suffix
Verb	None	ܢܶܟܬܽܘܒ	ܬܶܟܬܽܘܒ	ܬܶܟܬܽܘܒ	ܬܶܟܬܒܺܝܢ	ܐܶܟܬܽܘܒ	–
Verb + him	3ms	ܢܶܟܬܒܺܝܘܗܝ	ܬܶܟܬܒܺܝܘܗܝ	ܬܶܟܬܒܺܝܘܗܝ	ܬܶܟܬܒܺܝܢܳܝܗܝ	ܐܶܟܬܒܺܝܘܗܝ	ܘܗܝ
Verb + them	3mp	ܢܶܟܬܽܘܒ ܐܶܢܽܘܢ	ܬܶܟܬܽܘܒ ܐܶܢܽܘܢ	ܬܶܟܬܽܘܒ ܐܶܢܽܘܢ	ܬܶܟܬܒܺܝܢ ܐܶܢܽܘܢ	ܐܶܟܬܽܘܒ ܐܶܢܽܘܢ	ܐܶܢܽܘܢ
Verb + them	3fp	ܢܶܟܬܽܘܒ ܐܶܢܶܝܢ	ܬܶܟܬܽܘܒ ܐܶܢܶܝܢ	ܬܶܟܬܽܘܒ ܐܶܢܶܝܢ	ܬܶܟܬܒܺܝܢ ܐܶܢܶܝܢ	ܐܶܟܬܽܘܒ ܐܶܢܶܝܢ	ܐܶܢܶܝܢ
Verb + her	3fs	ܢܶܟܬܒܺܝܗ	ܬܶܟܬܒܺܝܗ	ܬܶܟܬܒܺܝܗ	ܬܶܟܬܒܺܝܢܳܗ	ܐܶܟܬܒܺܝܗ	ܗ
Verb + you	2ms	ܢܶܟܬܒܳܟ	ܬܶܟܬܒܳܟ	–	–	ܐܶܟܬܒܳܟ	ܟ
Verb + you	2fs	ܢܶܟܬܒܶܟܝ	ܬܶܟܬܒܶܟܝ	–	–	ܐܶܟܬܒܶܟܝ	ܟܝ
Verb + you(pl)	2mp	ܢܶܟܬܽܘܒܟܽܘܢ	ܬܶܟܬܽܘܒܟܽܘܢ	–	–	ܐܶܟܬܽܘܒܟܽܘܢ	ܟܽܘܢ
Verb+you(pl)	2fp	ܢܶܟܬܽܘܒܟܶܝܢ	ܬܶܟܬܽܘܒܟܶܝܢ	–	–	ܐܶܟܬܽܘܒܟܶܝܢ	ܟܶܝܢ
Verb + me	1cs	ܢܶܟܬܒܰܢܝ	ܬܶܟܬܒܰܢܝ	ܬܶܟܬܒܰܢܝ	ܬܶܟܬܒܺܝܢܳܢܝ	–	ܢܝ
Verb + us	1cp	ܢܶܟܬܒܰܢ	ܬܶܟܬܒܰܢ	ܬܶܟܬܒܰܢ	ܬܶܟܬܒܺܝܢܳܢ	–	ܢ

Peal Imperfect—Plural Verbs

Plural	Suffix	3m	3f	2m	2f	1c	Suffix
Verb	None	ܢܶܩܛܠܽܘܢ	ܢܶܩܛܠܳܢ	ܬܶܩܛܠܽܘܢ	ܬܶܩܛܠܳܢ	ܢܶܩܛܽܘܠ	–
Verb + him	3ms	ܢܶܩܛܠܽܘܢܳܝܗ݈ܝ	ܢܶܩܛܠܳܢܳܝܗ݈ܝ	ܬܶܩܛܠܽܘܢܳܝܗ݈ܝ	ܬܶܩܛܠܳܢܳܝܗ݈ܝ	ܢܶܩܛܠܺܝܘܗ݈ܝ	ܝܗ݈ܝ
Verb + them	3mp	ܢܶܩܛܠܽܘܢ ܐܶܢܽܘܢ	ܢܶܩܛܠܳܢ ܐܶܢܽܘܢ	ܬܶܩܛܠܽܘܢ ܐܶܢܽܘܢ	ܬܶܩܛܠܳܢ ܐܶܢܽܘܢ	ܢܶܩܛܽܘܠ ܐܶܢܽܘܢ	ܐܶܢܽܘܢ
Verb + them	3fp	ܢܶܩܛܠܽܘܢ ܐܶܢܶܝܢ	ܢܶܩܛܠܳܢ ܐܶܢܶܝܢ	ܬܶܩܛܠܽܘܢ ܐܶܢܶܝܢ	ܬܶܩܛܠܳܢ ܐܶܢܶܝܢ	ܢܶܩܛܽܘܠ ܐܶܢܶܝܢ	ܐܶܢܶܝܢ
Verb + her	3fs	ܢܶܩܛܠܽܘܢܳܗ̇	ܢܶܩܛܠܳܢܳܗ̇	ܬܶܩܛܠܽܘܢܳܗ̇	ܬܶܩܛܠܳܢܳܗ̇	ܢܶܩܛܠܺܝܗ̇	ܗ̇
Verb + you	2ms	ܢܶܩܛܠܽܘܢܳܟ	ܢܶܩܛܠܳܢܳܟ	–	–	ܢܶܩܛܠܳܟ	ܟ
Verb + you	2fs	ܢܶܩܛܠܽܘܢܶܟܝ	ܢܶܩܛܠܳܢܶܟܝ	–	–	ܢܶܩܛܠܶܟܝ	ܟܝ
Verb + you(pl)	2mp	ܢܶܩܛܠܽܘܢܳܟܽܘܢ	ܢܶܩܛܠܳܢܳܟܽܘܢ	–	–	ܢܶܩܛܽܘܠܟܽܘܢ	ܟܽܘܢ
Verb+you(pl)	2fp	ܢܶܩܛܠܽܘܢܳܟܶܝܢ	ܢܶܩܛܠܳܢܳܟܶܝܢ	–	–	ܢܶܩܛܽܘܠܟܶܝܢ	ܟܶܝܢ
Verb + me	1cs	ܢܶܩܛܠܽܘܢܳܢܝ	ܢܶܩܛܠܳܢܳܢܝ	ܬܶܩܛܠܽܘܢܳܢܝ	ܬܶܩܛܠܳܢܳܢܝ	–	ܢܝ
Verb + us	1cp	ܢܶܩܛܠܽܘܢܳܢ	ܢܶܩܛܠܳܢܳܢ	ܬܶܩܛܠܽܘܢܳܢ	ܬܶܩܛܠܳܢܳܢ	–	ܢ

Peal Imperative—Singular Verbs

Singular	Suffix	Masculine	Feminine	Suffix
Verb	None	ܩܛܘܠ	ܩܛܘܠܝ	–
Verb + him	3ms	ܩܛܘܠܝܗܝ	ܩܛܘܠܝܢܝܗܝ	ܝܗܝ
Verb + them	3mp	ܩܛܘܠ ܐܢܘܢ	ܩܛܘܠܝ ܐܢܘܢ	ܐܢܘܢ
Verb + them	3fp	ܩܛܘܠ ܐܢܝܢ	ܩܛܘܠܝ ܐܢܝܢ	ܐܢܝܢ
Verb + her	3fs	ܩܛܘܠܝܗ	ܩܛܘܠܝܗ	ܗ
Verb + you	2ms	–	–	ܟ
Verb + you	2fs	–	–	ܟܝ
Verb + you(pl)	2mp	–	–	ܟܘܢ
Verb+you(pl)	2fp	–	–	ܟܝܢ
Verb + me	1cs	ܩܛܘܠܝܢܝ	ܩܛܘܠܝܢܝ	ܢܝ
Verb + us	1cp	ܩܛܘܠܝܢ	ܩܛܘܠܝܢ	ܢ

Peal Imperative — Type I Plural Verbs

Plural	Suffix	Masculine	Feminine	Suffix
Verb	None	ܟܬܘܒܘ	ܟܬܘܒܝ̈	–
Verb + him	3ms	ܟܬܒܘܗ̱ܝ	ܟܬܘܒܝܗ̱ܝ	ܗ̱ܝ
Verb + them	3mp	ܟܬܘܒܘ ܐܢܘܢ	ܟܬܘܒܝ̈ ܐܢܘܢ	ܐܢܘܢ
Verb + them	3fp	ܟܬܘܒܘ ܐܢܝܢ	ܟܬܘܒܝ̈ ܐܢܝܢ	ܐܢܝܢ
Verb + her	3fs	ܟܬܒܘܗ̇	ܟܬܘܒܝܗ̇	ܗ̇
Verb + you	2ms	–	–	ܟ
Verb + you	2fs	–	–	ܟܝ
Verb + you(pl)	2mp	–	–	ܟܘܢ
Verb+you(pl)	2fp	–	–	ܟܝܢ
Verb + me	1cs	ܟܬܒܘܢܝ	ܟܬܘܒܝܢܝ	ܢܝ
Verb + us	1cp	ܟܬܒܘܢ	ܟܬܘܒܝܢ	ܢ

Peal Imperative — Type II Plural Verbs

Plural	Suffix	Masculine	Feminine	Suffix
Verb	None	ܟܬܘܒܘ	ܟܬܘܒܝܢ	–
Verb + him	3ms	ܟܬܒܘܢܝܗܝ	ܟܬܘܒܝܢܝܗܝ	ܝܗܝ
Verb + them	3mp	ܟܬܘܒܘ ܐܢܘܢ	ܟܬܘܒܝܢ ܐܢܘܢ	ܐܢܘܢ
Verb + them	3fp	ܟܬܘܒܘ ܐܢܝܢ	ܟܬܘܒܝܢ ܐܢܝܢ	ܐܢܝܢ
Verb + her	3fs	ܟܬܒܘܢܗ	ܟܬܘܒܝܢܗ	ܗ
Verb + you	2ms	–	–	ܟ
Verb + you	2fs	–	–	ܟܝ
Verb + you(pl)	2mp	–	–	ܟܘܢ
Verb+you(pl)	2fp	–	–	ܟܝܢ
Verb + me	1cs	ܟܬܒܘܢܝ	ܟܬܘܒܝܢܝ	ܢܝ
Verb + us	1cp	ܟܬܒܘܢ	ܟܬܘܒܝܢ	ܢ

Peal Infinitive

	Suffix	Masculine
Verb	None	ܡܶܩܛܰܠ
Verb + him	3ms	ܡܶܩܛܠܶܗ
Verb + them	3mp	ܡܶܩܛܠܶܗ ܐܶܢܽܘܢ
Verb + them	3fp	ܡܶܩܛܰܠ ܐܶܢܶܝܢ
Verb + her	3fs	ܡܶܩܛܠܳܗ
Verb + you	2ms	ܡܶܩܛܠܳܟ
Verb + you	2fs	ܡܶܩܛܠܶܟܝ
Verb + you(pl)	2mp	ܡܶܩܛܰܠܟܽܘܢ
Verb+you(pl)	2fp	ܡܶܩܛܰܠܟܶܝܢ
Verb + me	1cs	ܡܶܩܛܠܰܢܝ
Verb + us	1cp	ܡܶܩܛܠܰܢ

Appendix 7

Syriac-English Lexicon

ܐ *ālap*

ܐܒܐ	*abā*	father
ܐܒܕ	*ebad*	to perish, be lost
ܐܒܕܢܐ	*abdānā*	loss, waste
ܐܓܪܐ	*agrā*	payment, reward, wage
ܐܓܪܬܐ	*eggartā*	letter, epistle
ܐܕܢܐ	*ednā*	ear
ܐܘ	*aw*	or, else, than
ܐܠܐ	*ellā*	but
ܐܘܠܨܢܐ	*ulṣānā*	affliction, oppression
ܐܘܢܓܠܝܘܢ	*ewangeliān*	Gospel (Gk. εὐαγγέλιον)
ܐܘܪܚܐ	*urḥā*	road, way
ܐܙܠ	*ezal*	to go, depart
ܐܚܐ	*aḥā*	brother
ܐܚܕ	*eḥad*	to take, seize, apprehend; let out (aphel)
ܐܚܪܝܐ	*ḥrāyā*	last, extreme
ܐܚܪܢܐ	*ḥrinā*	other, another
ܐܝܕܐ	*idā*	hand
ܐܝܟ	*ayk*	like, according to, as
ܐܝܟܐ	*aykā*	where?
ܐܝܟܢܐ	*aykanā*	how? ("as" with *dālat*)
ܐܝܠܝܢ	*ayleyn*	which? ("those who" with *dālat*)
ܐܝܠܢܐ	*ilyānā*	tree
ܐܝܡܟܐ	*aymekā*	hence, therefore
ܐܝܡܡܐ	*imāmā*	daytime
ܐܝܢ	*in*	truly, so, yes
ܐܝܩܪܐ	*iqārā*	honor, glory, majesty
ܐܝܬ	*it*	there is, there are
ܐܟܚܕܐ	*akḥdā*	together
ܐܟܠ	*ekal*	to eat

ܐܰܠܳܗܳܐ *alāhā* God
ܐܶܠܘ *ellu* if
ܐܶܠܦܳܐ *elpā* ship, boat
ܐܶܠܰܨ *elaṣ* to compel, constrain
ܐܶܡܳܐ *emmā* mother
ܐܰܡܺܝܢ *amin* amen, verily
ܐܶܡܰܪ *emar* to say, speak
ܐܶܡܪܳܐ *emrā* lamb
ܐܶܡܰܬܝ *emat* when
ܐܶܢ *en* if
ܐܢܳܫܳܐ *nāšā* man, mankind, people
ܐܰܢܬܬܳܐ *atttā* woman, wife
ܐܰܣܺܐ *asse* to heal (pael)
ܐܶܣܛܪܰܛܺܝܳܛܳܐ *asṭraṭiāṭā* soldier (Gk. στρατιώτης)
ܐܶܣܰܪ *esar* to bind
ܐܳܦ *āp* also, even
ܐܰܦܶܐ *appe* face
ܐܳܦܠܳܐ *āplā* not even (*ap+la*)
ܐܳܦܶܢ *āpen* even if
ܐܰܪܥܳܐ *arʿā* earth, country, ground, land
ܐܰܪܒܥܺܝܢ *arbʿin* forty
ܐܪܳܙܳܐ *rāzā* mystery
ܐܰܪܡܰܠܬܳܐ *armaltā* widow
ܐܶܫܰܕ *ešad* to pour out, shed
ܐܶܫܬܺܝ *ešti* to drink
ܐܳܬܳܐ *ātā* miraculous sign
ܐܶܬܳܐ *etā* to come, bring (aphel)
ܐܰܬܪܳܐ *atrā* country, place

ܒ *bēth*

ܒܗܶܬ *bhet* to be ashamed; shame (aphel)
ܒܽܘܝܳܐܳܐ *buyāā* to comfort (pael), encourage (pael)
ܒܛܶܠ *bṭel* to be idle, stop (pael)
ܒܝܳܐ *byā* to comfort, encourage
ܒܰܝܢܰ *bayna* between, among
ܒܰܝܢܳܬ *baynāt* between, among
ܒܺܝܫܳܐ *bišā* evil, wrong
ܒܶܝܬ *bēt* between, among
ܒܰܝܬܳܐ *baytā* house
ܒܟܳܐ *bkā* to weep
ܒܰܠܚܘܕ *balḥud* alone, only
ܒܢܳܐ *bnā* to build
ܒܶܣܡܳܐ *besmā* ointment, incense, aroma
ܒܶܣܪܳܐ *besrā* flesh

ܒܥܐ *bʿā* to seek, search for, require, question
ܒܥܠܐ *baʿlā* lord, husband
ܒܥܠܕܒܒܐ *bʿeldbābā* enemy
ܒܩܐ *bqā* to examine, prove
ܒܪ *bar* outside of
ܒܪܐ *brā* son
ܒܪܝܬܐ *britā* creation
ܒܪܟ *brek* to kneel, bless (pael)
ܒܪܢܫܐ *barnāšā* human, person (*bar* + *naša*, son of man)
ܒܪܡ *bram* but, yet, nonetheless
ܒܪܬܐ *bartā* daughter
ܒܬܪ *bātar* after, behind

ܓ *gāmal*

ܓܒܐ *gbā* to choose, gather (pael)
ܓܒܐ *gabā* side, sect
ܓܒܝܐ *gabyā* chosen, elect
ܓܒܪܐ *gabrā* man, husband
ܓܕܦ *gdap* to blaspheme (pael), revile
ܓܝܪ *ger* for (Gk. γάρ)
ܓܘ *gaww* in, within
ܓܙܘܪܬܐ *gzurtā* circumcision
ܓܠܐ *glā* to reveal
ܓܠܝܢܐ *gelyānā* revelation, assurance
ܓܡܪ *gmar* to accomplish, fulfill, perfect

ܕ *dālat*

ܕܒܚܐ *debḥā* sacrifice, victim
ܕܒܪ *dbar* to lead, take, rule (pael)
ܕܓܠܐ *daggālā* liar, false
ܕܗܒܐ *dahbā* gold
ܕܚܠ *dḥel* to fear
ܕܚܠܬܐ *dḥeltā* fear
ܕܘܟܬܐ *dukktā* place
ܕܝܘܐ *daywā* demon, devil
ܕܝܢܐ *dayānā* judge
ܕܝܠ *dil* own, belonging to
ܕܝܢ *dēn* but, yet, for, then, however
ܕܝܢܐ *dinā* judgment
ܕܝܐܬܝܩܐ *diatiqi* covenant (Gk. διαθήκη)
ܕܟܐ *dkā* to cleanse (pael), be pure
ܕܟܝܐ *dakyā* clean, pure
ܕܟܪ *dkar* to remember
ܕܠܡܐ *dalmā* lest

ܕܡܳܐ *dmā* blood

ܕܡܳܐ *dmā* to resemble, compare (pael)

ܕܡܽܘܬܳܐ *dmutā* form, image

ܕܡܶܟ *dmek* to sleep

ܕܡܰܪ *dmar* to marvel, be amazed

ܗ *hē*

ܗܳܐ *hā* lo, behold

ܗܰܕܳܡܳܐ *haddāmā* limb, member

ܗܘܳܐ *hwā* to be

ܗܽܘܝܽܘ *huyu* that is to say / he is

ܗܰܝܕܷܝܢ *haydēn* then, afterwards, next

ܗܰܝܟܠܳܐ *hayklā* temple

ܗܰܝܡܶܢ *haymen* to believe, trust in

ܗܰܝܡܳܢܽܘܬܳܐ *haymānutā* faith, belief

ܗܳܟܘܳܬ *hākwāt* likewise, so

ܗܳܟܺܝܠ *hākil* thus, hence, therefore

ܗܳܟܰܢܳܐ *hākannā* thus

ܗܰܠܶܟ *hallek* to walk (pael)

ܗܦܰܟ *hpak* to turn, return

ܗܳܪܟܳܐ *harkā* here

ܗܳܫܳܐ *hāšā* now

ܘ *waw*

ܘܳܝ *wāy* woe!

ܘܳܠܶܐ *wāle* it is necessary for, right

ܙ *zayn*

ܙܒܰܢ *zban* to buy, sell (pael)

ܙܰܒܢܳܐ *zabnā* time, season

ܙܰܕܺܝܩܳܐ *zaddiqā* righteous, just

ܙܰܕܺܝܩܽܘܬܳܐ *zadiqutā* justice, righteousness

ܙܰܕܶܩ *zadeq* to be right, justify (pael)

ܙܗܰܪ *zher* to warn (pael), beware

ܙܟܳܐ *zkā* to conquer, overcome

ܙܳܢܝܽܘܬܳܐ *zānyutā* adultery

ܙܳܥ *zāʿ* to be shaken, confused, trouble (aphel), stir (aphel)

ܙܥܽܘܪܳܐ *zʿurā* least, little

ܙܩܰܦ *zqap* to crucify, lift up

ܙܩܺܝܦܳܐ *zqipā* cross

ܙܪܰܥ *zraʿ* to sow

ܙܰܪܥܳܐ *zarʿā* seed

ܚ *ḥēt*

ܚܒ	*ḥāb*	to owe, be condemned
ܚܒ	*ḥab*	to be loving, kindled, love (pael)
ܚܒܝܒܐ	*ḥbibā*	beloved
ܚܒܠ	*ḥbal*	to corrupt, destroy
ܚܒܪܐ	*ḥabrā*	companion, friend
ܚܕ	*ḥad*	one, a
ܚܕܝ	*ḥdi*	to rejoice, be glad
ܚܕܘܬܐ	*ḥadutā*	joy, gladness
ܚܕܪܐ	*ḥdārā*	neighbor, surroundings
ܚܕܬܐ	*ḥadtā*	new
ܚܘܐ	*ḥwwā*	to show (pael)
ܚܘܒܐ	*ḥubā*	love, loving-kindness
ܚܘܪܐ	*ḥewwārā*	white
ܚܘܪܒܐ	*ḥurbā*	wilderness, desolation
ܚܙܐ	*ḥzā*	to see, behold
ܚܙܘܐ	*ḥezwā*	appearance
ܚܛܗܐ	*ḥṭāhā*	sin
ܚܛܝܐ	*ḥaṭāyā*	sinner
ܚܛܝܬܐ	*ḥṭitā*	sin
ܚܛܐ	*ḥṭā*	to sin
ܚܝܒܐ	*ḥayābā*	debtor
ܚܝܘܬܐ	*ḥayutā*	animal
ܚܟܝܡܐ	*ḥakimā*	wise, prudent
ܚܟܡܬܐ	*ḥekmtā*	wisdom
ܚܝܐ	*ḥyā*	to live, save (aphel)
ܚܝܐ	*ḥayyā*	alive, living
ܚܝ̈ܐ	*ḥayye*	life, salvation
ܚܝܠܐ	*ḥaylā*	power, strength, might
ܚܠܦ	*ḥlāp*	for, instead of, on account of
ܚܡܪܐ	*ḥamrā*	wine
ܚܣܝܪܐ	*ḥassirā*	deficient, shame, reproach
ܚܪ	*ḥār*	to look, behold
ܚܪܝܢܐ	*ḥeryānā*	altercation, strife
ܚܪܬܐ	*ḥartā*	end
ܚܫ	*ḥaš*	to suffer, feel
ܚܫܒ	*ḥšab*	to think, deliberate
ܚܫܘܟܐ	*ḥešukā*	darkness
ܚܬܐ	*ḥātā*	sister

ܛ *ṭēt*

ܛܒܐ	*ṭābā*	good
ܛܘܒܐ	*ṭubā*	blessedness

ܛܘܪܐ	*ṭurā*	mountain
ܛܝܒ	*ṭayeb*	to make ready (pael)
ܛܠܝܐ	*ṭalyā*	youth, child
ܛܢܦܐ	*ṭanpā*	impure, defiled
ܛܥܐ	*ṭʿā*	to go astray (aphel), wander
ܛܥܡ	*ṭʿem*	to taste, partake
ܛܫܐ	*ṭšā*	to hide (pael)

ܝ *yūd*

ܝܒܠ	*ybel*	to conduct (aphel), lead away (aphel)
ܝܕܐ	*yade*	to confess (aphel), give thanks
ܝܕܥ	*idaʿ*	to know
ܝܕܥܬܐ	*idaʿtā*	knowledge
ܝܗܒ	*yab*	to give
ܝܗܘܕܝܐ	*ihudāyā*	Jew
ܝܘܠܦܢܐ	*yulpānā*	teaching, learning, doctrine
ܝܘܡܐ	*yawmā*	day
ܝܘܡܢܐ	*yawmānā*	today
ܝܠܕ	*iled*	to give birth to (aphel)
ܝܠܦ	*ilep*	to learn, teach (pael)
ܝܡܐ	*imā*	to swear (an oath)
ܝܡܐ	*yammā*	sea
ܝܡܝܢܐ	*yamminā*	right
ܝܣܦ	*ysap*	to add, increase (aphel)
ܝܨܦ	*iṣep*	to be anxious, careful
ܝܩܕ	*iqed*	to burn
ܝܩܪ	*iqqar*	to be heavy, honor (pael)
ܝܩܝܪܐ	*yaqirā*	heavy, precious, honor
ܝܪܚܐ	*yarḥā*	month
ܝܬܒ	*iteb*	to sit
ܝܬܝܪܐ	*yatirā*	better, greater
ܝܬܝܪܐܝܬ	*yatirāit*	abundantly, especially (or *yattir*)
ܝܬܪ	*ittar*	to gain, abound (pael)

ܟ *kāp*

ܟܐܐ	*kā*	to rebuke
ܟܐܢܐ	*kinā*	just, righteous
ܟܐܢܘܬܐ	*kinutā*	righteousness, justice
ܟܐܦܐ	*kipā*	rock, stone
ܟܕ	*kad*	when, while, after, as
ܟܗܢܐ	*kāhnā*	priest
ܟܘܟܒܐ	*kawkbā*	star, planet
ܟܘܡܪܐ	*kumrā*	priest
ܟܘܪܗܢܐ	*kurhānā*	ailment, disease

ܟܘܪܣܝܐ *kursyā* seat, throne
ܟܠ / ܟܘܠ *kull* all, every
ܟܠܐ *klā* to forbid, restrain
ܟܠܙܒܢ *kullzban* always
ܟܠܝܘܡ *kullyum* everyday
ܟܠܡܕܡ *kullmeddem* everything
ܟܠܢܫ *kullnāš* everyone (man)
ܟܡܐ *kmā* how many / much?
ܟܢܘܫܬܐ *knuštā* council, synagogue
ܟܢܫ *knaš* to assemble
ܟܢܫܐ *kenšā* crowd
ܟܣܐ *ksā* to hide, conceal, clothe, cover
ܟܣܐ *kāsā* cup
ܟܣܦܐ *kespā* money, silver
ܟܦܢ *kpen* to hunger
ܟܦܪ *kpar* to deny, renounce
ܟܪܐ *krā* to have sorrow, be sad
ܟܪܗ *krah* to be sick, weak
ܟܪܙ *kraz* to be preached (ethpeel), proclaimed (pael)
ܟܪܝܗܐ *krihā* sick, weak in faith
ܟܪܟ *krak* to lead (aphel), wrap
ܟܪܡܐ *karmā* vineyard
ܟܪܣܐ *karsā* womb, belly
ܟܫܠ *kšel* to offend, stumble
ܟܬܒ *ktab* to write
ܟܬܒܐ *ktābā* book

ܠ *lāmad*

ܠܐ *lā* no, not
ܠܐܐ *lā* to labor, toil
ܠܒܐ *lebbā* heart
ܠܒܘܫܐ *lbušā* clothing
ܠܒܪ *lbar* outside
ܠܒܫ *lbeš* to wear, put on (clothes)
ܠܘ *law* no, is not (*la+hu*)
ܠܘܩܒܠ *luqbal* against, near
ܠܘܩܕܡ *luqdam* before, formerly
ܠܘܬ *lwāt* to, towards, with
ܠܚܡܐ *laḥmā* bread
ܠܝܬ *layt* there is/are not
ܠܠܝܐ *lilyā* night
ܠܡܐ *lmā* why?
ܠܡܢܐ *lmānā* why?
ܠܥܣ *lʿes* to eat

ܠܫܢܐ *leššānā* language

ܡ *mīm*

ܡܐܐ *mā* one hundred
ܡܐܢܐ *mānā* garment, vessel
ܡܐܟܘܠܬܐ *mekultā* food (also *meklā*)
ܡܐܬܝܬܐ *metitā* advent, coming
ܡܕܒܚܐ *madbḥā* altar
ܡܕܡ *medem* something
ܡܕܝܢܬܐ *mdittā* city, town
ܡܗܝܡܢܐ *mhaymnā* believer
ܡܘܗܒܬܐ *mawhabtā* gift
ܡܘܠܟܢܐ *mulkānā* promise
ܡܘܬܐ *mawtā* death
ܡܚܐ *mḥā* to strike, smite
ܡܚܕܐ *meḥdā* at once, immediately
ܡܚܘܬܐ *mḥutā* wound, plague
ܡܚܫܒܬܐ *maḥšabtā* counsel, reasoning, calculation
ܡܛܐ *mṭā* to arrive, attain (pael)
ܡܛܠ *meṭṭul* because
ܡܝܐ *mayyā* water (pl)
ܡܝܬ *mit* to die
ܡܝܬܐ *mitā* dead
ܡܟܝܟܐ *makkikā* gentle, humble
ܡܟܝܠ *mekkil* now, therefore, henceforth
ܡܟܣܐ *māksā* tax collector
ܡܠܐ *mlā* to complete, be full
ܡܠܐܟܐ *malakā* angel, messenger
ܡܠܟ *mlak* to council, reign (aphel)
ܡܠܟܐ *malkā* king
ܡܠܟܘܬܐ *malkutā* kingdom
ܡܠܠ *mallel* to speak (pael)
ܡܠܦܢܐ *malpānā* teacher
ܡܠܬܐ *melltā* word
ܡܢ *men* from
ܡܣܟܝܢܐ *meskinā* poor
ܡܣܝܒܪܢܘܬܐ *msaybrānutā* endurance, patience
ܡܥܡܘܕܝܬܐ *maʿmuditā* baptism, washing, pool
ܡܨܥܬܐ *mṣaʿtā* middle
ܡܪܝܐ *māryā* lord, master
ܡܫܝܚܐ *mšiḥā* Christ, Messiah
ܡܫܡܫܢܐ *mšammšānā* servant
ܡܬܠܐ *matlā* parable

ܢ *nūn*

ܢܒܐ	*nbā*	to prophesy (ethpaal)
ܢܒܝܐ	*nbiyā*	prophet
ܢܓܕ	*ngad*	to beat (pael), lead, drag
ܢܗܪ	*nhar*	to shine
ܢܘܗܪܐ	*nuhrā*	light
ܢܘܟܪܝܐ	*nukrāyā*	foreign, strange
ܢܘܢܐ	*nunā*	fish
ܢܘܪܐ	*nurā*	fire
ܢܚ	*nāḥ*	to rest
ܢܚܬ	*nḥet*	to descend
ܢܚܬܐ	*naḥtā*	garment
ܢܛܪ	*nṭar*	to keep, guard
ܢܡܘܣܐ	*nāmusā*	law (Gk. νόμος [*nomos*])
ܢܣܐ	*nse*	to try, test, prove (all pael)
ܢܣܒ	*nsab*	to take, receive
ܢܣܝܘܢܐ	*nesyunā*	trial, temptation
ܢܦܠ	*npal*	to fall
ܢܦܩ	*npaq*	to go out, go forth, cast out
ܢܩܦ	*nqep*	to adhere, follow
ܢܦܫܐ	*napšā*	soul, self
ܢܨܪܝܐ	*naṣrāyā*	Nazarene

ܣ *semkat*

ܣܒܪ	*sbar*	to think, consider, hope (pael)
ܣܒܪ	*sbar*	to preach, declare (pael)
ܣܒܪܐ	*sabrā*	hope
ܣܒܪܬܐ	*sbartā*	message, good news
ܣܓܐ	*sgā*	to increase (aphel), be great
ܣܓܕ	*sged*	to worship, pay homage
ܣܓܝܐܐ	*saggiā*	many, much, very (also *saggi*)
ܣܗܕ	*sed*	to testify, witness
ܣܗܕܐ	*sāhdā*	witness, martyr
ܣܗܕܘܬܐ	*sahdutā*	testimony, martyrdom
ܣܘܓܐܐ	*sugā*	abundance, many
ܣܛܢܐ	*sāṭānā*	satan, adversary
ܣܝܡܬܐ	*simtā*	treasure
ܣܝܒ	*syeb*	to defile (pael)
ܣܟܐ	*skā*	to expect, wait for (both pael)
ܣܟܠ	*skal*	to understand, perceive (both pael)
ܣܟܠܘܬܐ	*sakluwtā*	error, wrongdoing
ܣܠܩ	*sleq*	to ascend, go up
ܣܡ	*sām*	to put, place

ܣܡܝܐ	*samyā*	blind (also *same*)
ܣܡܟ	*smak*	to recline, rest
ܣܢܐ	*snā*	to hate
ܣܢܩ	*sneq*	to need
ܣܥܪ	*sʿar*	to do, effect
ܣܦܝܢܬܐ	*spittā*	boat, ship
ܣܦܩ	*spaq*	to be sufficient, able
ܣܦܪܐ	*sāprā*	scribe, lawyer

ܥ *ʿē*

ܥܒܕ	*ʿbad*	to do, make
ܥܒܕܐ	*ʿabdā*	servant
ܥܒܕܐ	*ʿbādā*	deed, work
ܥܒܪ	*ʿbar*	to cross over (with ܥܠ = to transgress)
ܥܒܪܐ	*ʿebrā*	crossing
ܥܓܠ	*ʿgal*	quickly
ܥܕ	*ʿad*	until, up to, while
ܥܕܟܝܠ	*ʿedakil*	still, yet
ܥܕܡܐ	*ʿadmā*	until
ܥܕܢܐ	*ʿedānā*	moment, time, season
ܥܐܕܥܐܕܐ	*ʿadʿidā*	feast, festival
ܥܕܪ	*ʿdar*	to help, give advantage
ܥܕܬܐ	*ʿidtā*	church, assembly
ܥܗܕ	*ʿehad*	to remember
ܥܘܠܐ	*ʿawwlā*	unrighteousness
ܥܘܬܪܐ	*ʿutrā*	riches
ܥܝܢܐ	*ʿaynā*	eye
ܥܠ	*ʿal*	to enter
ܥܠ	*ʿal*	on, against, over
ܥܠܡܐ	*ʿalmā*	age, world, eternity
ܥܠܬܐ	*ʿeltā*	reason, cause
ܥܡ	*ʿam*	with
ܥܡܐ	*ʿamā*	people, nation
ܥܡܕ	*ʿmad*	to baptize (aphel), sink
ܥܡܪ	*ʿmar*	to live, dwell
ܥܢܐ	*ʿnā*	to answer
ܥܢܢܐ	*ʿnānā*	cloud
ܥܣܪܐ	*ʿesrā*	ten
ܥܪ	*ʿer*	to wake up (aphel), watch
ܥܪܒܐ	*ʿerbā*	sheep
ܥܪܣܐ	*ʿarsā*	bed, pallet
ܥܪܩ	*ʿraq*	to flee
ܥܬܕ	*ʿtad*	to prepare (pael)
ܥܬܝܪܐ	*ʿatirā*	rich, wealthy

ܦ *pē*

ܦܐܪܐ	*pirā*	fruit
ܦܓܪܐ	*pagrā*	body
ܦܘܡܐ	*pumā*	mouth, edge
ܦܘܩܕܢܐ	*puqdānā*	commandment
ܦܘܪܩܢܐ	*purqānā*	salvation, redemption
ܦܝܣ	*payes*	to convince (aphel), persuade (aphel)
ܦܠܓ	*plag*	to distribute, divide
ܦܠܚ	*plaḥ*	to work, labor, serve
ܦܠܚܐ	*pālḥā*	servant, soldier
ܦܢܐ	*pnā*	to return, answer (pael)
ܦܣ	*pas*	to allow (aphel), permit (aphel)
ܦܣܩ	*psaq*	to cut off, break (pael)
ܦܩܕ	*pqad*	to command
ܦܩܚܐ	*paqāḥā*	better, profitable
ܦܪܝܫܐ	*prišā*	Pharisee
ܦܪܥ	*praʿ*	to repay
ܦܨܐ	*pṣā*	to deliver (pael)
ܦܨܚܐ	*peṣḥā*	Passover
ܦܪܨܘܦܐ	*parṣupā*	person, face, aspect (Gk. πρόσωπον)
ܦܪܩ	*praq*	to depart, deliver, save (pael)
ܦܪܫ	*praš*	to separate, appoint
ܦܫܩ	*pašeq*	to interpret (pael)
ܦܬܓܡܐ	*petgāmā*	word
ܦܬܚ	*ptaḥ*	to open
ܦܬܟܪܐ	*ptakrā*	idol, image

ܨ *ṣādē*

ܨܒܐ	*ṣbā*	to want, will, desire
ܨܒܘܬܐ	*ṣbutā*	thing, affair
ܨܒܝܢܐ	*ṣebyānā*	will, desire
ܨܠܐ	*ṣlā*	to incline toward, pray (pael)
ܨܠܘܬܐ	*ṣlutā*	prayer
ܨܡ	*ṣām*	to fast
ܨܦܪܐ	*ṣaprā*	morning

ܩ *qop*

ܩܒܠ	*qbal*	to receive (pael), accuse, appeal
ܩܒܪܐ	*qabrā*	grave
ܩܒܘܪܐ	*qburā*	tomb
ܩܕܝܡܐ	*qdimā*	before
ܩܕܝܫܐ	*qadišā*	holy
ܩܕܡ	*qdam*	to go before

ܩܕܡ	*qdām*	before
ܩܕܡܝ	*qadmāy*	first
ܩܕܫ	*qdāš*	to sanctify, make holy
ܩܘܐ	*qwā*	to abide, remain (both pael)
ܩܘܪܒܢܐ	*qurbānā*	gift, offering
ܩܘܫܬܐ	*quštā*	truth
ܩܘܕܫܐ	*qudšā*	holiness, sanctuary
ܩܛܠ	*qṭal*	to kill
ܩܝܡܬܐ	*qyāmtā*	resurrection
ܩܠܐ	*qālā*	voice
ܩܠܝܠܐ	*qalilā*	little
ܩܡ	*qām*	to stand, arise
ܩܢܛܪܘܢܐ	*qenṭrunā*	centurion (Gk. κένταρχος)
ܩܥܐ	*qʿā*	to appeal, to cry out
ܩܪܐ	*qrā*	to call, read
ܩܪܒ	*qreb*	to draw near
ܩܪܝܒܐ	*qaribā*	neighbor, near, at hand
ܩܪܝܬܐ	*qritā*	village
ܩܪܢܐ	*qarnā*	horn, corner
ܩܫܝܫܐ	*qašišā*	elder

ܪ *rīš*

ܪܒ	*rab*	big, great
ܪܒܐ	*rbā*	to grow, increase (pael)
ܪܒܐ	*rabā*	great, master
ܪܓ	*rag*	to covet, desire
ܪܓܝܓܬܐ	*rgigtā*	lust
ܪܓܠܐ	*reglā*	foot
ܪܕܐ	*rdā*	to journey, proceed, instruct
ܪܕܦ	*rdap*	to follow, persecute
ܪܗܛ	*rheṭ*	to run
ܪܘܓܙܐ	*rugzā*	anger, wrath
ܪܘܚܐ	*ruḥā*	spirit, breath, wind
ܪܙܐ	*rāzā*	mystery
ܪܚܝܩܐ	*raḥiqā*	far, distant
ܪܚܡ	*rḥem*	to love, have compassion (pael)
ܪܚܡܐ	*rāḥmā*	friend
ܪܚܡܐ	*raḥme*	mercy, bowels
ܪܝܫܐ	*rišā*	beginning, head
ܪܫܝܬܐ	*rišitā*	beginning
ܪܡ	*rām*	to be high, exalted (aphel)
ܪܡܐ	*rmā*	to cast, put, place
ܪܡܐ	*rāmā*	high
ܪܥܐ	*rʿā*	to think (ethpaal), feed, tend
ܪܥܝܢܐ	*reʿyānā*	mind, idea

ܫ *šīn*

ܫܐܕܐ	*šidā*	demon, evil spirit
ܫܐܠ	*šel*	to ask, seek, inquire, salute
ܫܒܚ	*šbaḥ*	to commend, praise (pael)
ܫܒܥܐ	*šabʿā*	seven
ܫܒܩ	*šbaq*	to forgive, leave, allow
ܫܒܬܐ	*šabtā*	Sabbath
ܫܓ	*šag*	to wash (aphel)
ܫܕܐ	*šdā*	to throw, cast down
ܫܕܪ	*šadar*	to send (pael)
ܫܘܐ	*šwā*	to be worthy, equal, agree (ethpeel)
ܫܘܒܗܪܐ	*šubhārā*	glorying
ܫܘܒܚܐ	*šubḥā*	glory, praise
ܫܘܠܛܢܐ	*šulṭānā*	authority, dominion, power
ܫܘܩܐ	*šuqā*	marketplace
ܫܘܬܦ	*šawtep*	to partake, share
ܫܟܚ	*škaḥ*	to be able, find, happen
ܫܠܝܚܐ	*šliḥā*	apostle
ܫܠܝܛܐ	*šaliṭā*	lawful, permitted (pl. rulers)
ܫܠܡ	*šlem*	to die, be finished, follow, deliver
ܫܠܡܐ	*šlāmā*	peace
ܫܡܐ	*šmā*	name
ܫܡܝܐ	*šmayyā*	heaven, sky
ܫܡܥ	*šmaʿ*	to hear, obey
ܫܡܫ	*šmaš*	to serve, minister (both pael)
ܫܡܫܐ	*šemšā*	sun
ܫܢܐ	*šnā*	to depart, be mad (both pael)
ܫܢܬܐ	*šattā*	year
ܫܥܐ	*šʿa*	to narrate (ethpaal), play (ethpeel)
ܫܥܬܐ	*šāʿtā*	hour
ܫܦܝܪܐ	*šapirā*	beautiful, good
ܫܦܪ	*špar*	to seem good, please
ܫܩܠ	*šqal*	to remove, take up
ܫܪ	*šar*	to be strong, establish (pael)
ܫܪܐ	*šrā*	to loosen, begin (pael), stop, camp
ܫܪܒܬܐ	*šarbtā*	family, generation
ܫܪܟܐ	*šarkā*	remainder, rest
ܫܪܝܪܐܝܬ	*šarirāit*	truly
ܫܪܝܪܐ	*šarirā*	steadfast, true
ܫܪܪܐ	*šrārā*	truth
ܫܬܐ	*štā*	six
ܫܬܐܣܬܐ	*šetestā*	foundation
ܫܬܩ	*šteq*	to be silent

ܬ *taw*

ܬܐܪܬܐ	*tirtā*	conscience
ܬܒ	*tāb*	to repent, return, answer (aphel)
ܬܘܒ	*tub*	again
ܬܚܝܬ	*tḥeyt*	under
ܬܝܒܘܬܐ	*tyābutā*	repentance
ܬܟܠ	*tkel*	to be confident (ethpeel), trust
ܬܠܡܝܕܐ	*talmidā*	disciple
ܬܠܬܐ	*tlātā*	three
ܬܡܗ	*tmah*	to be astonished
ܬܡܢ	*tammān*	there
ܬܩܢ	*tqen*	to be restored, make right, restore (pael)
ܬܪܝܢ	*trēn*	two
ܬܪܥܐ	*tarʿā*	door, gate
ܬܪܥܣܪ	*treʿsar*	twelve
ܬܫܒܘܚܬܐ	*tešbuḥtā*	glory, praise
ܬܫܡܫܬܐ	*tešmeštā*	administration, service
ܬܐܬܐ	*titā*	fig tree